Occupational Psychology

Occupational Psychology

Murray Porteous

Prentice Hall

London   New York   Toronto   Sydney   Tokyo   Singapore
Madrid   Mexico City   Munich   Paris

First published 1997 by
Prentice Hall Europe
Campus 400, Maylands Avenue,
Hemel Hempstead
Hertfordshire, HP2 7EZ
A division of
Simon & Schuster International Group

Typeset in 10 on 12pt Plantin
by Dorwyn Ltd, Rowlands Castle, Hants

Printed and bound in Great Britain by
TJ International Ltd

Library of Congress Cataloging-in-Publication Data

Available from the publisher.

British Library Cataloguing in Publication Data

A catalogue record for this book is available from
the British Library

ISBN 0–13–359316–9

1 2 3 4 5   01 00 99 98 97

To the late Professor Ralph Pickford, Glasgow University,
who taught us that psychology was 'fun' as well as
'functional', and to Professor Peter Dempsey,
National University of Ireland, who 'broke the ground'
for others to grow.

Contents

Preface

This book has been written for students of psychology but also for those in other disciplines who take a course in work, industrial or occupational psychology as an 'outside' subject. There are many excellent textbooks in this area but unfortunately, almost all of them are American. This does not make them any less good, but the nature of college teaching in America is quite different to that in Europe. From my teaching experience in two American universities, I can well understand that a compendious fact-filled text is necessary for their situation. Our students are less likely to learn and regurgitate and our teachers are less inclined to follow a narrowly defined road. Consequently this book was produced out of a need for a European course guide, in the expectation that teachers and students would avail themselves of our library facilities to find much additional information suitable for their own purposes. I have never believed psychology was much use, unless it could do something and be seen to work. And learning does not exist until it can be utilised. To this end, students in all courses should be encouraged towards practical expression and experimentation with the subject they are learning. An attempt has been made to put practical activities at the end of each chapter, though I am sure others will be able to think up interesting ones more appropriate for their circumstances. There are many areas in which this text can be improved and the process has already started. Suggestion from users would also be most welcome.

'Work for the night is coming when no man shall work'

Overview of occupational psychology

Focus questions

What is occupational psychology about?

Why should you be interested in occupational psychology?

How can your working life be influenced by occupational psychology?

What do occupational psychologists and personnel managers have in common?

What is work?

The past few years have seen the toppling of the Berlin Wall, the reunification of Germany, the demise of the USSR and the establishment of the European Union with a market of 330 million consumers, many of whom are among the world's better-off. The prospects for a strong independent European economy which can compete with the United States and Japan is real. Our Europeanisation has cast a new light on our traditional territorial and ideological disputes. We are now more willing to share and celebrate our differences, rather than beat each other over the heads with them. Independence in an integrated framework is the new possibility within our grasp. The integration of economic, technical and communication systems is already well in progress. In line with this there is the prospect of a coming together of industrial policies, human resource management approaches and social welfare and educational systems. The retired, the less able, the unemployed, the current workforce and, perhaps most importantly of all, the future workers still to seek their first job, will all be subject to a new range of community policies.

One of the areas where harmonisation of policy will affect everyone is the working environment. For example, European wage rates ranged in 1991 from $2.75 per hour in Portugal to $17.50 per hour in Germany. Such wide differences will gradually diminish, as movement of people and industries continues. Some countries have minimum wage rates while others do not. The legal situation with respect to work and business differs considerably from country to country. An important force for unification lies in the way we treat workers. Occupational Psychology is a scientific discipline which attempts to understand and explain the behaviour of people in the workplace. While there are national differences in our psychology and behaviour, if a method works in one country it will be imported and adapted for use in other countries. A common European approach to the Psychology of Work can be expected to develop, along with the other areas in which policies are gradually coalescing. This text endeavours to introduce the reader to the main areas where psychology contributes to work and to relate that contribution to practical questions in the European workplace. The principal focus is the individual in the workplace, concentrating on the feelings and beliefs, training and treatment, selection and performance of individuals in the context of their working environment. The contribution from the study of Organisational Psychology will be considered where relevant, as we can rarely separate the individual from the environment when we are thinking of human behaviour.

Early development of occupational psychology

Occupational psychology is a relatively new field, dating from the 1900s when the increasing complexity of organisations brought to the fore the need for a 'people specialist'. Munsterberg wrote one of the earliest books in this area, in 1913, with *Psychology of Industrial Efficiency*. In this he was applying the relatively new science of psychology which had already made substantial contributions to education, mental health and the field of economics. He summed up his aims as follows, 'we ask how to find the best possible man, how to produce the best possible work and how to secure the best possible effects' (i.e. in the interests of business). However, he was also aware that he was at the birth of a new discipline and stated: 'The time when an exact psychology of business life will be presented as a closed and perfected system lies very far distant'. Today it is probably still as distant, as in the case of science generally; the more we learn, the more we realise we have yet to discover.

The message of Munsterberg and others in the early part of the century brought considerable hope to industrialists, management and governments. It was felt by many that the study of behaviour at work would lead to great progress. In some ways their expectations were fulfilled. Massive increases in productivity and efficiency have taken place over the years and psychology has made some contribution to the progress.

What is work?

We might think that the answer to this question is fairly obvious. However, there are great variations in patterns of work today and also in what might or might not be called work. According to Arendt (1958) the distinction between work and labour is that the latter is effort to satisfy the immediate needs of the body, whereas work produces items of lasting use and is a source of satisfaction itself. However, we may have to revise this sensible viewpoint. For many people, work is something to be avoided, for some it is the main source of pleasure in their life. For at least 10 per cent of the European labour force, work is something they are deprived of. In some countries, the Republic of Ireland for example, the figure has been around 17 per cent for the whole of the 1990s, with little sign of it dropping. It is only in 1996 that the British figure has started to drop slightly after a long period of increase. If work is so central to life, why are so many of our citizens without it? This raises other questions which we shall consider in due course. For example, what is the effect of not working, and what are the ways that people can be best prepared to do work? If everyone cannot have a job then, what is the next best thing and who should get the jobs available? Studies clearly confirm that having at least some form of academic qualification, while it is not a guarantee of work, considerably enhances an individual's prospects. Another good reason for you to study with the help of this interesting book perhaps!

Work comes in many forms: part-time, temporary, home-working, voluntary work, working for oneself, working for others, providing services, running bureaucracies, entertaining. On that last point, is a street busker working? Are you working if you sing a song in a pub and get a free drink for your efforts? Is an opera singer working? Is a bank clerk who sings in the semi-professional part-time choral society working when he sings in the annual festival? Work is normally conceived as involving some element of giving away control of the way one can distribute one's time and effort to someone else in exchange for money or its equivalent. People who propose that home-making duties are work would not take kindly to this definition though.

Early developments in the psychology of work

In Britain and Ireland the first really significant interest in the psychology of work appeared during the First World War. Government officials were concerned with the health and performance of ammunition workers and how these were affected by hours and conditions of work. Selection methods and training were also considered as important areas for investigation. Maximum output from the workers who were making the guns and shells was essential. The National Institute of Industrial Psychology (NIIP) was established in 1921 by the head of the Cambridge University Psychology laboratory, C.S. Myers. He was succeeded by another influential psychologist, Frederick Bartlett, who continued the efforts to link the factory floor with the laboratory in an effort to improve productivity and working conditions (Shimmin and Wallis, 1994).

As time progressed, the realisation grew that organisations were organic and each in its own way unique. The more static views of workers' personalities and abilities were gradually revised. During World War II, observational and behavioural methods of assessment and development of officers were established and the Tavistock Institute in London had a major role to play. This work was continued after the War with courses in management development and interpersonal relations training, which had a strong industrial following.

The classical approach to assessment and vocational guidance declined in the 1960s, resulting in the closure of the NIIP in the early 1970s. However, the company which bought it is now a multi-million pound enterprise and companies offering the traditional forms of selection assessment are again doing very well. Just as in clothes perhaps, the styles change and reappear at twenty year intervals.

The science of psychology has developed since the early days. Marvin Dunnette, a leading academic in this area, has pointed out that changes in the field of occupational psychology are evident in publications such as the *Handbook of Occupational Psychology*. In a comparison of editions from the 1950s with those of the 1970s, he concludes that the subject has matured and grown scientifically. The change is from practical, applied and specific studies, to theoretical, generalisable and research-orientated studies. The development has continued into the 1990s. The areas with which the subject is concerned continue to expand. Stress, organisational design and human–computer interaction are a few of the areas where interest has increased significantly. Statistical and theoretical advances in the Psychology of Measurement and Cognitive Psychology, to name but two, are changing the subject considerably.

Each factory's problem should not be seen in a unique way instead, general theories and ways of understanding based on psychological research are now available and are being continually developed. This developmental process applies in any scientific discipline within the confines of its methodology. Concepts are changed through experience, and theories are tested and strengthened. Results can then be applied to an ever-widening range of situations and more reliable predictions made.

If we look back in the history of many industries we see that many occupational psychology ideas are not new. For example, in the field of motivation and worker participation, in 1887, Proctor and Gamble introduced profit sharing. In recent times this has been seen as a new idea to improve worker motivation by increasing their psychological commitment to the firm. In the 1830s, Robert Owen introduced a crèche facility to enable women to remain at their looms. Today this is one of the frequent demands of women workers to permit equality of opportunity in access to work. However even at the present time, some countries in the European Union do not have recognised child-care facilities and/or any monetary support for those who need to use crèches to facilitate their employment.

Robert Owen had a philanthropic streak, but he was also motivated primarily by profit and his changes in conditions were for that purpose. He was very aware of the psychological and social effects of work, as the following quote illustrates:

> the overwhelming effects of the new mechanical power as shown by statistics would soon be the creation of riches in such abundance that the wants and desires of every human being might be more than satisfied. But under the existing system of distribution would benefit only one person in a thousand. This would generate evil passions and a premature social upheaval. (Volwiler, 1922).

It is interesting to consider that in some of our European countries the rich are getting richer at a faster rate than before and the poor are becoming relatively poorer and more marginalised. At the same time 'evil passions' are very much in evidence with increases in crime, vandalism, terrorism and general bad manners. So Owen was probably right. He was also right and ahead of his time in recognising the role that looking after his workers' more personal needs would play in industrial efficiency.

People have long held a suspicion of psychology itself and its application to the workplace has not always been welcomed. Almost fifty years ago, in 1948, an article in *The Manchester Guardian* newspaper (3 August 1948) reported that the Trades Union Council 'has begun a brisk campaign to remove traditional suspicions that the application of industrial psychology to production is a disguised way of tricking people into working harder for the same, or lower, wages'. Trade unionists were to be encouraged to adopt the more scientific approach to production and make the workplace more happy and efficient in order to raise the living standards of the British people. Why indeed should people trust or listen to psychologists? The only justification is if what they say or do really works and makes a real difference in the end to the worker or the employer. Occupational psychology is not like social work where there is an ever-increasing queue of 'customers', many of whom are grateful for anything they are given. Occupational psychology has to work and has to be about work. People can turn away from it tomorrow – it is hardly compulsory.

What has led to the growth of interest in occupational psychology?

External environmental influences have impelled the growth in the application of psychology to work. For example, there have been considerable changes in the social attitudes to work, and in people's expectations of the workplace. In earlier times, the ruling attitude was that the employer was king or even that a person was lucky to have a job. These views have been eroded by factors such as human rights legislation, trade union power and the recognition that a reliable and contented staff is the greatest asset a firm can have. The social and financial support emanating from social security legislation in advanced countries has also led people to recast their view of their relationship to work. People are not prepared to be exploited and most do not have to put up with bad treatment by employers such as their parents and grandparents may have experienced.

There have been many changes in the legal requirements which employers have had to fulfil. These changes are found in several areas such as sex and race discrimination, provisions for people with disabilities and health and safety standards. They have influenced the care, training and selection of staff, which have all had to become more sophisticated and effective. The expense and, unfortunately, the increasing likelihood of legal action in the event of a mistake, have forced businesses and organisations to improve the quality of their work environment and the care of their staff and customers. The ISO 9000 standards for quality in the workplace have had a major impact in encouraging companies to install systems and procedures of the highest quality, focusing on safety, reliability and customer satisfaction. Again, these kinds of changes cannot be implemented unless the workforce is positive and committed to working together for the good of the company and the customer.

It has dawned on managers that in many business situations people are the most important resource. The financial and accountancy aspects are still important and production and design are no less significant than they were, but without the right people in the right places, businesses will fail even if they have the best accountants and machinery in the world.

Having said that, we can clearly see that advanced technology, such as computers and robotics, is rapidly bringing about a change in the way work is organised. Many modern production line jobs consist of sitting watching an electronically controlled machine doing the physical work that ten years ago was done by hand. The human skills now required are those such as attention, manual dexterity and vigilance. Higher order cognitive skills are needed in workers whose job consists of recognising and diagnosing process errors, resetting machines and making sure production materials are available in time. These job changes have brought about a reconsideration of the question of job satisfaction. There is now a need to invent ways of preventing boredom and stress, which in their turn cause staff turnover and possibly accidents.

The market requirements for workers are changing rapidly in specific directions. For example, in the United States, employment projections up until the year 2005, have suggested that there will be a growth in the workforce of 22 per cent from 121.1 million to 147.5 million workers. More growth will occur in the executive–managerial and service sector jobs. Clerical and administrative jobs and those for assemblers, operators and labourers will continue to decline in number relative to others (Silvestri, 1993). These changes will bring about a different workforce and ways of dealing with them will need to change too.

Managers are becoming increasingly aware that psychology is relevant to work, because psychology is about people and their behaviour. How people think and how their ideas can be changed are crucial to how they will work. How they feel about things at work affects their commitment to work and reaction to stressors. How they can be trained to learn new skills affects their occupational longevity and their overall usefulness. How people's characteristics can be assessed and compared with one another affects employers' ability to choose who will work for them. In many areas the findings of psychology filter through to the workplace, sometimes disguised as something else, but there none the less.

Before considering some specific examples of applications of psychology, we will take a brief look at some of the methodological considerations involved in psychological research.

What is the scientific method?

In general and most of the time psychology attempts to adopt the 'scientific method'. This consists of a number of distinct steps beginning with a period of preliminary observation and examination of previous theories and findings. Then various hypotheses are suggested and an experiment is designed. A hypothesis is a statement linking two or more of the variables in the situation together, usually saying how they will be related to each other. The variables, which are the things that we measure or change, are divided into independent (we control these) and dependent (they change as a result of our experiment). Some aspect of a situation is manipulated (independent variable) and observations (dependent variable) are made and analysed.

The experimenter might then propose a new theory, or a minor change of an existing one, which seems to account for the observations made. Then the theory is tested in another experiment, and so on round the loop again and again. Results are reported factually and honestly at conferences and in journals and books and the scientific community can examine them and try to repeat the findings for themselves. Various elements are included in the overall situation to make the process have more weight. For example, samples are usually chosen to be as representative as possible of the population that is being examined. When measures or observations are made, steps are taken to make them as objective and repeatable as possible. Where necessary and possible, people or groups are assigned randomly to treatments so that their individual characteristics will not unduly influence the results one way or another.

Of course this is a long-winded and tedious process of an academic nature. In the real world, some people prefer to have an opinion and stick to it no matter what occurs. Usually if they are loud enough, rich enough or important enough, people have to listen to them anyway. For example, one manager in response to a questionnaire about selection techniques told us that 'final selection is always based on our own instinct' (Porteous and Hodgins, 1995). It would probably be very difficult to tell that sort of person that academic research had shown conclusively over fifty years that selection based on instinct was about as effective as selection based on sticking a pin in the list while blindfolded.

Nevertheless we will continue to research, experiment, observe, ask questions and try to spread our findings and theories into the practical context of the working environment. In the workplace itself, as more people with psychological knowledge and enquiring minds are employed, improvements will be introduced and new methods tried out.

The two main approaches of psychology

Psychology offers two principal methodological approaches with which it hopes to establish laws which will explain and predict at least some of the behaviour of people. The first one we will look at is the method of *experimentation*. The essential characteristic of experimentation is that one element in a situation is changed or held constant and the resulting effects on something else are observed. For example, we may want to predict how changing some condition of the workplace will affect some aspect of people's behaviour.

Sometimes we cannot actually change the conditions of work, but instead have to examine the effect of a variable where a difference is known to exist and try to determine whether that difference seems to be related to something else. Perhaps males and females, or young and old respond differently to advice of different kinds given during a counselling/training session. In this experiment we could have four

Example

Some companies, e.g. banks, multinationals and large private companies, have systems where staff can criticise and advise other staff about their behaviour and performance. These appraisal systems work by means of questionnaires and ratings, followed by feedback discussion. Appraisal can be in an upward direction where the workers give their opinions on the supervisor, or more often downward, and the appraisals can be anonymous or accountable.

categories (male/young, male/old, female/young, female/old) and the variable we are interested in is their response to advice. We might find a gender difference, a sex difference or an interaction effect. An interaction effect could mean that young females and older males took the most advice compared to young males and older females who between them took the least.

In a study in an insurance company Antonioni (1994) assigned subjects randomly to groups. Subordinates appraised managers, some anonymously and some not. The positive or negative aspect of the ratings was measured, as was the extent to which the appraisers felt comfortable doing the ratings. The results showed that anonymous raters felt more comfortable and the accountable raters gave higher ratings.

As an experiment this illustrates the following concepts:

- *Experimental control*: this is achieved by the random assignment of subjects to groups. By doing this, it is assumed that differences between people which might affect the results but which are not part of the experiment will be balanced out.

- *Dependent variables*: these are the ones that we are looking for the change in as a result of the procedure; in this case they were the level of the ratings, high or low, and the comfort of the raters.

- *Independent variables*: these were the levels of accountability, i.e. there were two levels, anonymous and accountable, there were two levels of job category, subordinate or supervisor, and appraisal could have had two levels, up or down, though in fact it had only one.

The second general methodological approach in psychology is called *correlational*. This set of methods has many applications in occupational psychology. In many practical situations in factories and offices, we cannot come in and get people to do things differently or to work in randomly assigned groups and then measure what happens when we change something. We have to take situations as they exist, measure a selection of variables across a group of subjects and examine whether one variable is predictive of another. Correlation coefficients are one way of examining the strength of the relationship which variables have to each other. An index ranging from −1 to +1 can be calculated, which is indicative of the extent to which two variables share the same rate and direction of change. For example, the more heat applied to a kettle of water, the faster the water boils, i.e. there is a negative correlation which would be high (as heat increases, time decreases). In the workplace more employee participation in decision making might lead to higher productivity, so there would be a positive correlation; more leads to more. A further stage in correlation is reached when we control for the effects of a third variable on the relations between the first two. This involves 'partial correlation' and offers many interesting possibilities.

In a study of this kind, Tett and Jackson (1990) made a number of observational measures of 'participative behaviour' from responses that subjects made to a paper and pencil work-related exercise. They then examined whether these measures were

> **Example**
>
> In selecting staff many companies use personality tests and exercises in situations called assessment centres. We could be interested in the way in which the behaviour observed in the situation is related to the apparent personality of the individual as described by a personality questionnaire. That is, do people actually behave as they say they do?

related to the subjects' scores on cognitive structure (prefers definite and certain information), autonomy (prefers freedom and no restraint) and dominance (enjoys being the leader) obtained from a personality questionnaire.

As is the case in many studies of this type, they did not find everything they thought they would. We will see later on that personality questionnaires are not very good at predicting single specific behaviours. The high scorers in cognitive structure scored low in participative tendencies, as they expected. However, high participators were high in both dominance and autonomy.

Another point worth making here, and which you will see the relevance of later on, is that correlational studies can sometimes be accused of being 'fishing expeditions'. If you have a large number of variables, and correlate all of them with each other, then purely by chance you will find some significant relationships. This is bad research. Research should start with a definite hypothesis based on previous work. What is being examined should be decided at the beginning, not at the end. Significance testing, which we have all grown up with, should be accompanied by more emphasis on replication. That is, another researcher or even yourself should repeat your study in another place and get similar results. This is good evidence for the truth or otherwise of a theory (Breakwell *et al.*, 1995; Kimble, 1996).

A methodological point

A methodological warning which is given by Bandura (1978) is called reciprocal causation. This refers to the fact that it is very difficult to separate out the actual cause of an event in a complex social setting. In the work situation the person is part of the situation and their behaviour changes the situation. Additionally, the person's perceptions of the situation may be having a crucial role in how they behave or report their behaviour. Despite this rather strong reservation, a large part of psychology involves seeing if one thing relates to another in a given situation. We try to be scientific and rational by controlling things as much as possible and by getting results repeated in other similar situations by other people. However, there is no point in pretending other than that in many respects psychology is a rather 'soft science'. Nothing is ever proven definitively and changing perceptions of psychology itself often bring about different ways of understanding and speaking about the subject matter. Those of us who have been 'doing Psychology' for many years, even notice the same subject coming around again with a new title, as if it had just been discovered. Despite this reservation there is no doubt that psychology has a contribution to make to the way we understand and operate in relation to work behaviour. It is also beyond doubt that thinking in a psychological way will make you better able to understand and relate to aspects of your own work and life. At the end of the day, the effectiveness of psychology is as much to do with the way it directs our way of thinking as it has to do with any rules or theories or prescriptions it might offer.

Applications of occupational psychology

Now we shall briefly look at a number of areas which the psychology of work is concerned with, in order to give you an idea of what the subject is about. You might also think of this as an appetiser and possibly consider, before you read any further, what might be in store.

Individual differences

Correlational techniques have led to the development of the psychology of *individual differences*, a subject with its roots in the late nineteenth century measurement laboratories of Wundt and Galton. This has led to the development of methods which help to assess people's characteristics. World War II gave a considerable impetus to this endeavour, in the area of selection and training of officers and soldiers. Individual difference variables can readily be fitted into experimental or predictive patterns, and so many psychological researchers have used this approach. For example, relating the vigilance and intelligence of radar operators to their success in spotting enemy aircraft has been studied with useful results.

Another example is honesty tests; there are many such tests and they are widely used. Surveys have shown that most of the pilfering /shoplifting in stores is carried out by employees. It is also true that the really significant losses sustained by organisations are due to the higher management. The psychologist who can accurately predict honesty in a socially acceptable manner will become a very rich person indeed. Most methods are based on questionnaires which people can answer dishonestly which creates rather a problem. However, we are developing ways around this particular snag. Electronic lie detectors are not socially acceptable on a wide scale and in any case not always very reliable.

Concepts such as vigilance, intelligence, manual dexterity and honesty are psychological constructs which we can measure and use in employment selection or in research. Their creation and development usually depends on correlational techniques as well as on a great deal of imagination and creativity on the part of the developer.

Personality and work

We can examine the relationship between personality and work and vice versa. The most common personality type in a particular work group was found to be: 'hesitant, mild, indecisive and non-demanding and also dependable, deliberate and amiable'. Fifty-five per cent of this group of employees describe themselves as sensing plus thinking types (Cusack, 1991). This finding mirrored those in similar studies done in the United States. According to the author of the test used in these studies (Myers–Briggs Type Inventory), these personality types stand a better chance of success in fields which demand impersonal analysis of concrete facts, such as law. The work group in question were policemen.

There is currently a debate on the whole question of whether personality tests can predict occupational behaviour at all (Blinkhorn and Johnson, 1990). We are very interested in this question, because if we could find particular people for whom a particular job was more suitable, then it would be very significant, i.e. perhaps they would be more successful, or less prone to nervous breakdowns or less accident prone. In various occupational areas these things can be quite crucial and involve great financial savings if we could get the predictions right. Consider how much it costs to train a policeman. What a pity if we were training a lot of 'mis-fits', in the true sense of the word.

While this serious scientific debate is going on, the use of graphology in person-nel selection is spreading and is particularly popular in some European Union countries. Solid scientific evidence that graphology is a useful predictor is lacking and the facts point in the opposite direction.

Although psychologists try to be scientific, objective and sceptical, in the real world people who have a chance of making money from a psychological idea or technique are not hampered by notions of scientific rigour or proof. In the commercial environment, something works if you can make money from it. Even in psychology this can be observed, where those who are objecting to some technique are selling an alternative of their own and simply seeking publicity and commercial space for their own product or service. And that is how it should be, otherwise we would be hog-tied and hamstrung and no one would risk doing anything. This is why occupational psychology is particularly interesting, it actually works and people pay for it and derive benefits!

Work design and measurement

The area of Ergonomics and the measurement of work performance has become more scientific from the 1920s when Frank and Lillian Gilbreth and Frederick Taylor laid down the principles of time and motion study. The ability to measure work has led into the areas of ergonomics and human factors. These areas of study are now central to industry and organisations. Measuring work and work study are sometimes called 'indus-trial engineering'. Oborne (1995) describes ergonomics as the amalgamation between three separate scientific strands, physiology, experimental psychology and engineering. Ergonomists attempt to design work so as to maximise the safety and reliability of the production process, to make job tasks easier to learn and to make workers feel more comfortable and satisfied. Occupational psychology and ergonomics are now separate disciplines, but they overlap in many ways and they both owe part of their nascence to something called the Industrial Fatigue Research Board which developed out of a committee looking into the health of munitions workers in the First World War.

Performance appraisal

One area which occupational psychology has been involved in somewhat less willingly than others is Performance Appraisal. Employers would very much value the ability to accurately and fairly assess the work performance of their staff. This information could then be tied in with promotions, training and rewards. Appraisal is both developmental, i.e. it helps to see where people can make progress, and for reward purposes, i.e. the best performers can earn a bonus. This is one of several issues in occupational psychology where the issues of the real world in the form of workers' rights, union agreements and employers' priorities have to be carefully balanced and negotiated. A valid 'psychological' way of appraising may be too time consuming or unacceptable and we may often have to compromise our principles. Research on performance appraisal has for many years looked long and hard at methods and then staff acceptability; now the focus is back to methods and with a more in-depth emphasis on the psychological processes involved.

Behaviour and work performance

These are affected by a multitude of interacting variables. In particular we can categorise them into three broad areas. These are abilities and personality, the social environment of the workplace and the role of training and experience. Abilities and personality are particularly relevant in the selection and placement of staff. Much early occupational psychology was involved in this area and this is still the case today. Methods of testing and assessment of job applicants is very much the speciality of the psychologist. Effective methods can save organisations millions of pounds over the years.

Humanistic values

As work has become more standardised and machinery more technically complex the 'human' input has been treated more seriously. The feelings, motivations and social relations of the worker are receiving more and more attention. A major influence from the early development of occupational psychology is the 'Hawthorne Studies' which began in 1924 in the Western Electric Company (Roethlisberger and Dickson, 1939). These pointed to the very strong possibility that the route to gains in productivity, etc., was not only to be found in the organisation and mechanisation of work but also in the psychological treatment of the worker, i.e. 'the people factor', and in improvements in lighting, rest, etc.

These studies, which have been extremely influential in occupational psychology, are also an example of something which can occur in psychology more often than we might like to admit. The actual results of the studies when rigorously examined were not really as plain as they are often quoted as being. But we have come to believe that they were something that they were not, i.e. an artefact has been created by mis-interpretation and exaggeration of a minor scientific finding. It so happened that at the time people needed the Hawthorne type of finding to advance worker's rights, and to combat the heavy implementation of assembly-line manufacturing with all its detriment to the human condition. It also enabled pioneering social psychologists to make an input outside the laboratories of the time (Adair, 1984).

Cross-cultural values

Integrating hard core unemployed people from the ethnic minorities in the United States has proved difficult, as their values are often found to differ from the white majority with respect to integrating with the organisation, attendance and performance. Orientation programmes had to be devised to change values and beliefs (Friedlander and Greenberg, 1971). An example from this side of the Atlantic is that multinationals have found that an automatic transfer of values simply is not possible. In recent surveys of the cross-cultural effects of management culture, it has been noted that there is a gulf between the treatment received and the treatment expected between managers and workers and between manager and manager. Different ruling value systems often clash, with negative results.

Counselling workers

In any workforce there will be unfortunate individuals who have problems coping either with their job or with their life outside of work. In some industries this has been met with a 'hard luck', 'shape up or ship out' attitude, but in many organisations, especially the state-controlled ones and those with national reputations, there has been an attempt to respond to people's problems. In many instances this has taken the form of Employee Assistance Programmes. These exemplify the human side of management and the possible application of the skills of psychologists. Originating with alcohol treatment programmes in large companies in the 1940s they have since expanded to fulfil many other employee welfare and counselling functions. Personal problems of employees can have a significant impact across a company. Recent cases have included nurses deliberately injuring and indeed killing patients. More mundane issues include absenteeism and lateness, as well as sabotage.

Stress

Workers' coping with and their response to stressful work environments bring us to the topic of stress at work. This is tied up with safety, absenteeism and well-being of workers and is a flourishing area at present thanks partly to Professor Cary Cooper of the University of Manchester Institute of Science and Technology. This issue is an intriguing one, as there is some considerable doubt over whether the idea of stress is a valid one in the first place. Concepts from social psychology, e.g. role conflict, have been used to explain and treat different types of occupational stress.

Leadership

There are numerous examples of the application of social psychology to the workplace. Among these is the study of leadership style, whether autocratic, democratic or charismatic approaches work better and in which circumstances. Another area is the study of organising and encouraging useful communication up and down the hierarchy in a group or organisation. Choosing teams and then finding the right way to lead the activities of the team is a current focus of interest. Team building and organisational change and development are growing areas of interest for occupational psychologists at the moment. Literally thousands of psychologists and others are employed in consultancy roles to make managers work better together and to transmit management philosophies and practices 'down the line' to production workers and supervisors. The growth in consultancy businesses in occupational psychology has been very considerable in the last ten years. Currently there are over 200 such businesses in the United Kingdom, whereas ten years ago there were only a handful. Organisations are 'de-layering' at present. The idea is to have fewer people to report to and fewer people overseeing other people. In place of the layers of management, workers are being trained to increase their own responsibility for their work and to communicate more with each other to solve the work-related problems which crop up from day to day.

Human–computer interaction

A recent influence from psychology is the Cognitive approach. This looks at work and people's behaviour in the workplace in terms of information-processing functions, such as remembering, recognising and associating pieces of information. Human factor specialists with a grounding in psychology employ ideas from research in memory, perception and learning. They will have an ever-increasing impact, especially as we move further into the information technology revolution. Questions of considerable importance in many fields at the moment include the following. How does memory affect the interviewing process? What kinds of instructions are more likely to be understood and even followed in relation to operating a piece of machinery? How should a training programme be designed for maximum effectiveness? These are mainly about cognitive issues, i.e. how will people best process the information? While computers are all around us and seem sophisticated, not enough thought has gone into making them usable. People have been asked to adapt to these awkward things whose design has been led by their technology and not by people's psychological capabilities. In some cases, this has been at considerable emotional and sometimes physical cost. The European Union at the moment is investing considerable sums of money in research on computer usability to address these concerns (Preece, 1994).

Health and safety

Cognitive psychology, psychometrics and correlational methods can all be seen as impacting on the area of safety behaviour, which itself is a combination of attitudes and personality, e.g. risk takers and decision-making. These psychological concepts are relevant in the workplace because of the considerable changes and legislation in the area of health and safety at work.

New work

In the forthcoming millennium, occupational psychologists will be heavily involved in the design of work and working lives centred around the great changes taking place in the availability and nature of work. Schaff (1985) pointed out that in Germany the idea of 'the fading away of work' is well established. New technology leads to reduced time working and so work loses its dominant position in structuring people's time and thus their perspectives on life. Work also loses some of its dominance, as early retirement and extended education eat away at its time demands. There is beginning to be a gradual incursion of leisure values and a general 'post-materialist way' of thinking. We have moved from the era of 'conspicuous consumption' when membership of the 'yuppie' culture was thought worthwhile and purchased with flamboyant spending on material goods. We are now entering the era of more balanced material consumption and more emphasis on improvement in lifestyle. How we relate to work will be one of the central themes of this change and occupational psychology can be expected to play an important role. It is becoming more important that work offers autonomy and is interesting, while the moral importance of hard work and pride in craftsmanship is declining (Cherrington, 1980). A technique known as job enrichment has gained in importance in order to counter the effects of this decline in the pride and moral value of work. New work meanings demand new ways of motivating workers.

Occupational psychology and professionalism

Occupational psychologists work in a wide variety of locations, from government training centres to marketing departments of cosmetic manufacturers. In Britain the profession as such is mainly under the wing of the British Psychological Society, Division of Occupational Psychology. Members of this division supervise and control entry to itself by means of the post-graduate degree in Occupational Psychology or its equivalent BPS post-graduate Certificate. The level of control over admission to the Division has increased over the years. Originally anyone with an interest in the subject could join the Division; now people need to be qualified and experienced. There are eight recognised areas in which potential members must demonstrate a degree of familiarity or qualification. These are human–machine interaction, design of environments, personnel selection, performance appraisal, counselling and personal development, training, employee relations and organisational development.

The European Association of Work and Organisational Psychology is a more informal grouping linking together occupational psychologists from various countries. Its aims are the dissemination of ideas, encouragement of education and research and the communication of findings via newsletters, journals and conferences. There are many other academic and professional bodies which have an input into the subject. The Institute of Personnel Development has a major role in the personnel and training fields for example.

Development of personnel function in industry

Personnel is part of the management function, which traditionally has been divided into financial, production and marketing, with a general manager overseeing all and also concerned with administrative and secretarial duties. The general manager or company secretary often took personnel under their wing and delegated many of the routine functions to a clerk. Personnel is now a main fourth area of management function in most companies. The main concerns of the personnel manager are the health and welfare of employees, their employment rights and conditions and their selection and training. The day-to-day life of a personnel manager is largely concerned with administrative work. Pensions, benefits, insurance, health, sick days, holiday rosters, overtime, bonuses and meetings are the core elements of the personnel manager's job. Much of what we will consider in this book enters the personnel function but unfortunately not at a very sophisticated level. Many companies are totally unaware of the value of good occupational psychologists. Being qualified in occupational psychology is not the same as being qualified in personnel.

Summary

This chapter has given you a brief overview of what occupational psychology is all about. It has included some elementary points about psychological research and also included some special warnings and guidelines for interpreting what you are told to believe by psychologists. It has emphasised that the future of this subject is bright and the need for specialists in this area is likely to expand considerably in the future. Even just a passing knowledge of the subject will be good for you in whatever career you choose to follow.

Activities

1.   **Consider a job you have done and discuss whether the application of psychology to it would bring benefits.**

2.   **Ask a personnel manager about psychology in their line of work.**

3.   **Talk to a selection of different workers about any of the topics so far mentioned, e.g. stress, performance appraisal.**

Further reading

Breakwell, G.M., Hammond, S. and Fife-Schaw, C.F. (eds) (1995) *Research Methods in Psychology*. (London, Sage).

Guest, D.E. (1994) Organisational psychology and human resource management. *European Work and Organizational Psychologist*, 4, 251–70.

Kimble, G.A. (1996) *Psychology: the Hope of a Science*. (Cambridge, MA, MIT Press).

Shimmin, S. and Wallis, D. (1994) *Fifty Years of Occupational Psychology*. (Leicester, British Psychological Society).

Addresses

British Psychological Society, St. Andrews House, Princess Road, East, Leicester, LE1 7DR. Fax +1162470787.

European Association of Work and Organizational Psychology, Secretariat, Coosemanstraat 100, 3010 Leuven, Belgium. Fax +32 16 25 7815.

Attitudes to work

CHAPTER 2

Focus questions

What are your attitudes towards work?

Why do some people seem to want more and more things to do while others are content to take a spectator role?

How can employers use an understanding of work attitudes to improve the performance of their companies?

What is it that helps us develop our attitudes to work?

Much of what we do in our work and careers is related to what we believe about work, how we conceive it, what its value is to us, etc. Whether a student studies hard or puts much effort into assignments is partly influenced by personal beliefs. Other import-ant influences include such factors as the time available, whether the subject is interesting and what the student's social priorities are. We could categorise these factors as resources (time), content and environmental pressures. These tend to be balanced and prioritised by the individual's attitudes and beliefs about their import-ance. At the end of the day, in the case of the student, an essay gets written or a chapter read, either in good time, at the last minute, or not at all. The student then has to rationalise. For example, they did not have the time, the chapter was boring, their granny died (for the third time). In the past two years I have had two students who have lost their final year projects because of a fire in their flats! People's beliefs and attitudes about work affect their performance in a similar way.

It appears that what we think and feel about work is a relatively stable and enduring construct which transfers from one work situation to another. That is, our job attitudes and beliefs, provided nobody tries to change them by training, are for the most part fairly consistent. This fact has a lot of serious implications for employers and for individuals and brings up the question of where we get those beliefs from in the first place. For example in a study over a five-year period (longitudinal) of 5000 middle-aged men, considerable consistency in their job attitudes was shown, even in cases where they had changed their jobs. Prior attitudes turned out to be better predictors of their expressed satisfaction than changes in their pay and or previous levels of satisfaction. That is, what they brought to the job in terms of attitudes was very important in determining how they felt about their job. It was even more import-ant than many of the situational aspects of the job itself (Staw and Ross, 1985). This has interesting implications for selecting staff and for training. If we want to have a happy and efficient workforce, we should look closely at their attitudes before we decide to employ them and after they have been taken on, we should construct aspects of the work environment that help to develop the 'right' sort of attitudes.

In relation to work, a set of economic and work-related beliefs have been studied over the years. These seem to have a clear impact on how different people and possibly different national groups approach the process of working. Perhaps they contain some explanation of why some people are 'workaholics' and others seem to be lazy, or as some managers might say, 'difficult to motivate'. Some of these con-cepts will be described and relevant research outlined in the following section.

Protestant work ethic

This concept is found in a wide range of social science literature. In psychology it is usually seen as being characterised by a belief in the importance of hard work, rationality, frugality and as a defence against sloth, sensuality and religious doubt (Mirels and Garrett, 1971). It is seen as part of our personality and it represents a tendency to behave consistently in a particular manner across many situations so that our level of work ethic will partly determine how we behave in the work situation.

If you look around your colleagues or fellow students, you may notice differences in certain behaviours in relation to their study and work habits. The person who is high in Protestant Work Ethic will be the one who saves carefully and does not waste things. You can see them writing on the back of old notes rather than buying a new notepad. They will appear to be always on the go and directed to getting something done. Unless you share their beliefs, you will tend to avoid them and find their company rather trying. The early dissenters and Protestants, many of whom came from Ulster, Scotland, England and Germany to found the United States, were characterised by this way of behaving.

The concept originated with the German sociologist, Weber. In 1904 Weber's theory stated that Protestant work ethic ideals and values were strong determining factors in the way capitalism made progress as the ruling ideology of prosperous states. Some main features in the way child rearing is carried out, have been associated with these ideals and values.

Measuring work ethic

Questionnaires are the generally accepted way of assessing how strong people are on Protestant work ethic. The various scales which measure work ethic seem to agree well with each other and show consistent relationships with other measures. This is usually taken as evidence that there is a valid concept. It could be that what is being measured has some kind of existence in the set of human traits. It may of course be simply a subset of another trait of a higher order such as conservatism; research is ambiguous on this question.

Work on the Protestant work ethic concept over the years has looked at its relation to various work beliefs and to behaviour. It has been related to differences in people's reactions to unemployment (Feather, 1982), those with high work ethic being more affected and reacting more strongly. Some people distinguish between work ethic and Work Involvement (Kanungo, 1982). People can identify very strongly with their particular job because of the extent to which their needs are satisfied by it. This might be because their needs are very salient in relation to the job. In another job they might be less involved or even not involved at all if their needs were not being met. The concept of work involvement would be measured by how people respond to such statements as 'Work should only be a small part of life', or 'The most important things that happen in life involve work'. This contrast may explain why some people will work like demons in training the street football team, or in getting people to support a motion for cycle paths but in their actual job, they are totally apathetic.

Beit-Hallahmi (1979) found that Protestant work ethic scores were related to religious self-identification (those claiming to be Catholics and Protestants scoring higher than Jews and agnostics) and ethnicity (whites score higher than blacks). Conservatives score higher than liberals and those who attend church score higher than those with unconventional beliefs or low church attendance. This was a study among students at Michigan University and we might therefore question its 'ecological' validity. That is, bearing in mind the environment in which it was carried out would its results apply in other, more real world settings? Tang and Tzeng (1992), in a study of 689 subjects from a mixed sample in the United States found that Protestant work ethic scores correlated with lower educational standing and with the support of the Republican party. There were no relations with gender or age though single people and the lower paid scored higher. Recent evidence in South America show considerable defections from Roman Catholicism. It has been suggested that these defections are related to the new modern industrial ethic of the country (Brazil).

Adrian Furnham of the Psychology Department in the University of London has published extensively in the area of measuring beliefs in relation to work and economics. In 1987, he studied whether work beliefs bore any relation to 'terminal' values. The main aim was to find evidence for or against the view of Feather (1985) that people have an overall cognitive–affective system which contains their values, work and other beliefs. Our values, which we develop through experience, underpin the beliefs that we also develop, making the experience that we have of life and work, etc., seem coherent and meaningful. Two hundred and fifty-six people from various walks of life completed a number of scales of beliefs and values. Furnham says they were not representative of the general population though not atypical.

Terminal values like freedom, equality, wisdom and instrumental values like ambition, helpfulness and honesty were given a scale value for each subject which depended on the ranking he or she gave to each of 18 values in each of the 2 sets. In total 252 correlations were calculated between the 36 values and the 7 belief scale scores. The principal findings were that some values were predictably associated with some work beliefs. Some background variables, i.e. age, social class and gender were predictive of values. Beliefs which were in favour of the capitalist societies' approved version of work, were in disagreement with the marxist beliefs and the leisure ethic. Another conclusion was that the work ethic concept is complex and the scales which measure it do not all agree. There is more to work ethic than can be contained in one simple definition. The above points about value systems should be borne in mind when we consider, shortly, Locke's widely regarded theory of satisfaction and motivation.

Need for achievement

William James was one of the first internationally recognised psychologists at the beginning of the twentieth century. His brother, Henry, was even more famous as a playwright and novelist. William (1890) in his famous *Principles of Psychology* made the suggestion that there was a relationship between personal striving and emotional well-being. His views have been influential for many years. McClelland *et al.* (1953), following on from James' theories, developed the idea that we all have a degree of 'Need for Achievement'. He saw this as a fundamental human trait. It tended to take over from the Protestant work ethic though 'nAch' only covers part of the concept of Protestant work ethic and perhaps is not too well founded or measured. In many experiments and research studies since he introduced the idea, it has been supported and has shown predictive relationships with achievement behaviours, both in the real world and in the laboratory. It has also been associated with early upbringing and socialisation experiences, e.g. how has success been rewarded in childhood and adolescence (Heckhausen *et al.*, 1985).

McClelland studied children's literature in different cultures for the presence of achievement-related concepts and showed that these were related to the growth or decline of capitalism and industrialisation. In a study of the state of forty nations in 1925 he found a correlation (0.53) between achievement motivation measured in this way and the growth in the consumption of electricity. In later studies exploring the concept, various researchers have found that high levels of nAch have been shown to predict important outcomes in management situations. Managers with a high need for achievement have been shown to be more receptive, flexible and enterprising. Wainer and Rubin (1969) found that output was related to high nAch across a number of firms in the one industry. Those companies whose staff had higher levels of nAch had better levels of output, other things being equal.

At the opposite pole is the need to avoid failure, which is quite closely linked to nAch as its mirror image. Rather than seeking situations in which they can succeed, people who are concerned with the need to avoid failure try to avoid situations in which failure is a possibility. They may be found in unchallenging job roles where there is no clear measure of performance and where promotion is achieved through serving time and not causing any stir.

Measuring nAch

The large volume of research on the need for achievement has produced many measures of the concept. Fineman (1977) lists twenty-two such measures (five projective, six scales from larger personality questionnaires and eleven specifically designed questionnaires), so the subject has been well studied. Projective measures are those in which a vague or ambiguous stimulus is presented to subjects and their responses are categorised according to a predetermined scheme. This is often a good way of getting information of a psychological nature as the subjects are not fully aware of what they are being asked and will be more revealing than if they are asked direct obvious questions, such as 'Do you like work?'. For instance if you were to be shown a picture of a man leaning on a shovel beside a large pile of rubble, what would you think? See later for an answer.

It has been suggested that nAch breaks down into a number of separate dimensions listed as work ethic (the desire to work hard), pursuit of excellence (aspiring to reach a standard of excellence), status aspiration (climbing the hierarchy, the need to be dominant), competitiveness (enjoying the element of competition), acquisitiveness for money and mastery (reinforcement obtained from successful problem solving) (Cassidy and Lynn, 1989).

Power needs

Power needs are also being increasingly studied and give some clue to satisfaction for some people. McClelland (1975) suggests that some people need to have an impact on others in a power, control sense. Apparently men with high power needs prefer competitive sports and read *Playboy* magazine! Two forms of power motive are observed in practice, Personalised Power and Socialised Power. The first of these is manifested in an interpersonal way, person to person, law of the jungle, etc. People seek control and dominance over others for their own sake. People with high socialised power needs believe that they are exercising power for the good of others. McClelland found that such people were in leadership roles in organisations. They might be bossy teachers or head nuns or charity workers who work with the weak and the vulnerable. Positions which give them control over other people but are under the guise of 'helping' are ideal for this person. In the working environment these people's needs may be satisfied, provided they can exercise these kinds of power over others. It should be said that they may not be obviously bossy, they can sometimes speak very quietly and be self-effacing provided nobody contradicts them or tries to impose their will on them.

In the area of work beliefs generally, there is a very large number of measures most of which are in the form of questionnaires. Cook *et al*. (1981) assembled together over 200 scales measuring various aspects of work beliefs and attitudes. For example, they list 29 measures which have set out to tap a person's commitment to paid employment. Anyone doing research in this area would find this book a useful starting point in their search for suitable measures.

Locus of control/attribution theory

Locus of Control is another very common psychological construct which mainly originated in the educational psychology area and has been adapted to research on work behaviour. It is defined as a generalised expectancy that rewards, reinforcements and outcomes in life are controlled either by oneself or by factors outside oneself, such as other persons (Rotter, 1966). Attribution theory is about how we attribute the success and failure outcomes of our behaviour. Do we blame or praise ourselves, blame our colleagues or our environment, for example the weather, the tools, the slow computer? There are numerous interesting correlates of locus of control. For example, training people with different levels of locus of control respond differently to feedback on their performance.

Spector (1988) reports a recent development of a Work Locus of Control Scale. Examples of items from this scale include, 'A job is what you make of it' and 'Getting the job you want is mostly a matter of luck'. As you can see from these examples, locus of control is about whether you think you are in charge of the happenings in your life. The more 'internal' you are, the more you think you are in charge, at the opposite end of the scale you would be inclined to believe that there is not much you can do about anything; it is all down to 'fate', i.e. you believe in 'external' control of reinforcement. Further study using this scale in a longitudinal design with students as subjects before and after they started work, showed relations between locus of control and various other work variables such as job satisfaction. Locus of control has also been shown to have some effect in the success of young people in finding work after leaving school and in the way people react to becoming unemployed. There is an accumulation of evidence that this variable is related to many outcomes of behaviour in education, work and career success.

Origins of values

Although this is a book on occupational psychology, we should consider how some of these belief and value systems originate. We come to the workplace already highly conditioned and organised, due to our earlier upbringing. Child-rearing practices of parents have been shown to be related to the level of Protestant work ethic which people display. These practices include encouraging independence, enforcing the delay of gratification, encouragement of rationality and mastery training. For example, in order to *encourage independence*, the child is allowed to make certain decisions on their own and to fail at times. They are not over-protected from the consequences of their own choices. They are made to wait their turn for satisfaction of their needs, rather than getting everything they want the minute they scream; this is *delay of gratification*. Then we have the *encouragement of rationality*. Everything has an explanation at some level, believing in luck or mystical influences on our fate is not acceptable. Finally we have *mastery training* where the child is made to finish tasks successfully and to feel pride in a job well done, no matter how trivial.

These practices allegedly lead children to have Protestant work ethic beliefs and so to develop high levels of achievement motivation. High achievers become successful entrepreneurs and create business and further the ideals and values of capitalist society. Of course, we are all familiar with the poor little rich girl or boy. The princess with the rich daddy, used to the exact opposite of the above treatment, who unless she gets a rich husband will achieve very little from her own resources. Or the playboy with all the material advantages, but whose only drive is pathological selfishness. These types would be at the opposite pole to high work ethic and would be unlikely to achieve much on their own initiative.

Frederick Jackson Turner in *The Frontier in American History* (1921) describes the typical frontiersman who pioneered the American West as optimistic, hopeful and with high levels of aspiration. They believed strongly that their children would surpass them in accomplishment and that the world was there to be improved. It has been suggested that they were influenced by some American Indian ways of child-rearing, which emphasise independence and self-expression in children. It was not uncommon for the early settlers to marry women from the Native American tribes. In Pensacola, Florida, the wealth of the community was established by the immigrant Scottish and English men who married women from the local Cree Indians. Their descendants then went on to develop the extremely profitable lumber and fishing industries, which produced many millionaires before the fishing stocks were exhausted and the forests cut bare. We might speculate that a combination of high work ethic combined with an intimate knowledge of the local environment and culture provided a very effective mixture.

Bronfenbrenner (1961) has proposed that there is a strong connection between parental occupational type and the way children were socialised at home. This then affects how they tend to behave in career settings later on. Different approaches to child rearing are associated with 'bureaucratic' and 'entrepreneurial' types of occupation. Bureaucratic parents are those who work in civil service-type settings or in the offices of large companies or banks, etc. They do everything by the book and take no personal risks. Whether they get a job finished on one day or the next will have little impact outside of their organisation and their main concerns are security and avoidance of blame. The entrepreneurial parent on the other hand is mainly a small tradesperson, owning a business, taking risks and struggling against the competitive and bureaucratic forces in the environment to provide for the family and the workforce employed in the business.

Meaning of work

Another variable which has been extensively studied and shown to relate to working behaviour is 'meaning of work'. It concerns our beliefs about work itself and how these beliefs influence the way we prioritise work alongside all the other aspects of our lives. Work meanings can be seen as shared interpretations of what people want and expect to get from work. They are part of the individual's social reality and they affect the way in which a person responds to the working situation. Usually a group of people who work well together will hold many of the same work beliefs. This has long been recognised by military commanders who try to instil the ethos of the corps to the new recruits. Those who hold different beliefs and refuse to change will find that they do not fit in and eventually they will crash out in one way or another.

Work meaning comes down to four basic areas of belief.

1. What work people will expect others to do, i.e. what is reasonable in terms of tasks or targets. How often have you heard people say they left a job because they were asked to do X?

2. How people are socialised at work, i.e. how they are socialised into a new work setting, what role are their personal views accorded, whether friendship is part of the work scene, to what extent are we responsible for our fellow workers.

3. How work is related to and integrated with other aspects of life, i.e. do we work to live or live to work?

4. How do people acquire the self-imposed monitoring standards which tell them that a job is well done or is finished?

The last of these is a most interesting one which deserves detailed study. Looking at different people doing the same job or doing a job-related selection test, I have often been struck by the differences in people's views of what the finishing position of the task is. Some people will do the task, put away or tidy the materials and sit back ready for the next task, others will do the task to an extent and finish at the first acceptable point, gaze round, watch others and seek environmental diversions. There is clearly a wide difference in peoples' views of when a job is done. These beliefs seem to be quite culturally dependent, and one of the first things immigrants to foreign cultures have to develop is a set of appropriate work beliefs.

Studies carried out in the meaning of work concept and how it varies in different societies have tended to use the following variables, derived from the above more general aspects: *work centrality*, which is the degree of importance that working has in the life of the individual at any point in time; to what extent do people put work above other aspects of their life such as their home, family and friends? Is work a principal source of satisfaction to them and does it form part of their identity as a person, or is it just a boring interruption in the way of more important considerations in life? *Work goals* are the things which people can achieve from working. Various jobs will differ in the array of work goals which they provide and which are possible to achieve. In the study of work goals, individuals are usually asked to rate the relative importance to themselves of goals and values such as the following:

Opportunity to learn

Good interpersonal relations

Opportunity for promotion

Convenient working hours

Variety

Interesting work

Job security

Physical conditions

Pay

Autonomy

Match between job requirements and abilities

That is, on a scale from say, 1 to 5, we must rate how important it is to have 'opportunity for promotion'. Some people will answer '1' as they have no wish for responsibility and more challenge, they are happy to be a small cog in a large machine. Others must get on, so they would check the rating scale at '5'. Jobs can also be rated as to the extent that they provide these goals to the general worker. This can be incorporated into job design, a subject we will touch on in Chapter 4.

Social norms about working are what we are taught to believe about what are the usual or normal, right and wrong behaviours which we find in the workplace. There are two main points of focus which are the 'entitlement norms' and the 'obligation norms' towards work. The entitlement norms concern underlying rights of individuals and the work-related responsibilities of society towards the individual. These would concern things about how people are looked after in relation to health and safety at work. Are they provided with adequate training and guidance? Are they looked after when they fall ill? Do they expect their child to be given a job in their organisation before someone else's child? These are just some of the examples of the kinds of things that we may or may not think we are entitled to obtain from work. On the other hand, the obligation norms represent the underlying duties of the individual to organisations and to society with respect to working. Will we work late if need be to gain a valuable order? Will we keep secret the business of the company we work for, or are we willing to sell information to a rival? If someone is stealing from the workplace, are we duty bound to report them?

Cross-cultural experience has clearly taught that work standards, culture and values do not transport across national boundaries very easily. Multinational companies setting up in other countries, for example, have had to modify their expectations and change some of their practices to fit in with the ruling norms of the local workforce. An American refrigeration company, when it initially moved into Ireland, started out with the instructions that everyone was to be on first-name terms, all staff were to be called 'partners' and there were to be open plan offices. Staff in various grades were to participate in work sharing across the traditional boundaries. After the honeymoon period, the 'partners' decided that they were 'workers', and bosses were bosses. They also decided that their jobs were not going to be done by unskilled people or managers. Some bitter disputes ensued which included the slashing of tyres of 'scabs'. In due course, even doors and partitions were put on offices and today the plant is typical of any other. Engrained attitudes are not changed by directives.

Research on the meaning of work

Extensive studies have been carried out over the last decade in several countries on the meaning of work question. Ruiz Quintanilla and Wilpert (1991) concluded, from examining the question in Germany between 1983 and 1989, that while working hours are contracting, work is still a source of satisfying economic goals, though it has begun to be seen as also a source of satisfying goals of self-expression. They also concluded that the arrangement of working hours will have to become more flexible as the working week approaches thirty hours, as many people may wish to do their stint in a three-day period. Job sharing will become more common and trade union attitudes to rostering, etc., will have to change.

Another question which they raise is what will people do with the extra time resulting from the shorter working week? Hours may contract but people's work beliefs may remain the same, so how can the two elements be reconciled? Experience in America suggests that some people will take second jobs. This has a 'knock-on' effect, which is that more marginal workers, that is, those with limited abilities who have difficulty securing work, are forced out more on to the employment margin than ever before. That is, people who might have been able to wait on tables or work behind a bar but might not be mentally or physically able for a full working day in an office or factory are being replaced by teachers trying to keep up a big mortgage or pay for a second car or a safari holiday in Kenya.

In the United States, a meaning of work study surveyed 1002 people in 1982. The sample was stratified by regional labour force representation. Interviewing was by telephone and the study was repeated with the same sampling method, though not the same individuals, in 1989. Findings were that there was little change in the areas of entitlement or obligation expectations of the workforce. In work goals there was a change in direction as more importance was given to economic goals particularly pay and promotion. Autonomy and physical working conditions were actually given a lower rating in the later year. The change in the economic area is thought to reflect the downsizing in employment levels of the 1980s. Overall there is no evidence that the US workforce are showing a dramatic change in their rating of the importance of work goals. In relation to the work centrality concept there is a clear shift to a small degree, in all age groups and all worker categories in the direction of lower centrality, except for the self-employed who remain at the same high levels (England, 1991).

Work centrality in Japan

Japanese people attach a high value to work and this ethic has developed from as far back as the early agrarian society of more than 1000 years ago. It has been a feature of the writings of famous Japanese philosophers from the thirteenth century. Building on this traditional work ethic, companies have attempted to train their new recruits further in modern work values.

A meaning of work study in Japan involving a sample of 4800 workers in 8 different companies reported that work centrality scores increase with the age of the worker. There was also a slight increase from the first period in 1982 to the second in 1988. The Japanese figures for work centrality are significantly higher than the European figures. However at the teenage end of the sample, figures are very similar between Japan and Europe. It is suggested that it is the intensive and well-planned training in the values of work which the company inductees receive that brings about the differences at the later ages. Remember of course that the training is given to

Japanese people who have lived in the Japanese culture and are ready to accept the orientation to work which is given to them at this time. The same training may not work in Newcastle-upon-Tyne. Japanese industrial training, while it consists mainly of technical training for the job, also lays a heavy emphasis on the human relations side. Trainees are encouraged to achieve the role of 'Shakaijin' meaning an exemplary social person. Work norms of the Japanese organisational systems such as unquestioned respect for seniority and lifetime employment are taught alongside the technical part. The work attitude transcends the barrier between work and non-work situations (Misumi and Yamori, 1991).

Contrary to popular myth, the Japanese school system is highly academic and boring and it is not a technical education. In fact it is very much a system which strongly inculcates 'attitude' and regimentation. Ichiro Izawa, president of the New Frontier Party and leader of the opposition in Japan recently said 'our education system remains stuck in the 19th century, emphasising rote learning and stuffing students with all sorts of relevant and irrelevant information' (*The Economist*, 9 March 1996, p. 24). It is somewhat strange that we in the West have this fantasy about the wonderful Japanese education system which we should be trying to emulate.

This brings us back again to the two points that have been stressed in this chapter. First, that national cultures contain quite different emphases on work attitudes and second, that attitudes predate and predict much of work performance.

International differences

Several researchers have tried to make sense of these differing value systems on a global scale. For example, Hofstede derived a number of dimensions from surveying IBM workers in forty countries and factor analysing the results of their responses to his questionnaires. The result has been widely regarded as a significant and useful description of the main variables in national culture, with relevance in many areas including the study of organisations. The four dimensions are as follows:

1. *Individualism–collectivism*: do people prefer to focus on their own personal goals or do they regard the goals of their social groups as important or more important?

2. *Masculinity–femininity*: refers to the dominant goal orientations in a society, whether they are towards success, money, material things conquering obstacles or more towards mutual care, nurturing, quality of life, integrating, understanding.

3. *Power–distance*: is the prevailing distribution of power accepted by the less powerful in the society?

4. *Uncertainty avoidance*: to what extent do individuals set up or accept social institutions and beliefs whose main result is to reduce the amount of ambiguity in their lives (Hofstede, 1980).

Buchholz (1978) proposed that five sets of beliefs about work were prevalent in Western society.

The work ethic

The humanistic belief system

The organisational belief system

The leisure ethic

Marxist beliefs

In the 'work ethic', work is seen as good in itself and bestows dignity on the person. Everyone should work hard to overcome obstacles, make their own way in the world and achieve success by their own direct efforts. Wealth is the index of success. In the 'humanistic belief system' work is for self-discovery and fulfilment as a human being, its main characteristic is meaningfulness and its main purpose is to help people to grow. The 'organisational belief system' values work to the extent that it benefits the organisation and serves group interests. The ability to conform and adapt to the group norm is more important to success than individual effort. In the 'leisure ethic', work is a necessity to produce consumable products and provide money. Fulfilment is gained through leisure which as far as possible should have precedence over work. Finally, 'Marxist beliefs' represent work as important because it allows for participation and contact, but work has been designed to benefit the exploiting classes and workers need to have more control over their work.

Buchholz's studies have shown how different national cultures, on average, emphasise these different beliefs to different degrees. This affects how productive and efficient they are and how they set about organising the process of working.

The Irish work ethic

A study compared responses to questionnaires on work ethic, achievement motivation and fatalism in a sample of Irish and American people. Among workers, the Irish showed lower achievement needs than the Americans, but there were no differences on fatalism or work ethic. Among students, the Irish were notably lower in work ethic and need for achievement but higher on fatalism. There is always the possibility that when people fill in questionnaires of this kind that they may answer to some extent in the expected direction, according to ruling stereotypes of their culture. It is often said that the Irish work much harder when abroad than at home. So attitudes can change with the context of the individual to some extent (Moran, 1990).

Attitudes on the flight deck

People's attitudes in the close interpersonal workspace of the aircraft cockpit have been intensively studied in the United States. Helmreich (1984) has found that traits clustering around 'achievement motivation' and 'interpersonal sensitivity' related strongly to measures of performance in air carrier operations. Evidence from the National Transportation Safety Board and the National Aeronautic and Space Authority has shown that attitudes about managing resources on the flight deck have a significant impact on performance in multicrew situations (Foushee, 1984).

Helmreich concludes that some significant attitude differences between first officers and captains were shown to exist. He suggests that these could usefully be included in training programmes and discussions. It transpires that many experienced pilots disagree on effective flight management. These disagreements are often related to attitudes to roles, responsibilities and communication. This is not only a useful potential application of occupational psychology, it is also an exciting thing to know if you are going to take a flight some time soon.

Many of the studies discussed above and many others in this area take questionnaire-type instruments and get people to complete them. It should be remembered that there is a great wealth of data about how people feel about work which may never be recorded in a questionnaire. Our beliefs about our jobs are not static and can even fluctuate from day to day depending on the outcomes of the day. Just the addition of a new colleague or a new set of responsibilities can bring about big alterations in a person's attitudes to their work. There are also many ethnographic types of accounts of working which present nuances of feelings, adjustments to work customs and environments which are very real, but more difficult to capture using traditional methods.

Summary

This chapter has discussed the different ways in which people can conceive of work as an entity in itself. People and cultures differ quite distinctly in some cases in what they believe about work. These differences can be reflected in the performance of their economies. As far as Gross National Product is concerned, psychology has a clear impact which economists may not readily accept. Developing economies and economies or work sectors which are in a state of transformation need to look at the attitude–belief component in the workforce. The actual measurement of these factors is difficult and not nearly as obvious as appears in this brief discussion.

Activities

1. **Discuss different kinds of jobs and try to define an ideal 'attitude' for each of them, using personal examples where possible.**

2. **Ask people about the upbringing style of their parents and relate it to their parents' occupational categories and their own career ambitions.**

3. **Compare a number of your friends on their evaluation of their work goals. How important are various work goals to them, which would they trade for more of another etc.?**

Further reading

Beynon, H. (1984) *Working for Ford*. (Harmondsworth, Penguin).

Heller, F. (1991) Reassessing the work ethic: a new look at work and other activities. *The European Work and Organisational Psychologist*, 1 (2/3), 147–60.

MOW International Team (1987) *The Meaning of Working*. (New York, Academic Press).

Terkel, S. (1975) *Introduction to Work*. (Harmondsworth, Penguin).

Answer to rubble question

You might think   He was lazy and had not done a stroke.

He had just dug a large hole and was taking a brief rest.

He was waiting for his mate to return with the wheelbarrow.

His girlfriend was just coming with a cup of tea for him as a reward for his efforts.

Try it on your friends. What does their response say about them?

Job satisfaction and motivation

CHAPTER 3

Focus questions

Are you a 'hard worker'?

What makes some people keen to work and others lethargic?

If a worker is satisfied will they work differently?

What kind of things can be done to make work more satisfying?

Have motivation theories added to our understanding of how people work?

Job Satisfaction has been a major topic in occupational psychology for over fifty years. In earlier times it was thought to be a subject with great potential for improving the contentment of workers and that output would improve as a consequence. Unfortunately, reality has caught up with this subject and it has been found to be much more complicated than its original proponents thought. So many of the hoped-for relationships between satisfaction and other things have not been consistently found.

For example, there appears to be no necessary relationship between satisfaction and Job Performance. A person may like the job and value it highly for reasons which may be quite unpredictable and not connected with performance, e.g. it might be on a bus route and around the corner from a relative's house and a co-worker might be an old friend from school. Many people are in jobs where the main aim is economic survival. This has such a high value and is easy to attain provided they tow the line, that they give little or no heed to what they actually do in the job. At the end of the day, the job is simply a source of income, and to talk about satisfaction in this context is of small relevance to the majority of the workforce.

Some people disparage the concept of satisfaction, saying that it is largely irrelevant for workers' day-to-day concerns. Hodson (1991) argues that job satisfaction ignores the emotional need states which underlie individual well-being and that it is theoretically naive. He maintains that going to a behaviourally based classification of workers, more firmly rooted in workplace settings and individuals' reactions to them would be more realistic. This would however be more difficult to examine practically.

In 1991, 10000 individuals in Britain were part of a random sample for the British Household Panel Survey. Among the many questions asked were some on job satisfaction. This provides a unique insight into people's views on the subject uncontaminated by expectancy effects which can arise in specific surveys of satisfaction for research purposes. That is, people's answers to the satisfaction questions in this case, are relatively independent of what they think people want them to say or what the survey is for. They were asked to rate their satisfaction with seven facets of their job: promotion prospects, total pay, relations with supervisors, job security, ability to work on own initiative, the actual work itself and hours of work. They were also asked to rate their overall satisfaction. Results were that overall women reported more satisfaction than men. This was thought to be surprising as many women's jobs are part-time, insecure and not apparently very rewarding, e.g. check-out operators. A possible explanation is that many women do not have to work and so those that do, really like it and those who are really dissatisfied can quit more easily than men. There were interesting differences in men's and women's ratings of specific facets of work, 34 per cent of women rated 'work itself' as the most important source of satisfaction compared to 24 per cent of men. As for 'pay' this was rated as the most important source of satisfaction by 19 per cent of men and 13 per cent of women. Age was related to satisfaction levels with a steady rise in satisfaction from the mid 1930s through the 1950s and 1960s. Higher levels of education were associated with lower levels of satisfaction, contrary to expectations and previous research. This could be due to job expectations being higher in the more qualified. It may also be a reflection of government policies in education and health and public service generally which

	Pay satisfaction	Satisfaction with the work itself	Overall satisfaction
7	20	41	32
6	14	22	27
5	17	15	19
4	20	13	13
3	10	4	5
2	5	1	2
1	13	4	3

have left many teachers, doctors and nurses less happy than they were in times past (Clarke, 1996).

Overall British people seemed well satisfied with their jobs. The table shows the percentage of people in the sample rating the three aspects from '7', the highest satisfaction to '1' the lowest.

One of the earliest surveys of job satisfaction was by Hoppock in a small American town, where he found that 77 per cent of the workers were very happy in their work. However, this condition of bliss was less prevalent among the un-skilled workers. This was in 1935 and, according to Viteles, in one of the first texts in occupational psychology, was the start of research in job satisfaction. By 1972, well over 3000 studies about job satisfaction had been published (Locke, 1976).

Satisfaction and performance

Job satisfaction is generally regarded as a set of feelings about work. It is job centred rather than being a personal trait, though individuals will be differently satisfied by the same job. It has to be considered along with other emotional factors, such as job commitment and job involvement.

If workers are satisfied, they should be motivated to perform better so perfor-mance will improve. Finding what motivates people will increase their job satisfac-tion because their needs will be met. This should mean that they will work better. So goes the expectation, but it is not necessarily so. However workers' needs and satis-faction should not be ignored; there are certainly good effects to be gained from a satisfied and motivated workforce. It is more than likely that a dissatisfied workforce will be problematic.

We would be primarily interested in job satisfaction if it could be shown in some way to be related consistently to job performance. However, job performance is not always directly related to worker behaviour; there are many contaminating factors clouding the relationship. Workers respond to incentives other than money and are even prepared to vote themselves out of a job if conditions are not acceptable.

Models of satisfaction

Early theories of satisfaction were simplistic and have since been superseded, e.g. the carrot and stick approach of scientific management (Taylor, 1911) and the ideas of the human relations school are now seen as oversimplified, apart from the fact that the Hawthorne experiments were confounded by other variables and the results were probably far from valid. An early study by Watson found job satisfaction was predicted by age, marital status and kind of job, e.g. shift work. Such relationships have only been occasionally and often only partially confirmed in subsequent studies.

There is little or no evidence over thirty years to show that job satisfaction is related to actual differences in job performance. The effects of satisfaction are much weaker than expected (Saal and Knight, 1988). Some evidence shows that satisfaction is related to performance where good performance is differentially rewarded (Iaffaldano and Muchinsky, 1985). That is, if people see that the good performers get a bonus, or more pay, then this seems to reinforce their positive feelings about their job performance. So both satisfaction and performance will be enhanced and will be related to each other to some extent.

Although job satisfaction may not be the answer to our problems Warr (1987) has said that it requires to be studied in its own right, not just for how it will affect the 'bottom-line'. Warr's 'vitamin' model suggested that there were nine ingredients which contributed to job satisfaction but that too much of some of them could have a negative effect. So satisfaction is worth aiming for, though its level may not be closely reflected by productivity. Apart from wanting to lead a satisfied workforce, the wise manager will realise that there is such a thing as a reservoir of goodwill which can be called on in difficult times. If workers feel satisfied with at least some aspects of their job, for example the way they are treated by management, then this might pay dividends at some time in the future.

A recent study examined whether satisfaction and liking for the job would predict a number of outcomes in a sample of newly hired nurses. The outcomes included turnover, lateness, withdrawal and change seeking behaviour. There was a relationship between satisfaction and liking and seeking to bring about change in the job. Turnover and intention to quit were also found to be related to the measures of satisfaction and liking. This model suggests that events trigger an evaluation of the work situation. This evaluation then brings about a feeling of relative satisfaction or dissatisfaction. The worker then seeks remedies and the best one is considered in the light of personal circumstances. Attempts to change the job included filing complaints and union activity (Rosse and Hulin, 1985).

Nurses are generally in short supply, so the ease of finding alternative work is perceived as high. The job is stressful and there are many opportunities for the development of interpersonal problems with doctors, supervisors and administrators.

Attrition among nurses is a considerable problem in many hospitals. In the above sample almost 50 per cent left in a twelve-month period.

There is some support for the idea that satisfaction is some kind of temperamental or emotional disposition. Observation would tell us that some folks are easily satisfied, whereas others complain and grumble at the slightest thing. This may have implications for staff selection as much as for job design. It implies that we choose jobs and choose to stay with and adjust to them, due partly to our temperament, as well as to the characteristics of the job itself, so that for many people job satisfaction is not only due to the job. In an unusual, not to say unlikely, study, Arvey *et al.* (1989) took more than thirty pairs of identical twins who had been reared apart and showed that the similarity between their scores on the Minnesota Job Satisfaction Questionnaire could be partly attributed to genetic factors. This might suggest that the ability to be satisfied is an aspect of our individual temperamental disposition, and may even have a heritable component.

Locke's value theory

This is a theory relating satisfaction to the extent to which a worker perceives work as providing what he/she wants, values or desires. This involves the idea of personal goal setting and intentions. The worker is seen as having conscious goals which they admit to and know about. Different kinds of goals are identified, such as task goals which are related to some sort of performance standard in the job. Goal acceptance is the degree to which the task goal becomes the conscious goal, and goal commitment is reflected in the amount of effort expended in achieving the task goals. Goal commitment implies the extension of effort over time towards the accomplishment of an original goal, and emphasises an unwillingness to abandon or to lower the goal (Hollenbeck and Klein, 1987).

E.A. Locke has been working in the field of satisfaction and motivation for some thirty years. In a series of laboratory studies (1963–1967), he and his colleagues established that success in a task was related to liking the task. Locke's view of the satisfaction construct is that, we cognise, i.e. sense, perceive and form concepts and we also think and remember (re-cognise would be reviewing and comparing our recalled remembrances). The cognitions that we develop are then related to our welfare, health and safety. We act, that is we select, decide and initiate. We come in time to recognise that certain values, which are actual and symbolic entities based on past experience, are for our good. Job values are the things we either find or would wish to find in our jobs. Our society in effect attempts to codify and preserve values which are beneficial to the commonwealth of people. (Hence, in the final analysis, we go to war over them.)

Job satisfaction is an emotional state. We arrive at a level of job satisfaction via the appraisal of our job's capability to let us achieve our job values. According to Locke (1990), 'a job is not an entity but an abstraction, referring to a combination of tasks performed by an individual in a certain social and physical context for financial and other remuneration' (p. 330). Individuals hold their values in a hierarchy and people differ in their values and in the importance they assign to them. They also differ in their perception of whether their values are being met. A further complication is that at different times their value hierarchy may change. If I win the lottery, I will keep working, but pay or security will no longer rate on my job value hierarchy. Goal commitment has played a significant part in various formulations of Locke's theory. A self-report measure of goal commitment with good psychometric qualities has been constructed (Hollenbeck *et al.*, 1989). It has been suggested that a discrepancy measure would be more effective as a measure of goal commitment than a pure self-report measure. The discrepancy would be that between a personal goal and an assigned goal. However, this kind of measure is not easy to validate and has problems from a measurement point of view, as well as unknown error due to individual differences in personal goal commitment.

Task and non-task values

A useful way of looking at jobs for purposes of satisfaction assessment is to think of them in terms of different kinds of values. These can be defined as task and non-task values. A job consists of a number of elements which are to do with tasks, yet every job occurs in a social and economic environment which entails a large number of non-task elements. Some people might have a really lousy job, but get to wear a nice uniform for example.

Task-related values that a person might seek on a job include different ways of valuing the actual parts of the job and their outcomes. They encompass 'task activity' which might include doing interesting things and 'task success' which may be obtained when some goal is achieved. This is a major source of satisfaction particularly when the goal is set by the worker. Likewise, the more challenging a task, the more satisfaction gained when it has been achieved.

Non-task values include pay, promotion and recognition, and they are mainly under the control of external agents. The theory also allows for individual differences in values. There are often actual differences in rewards that people receive for the same work, and more importantly differences in individual's perceptions of the same reward. A pay rise might mean a lot to one individual and very little to another, depending on their circumstances. There are differences in attitudes to performance and differences in the expectations that people have of likely future rewards (Locke, 1970).

Despite volumes of research correlating job performance with many variables there is a lack of a theoretical explanatory structure. The facts of relationships are mined by the dozen, but the 'whys' are not forthcoming. Too much research proceeded in the past without defining what was being measured or justifying the relationship that was being sought in conceptual terms. Much of the research by Locke and, also in this area in general, has been carried out in the laboratory or with students as guinea pigs and is very artificial. It is not possible usually in the real world to change people's jobs in such a way that their value relevance is affected.

Perspectives on motivation

Motivation, satisfaction and attitudes are all part of a set of beliefs and sentiments about work. It is often unclear whether the subject of discussion is a motivational aspect, an attitude or an emotional feeling or a belief. Motivation often overlaps with satisfaction, as a satisfied worker must theoretically have been motivated at some time. They are satisfied because some or all of their needs have been met. Of course their attitudes and beliefs about work which are part of their system of values, affect how and to what extent they can or will be motivated.

Theories of worker motivation may be classified as 'exogenous' where the influences affecting the behaviour of the worker are external to the worker and can thus be manipulated by the management. There are also 'endogenous' theories where the motivation is more internal and can only be accessed indirectly. This is the familiar Push or Pull effect in motivation (Katzell and Thompson, 1990).

Many approaches to motivation are based on the idea of psychological needs. These approaches vary according to the number, type and hierarchy of the proposed needs. If we have a need it is usually crying out to be satisfied. A popular need theory proposed five basic need categories arranged in a hierarchy; this was first proposed by Maslow, a psychoanalyst. Theories of human behaviour based on need had been proposed prior to Maslow and had formed a basis for various psychological approaches. McClelland's approach to achievement and Edward's approach to personality assessment (Edward's Personal Preference Inventory) were basically dependent on Henry Murray, the originator of the TAT (a well-known projective test from clinical and child psychology). Murray's need theory was complex, but Maslow achieved a digestible simplification (Hall and Lindzey, 1957).

Maslow's needs were physiological, safety, belonging, esteem and self-actualisation. People supposedly sought the satisfaction of the lower needs in the physiological and safety domains before moving up the hierarchy. Self-actualisation was basically an 'unsatisfiable' need. It was more a need to seek but never one to achieve. It concerned expressing oneself in more ways than one. It involved continual growth and transformation, reminiscent of the Buddhist's eternal search for enlightenment. Maslow's work has had a major impact in the way people have approached motivational questions though in real world practice, it has probably made little difference. The concept of self-actualisation has passed in and through common parlance. McGregor's (1960) 'Theory X–Theory Y' describing how people managed, had a major impact on managerial styles through popularised management books, and owed a lot to the hierarchy of needs concept. However, for many years Maslow's theory was not tested empirically. In practical terms it was almost not testable and not supported. Wahba and Bridwell (1976), in looking at a range of studies in this area, found that most research confirmed the existence of two broad need areas. The security/physical needs lay in one cluster and the self-development/personal needs in another.

Alderfer (1969) proposed ERG theory to provide a more adequate understanding of the phenomenon addressed by Maslow. Maslow's five sets of needs are not bounded distinctly and overlap depending on subjective definition. In Alderfer's formulation, 'E' stood for obtaining material existence needs, 'R' for maintaining relatedness with significant others and 'G' for seeking opportunities for unique personal development and growth. Compound needs could include some or all of the basic trio, e.g. promotion would bring material rewards, change relationship patterns and give opportunities for growth via new challenges. In this view, if higher order needs are not satisfied the worker lowers her expectations and looks for the next lower need to be met and is then satisfied.

Need theories in general

It has been found that Need theories are difficult to apply or research, though they certainly have some validity. The problems are that it is difficult to define and measure psychological needs accurately enough for research purposes across a wide range of people. Also, needs are generally too broad for practical applications though the idea of the hierarchy has been found to be useful.

If need theories push us, then Incentive theories pull us in the desired direction. Incentive theories emphasise the kinds of things which make work more rewarding, such as status, perks and titles. Probably the most well known of these is Herzberg's two-factor theory. Herzberg's position is that satisfaction and dissatisfaction are not simply opposite poles of the same continuum, but rather they are contributed to by two different sets of relatively independent factors. Herzberg hypothesises that people have two different kinds of needs in the work situation, 'Hygiene needs' and 'Motivator needs'. Hygiene needs are influenced by the physical and psychological conditions of the workplace, and would be met by co-workers, working conditions, supervision, interpersonal relations, salary, company policies, benefits and job security. All of these are closely related to the job context or the environment in which the job exists. The fulfilment of the hygiene factors is seen as lowering the possibility that dissatisfaction will occur, but not as leading to job satisfaction by itself (Herzberg *et al.*, 1959; Herzberg, 1966).

Motivator needs relate to the nature and challenge of the work itself and would be served by the responsibilities and actual job duties. These needs are fulfilled by motivator factors identified by Herzberg *et al.* (1959) as achievement, recognition, work itself, responsibility, advancement and the possibility of growth. They are concerned with the nature of work itself or with its consequences. Herzberg argued that intrinsic work factors (the motivators) can cause job satisfaction but not job dissatisfaction, whereas extrinsic factors (the hygiene factors) can cause job dissatisfaction but not satisfaction.

Herzberg's views are superficially attractive and convincing, but they have found only slight support in empirical testing. The theory suffers initially from being derived by interviews only (single method) and by being based on a small sample of engineers and accountants (limited representativeness). According to House and Wigdor (1967), other studies which use different methods to elicit the sources of satisfaction do not get results which coincide with the two-factor theory. In general, the motivator–hygiene dichotomy is more imagined than real. Nearly all of the studies designed to test Herzberg's theory which have not used his specific method and classification system have failed to support the theory. Individual differences are not taken account of in the theory, e.g. self-confidence and competence can make a lot of difference to individual work satisfaction, irrespective of the Herzberg factors. People react to and evaluate different motivators differently depending on their circumstances (Fried and Ferris, 1986). King (1970) shows that Herzberg has proposed at least five distinct variations of his theory over the years since its original appearance.

Landy (1985) expresses the view that while the two-factor theory does not predict satisfaction very well, it serves a purpose in that it represents the way people conceive motivation and explain it to themselves. It is a theory that many managers are familiar with, despite the fact that it does not seem to be provable. Overall satisfaction has to be a combination of satisfaction with different elements, whereas in Herzberg's theory it would appear that some elements would not have any significance. For example if supervision was good, then, because it only relates to dissatisfaction, it cannot cause satisfaction, so its contribution to satisfaction is apparently zero.

Reinforcement theory

Reinforcement theory has had a profound impact on psychology generally. It comes in a variety of guises from an array of theorists. The basic idea, which is central to all the theories and formulations, is that following the occurrence of some desired behaviour or a close approximation to the desired behaviour, a reward or even a hint of a reward comes along. Hang your coat up, you will get a 'Smartie'. The process of 'shaping' behaviour is a gradual one in which approximations to desired behaviour are elicited from the subject by presenting suitable stimuli and then the subject is rewarded each time their behaviour gets closer to the desired pattern. Although most of the recipients of this treatment have been laboratory rats or college students, it has been shown to be effective in company settings for example, where public posting of the results of safety drives over a period brings about an increase in pro-safety behaviour.

Financial reinforcement is not so frequently used, though it is effective in the form of bonuses and special payments for achievements beyond the call of duty. Surprisingly, research has shown that for most people pay is not contingent on their performance. Where it is and they are also aware of it being so, then pay can be an effective motivator up to a point. The results of most reinforcement paradigm interventions are that improvements in the desired direction are reasonably easy to obtain. However, unless the programmes are continued and developed and the behaviour more strongly supported, people revert to old habits fairly quickly. One of the vital areas where this has been seen in companies is in relation to pro-safety behaviour. Safety drives almost invariably produce results fairly quickly. But keeping the level of accidents down to the new level attained during 'safety week' is a much less easy objective.

Goal theory

This is popular, though there is much individual and situational variation in the setting and achieving of goals. Goal theory is not yet in any sense a complete theory, as there are too many exceptions and inconsistencies. It is found that if goals are set which are clear and acceptable and desirable and seen as such by the workers, then people tend to behave in the desired way. Important related concepts in goal theory are Feedback, which is the information people receive regarding the achievement of their goals. Central ideas which mediate between goal setting and behaviour are goal commitment and goal acceptance. They describe differences between people in the extent to which they take on their goals and seek to achieve them (Locke *et al.*, 1981).

A lot of research has been done on theories of goal setting. There are a number of specific and fairly well-supported findings which merit close attention. Various aspects of the ways in which goal setting is carried out have been shown to relate to outcome and performance. For example, individual goals are usually found to be more effective than group goals in achieving results either for the company or the individual. Where the worker personally 'owns' and has accepted the goal, better results ensue than where the goal is only held by a group of workers. Participation in goal setting is better than having goals assigned by a manager or supervisor. Interestingly enough, difficult goals lead to better motivation than easy ones. Carroll and Tosi (1973) suggest that many managers set goals for their subordinates that are too general. A practical outcome of goal-setting theory has been achieved in the widespread application of so-called Management by Objectives (MBO) principles. This is based on mutual agreed objectives for work performance designed between a worker and a supervisor. These are made clear and specific, as are the consequences of their achievement or non-achievement. The latter is unlikely providing the objectives have been set fairly. Results of programmes utilising MBO principles are positive in the large majority of cases (Rodgers and Hunter, 1991).

Equity and expectancy theories

Equity theories emphasise the balance between input and output from the job. Comparisons with other workers should not reveal disparities. Equity theories have been formulated by various writers, most explicitly by Adams (1965). Their relevance is mainly in relation to financial compensation. Each worker has inputs to a job situation, all of which they value and rate to some degree. They also receive outcomes from the job situation. The same applies to their co-workers. Positions of equity or inequity arise when the comparison between the person's input and output ratio with other people's shows similarity or not. The magnitude of the inequity will motivate the individual to act in some way to improve the situation. There are various options to choose from, e.g. work less hard, get another job, make a complaint, claim more pay, etc. The person can also work on the other person with whom they are comparing themselves or change their own way of perceiving things. For example, re-evaluate the outcomes of their work (Pritchard, 1969). If someone is permanently stuck in a job with no way to change it or get out, then they may view the satisfaction they get from the job as being more valuable than an objective assessment would indicate, e.g. an unpromoted burnt-out teacher might cherish the thought that he or she is 'educating the next generation of society' and so feel that his or her influence may shape future events. Adams' theory has received support from many realistic investigations in practical settings as well as from the usual experimental settings using student volunteers.

The development of equity theories is continuing. A revision of the theory, using a more explicit cognitive processing approach, is of current interest. A basic concept is 'procedural justice' which describes the fairness of the procedures used to allocate pay and bonuses. Equity might be an endpoint, but procedural justice impinges on the process and on people's perceptions of the process (Folger and Konovsky, 1989).

There are various expectancy types of approach to motivation, such as Lawler's Facet Satisfaction Model, which assesses satisfaction as the difference between what a worker feels they should receive in a particular area or facet of the work situation and what they do receive. It assumes workers are both rational and knowledgeable in relation to what they and others should and do receive. This view has yet to be widely supported by the evidence.

Summary

The many psychological theories of satisfaction and motivation have contributed to our conception of why people work and what they get out of work. But no one theory is generally accepted and they are all found to be less than adequate when put to empirical test in real work settings. Motivation and satisfaction are truly complex concepts, which in the case of the individual worker may change from day to day. It is an unusual person who is single-mindedly dedicated from beginning to end. It is also more common for people to change their perspective on their jobs as time goes on. So although these theories are interesting, they will not solve the puzzle of motivation.

Activities

1. **Discuss the differences in jobs, in terms of whether people set their own goals or not. Then reflect on the differences in performance expectations and supervision required.**

2. **Ask people about the aspects of their work which they find most motivating.**

3. **Compare a number of your friends on their individual levels of motivation for the different activities they engage in. Is their any evidence for a generalised state of motivation?**

Further reading

Clarke, A.E. (1996) Job satisfaction in Britain. *British Journal of Industrial Relations*, 34(2), 189–219.

Katzell, R.A. and Thompson, D.E. (1990) Work motivation. *American Psychologist*, 45(2), 144–53.

Locke, E.A. (1990) What is job satisfaction? *Organisational Behaviour and Human Performance*, 4, 309–36.

Steers, R.M. and Porter, L.W. (1991) *Motivation and Work Behavior*. (New York, McGraw-Hill)

Applications of satisfaction and motivation

Focus questions

Are you ever absent without good cause?

What factors make some people good attenders?

How can differences in performance between workers be quantified?

Should people be paid more if they perform better at work?

How are the pay rates for different jobs determined?

What are the main characteristics of jobs which affect how satisfied people are likely to be?

What can be done to prevent good workers leaving a company?

The practical applications of theories of satisfaction and motivation are to be found in the way we design and perform our work. If we are satisfied in our work and well motivated in its execution, then we are more likely to have a good attendance record. We will feel inclined to stay with our company and seek greater benefits and rewards through promotion. We will feel involved with our workmates and be more positive towards our customers. The way we are rewarded and treated at work will, according to equity theory for example, have the determining impact on the quality of our work behaviour. In this section, we discuss some of the practical outcomes and forerunners of satisfaction and motivation such as job design, absence, staff turnover and rewarding people for their efforts in a tangible sense.

Job design

Job design can have an important impact on a wide range of factors, such as safety at work, output, fatigue and satisfaction. It is important to improve the quality of working life where possible and one area where this can occur is in the design of jobs. Redesigning jobs has a number of indirect effects, such as easing problems created by promotional log-jams by redistributing tasks and changing the titles of jobs. Changing the content of jobs can make them more interesting and challenging. Jobs can be moved into different areas or positions in the organisational hierarchy, resulting in changed attitudes to the job. Redesign of jobs is being increasingly forced on firms, due to economic or technical changes. A considered and proactive approach to job design is a major contributor to the quality of work performance.

The traditional approach to job design has been to concentrate on machinery, work processes, physical layout and time expended for different tasks. In addition, it was thought desirable to encourage the maximum degree of specialisation. Industrial engineers used an operations process chart and, helped by cameras and observation, they carried out time and motion studies of the best workers. Their aims were to achieve the maximum degree of simplicity, to develop the most efficient pattern of movements, to set output standards and to develop accurate job descriptions. Such an approach has been found to have considerable drawbacks and to be associated with high turnover levels, boredom, low quality of work and high and constantly recurring recruiting costs. Looking at jobs from the purely mechanical efficiency angle is not the best approach.

Apart from the obvious considerations, such as reducing hazard and unpleasantness, and supplying the appropriate tools and procedures to make a job both safe and enjoyable, there are the psychological factors such as meaning and importance, which can be added to any job in the design stage.

Hackman and Oldham proposed a model of satisfaction and job design in 1976; this is sometimes referred to as Job Characteristics Theory. The five core job characteristics according to Hackman and Oldham are:

Skill variety

Task identity

Task significance

Autonomy

Task feedback

The five core job characteristics put forward by Hackman and Oldham permit the occurrence, to some degree, of three psychological states in the worker. These are Meaningfulness of the work, Responsibility for the outcomes of the work and Knowledge of the actual results of the work activities. The worker in the appropriate psychological state is then in the position to produce outcomes of work. These outcomes are categorised as work effectiveness, general job satisfaction, satisfaction with opportunities for growth and personal development and internal motivation. Internal motivation is the extent to which people experience personal satisfaction when they perform well at work. In addition to the three-part model, individual differences are acknowledged as the links between the parts are dependent on certain characteristics of the worker. These are the employee's knowledge or skill, the individual's particular growth need strength, and the extent to which the actual context of the work gives the worker satisfaction. As can be seen, there are many interactions possible here and every situation is in effect covered by some variation of the model or another. Usually when psychologists produce complex models, they find that in practice they fail to hold up as well as they had hoped. Although human behaviour is exceptionally complex, our ability to measure differences in behaviour is relatively crude and so our models are often not entirely confirmed, though they may well be true.

In the case of the Job Characteristics Model, the approach at confirmation has been to ask people to fill in questionnaires. The principle questionnaire has been the Job Diagnostic Survey designed by Hackman and Oldham (1975). Studies using this questionnaire have not been able to find good evidence for the existence of five separate job characteristics in jobs. Differences exist between studies, depending on the precise method used, such as the instructions given and the wording of the items in the questionnaire. Again, the effects have been mainly on people's feelings about their jobs and not so much on performance. This measure has been used very widely in this area of research.

The job characteristics can be combined together to give a global score for any job and this has been called the Motivating Potential Score. Clearly if all this worked, it would be very useful in the area of job design. Allowing for individual differences, we could obtain scores for jobs and manipulate these scores by changing job characteristics until an optimum position was arrived at. The workers would then produce their best work and be most satisfied in the various ways specified in the outcome part of the model. Research has suggested that the job characteristics are related to motivation and satisfaction outcomes, but less so to performance outcomes. Experiments have been carried out in actual job situations in which the core characteristics have been manipulated. Job satisfaction has been increased in 80 per cent of these studies to some extent, while productivity changes have occurred in relatively few (Kopelman, 1985).

An alternative view of job design is proposed by Campion *et al.* (Campion and McClelland, 1993). This proposes four broad strategies, mechanistic, motivational, biological and perceptual. Each approach would concentrate on different aspects of the job and would result in different outcomes. For example, the mechanistic involves breaking a job down to a minimum of basic simplified parts and incorporating as much automation as possible, so that the operator can have little skill and still function successfully. Advantages to this are high output, minimum wastage, minimal human resourcing problems and low wages. However, job satisfaction will be very low and absenteeism and turnover probably quite high. The motivational approach recommends putting variety and interest into jobs, with much of the key decision making devolved down to the worker. This requires that workers are more highly trained, and requires that selection systems are of high quality. Good back up and support are needed to reinforce the training and selection. All jobs should be considered from the point of view of our biological limitations and needs. Considerations of energy expenditure, the build-up and resolution of fatigue, appropriate break-time intervals, etc., are essential contributions to safety, health and well-being at work. Perceptual aspects of job design can cover a wide range and may often be taken for granted until something goes wrong. The consistency of signs, directions and instructions, the presence of clarity and consistency in failsafe procedures are all vital to the carrying out of tasks in a safe and efficient manner.

Job enrichment

An application of these ideas is in Job Enrichment, which consists of a large set of general job design improvements which are applied to the job design process and which have been shown to be effective in improving jobs. Aspects which are incorporated in job redesign are many and various. They include removing some controls and replacing them by more personal responsibility. For example, the individual has to check, measure or compare and then decide if a part is acceptable rather than passing it down the line for it to fail when fitted, or to be inspected by another person whose sole responsibility is quality. Individuals are encouraged to become experts in their own area. The individual's accountability for their job is increased and they become more strongly identified with their area of work in the eyes of their fellow workers and themselves. New and more difficult tasks are included in a job and the feeling of job ownership is encouraged. Informative feedback on the overall production process is improved as well as on the worker's own performance, and workers are allowed to become more involved in decision making as far as is feasible. Increased specialisation is encouraged while avoiding over-specialisation and boredom. There are many ways that a particular job may be enhanced to give the individual more say or more satisfaction without detracting from the output. Studies show this has a good effect on attitudes, but no clear consistent advantages regarding performance (Stone, 1986). Many applications have found good results from setting jobs in smaller inter-dependent worker groups; setting jobs within work centres which are clearly pur-poseful, i.e. profit centres, project centres; making jobs have more meaning in the context of the firm or product as a whole; reducing by environmental changes the level of stress induced in the work.

It should not be overlooked that not all individuals want job changes, and findings suggest that some personality types are more resistant than others, e.g. some people like clear authority and limited responsibility; others find working in groups unpleasant when they have been used to being on their own for a long time in their job; others find the uncertainty and ambiguity of the redesigned workplace difficult to cope with.

Robots and computer control

Many manufacturing jobs now involve computer-controlled assembly lines or robot systems. The question is how the jobs of the remaining humans can be designed to make them acceptable and even rewarding. Some studies have shown that increasing the decision making and training level of the line operators so that they are able to correct, reset and diagnose problems for themselves without having to call in the technical specialist has had considerable benefits at least in terms of the time taken to recommence production after a breakdown (down-time) (Wall *et al.*, 1990).

Research has suggested that if people are selected at the beginning or trained into accepting the motives and values of the organisation, they will be more satisfied and stay longer. This was demonstrated in a study in the American Telephone and Telegraph Company over a twenty-year period by Howard and Bray (1988). This issue is covered to some extent in the Realistic Job Preview. In most selection situations, there is an element of self-selection to enter a specific work situation. If workers perceive the values of the company are not in line with their own and that their needs will not be satisfied, they will be inclined not to take a job in the first place. Though in reality they will take the job and not stay very long or simply mess-up and be dismissed.

Absenteeism

Absenteeism is one area where the practical consequences of levels of satisfaction have been noted. The subject has been studied for over fifty years; Fox and Scott (1943) produced one of the earlier treatments of the subject. Absence can be and usually has been regarded as a managerial–organisational problem. That is, its causes lie in the organisation and its solution lies in the hands of managers. Another view less frequently researched is that absence, like any other behaviour, is an individualistic phenomenon with benefits and costs to the individual absentee. Here the solution would need to be found at the level of understanding the individual. Alternatively, just as we are being forced to think in a different way about work in order to cope with high levels of persistent lack of full-time employment opportunities, we should also look differently on absence from work (Porter and Steers, 1973).

Some people feel that there has been a lack of progress in research on absenteeism. The blame for this, they say, lies in the fact that the focus on the individual employee does not work. What has to be studied and manipulated is the organisational culture, which includes as a major constituent an 'absence culture'. This can be so strong that it swamps the influence of individual differences in many instances (Nicholson and Johns, 1985).

Absence is the failure to be present when that presence is expected by others. We can be absent from more than one situation simultaneously, but we can only attend one place at a time. We may not be at work, but we may also be missing from the tennis game we had arranged to play because we were present at the garage getting our puncture repaired. Our work absence was planned, our tennis absence was involuntary. Although absence and attendance seem to be opposites, that is not the case.

Absence has been viewed with both a narrow and a broad focus. For example, Hulin and others have suggested that absenteeism is part of a broader construct which describes an individual's social construction of work and his or her role there. Other related terms within the broad construct would be 'avoidance of work', 'withdrawal from the work role' and 'adaptation to the work environment'. We can also include persistent lateness, excessive breaks, various kinds of work sabotage and stoppage and engaging in or inciting industrial disputes as part of the broader construct which contains absenteeism. There is a strong case both methodologically and practically for seeing absence as much more than a failure to 'clock-in'. It can be a failure to be a member of a committed workforce, through complete withdrawal, lack of positive participation or counter-productive participation. This is an extension of the concept which may allow control models and explanatory models of absence to be more widely applied. One thing is clear and that is the costs of absence. A report in 1990 suggested that absence cost the US economy $40 billion in a year. Hours lost due to absence equal 40 per cent of hours lost due to unemployment.

Absence control

All companies would wish to control absence. Currently there are three approaches to the problem of absence reduction. First, there is a model which attempts to reward attendance in some programmed way; this is called the operant approach. Rewards follow or 'are contingent on' acceptable behaviour. This is probably the most common approach; it is both transparent and understandable to the worker.

The second approach involves prevention programmes. They focus on the worker's ability to attend and try to improve that ability. By paying close attention to attendance constraints in the worker's life or environment and dealing with these appropriately, attendance can be improved dramatically. These constraints or hindrances could include transport problems, a sick child, excessive drinking, etc.

A third policy is based on organisational culture, encouraging a shift in staff perceptions towards a view that the organisation is very specifically attendance orientated. The last approach is yet at the theoretical level, with little empirical evidence to date (Nicholson and Johns, 1985). In a practical situation as opposed to the abstract academic one, a personnel manager would most likely engage in all three strategies simultaneously.

Approaches to absence control	
Operant approach	Reward good attendance
Prevention approach	Remove attendance constraints
Organisational approach	Develop beliefs and attitudes about attendance within the company

Some people have grown up in families where a strong example or strong pro-attendance norms have been handed down. Others may have had strong moral feelings of obligation instilled in them. In some households, strong environmental constraints make absence a very uncomfortable choice. For example, the wife or mother literally forces the worker out of bed and out the door, and dares him not to go to work. Could cultures with less strong matriarchal figures have higher absence rates?

Defining and measuring absence

Absence is usually seen in one of two ways, though in absenteeism research there is a perennial problem in defining absenteeism (Driver and Watson, 1989). There is involuntary absence caused by factors beyond the control of the employee and usually of a longer term. A measure of this is the time-lost index, which is the number of days lost over a specific period. Many frequently absent workers are absent for a day at a time, while the infrequently absent may be absent for serious problems of health and so be away from work for weeks. For example, in The Netherlands, a study showed that absences of six weeks or longer account for 10 per cent of all occurrences of absence, but for a total of 50 per cent of all the days lost.

Voluntary absence reflecting the employee's deliberate choice can be measured by the frequency index, which is the number of absences in a specified period, regardless of duration, and usually represented by short-term absence with repetitive occurrences. Smulders (1980) suggests that employees play an active part in taking on and maintaining the 'sick role'. It is clear that the same illness or accident does not result in the same amount of absence for different workers. The process of becoming absent after becoming sick involves a transition from a well state to a state of illness, through a coping process, then finally into the sick role. Various factors, some of them controllable, interact with the process and determine the occurrence and the length of the absence. These include predominantly, shift work, working conditions, access to a medical advisor and ongoing guidance and support while sick.

Studies have shown that frequency and duration are influenced by slightly different things. Frequency is related to tenure, task, workgroup and conditions, and leadership style, shift work and benefits. Duration is mainly affected by age, personal and medical guidance and working conditions. This means that approaches to absence control have to be initially diagnostic and then selective about the point of attack, though working conditions are likely to be a major factor in all absences.

Some researchers prefer to work with a variable which they label 'attendance' rather than with the variable 'absence'. This reduces one of the disadvantages of using the absence concept, which is that the recording of attendance is more accurate than the recording of absence. In recording absences, there is a large subjective element in deciding if time lost is actually an absence. In situations where there are incentives or consequences following on absence, it has been shown that recording can be significantly affected. It has been found that where managers and co-workers respond negatively to absent colleagues, this is effective in reducing the occurrence of absenteeism. This was shown in a study among nurses (Rosse and Hulin, 1985). In some such settings, the opposite response is taken where tacit covering up for absent colleagues takes place on an informal *quid pro quo* basis and so encourages excessive absenteeism.

Both Dalton and Perry (1981) and Winkler (1980) found that firms with an allotted paid sick leave entitlement experienced more absences. In situations where the sick days had to be used up or otherwise lost, absences were correspondingly periodic. So voluntary absenteeism was a function of organisational arrangements. Workers could exchange work for leisure at no cost and tended to do so. Where there was, as it were, an 'absence incentive', workers duly responded in the logical way. Farrell and Stamm (1988) also found that absence policies were related to absence levels.

Absenteeism has been called a precursor to turnover (Jackson, 1983) and an alternative to turnover. Clegg (1983) noted the relation between lateness, absence and job dissatisfaction.

A prominent model of absenteeism is that of Steers and Rhodes (1978).

Attendance motivation is a function of	Job satisfaction X
	Pressure to attend
Attendance is a function of	Attendance motivation
	X ability to attend

This is saying that everyone has a certain level of desire to attend, though in some cases it may be slight. This desire is made up of the extent to which they perceive the work which they are attending will satisfy their needs. In the case of the majority, this is the need for money and therefore 'that will do, thank you'. Pressure to attend will be an added force, perhaps the threat of unemployment or the wife's tongue. This equation will not guarantee the workers' attendance if their car fails to start or they have such a hangover that their legs refuse to function. So we must include the 'ability to attend' as an additional factor.

Factors influencing absence

Three other areas been shown to have an influence on attendance: job involvement, perceptions about fairness of pay and involvement with alcohol (Brooke and Price, 1989). Muchinsky (1977) stated that there was a consistent negative relation between absenteeism and satisfaction. However, the relationship is at best small and other factors predominate. In general, less-absent employees tend to be older, married, in higher status jobs, have good self-esteem, high felt responsibility and belong to a cohesive work group (Keller, 1983). Also associated with absenteeism is gender. Several studies give females as being more likely to be absent (Flanagan et al., 1974; Garrison and Muchinsky, 1977; Johns, 1978; Blau, 1985). However, this has been found in other studies (Markham et al., 1982) to be mainly in the winter when children get sick. Number of dependants is also a factor here. Workers' performance is also related to absence. In a review of forty-six separate studies, there was a slight overall relationship between poor work performance and absence. It is a little unclear, though, whether an intervening variable may be that supervisors would rate people less highly if they tended to have an absence history, and as their work performance is often judged by ratings, this would obviously cloud the picture. However, in this case, looking exclusively at performance ratings derived from actual objective performance, the relationship between absence and poor performance remained (Bycio, 1992).

Easily the best predictor of absenteeism is past absence. A second predictor is the cohesiveness of the work group (Ivancevich, 1985). More research is now facing the question, 'why are some people never absent?'. The in-depth study of why some children in deprived families living in criminal environments do not commit crimes similarly seeks the 'immunising' factors. The behaviour of management is also a factor. A study which appears to show this compared workers' absence records in relation to the management response to a transfer request (to another department, job or factory) which they had or had not made. Those whose transfer request was granted were absent almost half as much as those whose requests were turned down. They were even less than those who had not requested a transfer. This might suggest that responding to a worker's felt dissatisfaction has an effect on their attendance (Dalton and Mesch, 1992).

The smaller the workgroup the less the absenteeism (Markham et al., 1982). This has a parallel in other areas, e.g. in schools where people are recommending the retention of smaller schools for the psychological benefits which they bring. This has been called 'undermanning theory', and it appears to work because everyone in the smaller group feels they have a role and are important.

Practical approaches to absence control

Most companies take absence very seriously and have instituted procedures for the monitoring and reduction of the problem. Aer Lingus in 1989 announced a 50 per cent cut in absenteeism on implementation of an attendance bonus. General Motors (GM) in the 1980s had, in common with many other large traditional manufacturing organisations, a high level of absenteeism in a minority of its employees. A three-pronged attack on the problem was instituted with the cooperation of the unions at the Delco-Remy plant of GM. This had the effect of reducing controllable absence from 4.5 per cent in January 1980 to 2.1 per cent in January 1984. The general strategy was as follows:

1. Increase the cost of absence to the employee by tying benefits directly to the hours worked.
2. Enforce contractual disciplinary procedures, *re* absence.
3. Educate employees regarding the true costs of absenteeism to the company and to themselves and arrange for a mechanism whereby the savings made by absence reduction are distributed to the workers.

Monitoring of absences

Delco-Remy used a 'Close the Loop' system, whose objectives were first to attack voluntary absence and second to provide a review for upper management of those employees having chronic patterns and the attempts made by their supervisors at absence control. A third strand in the attack was to institute a reliable method which would provide accurate data for measuring absenteeism. This involved an absentee coordinator who reviewed all reports from supervisors and from their superintendents, tracked missing reports, assisted supervisors in compiling reports and monitored trends in absence. In addition, the programme also included the following procedures which were highly publicised.

Employees with over 20 per cent absence in a six-month period were personally identified and the list was 'purified' by removing legitimate involuntary absence. Next, counselling and a warning were given to the remainder, pointing out the possible loss of benefits which would follow continued poor attendance. If a person was on the list in the second six-month period, they lost benefits and were counselled again. Finally, a continuation of the absence pattern resulted in disciplinary procedures (Dilts and Deitsch, 1986).

Treating the individual

It has been found that an individual's absence behaviour can be substantially improved by fairly inexpensive but sophisticated intervention using a training in self-management technique formerly used with substance abusers (Latham and Frayne, 1989). An experiment to test the method was set up using forty carpenters employed in a government agency. They were split into control and experimental groups and results were monitored over three, six and twelve months. The training programme involved each worker setting long- and short-term goals for attendance. Next, they each wrote their own contract with themselves including rewards and punishments. They monitored and recorded their own attendance and gave themselves the incentives. They had regular meetings with the trainer and argued out any problems with the programme. The experiment achieved significant improvements, which were maintained over a twelve-month period.

Turnover

Turnover is the proportion of staff leaving an organisation in a given time period. Turnover research is important to the organisation for several reasons. These include the improvement of the effective management of the available resources and the avoidance of the turmoil to the business and to the other workers when someone leaves. Another aspect of the subject is the careful and planned management of layoffs, i.e. necessary turnover due to business cycles or changes in production process or content. Early retirement or first in–first out policies of layoff do not target people in terms of their abilities or contributions to the company. Hence, unplanned policies can leave the company weak or understaffed in a critical area. A company which was once one of the world's most profitable manufacturers of decorative glassware was faced with market downturns in the 1980s due to weakness in the dollar and lack of American tourists. They had to trim the fat off their workforce, which had grown steadily over the past decade. They offered generous redundancy packages and were initially pleased with the number taking them up. Unfortunately too many of their most skilled key workers took the offer. When the upturn in the market occurred some years later the company were not able to respond as quickly as it would have wished.

Although turnover is a costly organisational problem, it is not all negative. Levels of turnover often look worse than they are, as they include a number of cases which are not costly losses to the firm. Two factors moderating the costs of turnover are the replaceability and evaluation of staff. The organisation may in fact encourage the turnover of unsatisfactory staff rather than go to the extent of sacking, which may be complicated. Dalton *et al.* (1981) called this functional turnover, because it was useful to the company. Dysfunctional turnover occurred when highly valued people left in circumstances which might have been avoided. Some turnover is unavoidable due to family reasons, health or personal circumstances and should be counted separately when evaluating turnover policy and its effectiveness.

Turnover may be viewed as occurring into or out of the firm. People changing jobs internally may be viewed as examples of turnover. The March and Simon hypothesis states that a voluntary choice to leave an organisation depends on the individual perception of the desirability and the ease of movement. In a study by

Jackofsky and Peters (1983), the interaction of the two was found to be predictive of turnover. Another model of employee turnover decision making suggests that dissatisfaction is not the main reason, but only a precursor which may be the first stage in a 'looking around' process. The job market is obviously a crucial factor in the decision to quit (Mobley *et al*., 1978).

Turnover culture

The organisational culture includes elements of what might be called 'turnover culture'. For example, many large accountancy or law firms have many people joining in the knowledge that most of them can never be partners. Eventually they leave to join client companies or start their own firms. In contrast, the Civil Service or the banks have a different culture with respect to turnover of staff. Once someone joins these organisations, they tend to view themselves as in a stable job situation for life.

Turnover of staff is a phenomenon bound up with the organisational culture. Turnover at the individual level is connected with many perceptions and decisions. Satisfaction on the job is important, followed by a reading of the overall intentions of the company and the state of the job market. People must then form and implement intentions to search for a new job, and finally decide to go. Even then the person may have to have considerable resolve as at the time of the decision to leave, the company may offer inducements to stay, which have to be resisted. All of these behaviours take place within the company culture, which includes the way they manage turnover, replacement policy, retraining, promotion and performance monitoring.

The formation of personal decisions to leave or stay is influenced by many factors within the organisation. Realistic job previews and early socialisation efforts can increase feelings of trust, loyalty and belonging, as well as sympathy with and acceptance of group or company goals. Selection patterns are important, such as whether promotion is from within or not. The kind of training and personal development offered affects decisions. It is found that task-specific skills and ability training are more conducive of retention than general skills training and attitude formation exercises. Pay is a major feature in the calculation of the turnover decision; satisfaction with pay has a big impact on reducing turnover. In general, lower paying industries have larger turnover rates. Age has also been found to be highly relevant. The age profile of the organisation influences decisions and it is the younger worker who is more inclined to seek new opportunities and also has the freedom to take them.

Measuring the value of good performance

More effective workers make a lot of difference to a firm, and successful companies recognise this fact and seek to improve their workforce. Ways of doing this include getting the right ones in the first place, keeping them and finally training and developing them. In essence, this is what a large proportion of occupational psychology is about.

The general principle of employing people is that they are worth more to the firm than the money they are paid; otherwise the firm goes bankrupt. There are exceptions to this rule, of course. For example, if you consider the many jobs in non-commercial settings such as teaching, lecturing, social work, public services and offices of public utilities and councils. People can perform relatively poorly in many such jobs for years and get away with it. Rewarding good performance in these jobs can be just as difficult as reacting to bad performance. It is a fact that in some situations the difference between the best and the worst worker is a factor of '5'. This ratio was established by Hull (1928) and no one has seen much need to change it since, human nature being what it is. This means that, in the extreme case, the best worker will be five times more productive than the poorest one. A firm which is carrying more than its fair share of the poorer workers will have difficulty surviving for long in a competitive market. But can performance be accurately measured and can it be fairly rewarded? There is no point in paying out bonuses to some if the others are going to be so upset that they sabotage production to get their own back.

Boudreau (1983) contends that managers in the human resource context must learn to appreciate the utility concept and the 'dollar value' of a worker in order to make comparisons and evaluate the workforce and any proposed changes in it.

Although psychology is a 'people' business we must not forget that the performance of people is central to business. Utility, which is discussed in more detail elsewhere, refers to the contribution in cost–benefit terms of a worker or a selection device, or anything else for that matter. However, usually we need to quantify the value, which something is producing to compare against the cost of acquiring it, to know if there is a benefit. I can hire a JCB and driver at a thousand pounds a day or I can hire twenty workers and their shovels at the same cost. Which produces the better benefits? Will more earth be moved by the machine? Will I have fewer problems with insurance, etc.? If I avoid a lot of staff, what happens if the machine breaks down? These are questions which must get answered, along with many similar ones in order to stack up both sides of the utility equation.

Methods have been developed to measure the difference between the best and poorest workers in actual money terms. One of the most well known is that proposed by Schmidt and Hunter (1983). They define the best worker as being represented by output at the 95th percentile. That is, if all the outputs are placed in order and the cumulative percentage of people at or below each level is calculated then the person at the 95th percentile is above 95 per cent of their co-workers in the distribution of outputs. The worst level of performance is defined as being at the 5th percentile. The usual ratio of outputs at the 95th and 5th percentiles across many occupations is around '2'. That is, the better worker is at least twice as productive as the poorer ones. The same will apply to absenteeism. The worst will be absent at least twice as often as the best. Of course a few people are never off. They are above the 95th percentile. And some are rarely there; they are at the less than 5th percentile level.

Schmidt and Hunter's rational estimate technique was developed to quantify in money terms the value of workers. SDy is the standard deviation of employee productivity. This is a statistic which represents the relative extent to which any set of figures (data, e.g. wage rates) is spread out from lowest to highest. If SDy is small, then there is little difference between staff, due perhaps to the nature of the work, i.e. anyone can do it well or there is no pressure on performance. A standard deviation of +1 is at a 'good' level of productivity and -1 is 'poor'; with the mean being exactly in between. They applied their method to budget analysts in United States Government service and found a difference between good and average performers of $11 000. Schmidt and Hunter's rule of thumb states that SDy is between 40 and 70 per cent of salary, on average. This means that the difference between a good and a poor worker in productivity will be almost equal to one year's salary. The essential point is that the difference between good and bad workers is considerable and that there are methods which can put a monetary quantification on that difference. Of course getting back to the real world, most employers will tell you that they know that, but they cannot do much about it. Alternatively, sensible employers who are in touch with the situation will recognise their good workers and make sure they are treated better and encouraged to stay in various non-explicit ways.

Job evaluation

Job Evaluation is one basis for establishing compensation levels, i.e. pay rates or salary levels. Establishing equitable pay rates is a major task for which a number of standard methods have been devised. At the basic level, wage rates are set by industry standards and in many cases they are laid down by national agreements, though in practice many firms pay over the agreed figure. In most countries, national surveys are continually being carried out by both employer and worker organisations in an attempt to define accurately the current going rate for a job. Such information is sent out in a monthly bulletin to all subscribing organisations. The trade unions and the employers' organisations are both, separately, highly involved in this area.

McFarland (1977) reported on a field study and literature search of methods used in manpower costing. The findings were that there was a wide range of ways of implementing policy, but that theoretical and statistical methods were in the minority; most companies adopted a seat-of-the-pants procedure or none at all. Mechanisation had reduced the impact of direct labour costs as an important factor, and also operating time standards, which constituted the basic tool, were not able to be applied in many jobs. There was worker resistance to the application of standards and which were said to have a negative effect on morale. Some companies reported great savings through ordinary job and time data collection procedures, but they found the process itself rather expensive.

In putting a monetary value on jobs, the basic factors usually involved are as follows:

1. Degree of skill or training required.

2. Degree of danger or distasteful, dirty element in job.

3. Amount of time, energy, or effort demanded and responsibility.

4. Relative equity in the firm between different jobs.

These factors have to be quantified and this usually involves some kind of subjective judgement or the use of rating scales. Other external factors which come into the equation are the scarcity in the job market of the type of person and skills required; the actual real importance to the firm of the job involved and the cost of replacing people when they move on to another job. National wage agreements which lay down guidelines for wage rates have also to be taken into consideration.

The most widely used systems in large-scale industrial settings are based on the point system or the Factor Comparison System. These systems involve a number of steps such as the following: a set of factors is drawn up which are involved in all the jobs being evaluated. There will usually be around ten to fifteen of these. For example, they might be education, experience, responsibility, complexity, supervision required, accuracy, monotony, etc. For each factor a range of descriptions is written to exemplify different levels at which the factor would be found, from the lowest to the highest degree of presence for each factor. These are called the degrees for each factor and are usually on a five point scale. For each factor, the five degrees are given a value or weight on a scale. This is done by a committee of management or worker representatives and other relevant people.

All jobs are then evaluated to the extent that each factor is required. The total sum of points is then calculated for each job and this is translated into a monetary value. Thus the job itself is not actually priced, but each individual level of each factor is, and the final quantitative evaluation of each job is based on the particular makeup of factors in it.

Such methods may seem rather cumbersome and in practice there is likely to be much short circuiting of such proposals; however the standard methods at least ensure the appearance of fairness and objectivity in comparison. Differences between methods are found in whether the comparisons are made within firms or within industries, whether individual factors are priced or jobs as a whole, and whether a ranking method or a more global classification method is employed.

Other approaches to rewarding workers

A Maturity Curve Compensation approach is sometimes used in placing the pay level of professional and executive staff. This involves factors such as experience, and academic qualifications being related in a graphical way to salary levels. The 'Cafeteria System' of allocating rewards is used where for one reason or another money cannot be paid in compensation or where more money is not attractive to employees.

Some firms have found that a 'cafeteria system' of compensation has considerably changed the status quo in regard to issues such as turnover, output and absenteeism. This works through offering benefits to the worker, with or without an element of choice. The company car is the most common example, now being offered to workers who do not actually require a car for the carrying out of their duties. These benefits are particularly useful in attracting highly skilled staff, or retaining the loyalty of present qualified staff.

At the end of the day, some general facts are true in the area of compensation. The first is that although we work for money, in many cases money is not a major motivating factor affecting worker behaviour. In some cases the opposite is true, as the more money workers earn, the more relaxed they feel when it comes to taking a day off. An American miner, when asked why he came to work for four shifts when five shifts were expected, replied 'because he couldn't afford to come for three shifts'. That is if he could earn enough to cover his living expenses by working three shifts, he would have preferred to do so. He was exchanging leisure for money, in effect.

Pay for performance

Good pay and reward schemes are thought to enhance retention of employees and encourage recruitment of superior people. While the evidence again is unclear, the hypothesis is quite tenable and not contradicted by findings. High wages generally are associated with low turnover, so the effect of merit pay is likely to be the same. Merit pay plans are typically implemented by a merit grid. In large organisations, such payments are generally given as a percentage of salary and distributed annually. Merit pay is applied to an individual in response to some special performance on their part. It is usually a permanent increase and based on ratings or evaluations. In some situations, it has been found to counteract cooperative working. The most recent survey (US), suggests that 95 per cent of private sector firms have merit pay programmes for eligible workers and 75 per cent for non-union hourly paid employees, so it is a widespread phenomenon.

In Japan, because of the constraints of strong employment security which is now becoming a problem in the large corporations, there is a move to more competitive appraisal and reward practices. For example, All Nippon Airways, Japan's second largest passenger carrier, has put 6800 technical and administrative staff on a form of MBO. Skill development goals are specially designed into the process of goal setting (Morishima, 1995). Usually the Japanese are paid on a skill grade system, where pay is partly calculated on what an employee is capable of doing, after detailed assessment of skills and knowledge.

The United States Government established an investigation in 1989 to look at pay for performance issues and to determine the applicability of commercial practices to the Federal Service (Milkovich and Wigdor, 1991). The main conclusions were that, although the evidence was not as strong as they would have liked, variable pay plans (share options, profit sharing, bonuses) seemed to bring about enhancements in performance. It was not clear whether merit pay actually enhanced performance and no conclusion was possible. It was noted that in some situations merit pay caused envy and discord when the merit judgements were not agreed with.

The organisational context has a vital role in whether performance appraisal or pay for performance can be made to work or be instituted successfully. Three contextual factors were found to be important. These were the nature of the work, the congruence of organisational structure and culture with performance appraisal and pay for performance policies, and relevant external factors such as the economic climate, laws, union policies and political forces.

Variable pay includes profit sharing and it keeps the proportion of labour costs to earnings constant. They are made as one-off payments and are largely out of the control of the workers and depend on management decisions. They are often insignificant amounts, as they have to be spread out widely. They also get paid to all regardless of individual differences in effort, etc. A major question has been whether it is the actual pay that affects the performance or whether it is the changes in organisational culture which are entailed in implementing the policy that bring about the main effect. Paying people different amounts by whatever method for roughly similar jobs means that trade union influence has been dissipated. It also involves a more observant and aware supervisory staff and clearer expectations need to be set for workers. Effective ways of assessing performance may have to be implemented and this involves getting to grips with what people are actually supposed to be doing. All of these factors can enhance productivity whatever the pay rewards may turn out to be.

The pay for performance schemes in the United States Federal Government Service are said to have been a failure. They have not worked, as employees have been sceptical and there is never enough money available. The evaluations of merit are also very suspect and tinged with suspicions of discrimination.

Milkovich and Wigdor concluded that for a pay for performance system to work, there needs to be the following essential elements in place otherwise the system can do more harm than good.

Necessary	Otherwise
Sufficient funds must be available to give meaningful rewards	The system becomes pointless
A credible performance system which works and is believed in by workers	People become cynical and think favouritism rules the system
A known link between performance and reward, understandable and clear	People become disgruntled and feel cheated
Reward for appraisers who do a good job and act impartially	Lack of recognition and feedback may lead appraisers to reduce their effort

There are many other factors involved in work which people find rewarding and this is especially true as workers get older or more senior in their firm. Other considerations have to be kept sight of by the manager of a company in relation to pay, apart from who gets what. For example, there is a phenomenon called 'Wage Compression' which occurs where labour market conditions change and higher entry-level wages are paid to certain grades than were paid previously, leading to a much narrower band of wage differentials between grades. This can have various adverse effects. On the other hand, 'Wage Drift' can also occur due to factors outside the firm, which can lead to jobs being under or overvalued in relation to others or to their former position. In the 1980s in London, energetic young men (mainly) who were good at arithmetic and quick on their feet were making fortunes in the newly liberated Stock Exchange. There was enormous wage drift compared to people who had worked in the Stock Exchange all their lives doing the more mundane, yet essential tasks. At the current time, this particular bubble has burst and the Porsches have all been repossessed, so the drift in a sense has drifted back again. Another pressure has emerged recently in relation to highly qualified software programmers, who are currently very difficult to recruit.

Summary

Job design is an important and somewhat overlooked aspect of occupational psychology. Putting together the right combination of factors which make up a job has potential for affecting performance, though most effects are shown on satisfaction. Attendance at work is an issue which has been clouded by difficulties in definition, organisational policies and politics and low-quality record keeping. Preventative programmes prove to be highly effective if they are rigorously maintained, otherwise, absence creeps back to former levels. Absenteeism and turnover are closely linked. A healthy turnover policy should be the goal of all organisations. It is often the basic commonsense approach which is applied to pay and reward issues, though there are more sophisticated ways of calculating pay rates. Performance levels are very wide and there are many alternatives in rewarding performance. In general, pay for performance brings as many problems as it solves, unless it is implemented in a very careful way.

Activities

1. **Consider the job of student or lecturer as a subject for job evaluation.**
2. **Who in your group or any other group you are in is likely to be absent? Discuss the factors which are behind this lack of attendance.**

3. **Try to calculate the costs of absence or turnover in an organisation.**

4. **Try to find an organisation with an absence control policy and discuss this with the individual concerned in implementing it. Evaluate its success and its consequences.**

Further reading

Blumberg, M. and Pringle, C.D. (1982) The missing opportunity in organizational research: some implications for a theory of work performance. *Academy of Management Review*, 7(4), 560–9.

Bycio, P. (1992) Job performance and absenteeism: a review and meta-analysis. *Human Relations*, 45(2), 193–220.

Clegg, C.W. (1983) Psychology of employee lateness, absence and turnover: a methodological critique and empirical study. *Journal of Applied Psychology*, 68, 88–101.

Dalton, D.R., Kratchardt, D.M. and Porter, L.M. (1981) Functional turnover: an empirical assessment. *Journal of Applied Psychology*, 66(6), 716–21.

Martocchio, J.J. and Harrison, D.A. (1993) To be there or not to be there?: questions, theories, and methods in absenteeism research. *Research in Personnel and Human Resources Management*, 11, 259–328.

Milkovich, G.T. and Wigdor, A.K. (1991) *Pay for Performance*. (Washington DC, National Academy Press).

Wall, T.D., Corbett, J.M., Martin, R., Clegg, C.W. and Jackson, P.R. (1990) Advanced manufacturing technology, work design and performance: a change study. *Journal of Applied Psychology*, 75, 691–7.

Performance appraisal

Focus questions

What is meant by performance appraisal?

Have you ever been appraised?

What do workers feel about performance appraisal?

What are the main purposes and practical problems of appraisal?

What are the main methods used in the process?

Performance Appraisal generally aims to assess the employee's contribution to the organisation and to provide goals to aid further improvement in that contribution. In many respects, performance appraisal is central to most organisations, if not in practice, at least in theory. An organisation which ignored the performance of its workers would not last very long in a competitive environment. The process of performance appraisal is anything but smooth.

In our own personal lives, we make appraisals (i.e. examine and evaluate) of the performance (i.e. behaviour) of our friends, relatives and people we have to interact with. We consider the question, 'is their behaviour acceptable?'. If it is not, we have the dilemma of whether to tell them (feedback) or not. We may also try to change them (training). And we may, if we have the option, stop seeing them (termination). We may pay less attention to them (reduce rewards) if we are not actually able to stop seeing them. The situation mirrors in some ways that of the commercial company needing to assess and react to its employees' behaviour.

There are various definitions of performance appraisal, for example, 'The systematic description of an individual's job relevant strengths and weaknesses'. In a recent book, Smither (1988) defines performance appraisal as 'the evaluation of employee performance in the light of predetermined standards'. Employee performance is central to all definitions, and some method of assessing or gauging that performance is implied. Where definitions vary is in the emphasis they happen to place on the employee's development or on the company's benefit.

Performance appraisal should be a central part of the occupational psychologist's work, but its acceptability is marginal among both workers and personnel people. Heneman (1975) stated that workers and supervisors are often suspicious of appraisal systems. They tend to question the use to which the information is put. In many companies, particularly where there is strong and traditional trade union power, the use of performance appraisal is banned altogether. There is an in-built assumption in performance appraisal that workers perform differently and that an individual's performance is improvable in some way. There are implications that some workers are less effective than others; this leads to the question of what can be done about that, and one answer to that question is to replace them. Thus, the very acceptance of performance appraisal leads on to the possibility of a situation which is unwelcome to unions and workers.

Napier and Latham (1986) carried out an interview study on a small sample of managers, superintendents and supervisors. They asked the sample if they believed that performance appraisals were related to pay, promotion and training; how they were affected by giving performance appraisals; whether they received any rewards or recognition for good appraisals and finally how were they affected by the performance appraisals they received. Results showed people in general were clear in regard to the purposes of performance appraisal, but that many managers saw little practical value in performance appraisal and were reluctant to be involved. They were often concerned about their ability to be fair to the worker and also that they lacked day-to-day contact with the people they had to report on. Little feedback was given to raters as to the accuracy or effectiveness of their ratings. A widely held opinion was that appraisals were carried out much too infrequently.

Various studies have stated that appraisers see little value in conducting performance appraisals. In some circumstances, giving negative appraisals can result in negative consequences for the appraiser. In many companies, the occasion of the annual appraisals is a tense and nervous time for both workers and supervisors. Fully implemented performance appraisal systems, as a formal part of the managerial procedures, are less common in British and Irish organisations, though this is changing rapidly. They are almost universal in American firms. Large organisations such as banks use them extensively. In such situations there are promotional opportunities all the way up the hierarchy and many candidates are in line for promotion each year. Consequently some system which is relatively open and fair has to be used for the sake of staff morale. A leading manufacturer of cement products in Britain and Ireland was recently visited by a student doing her personnel policy study. She discovered that they had no system of performance measurement or appraisal. When she asked why this was, she was surprised to learn that it was not because the unions were opposed to it, but because the management did not want to be tied down to specific numbers, rates, etc., which they felt would have significantly limited their freedom of action. So whether a company has a performance appraisal system may not always be for the commonly stated reasons of worker acceptance or union resistance.

McDonald's hamburger chain has a regular system of appraisal linked to rewards. The situation here is that there is a multiplicity of staff at the same level and the work is boring and intrinsically unrewarding. Some fair and transparent system is needed which rewards staff, but also controls staff and identifies the unsuitable quickly and fairly. Performance appraisal is a management device for processing staff both upwards and outwards. It also provides a form of motivational calculus rather like the Boy Scouts; people earn badges and recognition for doing fairly pointless things better than anyone else.

Most of the work in performance appraisal has been focused on non-managerial jobs. Management jobs are more difficult to define. They are often very varied and involve reacting to circumstances and taking risky decisions. They are less circumscribed than the average process operator's job, for example. They are also politically more difficult to examine. Many management jobs have some form of MBO controlling eventual rewards, and failure can be responded to by termination. Even success can be met by termination if a company board sees the need.

Purposes of performance appraisal

Performance appraisal has a number of clear and useful functions to fulfil for the organisation. Primarily, it forms the basis of the organisation's punishment and reward system. Decisions regarding termination, promotion and bonuses can be related to performance appraisals. Based on appraisals, an individual can be given a higher bonus or moved on to the next step in the promotional ladder. Because of this, performance appraisal should provide a good platform for employee motivation. Employee performance is a major criterion in evaluating selection decisions and examining the validity of selection tests. We need to know if we have selected the right people to some extent, and whether the tests and procedures used at selection are good predictors of performance. Having some regular estimate of an individual's performance is therefore helpful in validating selection procedures. It provides information for training programmes and for the guidance and counselling of employees in the areas of career planning or improvement. It can identify workers' views about many things, such as organisational effectiveness and problems. It aids productivity by enabling goal setting to be done objectively, and enables information to be gathered on the production process. A clear idea can be gathered of what the typical worker is able to do, given the time and resources available.

Eichel and Bender (1984) studied 500 American companies, and established that the main uses of performance appraisal were in wage and salary determination, counselling and evaluating the need for training. Whereas Long (1986), in a survey of British companies, found that the main uses of performance appraisal were seen as assessing training needs, reviewing performance and improving future performance. Only 40 per cent of the firms surveyed used the results to determine pay increases. On this side of the Atlantic there is not the degree of flexibility in altering pay rates or paying people different amounts for doing essentially the same job. In reality, the relation between pay and performance (in managers), is obscured by many other factors and is not a direct one (Markham, 1988). This issue has recently come to the fore in Britain, with the extremely generous pay awards and bonuses being awarded to heads and senior staff in privatised utility companies. It has been seen as very difficult for the boards of these corporations to justify empirically these presents to themselves and their colleagues.

Practical problems with performance appraisal

Problems arise with performance appraisal systems in both methodology and acceptability. There is a wide choice of methods and the better ones are very time consuming, while the poorer ones are probably worse than nothing at all, as they give rise to many difficulties. Refusal to cooperate is not uncommon. This can be expressed by subtle forms of sabotage, e.g. giving everyone the same rating, losing the forms, etc. A successful performance appraisal system very much depends on the organisational climate and the preparation and presentation of the system.

Problems of a political and interpersonal nature are frequent and no methodological developments will ever eradicate them. For example, a pressing and ever-present problem is that workers with good ratings may be lost to the department of the supervisor giving the good ratings. Thus the supervisor ends up being a perpetual trainer and the performance of the section suffers. On the other hand, if a supervisor is giving consistently poor ratings, this may reflect on the supervisor.

Why are the workers so poor? Is this not the supervisor's fault? Many people find it difficult to make adverse judgements about others and sometimes people are damned by faint praise. Good performance appraisal is very time consuming, bad performance appraisal damages morale and relationships. Lack of clarity can exist as to the aims of the exercise and this can be experienced by both worker and supervisor. These are all problems to do with perceptions and emotions. In other words, they are psychological problems which in the organisational context can become political.

Acceptability

Although procedures can be forced on workers, they work far better if there is worker acceptance. A major task of the manager is to design the performance appraisal system so that it gains some degree of acceptance. Research has shown that increased acceptability results if performance is evaluated frequently, that is at least twice, and up to four times a year. If employees have the opportunity to express their personal feelings at the appraisal interview or on forms, this has been found to be helpful. Acceptability is improved the more familiar the supervisor is with the job and the worker's personal situation. Finally, it helps to set new goals based on the performance appraisal interview. The fact that there is a meaningful job-related conclusion to the process, which gives guidance and a future perspective, makes the pain of taking part in it somewhat more bearable. Perhaps most important of all is the requirement that the senior management are fully behind the scheme and take its results seriously and in a positive rather than a punitive way.

A lot of research into acceptability consists of case studies and anecdotal reports. There is also a considerable proportion of laboratory-based findings. There is no research in the real-world context which can be reliably interpreted as proving anything conclusive (Roberts, 1994). Roberts carried out a study on performance appraisal systems effectiveness among 800 municipal government personnel departments in the United States. The main finding was that factors called 'information validity' and 'employee voice' were most influential in explaining perceived employee acceptance. Goal setting and employee participation in goal setting and criticism of results were seen as fairly important. The design of rating forms and the setting of performance standards were not significant predictors of employee acceptance.

Employee Voice was defined as the employee having a participatory role at the appraisal interview, being involved in goal setting and having a say in performance standards. Having a good quality feedback mechanism, in which discussion was allowed, was also part of this factor. Information Validity consisted of the perception of the truthfulness of the information being used in the process. There was a positive perception of performance standard quality and a perception that performance ratings had an impact on decision making. That is, the standards were real, attainable and well defined, so that both worker and supervisor could recognise them.

Factors involved in Employee Acceptance	
Employee voice	Information validity
Worker has participatory role	Truthfulness of the information
Worker is involved in setting standards	Performance standards have quality
Feedback mechanism is two-way	Performance ratings affect decision making

Criteria

A major problem is the establishment of acceptable and valid criteria on which to judge people. Theoretically, a criterion is a dependent measure used for judging the effectiveness of people or organisations. It is an outcome or result of some kind which could be behavioural, personal or criterion referenced.

Performance criteria	
Behavioural	What a person does in actual task performance
Personal	What a person is or seems to denote through behaviour
Criterion referenced	Whether an actual landmark point is reached

Or another way in which this has been viewed is in terms of performance of tasks carried out, effectiveness of performance and context or environmental aspects affecting performance.

Criterion contamination

Criterion contamination occurs where extraneous factors which are not relevant to the job task are included in the performance appraisal. Contamination may be due to bias of many kinds. Similar problems of bias exist in the performance appraisal situation as in the interview, i.e. leniency: a tendency to be overgenerous and uncritical; halo: a tendency to make global judgements and not differentiate judgements in every item; central tendency: opting for the average every time, i.e. taking safe options. Numerous methods have been adopted in performance appraisal in order to reduce the effects of these and other biases.

Setting

Another important aspect of performance appraisal is the setting, e.g. where the setting is bodies such as the police, armed forces, banks, etc., there is the chance that economical and relevant methods can be devised. Ideally the setting should contain large numbers of people, a stable workforce and resources for development and validation, as well as clear and consistent job specifications. In other jobs, e.g. shop assistants, engineers, salesman or labourers, people change their jobs frequently, the content of jobs can change abruptly and the outside environment can be a major influence on job success.

Objective indices

Objective indices, such as cost-related criteria or other objectively quantifiable measures, appear to be accurate and fair, but omit many important considerations. They are also difficult to apply to people who have no obvious commercial output or product, such as teachers or nurses. Examples of objective criteria include units produced, quality control data, absences, failure to complete assigned work, number of sales, calls and amount of new business. These criteria can be affected by chance factors such as seasonal fluctuations, market forces, tools and machinery in use.

Objective data from personnel files such as rewards, disciplinary events, etc., are usually so incomplete as to make their effective usage minimal; not every worker has an entry in every category and some have none. 'Objective' performance measures tend to focus on outcome and can involve making false attributions based on subjectivity, e.g. the cause and effect sequence. It is possible to overlook the critical behaviours involved.

Legal issues

As with much of occupational psychology, the psychology must often take second place to the legal considerations, which are often very strong. Legal cases have been critical of performance appraisal and some performance appraisal schemes have been accused of operating disguised employment tests and of discriminating between people on invalid or irrelevant criteria. They have been accused of using purely subjective factors which could lead to prejudiced judgements and may be based on no more than the whim of supervisor. This is especially problematic where layoffs or promotions or rehiring are based on performance appraisal results. A 1978 Act in the United States has set standards for the conduct of appraisals. It states that employees should participate in determining the critical job elements. Evaluations should be based on job analysis requirements only and not on any arbitrary personal views of what the job is about. It also suggests that rewards should be tied to performance and appraisals should take place at least once a year. In the event of an adverse decision, thirty days' notice should be given and there should be a right to reply.

Research

Research on performance appraisal has moved through several distinct phases. It was initially concerned with the psychometric qualities of rating scales, such as their reliability, validity, freedom from bias and practicality. Psychometrics is the statistical and methodological side of psychological assessment and rating scales are a form of assessment instrument, as we shall see later. The focus then shifted to counselling and developing employees, and on the need to separate administrative features from developmental ones. Currently, attention has shifted back to the rating process itself, with a close study being applied to the cognitive processes of the rater. Cognitive processes concern aspects such as the ways in which the rater conceives performance. For example, what model is held in the head of the rater in relation to work performance and the job which will enable a judgement to be made and where does that model come from? How does the rater remember or recall significant performance? What particular aspects of performance emerge in the rater's conception which are then used for comparison purposes?

Rating research

One important characteristic of the rater is race. There does appear to be some effect of race in performance ratings. In a review of seventy-four studies in this area it was found that both black and white raters tended to give higher ratings to subjects of their own race. Some of these effects were possibly due to real performance differences. In the same review, gender effects were not generally found to be significant and age effects slight (Kraiger and Ford, 1985). That is, whether the rater and worker were male or female was not reflected in the ratings given. Nor was bias particularly evident on the basis of a worker's age. Raters who are more cognitively complex tend to be less lenient, and show less halo and range restriction (Schneier, 1977). Cognitive complexity is something akin to what we used to call intelligence. It involves the capacity to see more than one side of a situation and to hold several concepts in mind at the same time and make judgements about them. Halo is the tendency to give similar ratings to an individual's performance in a number of separate dimensions even though the performances are at a different level of quality. A noticeable level of performance, either good or bad, in one area influences the way the other areas' performances are rated. Range restriction, in this context, involves using a rather limited range of different rating levels to someone. So Schneier is saying that there is evidence to support the commonly held suspicion that some people give qualitatively different ratings due to their personal process of making judgements. As people gain more experience in the job, it has been found that their ratings become more reliable.

Bernardin and Beatty (1984) report on studies on interrater reliability in performance rating. It is important that raters of the same person agree to a reasonable extent on their judgements, otherwise the system is arbitrary and unfair. A worker's performance ratings would depend too much on who is doing the rating, for example. The overall level of agreement between raters is said to be 0.7 and somewhat above that between supervisors. As we compare different levels of the organisation, agreement between ratings is still present but to a lesser extent. For example, the correlation between peer and supervisor ratings is around 0.6; self-ratings correlate with peer ratings around 0.4 and similarly for self with supervisor. That is, as has long been suspected, an individual tends to disagree with the performance rating they are given by their supervisors.

Self-efficacy

Another theory of why performance appraisal is not fully effective may be found in terms of Self-efficacy (Bandura, 1982) and expected outcomes, rather than in the more complex areas. The extent to which people feel competent and in control of the situation has a bearing on how they feel about the outcomes of their behaviour. Performance appraisal may be poorly carried out because appraisers do not feel they have the means to do it properly (low self-efficacy), or they may feel that the organisation will not act on their appraisals anyway, even though they are well done and reliable (high self-efficacy). Appraisal behaviour must relate to rewards. And it must be perceived to be so related by the appraiser and the appraisee. People doing appraisals must feel that there is something in it for them. They must feel supported and recognised for their efforts and the results of appraisals must be seen to mean something to the participants and the organisation.

Studies have shown that where conditions in an organisation result in people having perceptions of high self-efficacy and, at the same time, low outcome expectancies, resentment is caused. At the same time, protest will occur and efforts to change existing practices in the organisation will take place (Hobson *et al.*, 1981). This applies to performance appraisal in the way in which non-cooperation can be engendered and people can protest at having to do the appraisals. Nothing annoys students more than when they hand in essays on time but they do not get them marked for months. Then when they eventually do get returned, there is only a mark and no comment at all on them. The better students feel more resentment than those who are only going through the motions on a particular course.

Training raters

Landy and Farr's (1980) review says that training raters has only a marginal effect. Other views emphasise the cognitive modelling of the appraisal process and consider the value of a shared 'meaning perception' on the part of raters, something which can come about through training. Feldman (1986) concluded that rater training is not very effective in increasing the validity and accuracy of ratings. Unless the system is complex or the rater lacks job knowledge, training adds little. People need to know what they are doing and to have some basic concepts about observing and judging, i.e. instruction at least, if not an outright planned training course.

Smith (1986) reviewed twenty-four studies on performance appraisal training, comparing them by content and method of training. The three general approaches to the content of training are rater error training, performance dimension training and performance standards training. In rater error training, examples of errors are shown and discussed. In performance dimension training, the main focus is in enhancing familiarity with the dimensions used for rating. This is often achieved through in-depth reviews of the scale and sometimes in the actual construction of the scales. Performance standards training involves evaluating the performance of the raters. Trainee raters are compared with trained examples or with a desired model.

Methods

There is a considerable choice between supervisors, management, peers, clients or self in who fills in the forms for performance appraisal. Studies suggest that in over 90 per cent of companies supervisors or middle management usually carry out the performance appraisal. They normally have first-hand knowledge of the job, the working conditions and of the person being assessed. Performance appraisal involves top–down evaluations in 95 per cent of cases (Finn and Fontaine, 1984). That is, there is very little upward evaluation of management by staff, something which would probably have a much higher payoff for the company than the usual format.

Peer ratings are said to be both reliable and useful and to give high agreement (Siegel, 1982). Korman (1968), after reviewing literature says they are very good predictors of future job success. They are also said to be relatively free of bias and to be valid. However, negative peer ratings are difficult for people to take and as such can damage the cohesiveness of a work group, and result in problems between workers. Some possible solutions to these problems with peer ratings are to make the ratings confidential, discussing them only with the individual concerned while collecting feedback from the individual. The behaviour being rated should be objective and group ratings should be amalgamated, so that no one in the peer group can be identified as the one who gave the bad rating.

Subordinate or client rating is often used in an informal sense at least. Sometimes when you go into a restaurant or hotel you will find a 'comment card' to fill in. After class and usually just before exams, your lecturers may give you a rating form to complete so that you can pass a confidential opinion on their performance. This is quite common in colleges and can provide useful feedback to teachers. Students' views on what constitutes 'good lecturing' however may not be very consistent and may tend to emphasise only part of the role. For example, did the lecturer give you an idea of what was coming up on the exam paper? Did they give you copious amounts of handouts of notes, so you did not have to come to class at all? In this connection, evidence shows that the purpose of the ratings can make a major difference, e.g. if for salary, promotion or guided self-development. Client-based appraisal is also applicable in the public services. It has been used in evaluating some aspects of the work behaviour of policemen in the United States, for example.

Subordinate appraisal of managers (SAM), has been recommended as part of a multitier appraisal system. Only a few companies use SAM, but in those that do the performance appraisal system wins more positive endorsement than is usually the case. Subordinates are in an excellent position to evaluate managers, but there are many practical and political problems to overcome (i.e. training and experience of raters, adequate job and organisational knowledge, loss of authority, rewarding weak managers for political reasons). Research has shown that there is reasonable accept-ance of the SAM process by managers and supervisors, though only subordinate groups felt they should be used for reward purposes as well as development. That is, the managers were not too happy that their bonuses, etc., could be controlled in any way by the lower orders (Ash, 1994).

Self-appraisal is the most acceptable form of performance appraisal, but unfor-tunately we are not all equally capable of self-criticism and our self-perceptions are often far from accurate. Also, if appraisal is linked to salary increases, people are unlikely to be free from bias. Self-appraisal combined with goal setting is common and found to be acceptable. It should take place at regular fixed intervals. It improves motivation and reduces defensiveness; its frequency makes it seem like part of the job. In practice, it has been found useful as it gave the employee more understanding of the job requirements, and information for job development. It may be seen as more appropriate where the worker is in isolation or possesses special skills, for example in many professional contexts, vets, technical specialists, etc.

Various forms of self-appraisal are found quite often in combination with other forms. Mabe and West (1982) show that the accuracy of self-assessment is related to intelligence, high achievement status and internal locus of control (the feeling that the individual is in control of things and not outside forces or other people). It may lead to inflated scores, especially where tangible rewards are connected with the results. Self-appraisal has been shown to be advantageous in conjunction with a Behavioural Observation Scale approach, that is, where specific job behaviours are incorporated in a list and people have to respond to each element on the list.

Another variety of self assessment is Feedback-Based Self-appraisal, where it is recommended that ratings are based exclusively on formal and informal feedback re-ceived from supervisors over a period of time. This is an aid to reduce ambiguity. The worker is supposed to make a collection of these supervisory comments over a period and detail personal responses to them over the same period (Steel and Ovalle, 1984).

The process of performance appraisal

The logical basis of performance appraisal is in Job Analysis from which criteria are developed on which the performance appraisal can be based. Hence, all performance appraisal is essentially a three-part process: job analysis, standard setting, and per-formance appraisal. Traditionally, performance appraisal research has used the psy-chometric model and standards. However, there are at least two critical differences between tests and performance appraisals. First, in the performance appraisal the 'test' and the person are interlinked. Second, the context is not standard, each ratee is a separate situation and the 'score' involves interpersonal judgement and perception unique to each case. Another contribution to how we should view the overall occur-rence of job performance is provided by Blumberg and Pringle (1982). They describe performance as being the result of the interaction of Opportunity, Capability and Willingness. Trying to measure performance without first examining and taking into consideration the levels of these attributes would be unwise and unfair. The opportunity to perform effectively is not evenly distributed in a workforce or company. There are many environmental variables which both enhance and diminish the performance of individuals. Capability and willingness, in an individual worker's case, may be the result of inadequate training or years of poor feedback and motivational features in the worker–supervisor relationship.

Appraisal itself consists of both an Observation process, i.e. what is done and a Judgemental process, i.e. how well it is being done. It is feasible to separate the two parts and have the behaviour recording done by one individual and the judgement process by another. This has been shown to have some advantages. Both observation and judgement are subject to bias, and attempts to reduce this involve moving to more objective indices of performance, involving workers much more in the process and training raters. The common methods vary along a number of dimensions. These include complexity, time required, rater control, usefulness for feedback purposes and acceptability.

Practical approaches

According to Borman *et al*. (1991), there are four general approaches to performance rating in job and training situations: objective measures, rating scales, job sample proficiency tests and job knowledge tests. By and large, experience suggests that often the first two are encountered and rarely the latter two. In the past, methods have included Ranking and Forced Distribution, which is only a more sophisticated form of ranking. These are relative methods, as they compare one employee with another. They would have low acceptability, and probably not give a valid reflection of a person's performance even if they could all be compared on the same scales, which is unlikely. They are very much out of favour and were in fact banned in the United States in 1978. Rating is the most frequently used method, amounting to around 72 per cent of all cases (Landy and Trumbo, 1980). Rating methods are many and various, including descriptive reports, behaviour checklists, critical incident technique, graphic rating scales, mixed standard rating scales and behaviourally anchored rating scales. Some of these are briefly outlined in the following section.

Behaviour checklists/graphic rating scales

Behaviour Checklists/ Graphic Rating Scales consist of a list of job-relevant behaviour items and usually a five-point scale is used for rating each item. There are various ways of presenting these. The main version is to give a line with equally spaced intervals on it, hence the name graphic. Each scale point has a label, e.g. very often, frequently, etc.

An example is given by Albert *et al*. (1986) where an operator evaluation scale of twenty-five items on a four-point scale for use in the textile industry had good validity, reliability and consistency across samples. It produced four meaningful factors of operator work behaviour: Assertive Commitment, Identification with Significant Others, Sense of Responsibility and Productivity/Industriousness. Worker's performance could be reasonably well evaluated by using this questionnaire. The four dimensions were meaningful and could be used in development as well as appraisal.

Another example from a study of police performance illustrates the fact that, although these types of instrument contain many apparently differing dimensions for rating, they often boil down to a few major ones which can be more easily handled for research and other purposes; Beutler *et al.* (1985) for instance, carried out an analysis of supervisors' ratings of US police officers which produced two principal dimensions, Interpersonal Ability and Technical Proficiency, from a large list of apparently independent rating items.

Advantages of the behaviour checklist method are as follows:

Easily computerised

Reliability and validity can be assessed

Little training is required in their use

Readily transformed into numerical summaries

Readily updated and improvable.

Forced comparison methods

In this method two statements which have some degree of equivalence in desirability for example, are taken and the rater has to choose the one most like the subject. This method has some problems, i.e. comparison between people is unreliable. However, leniency errors and subjectivity are avoided or reduced and scales can have an empirical basis to them. They also avoid rater bias to an extent and they look sensible. They are however difficult to score and raters are found to occasionally object to various aspects, such as being forced to choose, and also to the difficulty of choosing between alternatives, when they may well want to express an opinion about both.

In a forced choice method used in the US Army, statements are presented in groups of four, two descriptive of an effective worker and two of a less effective worker. Social desirability is controlled for by putting statements of equivalent social desirability in the same group. In each group the rater has to make a choice of the one statement most like a person and the one statement least like them.

Critical incident technique

Critical Incident Technique was introduced in 1954 by Flanagan and is still quite well regarded in the literature, though this kind of approach, while giving psychometric quality, tends to miss essential elements of jobs and does not match supervisors' concepts. Relevant workers or supervisors have to make a list of critical incidents which distinguish between good and bad performance on a job, over a period of time, as they occur, for each employee. At the end of the period the assessment is based on these descriptive incidents. This has the advantage of being relevant, unsophisticated and good for feedback and counselling purposes, but on the other hand, it can be highly time consuming and impossible in many situations where observation is not feasible, or where there are too many people under one supervisor. It is subject to bias, selectivity in perception and to chance.

Behaviourally anchored rating scales

Behaviourally Anchored Rating Scales, which were introduced by Smith and Kendall (1963), are an adaptation using the critical incident technique as a basis. They differ from ordinary rating scales in a number of ways, the most obvious apart from their construction details being that at each scale point there are behaviour descriptions rather than adjectives, numbers or trait labels.

The basic methodology of putting together behaviourally anchored rating scales is time consuming and complex. It involves collecting lists of good and bad job performance incidents from workers and supervisors. Latham and Wexley (1981) suggest interviewing 30 people and collecting about 300 incidents. The incidents then have to be rewritten to make them as objective as possible and expressed in terms of observable behaviour wherever possible. A sample of experienced people, who may be experts in the job or subject matter, then group the incidents into job-relevant classifications. Next, the list of incidents is given to another group who are asked to say which of the stated classifications the items fall into, which is called 'retranslating'. The most consistently classified and useful incidents within each of the dimensions are identified. Ranking or rating procedures are then used to obtain a scale value for each incident. Finally, a scale is assembled so that there are at least 7 or 8 incidents fairly evenly spread out along the range of scale values.

The scales look like a particular behavioural class, e.g. serving a customer and a number of behavioural descriptions at different points on a scale. The rating process then gives the individual a position on each scale with respect to job-relevant behaviours expressed in a job-relevant way.

Mixed standard scale

The Mixed Standard Scale has many advantages over the ordinary graphic rating scale (Blanz and Ghiselli, 1972). Items relating to different areas of performance and to different levels of performance are mixed together. Three statements are used for each job-relevant behaviour: good, bad and indifferent. Thus there is a mix in terms of their significance for the overall assessment and in terms of their positive and negative import. The rater has to indicate for each item whether the worker is better than, the same as or worse than the description given.

This method has a number of advantages; for example, it can reduce bias and some of the common errors such as halo effect or response set which can otherwise occur. It makes inconsistent rating very obvious. However, scoring is more difficult to handle and sophistication is required on construction; the task can make some raters refuse to cooperate, presumably because it is more demanding and contains the element of self-checking for consistency.

The sum and substance of thirty years' research on the subject of alternative methods of appraisal rating is that no single method is superior in all circumstances and people revert to the simple and tried methods of rating or descriptive reporting. The psychometric superiority posited for behaviourally anchored rating scales is now thought to be questionable, though it does have the advantage of the involvement of a large number of key personnel.

A model of the performance appraisal process

The study of appraisal as a systematic process has resulted in the posing of a number of research questions, e.g. the meaning of behaviour/appraisal to participants, especially raters; the relevance of specific behaviour to overall ratings; the handling of inconsistency in performance especially of extreme people who are rarely always bad or always good. This model represents the ideal and attempts to model the cognitive processes that underlie performance appraisal. There are three parts to the process (Borman, 1978):

1. The rater observes behaviours that are relevant to the job. The rater needs to know what critical job behaviours are and have access to the behaviours which are critical to success. It would not for example be sufficient to hand the rater a list. The behaviours would have to be demonstrated and their significance to the performance of the job explained.

2. The rater makes an evaluation of each behaviour. Each behaviour should be rated independently avoiding the very common halo effect and the global rating effect.

3. For the final step, each evaluation is weighted according to the importance of the behaviour for job performance and a final single rating is arrived at for a performance dimension. There may be numerous performance dimensions.

Development dialogues

A suggestion has recently been made that Development Dialogues should be substituted as an alternative to performance appraisal (Larsen and Bang, 1993). Development dialogues are recurrent planning sessions, during which a superior and subordinate on equal terms discuss future job tasks, training needs and career plans. The system is widely used in Denmark and other Scandinavian countries. The areas covered by dialogue can include:

State of employee's present performance and motivation

Which parts of the job are liked/disliked

What changes are coming in the job?

What kind of training or educational support is needed?

Which other jobs in the organisation are interesting to the employee?

What are the career plans and realistic possibilities of the employee?

Summary

The goals of performance appraisal are to measure a person's performance on the job and to create an evaluation system to advance the operational functions of the organisation. Findings in the measurement area are that job analysis and setting standards for performance are important, but cannot replace managerial judgement. Supervisors are good judges of performance. To achieve even modest validity performance, dimensions need to be well chosen and clearly defined. The actual scale types and rating formats used make relatively little difference to the quality of performance appraisal.

Performance appraisal can motivate employees provided supervisors are trusted and knowledgeable. The results are influenced by the use to which performance appraisal is put (e.g. pay, research, development). Trying to refine and perfect performance appraisal systems at great expense is pointless. They should be regarded as a backup of good quality management judgement.

Activities

1. **What items would be in a behaviour checklist for the performance of a student, assuming it could be regarded as a job? Try to put together such a checklist.**

2. Discuss with some people with experience exactly how appraisal is carried out and how it is accepted in their company.

3. Consider any job or jobs and try to determine in consultation with a job holder what are critical job behaviours, both positive and negative.

Further reading

Antonioni, D. (1994) The effects of feedback accountability on upward appraisal ratings. *Personnel Psychology*, 47(2), 349–56.

Ash, A. (1994) Participants' reactions to appraisal of managers: results of a pilot. *Public Personnel Management*, 23(2), 237–56.

Cascio, W.F. and Phillips, N. (1979) Performance testing: a rose among thorns. *Personnel Psychology*, 32, 751–66.

Friedman, M.G. (1986) 10 steps to objective appraisals. *Personnel Journal*, 66–71.

Latham, G.P. and Wexley, K.N. (1981) *Increasing Productivity Through Performance Appraisal*. (Reading, MA, Addison-Wesley).

Napier, N.K. and Latham, G.P. (1986) Outcome expectations of people who conduct performance appraisal. *Personnel Psychology*, 39(4) 827–37.

Training

CHAPTER 6

Focus questions

What is the significance to the country and industry of training?

How can we get the most out of training resources?

How can we go about finding out who needs what kind of training?

Is there a difference between training and education?

How would you decide if training was good value?

What are the alternative ways in which training can be delivered?

Training is a complex subject with many different aspects to it. It is a major discipline in itself and is likely to become even more so as time goes on. Training opportunities are the key for a very large majority of individuals to gain the satisfaction and rewards that are associated with work.

Training is concerned with basic adult learning processes. It focuses on the development of theories and methods to describe and specify the training needs of organisations. It concentrates on carrying out effective training, and evaluating its effects in the complex organisation. Interrelationships between organisational factors and the success of training interventions are also a crucial area. Designing training methods is complex, with many competing theories and approaches. Training has a major impact on a wide range of social issues, such as those affecting the hard-core unemployed, ageing workers and people entering non-traditional careers (Goldstein and associates, 1989).

Training has been defined as a planned activity aimed at increasing the knowledge, skills and abilities of employees in order to increase their contribution to the organisation which they currently or will in future work for. To put it another way, 'Training is a planned learning experience designed to bring about permanent change in an individual's ksas where "a" will include attitudes' (Campbell *et al.*, 1970). The predominant view of training has been that it consists of three parts: training needs assessment, training design and training transfer. These involved establishing what had to be done in training, finding the best way of doing it and finding out what the effects of the training were.

'KSAs' is an abbreviation frequently encountered in training as well as in selection. The individual parts are defined as follows.

■ 'K' = Knowledge: This is the content of technical information needed to perform adequately in the job; it is generally obtained through formal education and or on-the-job experience. Knowledge is necessary, but not sufficient for job performance. As we all know, there are some very knowledgeable professors who do not perform certain aspects of their jobs very well.

■ 'S'= Skills: These are specifically acquired and developed psychological and physical motor processes which are necessary to perform the job requirements. They include interpersonal processes such as listening, communicating and accommodating to other people, as well as the more obvious things such as being able to program in C++ or to put a frame around a picture. It is also vital that the individual possesses the skill or the facility to select from a repertoire of possible behaviours the one which is most appropriate in the circumstances.

■ 'A'= Abilities: These are basic cognitive factors which represent the individual's present capabilities or stage of development and on which further achievement can be grown. They include such things as verbal fluency, memory for faces and names, speed of reasoning with numbers. Fleishman and Quaintance (1984) defined 'abilities' as 'general capacities related to the performance of some set of tasks'. They are viewed as relatively enduring attributes of the individual, which are developed through the combined effects of genetics and experience. As noted above 'a' may also include attitudes. In many training situations, the task is often, initially at least, for people to relearn the reasons for working; to relearn the attitudes which enable people to accommodate to being told what to do and to being expected to do it all day. It is not enough to know things, to be able to do things and to be able to understand and learn things. A worker also needs to behave appropriately, that is to fit into teams, to address customers properly, to represent the company in a positive manner.

Historical

Taylor's 1911 treatise entitled *Scientific Management* was one of the early management books. It included, as the two crucial aspects of staffing, the selection of the best workers and their extensive training. Equally early on, Munsterberg (1913) also noted the importance of training. The first modern systematic treatment of training as such is generally regarded as that of McGehee and Thayer (1961). This presented in detail various approaches to the analysis of training needs which are still in use today. Glaser (1982) brought the focus onto cognitive issues in the learning process, how people think, memorise and organise their learning, and also to needs assessment from an educational standpoint and to criterion development, by which learning and training could be evaluated and so improved in the future.

Campbell (1971) was critical of the low-level ad hoc nature of training research and the delivery of training; certainly the profession of educational psychology and the teaching profession were well in advance of the industrial trainers in their application of psychology and the systematic analysis of learning and teaching. Industry and organisations have always tended to put production and profits first, to the detriment of long-term viability and staff development. However, this has rapidly altered in the last decade or so.

One of the most widely respected writers in training, Irwin Goldstein (1974), brought out a text which took a systems approach. This is a very influential theory which has found applications in many disciplines not only the scientific field, but also politics and economics. Every functional entity or operation, from the workings of the human body to the manufacture of pins to the putting of a human on the moon, can be seen as a system. Systems are composed of subsystems which are interrelated; larger systems are composed of smaller systems; systems have interdependent components; changing a component changes the systems at different levels. How something is understood and operated upon depends on what part of the system the viewer is standing at to achieve their viewpoint.

The worlds of education and training were to a certain extent wedded together, having been divorced many years previously, when Gagne and Briggs wrote an influential text on instructional development in 1974. They formally put in place a whole methodology for the design of training and the evaluation of its delivery. In 1980, Goldstein stated that considerable progress, both technically and practically, had been made in the area over the previous decade. In 1986, Goldstein revised his earlier book, updating it in assessment, evaluation and techniques based on the developing literature. Most recently, he brought out the third edition in 1993. The academic standing of the subject has developed slowly, becoming more theoretical, interfacing more completely with modern developments in psychology and education, to bring industrial training away from the greasy overalls and 'sitting next to Nellie' phase of its early development.

Traditional views of training have moved on and the area is now thought of as human resource development. It now includes a wider perspective on bringing about changes in people under headings such as management development, developing interpersonal skills in workers and developing and improving attitudes and commitment to the organisation.

Training professionals contribute to short- and long-term staffing plans, and also to the career development and opportunities of staff. They are also involved in redeployment of redundant staff, or in the retraining of staff whose jobs have been overtaken by the advances of technology or competition.

Training is undeniably a psychological area. At its base lies the psychology of learning and individual differences in how people learn; also involved are areas such as the technology of evaluating learning, and the social psychology of organisations, etc. Recently the traditional training model, often called Instructional Systems Design since Gagne and Briggs, has been forced to incorporate the approach of the cognitive psychologists. Highly complex, technical jobs now consist of much more demanding tasks from a mental load point of view and approaches to training have to be correspondingly more sophisticated (Ford and Kraiger, 1995).

The growth in training

Due to technological change and demographic factors, training is a major growth industry. There are a number of reasons for the increased emphasis on training. Training requirements are now becoming more frequent components contract between unions and employers. In some countries, training serves as a device for bringing about a reversal of the employment effects of past discrimination, such as against women or the disabled. Population changes indicate a decline in the rate of growth of the workforce, so in effect individuals need to be recycled into other jobs when their existing job becomes redundant. Jobs are also becoming more complex in the cognitive demands which they make of workers.

At any one time, 22 per cent of the population of Europe are in some form of education. And more than 10 million undergo some form of training every year. In France, for example, in firms of over 2000 employees, 34.9 per cent of employees are subject to training every year (*Delta News*, 1990). In Germany there is a dual education system which involves most 16 year olds signing an apprenticeship contract with a local firm. They work part-time for low wages and attend a trade-related school for the rest of the time. German companies spend about 30 billion pounds a year on this scheme and pay the teachers' salaries.

In America, Motorola Inc. (Schaumburg, Illinois) in 1985 devoted more than a million hours to training 25000 employees. In 1986 they invested 44 million dollars in training and education. Like many multinational companies, they have a purpose-built centre for training (The Galvin Center), with 12 classrooms and a 180 seat auditorium (Wagel, 1986).

The current situation in Ireland is summarised in several reports (Price Water-house Cranfield Project, 1992). From the latter we learn that the number of days' training received per annum by employees in different categories tends to decrease as we move down the employment hierarchy. Irish organisations do not value manage-ment development or devote significant resources to it. Managerial employees re-ceive, on average 3–5 days (36 per cent) or 5–10 days (32 per cent), and those in the private sector do significantly better. In the clerical and manual grades, 15 per cent of them receive no training, from 40 to 50 per cent receive 1–3 days and 20 per cent receive 3–5 days in the year.

Roche and Tansey (1992) reported that approximately 50 per cent of employees had received some training in the previous year; 21 per cent received off-the-job training, and only 11.6 per cent received more than four days training off-the-job. The highest incidence of training was among apprentices, who were in the process of gaining their craft. Only a third of qualified craftspeople received training on an ongoing basis. Professional and technical people ranked second highest in the amount of off-the-job training received. Almost 20 per cent of supervisors received more than four days' off-the-job training. While 30 per cent of managers received some off-the-job training, only 17 per cent had more than four days of off-the-job training. The amount of off-the-job training was lowest among administrative and clerical people, craftspeople and operatives.

Large firms undertook much more training than small firms. In firms employing more than 100 people, 91 per cent of managers and 82 per cent of supervisors had received some training in the previous year. This compares with 24 per cent of managers and 9 per cent of supervisors in firms employing 1–10 people. Service sector employees got significantly less training compared with those in manufactur-ing and construction.

International comparison of training

Comparisons can be made between countries in terms of the percentage of the payroll that is spent on training. In the United States, the figure is about 1.4 per cent, in France 2.1 per cent and in Germany 2.9 per cent. The Irish figure is estimated to be about 0.9 per cent. International figures also suggest that about one-third of expenditure on training is devoted to management training.

The future needs of the workforce for training are large and growing. For ex-ample Wexley (1984) estimates that office workers will have to be retrained five to eight times during their working lives. Employment skills in the technical areas are reckoned to have a life expectancy of ten years. Apart from technological change, other factors are bringing about the need for training. As industries close and open, redundancy and structural employment create training needs. School-leavers require industrial, commercial and technical training. Demographic changes are evident in some countries. Particularly in the United States and Germany, the gradual ageing of the population means that companies are actively seeking the return to work of older people.

In Britain and Ireland, significant increases in the labour force participation of women in middle age after families are at school have been evident. The large-scale closures of industries such as shipbuilding, steel production and coal mining have led to corresponding increases in training establishments as efforts are made to re-equip the former workers for new opportunities..

Why training is useful and desirable

Training delivers a number of competitive advantages to the firm. First, it is cost effective; firms find that money spent in training is usually recouped in increased efficiency. Second, there is also the pleasant fact that training expenses can be set against company tax liability in many situations, depending on the government policy which is applicable on the day in question.

Increased competition means that the highly trained workforce will survive while others fail. Training brings about clearly recognisable changes in staff morale and feelings of competence, as well as tangible benefits in technical competence. It is quite apparent, by observing the behaviour of the staff, which company has an active and effective training policy and which is moribund in that regard.

A major contribution of training is that it makes people more adaptable. In many situations, of which assembly line or product building is the most obvious, there are great benefits to be obtained from workers being able to do some or all of the jobs on the line as well as their own. 'Cross-training' or 'multiskilling' are names given to the concept of developing workers to fill others' roles. Apart from filling in when others are absent or on a break, there are other advantages. Quality checking is improved as people are more aware of the standards for the previous operation. Morale is improved as difficult jobs are shared, workers are more tolerant of their colleagues' mistakes and a feeling of team working is developed. The concept of 'lean production' involves this process.

Training is an option to recruitment. Recruiting and training new staff is expensive and time consuming and full of pitfalls. Productivity can be improved if scope can be found for combining jobs by redesigning them and redistributing tasks. People can be taken out of semi-redundant roles and used to the full after retraining. Existing staff know the company culture and have a mature view of the company goals and ways of working. New people have not only to learn a job, but also the social and political environment of the factory or office.

Training is the quickest way to adapt to environmental demands. The external environment changes with respect to a wide range of factors. For example, legislation in the areas of safety and quality, competition from other sources of the product, component suppliers changing their products or delivery cycles and customers requiring a sudden change in specification. There are many other ways in which the environment will impose the need to adapt on a company and a flexible well-trained workforce will cope with these demands much better.

Evaluation of training initiatives

Another set of views has been emerging recently on several large-scale evaluations of various training initiatives. All over Europe and America, countries are trying to respond to the employment situation by instituting training programmes; unfortunately it is becoming clear that much of this investment is relatively unproductive. Training is popular. It improves the unemployment figures, it should give more technically competent people a better chance of finding work, it increases the demand for education and of course the taxpayer is paying anyway.

The OECD in 1994 reported that broad government-sponsored training programmes for the unemployed had in reality a very marginal effect on their job prospects after training was finished. In America, 5 billion dollars are spent by the Department of Labor in schemes for the disadvantaged to equip them for work. Evaluating such schemes, Heckman concluded that they had no benefit for the under 21s, and only a limited benefit for adults such as mothers returning to work. Private schemes linked to particular businesses did best in terms of results and employment gained.

A large-scale project in Britain (Youth Training) enrolled over 200 000 16–18 year olds. Half of the participants dropped out before completion and the unemployment rate among the completers was worse than for the age group as a whole. These results are not necessarily the fault of the training scheme. It is likely that the hardest-to-place people are on these schemes in the first place. In several European countries, governments have set up organisations such as the Training and Enterprise Councils (TECs) which contract out to private organisations, to provide training suitable for the locality. This has some advantages, in that it has made training potentially responsive to local needs and it has put the supply of training on a more competitive basis. One disadvantage if the schemes are not adequately monitored, is fraud. Recently a number of organisations providing training have had to reimburse money because their trainees did not finish courses for which full payments were claimed. The police have been involved in investigating possible fraud cases in this area (Department of Education and Employment, 1996).

In Ireland, one of the many training initiatives of the government is the Community Employment scheme for people who have been unemployed for over a year. This gives people work experience in projects which have a benefit to the community. In a study of this scheme, participants reported in the ratio of 6 to 1 that they thought the scheme was worthwhile, though actual training was received by just under 70 per cent of them (Burke *et al.*, 1995).

In America, Canada and Australia, quite successful schemes have something in common. That is, they connect trainees with firms and focus on the skills required for jobs in these firms. The partnership of training centre and employer jointly prepares the trainee for a job. British retail companies provide industry-specific courses, in which trainees are attached to a store and follow a course taking them to a qualification under the NVQ system, e.g. Tesco have a 30-month course for 18 year olds called Career Select from which graduates will feed into the lower rungs of management with prospects for the future. Sainsbury have a retail Trainee Scheme for 16 year olds, which after a number of other courses allows trainees to take degrees by distance learning in the management of retail stores area.

Many training schemes suffer from two drawbacks. One is that the trained workers are far too expensive after they come out of their training and therefore the effect on the unemployment figures is less than might have been. The second is that many participants, school-leavers and unemployed, etc., have very low levels of literacy. Employers' organisations in Britain have frequently made the point that school-leavers are often illiterate and incapable of doing anything much (*Industry in Education*, January 1996, UK). The employers would be happy to train them if they could get a reasonable base to start from. The problem is widespread. In Sweden, 1 in 12 men could not understand the instructions on an Aspirin bottle, in The Netherlands it was 1 in 10, in Germany 1 in 7 and in the United States 1 in 5 (OECD, December 1995).

Corporate setting

The overall effectiveness of training has been found to depend very strongly on the visible commitment of the management to the content and objectives of the training programme. This has been termed the **commitment approach** and it must not be overlooked. It involves getting management support for the training programmes and establishing a positive institution-wide perspective on training (House, 1967). Workers and management must agree that the outcome of training will be progress in the company, and that there is recognition for trained personnel. Workers who take the trouble to learn new skills and adapt to changing demands should be rewarded in some way for their effort. They have improved their value to the company, and if the company fails to recognise this, then morale becomes sour. A training programme should reflect the company's goals. If a company emphasises quality and technological progress to its customers, then its training programme should be similarly designed.

Determining training needs

Since 1961, the training process has been conceived as falling into three segments: needs assessment, design and delivery and evaluation (McGehee and Thayer, 1961). In many situations, the need for training is obvious, e.g. a new machine or process is to be used, wastage is too high, customers are complaining or deserting in large numbers to a competitor, etc. Nevertheless the Training Needs Analysis (TNA) phase is essential. It provides information on where training is needed in the organisational structure. It helps to make an initial determination of what the content and aims of the training programme should be. It helps to identify who needs the training and in what specific skills and knowledge training is needed. It is therefore a necessary discipline and training should really not proceed without it. Training has to be placed in an organisational context. 'Quick-fix' style training, without support, development and evaluation, is minimally effective. There are three standard viewpoints from which TNA is normally approached: organisation, task and person.

Organisational analysis

This treats the organisation as a whole and considers first, questions such as, what are the goals? What are the obstacles to the goals? What are the staff discrepancies which will hinder goal achievement? How can training fill the gaps? Second, where are the inefficient units? Third, where are the areas in which future change and technology will necessitate new skills? Thus on an organisation-wide front, TNA is done in tune with a projection into the future. Organisational analysis includes looking at efficiency indexes, productivity records objectives, resources and allocations. An assessment must be made as to whether training is the way to accomplish the organisational goals.

Managers need to have greater awareness of training needs, so that they know what has to be done and can relate more effectively to training consultants and specialists and so they can evaluate whether a training job has achieved anything for them. Frequently problems are misdiagnosed and irrelevant training is called for.

A number of problems occur regularly in managers' decisions about training. The manager's self-perception is a crucial interfering factor, especially in the situation where a person has built up their own business from the ground. They can have difficulty accepting feedback and perhaps negative information about the quality of their operation from an outsider or from a 'young pup'. Environmental turbulence forces wrong decisions. Sometimes decisions are made for effect or in haste, rather than in relation to facts. Vital facts are misperceived or vital data is overlooked, especially if it comes from a low-grade source. The manager's judgement may also be affected by problems such as low self-esteem, anxiety and depression (Russell and Wexley, 1988).

Time orientation can be a key factor that differentiates among departments in an organisation (Lawrence and Lorsch, 1967). Organisational departments see time as a span or interval for receiving definitive feedback about the results of work and depending on what work they do, they will view the time intervals differently. The Accounts Department may work in terms of weeks, Delivery in days and Production in hours. The training and development specialist may even view time in terms of months or years (McGrath and Rochford, 1983). Scheduling, coordination and allocating resources when determining the need and provision of training can lead to conflicts.

Operations or task analysis

Managers and supervisors are asked to specify training needs in relation to the operations or tasks which are needed to be carried out. There is evidence that the perceptions of different members of the workforce will give varied answers under this heading (McEnery and McEnery, 1987).

Research on task analysis has typically focused on the individual level, mainly by means of responses to task inventories suitable for application to various job clusters. Organisation and subunit aspects are largely ignored. Two constructs relevant to task analysis are Technical Error and Situational Constraints. There are many situational constraints which have a potential to affect work performance. These include job information, tools and equipment, materials, finance, services, personal preparation, time and physical conditions (Peters *et al.*, 1985).

Person analysis

Person analysis involves assessing training needs in terms of the individual's behaviour. This can be allied to performance appraisal and to self-appraisal. Individual learning agendas have been used where the worker specifies and examines their own training needs. They may then contract with the firm in relation to training provision and their input to the company. It has been suggested that personal and corporate benefits are to be gained if workers are involved in writing a 'future job analysis'. This serves to prepare people for what they will be doing years into the future rather than right now. This is sometimes called 'updating'. Two major constructs are Skills, which includes knowledge, education and ability and Climate, which subsumes attitudinal aspects, perceptual component/interpersonal relations and support.

Some companies have computerised the results of person analysis by way of personnel inventories. These are comprehensive databases of skills and training levels of staff. When vacancies or new requirements arise in an organisation, the job specifications can be used to query the database and possibly reveal that people working for the company already have the relevant KSAs, or can be relatively easily upgraded.

Organisational analysis identifies where training is needed, Task analysis determines the activities performed on the job and describes the job conditions; from this, information on the skills and knowledge required is obtained. Hence, the training programme requirements are established and can be related to the existing skills of the workers or trainees. Much of the literature has focused on the techniques for gathering information (Moore and Dutton, 1978). It is thought that the increasing focus of cognitive psychology will lead to a vertical integration between job tasks and cognitive processing by people, rather than as at present with the job tasks and the people skills being horizontally juxtaposed, as it were (Ford and Kraiger, 1995).

Training systems can be conceptualised as existing on three levels: the individual, the training department and the organisation. Each of these has its own perspective on training. Not only that, but organisational goals may or may not be achieved, due to poor individual skills, knowledge or attitudes, e.g. poor communication between levels, organisational, subunit and individual. The very goals of the organisation may be misperceived, due to traditional versions of reality, avoidance of reality or inability to act organisationally, e.g. organisational climate, workgroup processes/integration of workgroups. 'The failure during TNA to analyse goals from different operational levels has important implications for effective training' (Hinrichs, 1976).

Delivering training

There is a considerable range of ways in which training can be delivered and received. There is a growing number of consultancies who provide training packages. Many firms have a training department, which provides home-grown courses and contracts with outside suppliers of training. Larger companies often have their own residential centres, though many divested themselves of these in the 1980s. They found that they could not afford staff to be off the job for the amount of time required by the residential centre. When Dixons took over Currys, their Personnel Manager felt that such centres were too removed from reality and recommended 'focused training' by line managers, who receive instructional packages from head office and deliver them to staff in the store.

Advantages of residential training

There are many benefits to be gained from delivering training on a residential basis. There is the lack of distraction from customers and job demands, which is a major plus. Even in the on-site training room of a company, people can be hauled away to answer queries, etc. In the residential setting there is a better level of social mixing, relaxation and the chance to develop a group ethos. People can often be forced to face problems because they cannot just sit quietly until home time. There is a more exclusive focus on tasks.

Product training

Manufacturers of high-technology equipment provide training as part of the after-sales package, and in fact this is one of the selling advantages of a product which often swings the sale of an expensive piece of equipment.

Government-sponsored training schemes

Government agencies provide training, in purpose built training centres. In Britain over the last fifteen years there has been considerable dismantling and reconstruction of training schemes. Some workers in these schemes have by now worked for around ten differently named organisations, but remain doing roughly the same thing in roughly the same place; that is, those who can stand all the disruption and name changing. The majority of schemes are now offered by TECs, which are privately run companies which contract with the government to deliver training. In 1996, over one and a half billion pounds will be paid over to these companies. The best of them are said to place under half of their clients in work at the end of courses, while the average figure is around a quarter. Such success rates are highly dependent on the surrounding economic environment.

Colleges are increasingly showing a commitment to industrial and commercial training. For example, many courses in European colleges are funded by the EU Advanced Technical Skills Programme. The Open University in Britain pioneered the provision of Higher Education through television and distance learning, a model which has been copied and developed worldwide. With the penetration of technology, e.g. teleconferencing, training course packaging has become very flexible. There is for example a growing market for training packages on CD-ROM which people can take at their desk on their computer. This is particularly relevant in accountancy and law, where changes in legislation and budgets of governments bring about instant changes in knowledge requirements. Regardless of how it is delivered, the training itself has to be designed first. There are a number of steps and principles underlying this.

Training design

Training will be less effective unless an attempt is made to design the exercise according to accepted principles and in accordance with the organisation's objectives. Goldstein's model of the training process is typical and includes the three essential phases, planning, implementation and evaluation.

The first step in training design involves stating the objectives of the programme in broad terms and specifying how these objectives will be achieved. We then require detailed specific learning objectives which describe the particular tasks to be learned. For example, the tasks are analysed and divided into distinct components; components are independent elements which are essential to the carrying out of the tasks; when these components have been learned, the skills involved will be transferable to other tasks; the learning of components has to be sequenced in a way which is logical and facilitates learning. Following this, each component must be trained and integrated.

Application of learning principles

Learning style

People learn differently, and some consideration may be needed for this. Some are predominantly experiential learners and benefit most through doing things as a first step. Others prefer to read or hear about the task and dissect it in their imagination; they would be more abstract/verbal learners. In the learning situation, some people are very dependent types who require detailed coaching and feedback, whereas others much prefer to have minimum guidance and more time on their own. In most training programmes, there will be a mixing of teaching modes which will accommodate everyone to some extent. But it may be one cause of dropping out from training programmes that the mode of delivery did not suit an individual's learning style (Noe, 1986).

Questionnaires have been devised which may help in this area. *The Learning Style Inventory*, first published in 1976 and revised in 1985 (Kolb, 1976, 1985) is based on Kolb's (1981) experiental learning theory. Based on two learning dimensions, Concrete/Abstract and Active/Reflective, we can obtain four learning style preferences, Converger, Diverger, Assimilator and Accommodator. A person's Learning Style preference can be identified by means of an adjective checklist (Willcoxson and Prosser, 1996).

Trainability

Individual differences exist and are obviously important in the area of 'trainability'. People differ in factors such as ability, personality and motivation. It is possible to take a trait approach, and assess individual differences on these factors. Trainability has been described as a function of ability, motivation and perceptions of the work environment (Porter and Lawler, 1968). Motivation is made up of components which energise, direct and maintain behaviour (Steers and Porter, 1975).

Trait approaches are probably not sufficiently predictive to be taken seriously in a practical context, unless the context is like the armed forces or a government agency, where large numbers of people have to be processed through an assessment programme into a training programme. In the more skill-based industrial context, it has been found that miniature training programmes are more predictive. The miniature training package consists of a small selection of training tasks which are representative of the overall programme. These are given to the applicants and their performance is evaluated. This approach also allows flexibility and adaptation to the individual learner, whereas the global trait assessment is a little rigid in comparison.

Knowledge of results (feedback)

Decisions have to be made about knowledge of results; when, how much and in what form. In some cases, feedback is built into the task and no external feedback is needed. For example, learning to throw a pot on a potter's wheel is a situation where verbal instruction is fairly pointless and the slithering pile of disobedient clay tells you exactly how you are doing. This is direct physical feedback. Flight simulators are another example of a training device which provides feedback without wasting lives and materials.

Informative feedback tells the learner why they went wrong and how to put it right or improve. People vary in the extent to which they will accept feedback, and in the extent that they will profit from it. Too much feedback has been found to be counter-productive. This is especially true of beginners, who become confused by an overload of information in an area where they are only just gaining familiarity with the tools and terms of the trade. It has been found extremely beneficial to combine feedback with goal setting. It should always be positive, emphasising the good points of performance. It should deal with and prioritise areas where improvement is most possible.

Transfer of training

Transfer is the most important aspect of training programmes. If training does not transfer from the setting of the training programme to the workplace, then the training is useless and if it does not transfer from one task to another, it is less useful than if it did.

The following steps **(O-P-R-A-M)** have been shown to increase the probability of transfer taking place.

Overlearning of skills: Skills should be practised past the point of proficiency, i.e. do not stop when 'you have got it'.

Principles should be emphasised until they are well understood. It is much better to know why something is done or works, not just how to do it.

Realistic simulation: Make the training situation as similar to the work situation as possible. If possible, deal with real situations, real customers, etc.

Adaptive: The training programme should contain aspects where something does not always fit or work out right as it should. This forces the trainee to adapt the material to the context or situation. By seeking their own solutions outside of the common procedures, the trainee learns far more and transfer is enhanced.

Monitoring: Newly trained staff should be subject to an in-depth and frequent follow-up programme until the effects of training are well established. It is quite common, especially when there is any form of outside pressure for the trainee to relapse into trusted old but inefficient methods. It is also even more common to assume that once someone has done the training course, they are qualified to operate the machine. In many cases, real learning only begins after the training and when the individual is exposed to the vagaries of reality.

Practice and rehearsal

Various forms of rehearsal are advantageous, and some are more relevant in some situations than others. 'Walk-through' involves the trainee being taken through each step separately and slowly, allowing them to build up a practical picture of the process before learning the individual parts. 'Imaginal rehearsal', now widely used in sports and athletics training to good effect, involves the trainee picturing in their imagination the possible scenarios and outcomes of the job or training situation. They are asked to visualise different situations and to see themselves in a reactive mode in relation to what is happening. 'Observational rehearsal' involves the trainee watching as the expert performs the task.

Practice is vital in the learning of any skill, yet fatigue should be avoided. Different forms of organising practice are available but in general advice has been that practice should be distributed, with regular recovery periods. That is, practice should take place often in smaller doses rather than for a long time infrequently. Changes of tasks should be introduced regularly. This helps the consolidation of learning to take place, whereas concentrating on the same task for a long time is counter-productive, as fatigue builds up and learning can be lost. Practice is also very beneficial if the circumstances and settings of carrying out the tasks is changed slightly every time.

Motivation to learn

Steps which improve trainee motivation and maintain it are important. Experienced trainers are aware of crisis points in training programmes, where a boost is needed to help flagging spirits. Goal setting has an important contribution to make to maintaining motivation. Competition between individuals or training groups helps.

Behavioural theory has suggested and proved the importance of reinforcement: providing training in small units, encouraging active participation from the outset, as opposed to passive watching, frequent practice and overlearning. Social Learning theory has developed and contributed a number of principles, such as behavioural modelling, the importance of confidence building, allowing success to be gained quickly by possibly watering down the task and gradually refining it and making learning meaningful. Behavioural Modelling was developed for application in clinical psychology, especially those concerned with phobias. The sequence of events in the training setting is as follows.

Introduction	This reviews the relevance of the behaviour to be modelled, setting out examples and discussing options
Observing	A skilled 'model' carries out the actual behaviours in an acting setting or in a real setting, and is observed, often by means of video film
Producing	The behaviour is carried out in an artificial setting and later may be progressed on to more real situations
Feedback	The tutor and fellow trainees who have watched the performance give detailed comment and advice
Evaluation and review	Possibly after some real field experience, the trainees will reconvene and discuss again aspects of the modelled behaviour and outcomes

Behavioural modelling has applications, particularly in supervisory training, development of leadership skills and in jobs dealing with the public. Many major banks and building societies, for example, have in their training centres a mock bank counter and actors come in and play the role of awkward customers. All the different scenarios of the counter clerk's life can be modelled and they are given the chance to be in the situation in the training centre. Modelling needs to concentrate on the specific and observable. Behaviour is generally broken down into its parts in sequence and praise is given regularly in response to the correct carrying out of specific parts of the role. Follow-up input from trainers has also been shown to be vital for new behaviour to be maintained. It has been employed successfully in numerous large corporations since the demonstration of its utility in General Electric in 1974 by Goldstein and Sorcher. The turnover of unskilled workers was reduced in this instance from 72 to 28 per cent. Simulation training consists of an artificial representation of a real-life situation, requiring the trainee to react in the real mode, similar to the above. Other examples include case analysis, role play, in-basket exercises, business games.

Information presentation

There is a variety of general ways in which training information can be presented to trainees. The conference method, frequently used in more academic areas, contains feedback on attitude and performance. Trainees may lead a session, prepare a topic and the group may be given the agenda. This method works with small groups and allows immediate feedback and the sharing of ideas and information. Group cohesion can develop, as opposed to competition, and this has been shown to enhance learning.

Programmed instruction

This is a highly structured individualised learning method, based on the theories of Watson and Skinner. It breaks down learning into very small units and requires responding at every single stage by the learner, then immediate feedback of results. Information is usually provided in a self-paced manner, where the learner works through the materials and self-tests as they go along. Each piece of information is presented in the form of a 'frame'. There are usually questions immediately after each frame and, depending on the subject's response to the question, the programme will go on to the next piece of information or go back and review the past information until learning has been demonstrated. For courses which have no fixed starting time, are required to be repeated without much warning, and are relatively easily specified, programmed instruction is ideal.

Lectures

Most research on formal lecture-type presentations has shown that 90 per cent of what is said has been forgotten within hours of the lecture and almost all within a few days or weeks. Lecturing is probably one of the most inefficient information communication procedures ever devised by man, yet it is practised widely by some of the more intelligent people in our society and not only that, they get paid for doing it! Lectures do, of course, ensure that everyone gets the same starting information and guidelines, and they often imply that further independent work is expected of the student.

Commenting on the training of pilots in the United States, one expert has said,

> lectures, media presentations and self-study programmes are less than optimal approaches because they fail to provide challenges and responses to individual's engrained beliefs and because they do not examine the linkage between attitudes and behaviour. The most effective approach should probably include factual presentations on the body of factual data now available, moderated group discussions, and behavioural exercises including the use of full mission flight simulations designed to present problems requiring close co-ordination.

This is being done in many versions of Line Oriented Flight Training (LOFT) (Helmreich, 1984).

Applications of cognitive psychology in training programmes

Most current training programmes derive their principles from the behaviourist tradition that dominated the world of learning until the 1960s. Training programmes have been mainly empirical in their design, i.e. do they appear to work? Currently the behaviourist orientation is being replaced by a cognitive one, though the truth is that, as in the 1970s, the application of psychology theory is very much an ad hoc phenomenon. There is no fine-tuned cognitive training method which is based from beginning to end on cognitive theory. People who design training will always have to be empirical.

Individual attributes and training

For the most part, training design tends to ignore individual differences and aims to provide a uniform training programme for all (one size fits all). Partly justifying this approach is that job training is for people in particular jobs and it may be assumed that they have similar ability levels and aptitudes, e.g. electricians, astronauts, etc. Job selection processes are guided to a large extent by ability and aptitude and previous performance. However, this is ignoring the vital fact of the individual as a learner and confusing it with the individual as an employee.

Some facts are fairly well established and accepted by most people, though there are a few people who remain unconvinced. Quite distinct differences exist in aptitudes, motivation, interest and prior history, which influence performance and response to and attrition in training (Ghiselli, 1973; Gettinger and White, 1979).

Certain types of instructional environments facilitate learning in certain classes of individuals. Unfortunately, findings are ambiguous and we are not nearly clever enough yet to make adequate specifications of the environmental and individual features that are involved in such a manner that they could be used in a practical way. Learner characteristics are so significant to training results that training should be designed to take them into account (Goldstein, 1986), but this advice is more ignored than it is followed. The primary problem is twofold; first, the variations between individuals cover a wide range of abilities, many of which are either not recognised or not well defined. Second, the characteristics of training programmes are also not clearly specifiable. So to build a training programme which interfaces with specific learner characteristics is impossible, or at least very difficult in any precise and reliable sense. Many people, among whom Fleishman is a leading figure, are trying to make this happen. We have taxonomies of learner characteristics and also taxonomies of tasks. Theoretically the two can meet each other and be married. Much of learning theory is based on research with children and in the context of educational psychology, or in experimental cognitive psychology. There is much need for an adult training theory of learning.

Special attention is needed in the training of older workers. They are becoming an increasingly relevant sector of the economy in some countries, as the replacement ratio of the population is falling. Older workers present a special problem for trainers, because they are experienced and know a lot already, they have different attitudes and self-concepts about learning which may interfere with their training and their abilities may be in a state of relative decline in certain areas. Activity learning was thought most appropriate for older workers, as it involved less memorisation and was practical and it avoided the didactic style of training (Belbin and Shimmin, 1964). This was later modified and presented as the Discovery method. In turn this developed into the CRAMP method, with beneficial results (Downs and Roberts, 1977).

C   Comprehension

R   Reflex

A   Attitude

M   Memory

P   Procedure

The major problem with training older workers appears to be in the area of motivation. This can be addressed in the design and presentation of the programme. Older people are probably better off if trained in a group of older people rather than in a mixed-age group. In many cases longer time to learn should be allowed and more time to practice in self-paced ways is beneficial. At the end of the day, the actual results of training older people seem to differ little from that found in the case of younger trainees (Sterns and Doverspike, 1989).

Training has to be validated

Training is set in an industrial context with all the management and financial implications and it has to be seen to work. One of the more amazing facts from the business world of takeovers, gurus and high technology is that the most basic aspect of any training system, which is 'Did it work?' is ignored almost universally. This is especially true of expensive management and staff development courses, which are sometimes regarded by their participants as little more than expensive ways of restating the obvious, without the benefit of explicit training design methodology.

A broadly held view is that there are four classes of training outcomes.

---

a   Trainees reaction to programme content and process

b   Knowledge and skill acquisition

c   Behaviour change

d   Improvement in tangible organisational or individual outcomes

---

These features need to be followed through over time with more than the happy faces sheet at the end of the training session.

The future

Training is vitally important, yet it is hardly at first base when it comes to effective methodology and professional recognition. In most companies the trainer is usually a former assembler or operator who has stood out for ability or enthusiasm. The training manager could be anyone depending on pure chance. Kenneth Wexley (1989) had the following comments to make regarding the status and future of training. It makes no sense to follow fads or to keep up with the Jones's in choosing training programmes. It is imperative to have effective TNA. Second, 'at this time we know relatively little about the design of training programmes'. Training requires that the best most trainable people are selected, that the best method is used and that the method maximises transfer. The focus in the future will be on retraining people, on older workers, and on upgrading people. On evaluating the effectiveness of training programmes, he says that this has been largely done by anecdotal evidence. This results in certain training programmes becoming institutionalised and staying around long after their usefulness has expired. Finally, in the future the need to use a cognitive perspective, especially in high-tech areas of training will grow. Considering that he has been a leading academic in this area for over twenty years, these are indeed sobering thoughts.

Summary

Training has a vital role to play in the development of efficient and profitable organisations and in the furtherance of the personal goals of millions of individuals. Considerable growth is occurring in the field of training at this time and will do so, for the foreseeable future. Training delivery has many options. For many technical jobs, the best appears to be a form of combined job training with technical skills training. Much of training is poorly evaluated or followed up with regard to its effectiveness for the company. This is especially true of much management training. Computer technology is bringing rapid changes to the training delivery end, but the basic work of good training design will always be essential and not something that can be easily mechanised.

Activities

1. Discuss the different types of training experience that you and your classmates have had from various perspectives, such as relevance, delivery, design and evaluation. Which was the best to date?

2. Ask people in industrial settings about the way training is organised in their company and about its follow-up in terms of what has been learned.

3. Try to find someone who has been on a management development course and compare the experience in terms of the basics of training course delivery and evaluation.

4. Discuss with a training officer in a company the role and the support it gets from the company in facilities and finance. What improvements are thought necessary?

Further reading

Goldstein, I.L. and associates (1989) *Training and Development in Organisations*. (San Francisco, Jossey-Bass).

Goldstein, I.L. (1986) *Training in Organisations; Needs Assessment: Development and Evaluation*. (Monterey, CA, Brooks-Cole).

Wexley, K.N. (1984) Personnel training. *Annual Review of Psychology*, 49, 61–73.

CHAPTER

Selection: some theoretical considerations

Focus questions

What makes selection successful?

What are bias and fairness in the selection context?

How can we tell if selection really did pick the 'right' people?

Is selection valuable?

If people did not vary, there would be no selection problem. A group of subjects chosen at random from any sample of applicants would be as good as any other. But people vary from one another in many ways, and some of these are relevant to performance in a job setting. People who have to make a selection from a group of applicants for a job vacancy are faced by a complex problem. First, they have to determine the key aspects of the job in performance terms. Next, they have to find a way of separating out people in terms of their potential for performing these aspects. Finally, they have to make a choice which is seen to be fair and in keeping with the information they have collected.

Selection testing, interviewing or other forms of assessment are carried out and provide a basis of information on which to make a decision to accept or reject a candidate. There is a distinction made in the assessment of people, which originated in clinical psychology, but which is equally applicable in occupational psychology. That is between a sign and a sample. Much of what we do in assessment is to collect data which stands for something else or is a 'sign'. An intelligence test result does not tell you that someone is good or bad at academic activity, but it is a pointer as to what to expect. Another focus of attention is towards samples. Here we can look at the actual behaviour, or a close approximation of it, and get an idea of what a person can actually do. The 'signs' approach is more generalisable, easier to assess reliably, more objective and probably cheaper to run on large groups. 'Sample' types of indicators are more valid and job related, more subjective and in all likelihood more expensive (Meehl, 1954; Wernimont and Campbell, 1968).

Issues involved in decision making

Acceptance ratio

If you have gone to a great deal of trouble interviewing and assessing a number of candidates for a job and possibly paying one of their air fares from Australia, then you sincerely hope your choice is going to work out successfully. However, of the many interesting sequels to the selection decision, the first one is perhaps a little unexpected and that is that the appointed candidate may not accept the offer. According to a US College Recruiting report in 1983, acceptance applies to 60–70 per cent of job offers. For less skilled jobs, the acceptance ratio approaches 95 per cent. In a fluid employment market, people with low levels of skill will be happy enough to move around from job to job for a bit of variety or to improve the 'irrelevant' aspects of the job for themselves, such as travelling time or congenial company. On the other hand, when jobs are scarce, the acceptance rate for job offers will increase considerably. This has been the normal state of affairs throughout the 1990s and is likely to continue for the next decade. In highly paid and highly skilled jobs, people are sometimes unwilling to move but willing to go for interviews. They do this for various reasons, such as putting pressure on the boss or visiting interesting places or even for industrial espionage purposes. Two senior lecturers who were candidates for a professorship in my department were successively offered posts, turned them down and were promptly given personal chairs in their own universities.

Successful selection?

Selection is a bit like fishing, where a particular bait and casting technique are suitable for a particular stretch of water or for a particular species of fish. Fishermen learn what works; we might question whether occupational selectors do. How can we judge if a selection was successful? After someone accepts a job offer, they will turn out to be a success or failure in work performance terms. Success or failure might be expressed in terms of tenure, i.e. do they stay with the company for any length of time, or do they move on fairly rapidly? This poses the questions, were they badly selected, was their induction into the company poor or was the job unrewarding? Productivity could be the measure of success, and poor productivity might not be down to the person, but due to the equipment or materials they had to work with. In some basic low-skill jobs, just the absence of adverse behaviour might be regarded as a sign of success, i.e. do they turn up regularly and on time? These examples represent an important issue, which is the choice of performance criteria which are valid and can be reliably assessed. Job success is an elusive idea, which is sometimes very subjective and prone to bias. The kind of criteria we use are obviously critical to confirming whether the selection was good or bad.

Job analysis

All test use should be preceded and dependent on systematic job analysis. If this is done, then we know that the test relates in some way to criteria which have been derived from the job analysis and personnel specification. At the same time, we might not want to be too job-specific. There is an important point here, which is that a company may not only be selecting someone for the present job, but for future jobs at a higher level. Selection for potential as well as for actual performance is important.

Job criteria

The various kinds of job criteria used in studies of selection validity, promotion and response to training are invariably difficult to get accurate and complete measures for. The kinds of criteria normally used are:

1. Ratings by supervisors	Subjective response to an employee rating scale
2. Objective measures of productivity	Number of customers seen, sales made, tyres repaired
3. Measures of behaviour	Absenteeism, accidents, turnover, punctuality, cooperation
4. 'Hands-on' measures	Work samples, drawings and designs, objects
5. Job-related knowledge tests	Legal knowledge, police procedures, postcodes

There are various psychological criteria by which we can judge the criteria. Does the criterion represent a characteristic which is due to the individual and not to the group they are in or the setting they have to work in? This is an important and sometimes rather elusive criterion. We often attribute people's lack of success to them, when in fact they are doing their best in difficult circumstances. Is the criterion in the individual's control and related directly to their abilities? Another important point is, can we get access to reliable estimates of the criterion or are we just asking someone to guess at it? It is also important that workers vary at the job performance criteria. Just as in selection, if there is no difference between people then we do not need selection or job performance criteria. The time at which we take our measures may affect what we find out. People's performance has been shown to vary, and it is also affected by external factors on a temporal basis, so adequate sampling of performance over time must be considered.

Selection outcomes

Decision theorists have assisted us by neatly grouping the outcomes of the results of the selection process into four categories, which combine the judgement and the performance outcome. These are true–positive, false–positive, true–negative and false–negative. The prediction of performance can be either positive or negative and the outcome is true or false vis-à-vis the prediction. So false–positive is where a person is predicted to be a good worker (the interview rating was positive) and turned out to be a poor worker (in practice the outcome was bad, so the prediction was false). The worst eventuality in the firm's eyes is a false–positive. Here the selection process suggested that the candidate would be a good performer, but this turned out not to be the case. If there are too many false–positives, then the firm is bound for disaster and needs to change something fast, probably their recruitment officer or their psychological test specialist. A false–negative is what you or I are when we are turned down for a job. That is, the panel rated us negatively, but of course they were wrong. When we eventually got a job, we did quite well showing that their prediction was false and we should have been a positive. The same might apply to the editor or reviewer of a book. It might be rated as a negative, but when another publisher gets hold of it, it is a success. Fortunately, for many people the consequences of our selection rejections rarely come back to haunt us, but the failure of our acceptances do. This is why people feel more comfortable rejecting people than appointing them: no risk.

In filling positions, we have two starting parameters which apply to all jobs: Base Rate and Selection Ratio. Base rate is, effectively, the chance of success on the job in question. If it is very high, then there is little or no need for a selection process at all. Just choosing applicants at random will be as good as anything. For example, it has been calculated that if the base rate is 0.8 then a selection process must have validity of 0.45 to produce just a 10 per cent improvement of selection accuracy over random choice. That is, the ability of the selection method to predict any differences in job performance must be very strong, since most people will not fail. Getting a selection method to find the rare people who are bound to fail is difficult. Jobs with very high base rates are boring and meaningless and suitable only for people with low levels of ambition or ability. At the other extreme, where the base rate is very low, the selection method still needs to be very accurate to be of any use. A better strategy would be to employ people on probation and monitor their performance closely. Selection methods contribute most to improving the effectiveness of decision making when the base rate is around 0.5.

It was thought by industrialists such as Henry Ford that deskilling and assembly-line production would mean that workers of the lowest skill levels could be employed, paid the minimum, treated badly and be easily replaced if they gave trouble. This method worked for a number of years, for as long as there were hordes of immigrants coming to America, or soldiers returning from the War desperate for any job. In the long run, industries of this type were doomed to failure and have since largely been replaced or have changed their methods.

The selection ratio is the ratio of job vacancies to applicants. If 100 people apply for 99 jobs, and the selection ratio is nearly 1, then there is clearly little point in selection procedures. When the selection ratio is low, a test with even modest validity can make a significant contribution.

Tables are available which indicate the proportion of successes that can be expected, given the validity of the test, the selection ratio and the base rate (Taylor and Russell, 1939). If a test or selection method had zero validity, then the success expected would equal the base rate. That is to say, the selection method is not improving the chances of success over base rate and a random choice would be as good. With a higher selection ratio, the selection method validity must be correspondingly higher to improve success rates. If the selection ratio is quite low, then the method validity can be fairly low and still lead to reasonable success rates, i.e. if you are only choosing 1 out of 100, you need to be pretty unlucky to get a wrong one, though it is not impossible and will occur in situations where patronage or other irrelevant criteria have an influence in selection.

Probationary periods in selection

It was stated above that the use of a probationary period had some advantages, especially when the base rate was low. In some situations, the probationer has the option of withdrawing, e.g. the Armed Forces; in others, the employer is more likely to exercise the option of withdrawing the job offer, e.g. university lecturing. In the United States, government agencies across all states showed the mean rate of termination after probationary period to be 5 per cent. While this is not very high, it is considerably higher than the rate of unsatisfactory performance in existing employees. This suggests that, because it is much easier from a legal and personal standpoint to terminate probationary employees, this rate is a truer reflection of performance in government jobs. Most states had probationary period; thirty-four out of forty-four replying to a survey had a probationary period for at least 50 per cent of staff (Elliot and Peaton, 1994).

Bias

Over the years it has been evident that people from different racial groups perform differently on cognitive tests and such tests have been accused of being biased. Companies have been sued for using them in selection and have therefore become wary about using them. In a situation where a particular ability, as measured by a particular test, cannot be shown to relate significantly to job performance, such a test should not be part of the selection procedure. Tests are biased if given equal levels of qualification, experience and ability to perform, people from one ethnic or social group perform less well on average than people from other groups. A test of physical strength could not be called biased just because women score less well than men. On average, men are physically stronger than women. However, if the test results predict job performance differently for men and women, then it is biased. It is not saying the same thing about the different groups. It may not have been adequately normed or developed, taking into account the group differences that exist. Unfair discrimination or bias exists when members of a minority group have lower probabilities of being selected, when if they had been selected their probabilities of performing successfully would have been equal to those of a non-minority person (Arvey and Falvey, 1988).

Bias is normally associated with race or gender, but there is also age bias and recently a more interesting subject altogether, that of discrimination on the grounds of body weight. Body weight has until recently received limited attention as a source of bias. The predominant Western cultural stereotype of overweight people is that they have defects of will-power, character and responsibility. The obese are viewed as emotionally impaired, lazy and selfish. On the bright side, the fat person has been stereotyped as jolly and fun to be with. These stereotypes are wrong and basically unfair. The effects of this unfairness can easily and inadvertently transfer to the employment selection situation. This has been demonstrated in an experiment, in which pictures showing the hands filling in an application form were shown to subjects. The application forms completed by the fat hands were less favourably rated (Larkin and Pines, 1979). In another study, fat or thin photographs were attached to identical CVs and anti-fat discrimination both in those called for interview and in hiring was observed (Benson et al., 1980). Obese women are probably worse off than obese men. There is some empirical evidence that overweight people are less preferred in sales positions but equally preferred for indoor clerical jobs. Student judges were presented with video stimuli consisting of the same actors playing fat and thin people (using makeup, etc.). They were shown as applying for two different jobs, one in sales the other in computers, and they were of both genders. Findings showed that weight affected the preference for hiring and the effect was greater for female applicants (Pignitore et al., 1994)

Of course, while there is probably discrimination in regard to body weight, there may be perceivable personality and attitude differences in the population of over-weight people cause by self-concept. There is no denying the importance of body shape to self-concept. We carry around in our heads a representation of our bodies, some-times an inaccurate one, called a 'body schema' and some people have a resultant emotional reaction of being satisfied/dissatisfied with this perception of body shape. This may well affect how some people behave at interview for example.

Fairness

There are many ways in which we can be unfair. Mainly, fairness implies that everyone has an equal chance to do their best in the selection process and that the results of the process will be regarded in the same way for everyone when the decision is made. So if we set up a decision rule that you have to score 20 out of 25 on a knowledge test, then everyone who attains that level must be passed on to the next phase of selection.

We cannot decide after the tests are taken that we do not want any red-headed people, even though they pass the test. Also everyone entering the process will have been informed that a knowledge test will be set and what areas that test will cover. As far as possible, they will all have had an equal opportunity of gaining access to the knowledge involved. For example, if the job was for a salesperson in a company selling pumps, it would not be fair to ask every candidate to describe the range of pumps made by the company if some of the candidates already worked for the company.

Psychometrics

In the use of tests in selection, a number of basic guidelines should be observed and a number of principles understood. Tests derive their authority or face validity from being specially prepared, officially formatted in terms of answer forms, etc., and looking relevant. Sometimes this authority is rather spurious. The glossier the cover, the more suspicious you should be.

Every test has characteristics which can be used to help us decide if it is usable as a test. These characteristics include reliability, which is the extent to which the test will repeat the same result if given again to the applicant. It is also measured by the extent to which the test is internally consistent. That is, the separate parts of the test tend to grade people in the same relative order. If an interview panel were to be regarded as a test and the separate members of the panel regarded as parts of the test, then it is easy to see why interviews lack reliability, since different people on the panel can often rate the candidates differently.

Validity is the second major area of concern which psychometrics has brought to the selection situation. Validity represents, quantitatively, the extent to which a selection method gives a true and accurate representation of what it is claiming to represent. A weighing scale is invalid if it gives you the wrong weight. It may be invalid and reliable if it gives you the same wrong weight every time. If it gives you a different wrong weight every time, then it is invalid and unreliable. If a selection method does this then obviously it is useless, but how will the selectors know that the method is useless?

Appropriateness of norms

Most tests are normative, though in training situations tests are often criterion related. Normative means that a standard has been set in earlier stages of developing or using the test (in the case of 'in-house' norms), which allows the test user to relate a person's score on the test to a set of scores obtained by a sample of people similar to the test taker. That is, the average performance and the range of performance for a representative group of subjects has already been established. These figures are often translated into 'percentiles', which are figures from 1 to 100 representing the percentage of the normative sample scoring at or below a given score. Norms must be appropriate for the group of subjects being tested. They should be reasonably up-to-date, i.e. under ten years old, and they should have been collected in the same country they are being used in. This is important in the case of foreign tests which are translated and used in other countries. Neither the norms nor probably the test itself can be considered appropriate until much development work has been done.

Validation of selection methods

Two types of validity used in employment studies are Predictive and Concurrent validity. It is essential to demonstrate and maintain the demonstration over time, that a selection method is effective. Predictive validity is preferable and ideally involves testing every job applicant, hiring every applicant, waiting for a period of months until the criterion could be reliably assessed and then correlating the scores of the predictor, i.e. test result and the criterion for all the workers. Of course this does not happen in a commercial situation, though it can happen in the Armed Forces to some extent. Normally only a proportion of applicants are taken on and so full data is not available on the job performance of those who are rejected. This causes a phenomenon known as Restriction of Range. The effect of restriction of range is to attenuate (make smaller) the correlation between tests and performance criteria. Fortunately there is a formula to cope with this, so restriction of range can be compensated for in calculations of test validity. Concurrent validity takes the test and a criterion measure which has been obtained at the same time, perhaps on current employees, though again there is a problem of restriction of range to cope with.

Predicting job performance from ability and aptitude tests

Statistical analysis of aptitude and ability tests has shown that underlying the performance of people are a number of within test factors (setting aside for the moment the within people factors). Each test that exists can be shown to be assessing a particular collection of factors, so that a verbal test will have more of the verbal factor than the numerical one and so on. A general test factor has been identified and called 'g'. It refers to what we think of as intelligence, though it is really the engine underlying intelligence, because much of our intelligence is dependent on culture, education and opportunities. 'g' is the basis of our power of reasoning across a range of different kinds of contents and subjects such as words, numbers, abstract symbols and diagrams.

It has been shown that 'g' is the most valid predictor of job performance in many job situations. Specific job knowledge tests provide minimal additional predictive power, (McHenry *et al.*, 1990; Ree *et al.*, 1994). In a sample of 78 041 airmen in 82 jobs, 'g' was the best predictor; specific abilities and job knowledge tests gave an average increase in predictiveness of only 0.02 (or say 4–5 per cent) (Olea and Ree, 1994). Based on factor scores from the multiple-aptitude battery used by the United States Air Force, the strongest predictor of flying and navigation is the 'g' factor. Technical knowledge tests and scores on specific factors are minimally effective. This is rather difficult for people to accept as it seems to contradict common sense, but it is now an established fact.

Selection for training

Selection for training is sometimes different and validity levels vary. Robertson and Downs (1979; 1989) reviewed a large number of studies in this area and conclude that selection for training often gives higher levels of validity than selection for jobs. In selection for training purposes, work sample tests are often used. However, though people may do well in training and pass with flying colours, the situation can change once they are confronted by the complexities of the real world. For example, a test developed to select pilots, bombers and navigators correlated well with the recruits' performance in training situations. But after using the system for several years in actual combat, it was found that the hit-rate of bombing was poor, and that the selection tests had no relation to success in hitting targets (Jenkins, 1946).

Content validity

Lawshe (1975) advocated a strategy called content validity analysis, which determines the extent to which the behaviour elicited by the test is the same as or similar to that required by the job. Obtaining the Content Validity Ratio is usually a judgemental procedure rather than a statistical one. A number of judges, who may be supervisors, are asked to review the test content and job specifications to see if they agree how relevant a given test or question appears to be. The ratio involved represents the number of favourable opinions over the total of opinions. A typing test is obviously content valid for a job as a typist. However, if the typist also has to answer the phone, greet customers and keep appointment diaries for ten people, then there are other skills required and the typing test is only valid for part of the job.

Portability of validity

As noted above in relation to norms, many tests are constructed on the basis of studies of college students, army samples or samples in the United States. There is a major risk that the predictions of job performance that might hold in these samples would not be attained in Europe. Any tests used here should ideally be constructed here, or at least their adaptation and validity carried out here and fully reported in British, Irish or European academic journals.

Meta-analysis

In the literature of selection, the term 'meta-analytic' study is encountered regularly. These are studies which take the essential data of a number of separate validity studies. This would include the correlation between a predictor (a test or rating) and a criterion, the sample size and the reliability of the measures. By statistical means, the data from all the separate studies are amalgamated to produce a global estimate of the validity of a specific method. Some apparently significant meta-analytic studies have been reported in recent years. These have given the average validity of interview methods as 0.14 and of ability tests as 0.53 (Hunter and Hunter, 1984). Thus the average correlation across a number of studies was, in the case of the interview, nearly negligible and similar to that for references. Some doubts are expressed by experts in relation to meta-analysis. It is said that they are often used to make up for a number of methodological faults or limitations in studies, or to overcome these faults by assumptions which cannot be proven about individual studies (Eysenck, 1994). Despite that, they are widely quoted and welcomed by selection psychologists as they have consistently suggested that most selection methods are actually more valid than we thought before, hurrah!

Validity generalisation

It has been said that too much of test validation was situation-specific and could not be applied outside of the particular validation situation or to prove that the validity coefficients were small and very variable, suggesting that test validity was both weak and inconsistent.

Pearlman *et al.* (1980) pointed out that validity between a test and a criterion was affected by three factors, each of which reduced the calculated value of the validity statistic. These three factors added variance to the measures, which was not due to the test itself, but had the effect of reducing the correlation between the test and the criterion.

The biggest source of unwanted variability was in the criterion measure itself, especially when these were the sort of subjective supervisor's ratings often used. Also, there was almost always range restriction, which limited the true range of genuine test and criterion variance. There was the inevitable reliability of the test itself, which unless the test was very long or unidimensional and factorially well saturated would always be a consideration. Added to these effects was the inevitable sampling error which was variance due to unavoidable random factors. This grows less as the sample size increases. The combined effect of all these factors was to depress test-criterion validity.

Standard deviation in any distribution of test validities, due to the combined effect of the three artefacts alone when the sample size was 50, was 0.164. Thus if a researcher had a large number of test validation studies, they would have to compute the variance of the distribution of validities and subtract the above artefactual variance from this total. If the remainder was essentially zero, the hypothesis of situational specificity could be rejected. That is, there was an allowable amount of variability in validity coefficients which could be legitimately ascribed to factors independent of the validity of the test. So in general, test validities were much stronger than was usually apparent (Pearlman *et al.*, 1980).

A pattern is emerging in validity studies, according to Smith and George (1992). This is related to 'point to point' validation theory (Asher and Sciarrino, 1974). They emphasise that for good validity there must be a strong relationship between job content and the selection method content. Another approach to validity assessment involves a statistical procedure called Multiple Regression Analysis. This calculates a prediction formula which contains weights for each relevant variable. Knowing an individual's scores on the prior-measured variables permits a prediction of their likelihood of success to be made, assuming that we already have a regression formula from previous selection. Each variable, i.e. test score, interview rating, etc., is multiplied by its weight derived from a previous sample or research. Rather than assigning complex weights, it has been found just as efficient, especially with smaller samples, to use unit weighting; this obviously assumes that the numbers are scaled to the same value range, otherwise adding them together would produce strange results. Suppose we scored the interview out of 100 and the job sample test out of 10, the people who were brilliant at the interview and useless at the job sample test would score better than those who were a little weak at the interview, but practically very competent.

It should also be noted that such formulae need to be updated regularly, as the determinants of occupational criteria change, e.g. turnover is greatly affected by conditions in the labour market. As more variables are entered into a multiple correlation, it is possible to arrive at an apparently valid result when none in fact exists. In some cases, a prediction formula may operate better for one subgroup than another, i.e. its effects are moderated by some extraneous variable. This is something that has to be looked out for, as prediction may appear OK for the group as a whole but be quite invalid for some specific subgroups. This is especially relevant and a cause for concern in situations where there is a mix in the applicant sample of people from widely differing backgrounds. Predictions for genders, ages and races need to be individually validated or cross-validated to be more precise.

Utility

The costs and benefits of particular decisions can be estimated. In the selection context, the association between the costs of the selection process and its accuracy on the one hand and the value of job performance on the other has been investigated, resulting in the concept of Utility. This is an estimate of how useful the method is in terms of the financial payoff gained from its use. In practice this simplifies down to the question 'What does it cost the firm to make a mistake?'. The utility of a selection device has been defined as 'the degree to which its use improves the quality of the individuals selected beyond what would have occurred had that device not been used' (Blum and Naylor, 1968).

Various approaches to quantifying the concept have been made over the years beginning with Hull (1928), advocating the use of the index of forecasting efficiency as a means of evaluating the utility of a selection device. This index was a function of the correlation between the device and the performance criterion. This was superseded when the Taylor-Russell (1939) method incorporated the addition of variables pertaining to the situation of the selection. These were the selection ratio and the base rate. Their formulation required the base rate to be dichotomised (successful/unsuccessful), which can be arbitrary and often loses information. Most workers are not totally successful or unsuccessful. In practice they can be retrained or transferred to other tasks. The model is appropriate where differences in ability beyond the minimum necessary to perform the job do not yield differences in benefit (e.g. clerical jobs) or where differences in output are believed to occur, but are presently unmeasurable, e.g. caring professions. Another approach is that of Naylor and Shine (1965) which, unlike the Taylor-Russell model, does not require that employees be dichotomised into 'satisfactory' and 'unsatisfactory' groups. Less information is required to use this model of utility. Like the Taylor-Russell model, it does not formally integrate the cost of selection or money gained or lost into the utility index.

Cronbach and Gleser (1965) extended utility to cover classification and placement as well as selection. They expressed utility on a monetary scale using a scaling factor to translate criterion levels into money terms, and a term for the costs of the selection programme is included. The scaling factor (SDy) is the value of a one-standard deviation difference in criterion level. That is how much more productive in actual value is the worker at $+1$ standard deviation above the average performer. The model assumes that the relationship between test scores and job performance is linear and test scores are normally distributed.

Boudreau (1989) refers to the 'raging debate' on the proper measurement method, but argues against exerting much research effort on this, since research to date shows that it cannot be determined which estimate (if any) is correct. He found substantial uncertainty associated with utility estimates, and that uncertainty stems largely from measurement error in SDy. Investigating this issue means changing the focus from measurement towards uncertainty and risk in the decision situation.

In a given situation, productivity gain under the conditions of selection ratio and the standard deviation of performance sets the baseline of maximum utility. So a selection device with 0.5 validity would yield half the utility of one with validity equal to the theoretical maximum of 1. In effect, most sophisticated selection devices will yield a utility advantage given suitable conditions of selection ratio and performance variation. Where there is a large and varied applicant pool and performance on the job varies widely but is correlated with the selection device to some extent, then using the device can be of potentially great financial value (Landy *et al.*, 1982).

In a practical context Schmidt *et al.* (1979) estimated that with a 50 per cent selection ratio, the US Federal Government could save 376 million dollars over ten years by using a cognitive ability test to select computer programmers. In a similar vein, it has been calculated that savings of 15 billion dollars per year could be made by using ability tests for selection at entry level (Hunter and Hunter, 1984).

Summary

Selection is a process which can go wrong in many different ways, some of which are obvious, but some of which are hidden and might not surface for years. The success of selection can be measured in various ways, including those which are more statistical and those which are based on monetary values. Validity is a key aspect of all selection methodology. Selection methods have more validity than is commonly believed. Part of their apparent lack of validity is due to the poor levels of validity in the criteria used to judge them. Selection can easily be both biased and unfair and great care needs to be taken to ensure procedures prevent both occurring. Whatever selection method is employed, the same technical criteria can be applied to the process. Because selection is the entry to most organisations, it is vital that it is done well.

Activities

1. Discuss how validity might be assessed with respect to different kinds of jobs.

2. In your own particular kind of job, consider the kind of criteria that might be used to judge whether the right people had been selected.

3. Compare a number of jobs from the point of view of the costs of poor selection. Discuss with any business owner or manager whether poor selection has ever cost them money.

Further reading

Arvey, R.D. and Falvey, R.H. (1988) *Fairness in Selecting Employees*, 2nd edn. (Reading, MA, Addison-Wesley).

Eysenck, H.J. (1994) Meta-analysis and its problems. *British Medical Journal*, 309, 789–92.

Herriot, P. (1989) *Assessment and Selection in Organizations*. (Chichester, Wiley).
Hunter, J. and Hunter, R. (1984) Validity and utility of alternative predictors of job performance. *Psychology Bulletin*, 96, 72–98.
Pearlman, I., Schmidt, F.L. and Hunter, J.E. (1980) Validity generalisation results for tests used to predict job performance and training success in clerical occupations. *Journal of Applied Psychology*, 65, 353–406.
Smith, M. and Robertson, I.T. (1989) *Advances in Selection and Assessment*. (Chichester, Wiley).

Selection process and practice

CHAPTER 8

Focus questions

What is the role of selection methods in human resource planning?

What are the real costs of selection?

Why is there a growing interest in selection?

What are the legal and practical issues involved?

What methods are used, and to what extent?

How can selection methods affect me?

> The first estimate of his (the prince) intelligence will be based on the character of the men he keeps about him. If they are capable and loyal, he will be reputed wise, for he will have demonstrated that he knows how to recognise their ability and keep them loyal to him. If they are otherwise he will be judged unfavourably for the first mistake a ruler can make lies in the selection of his ministers.

This quote comes from a book written in the sixteenth century (*The Prince*, Machiavelli), which for many years was a kind of bible for statesmen and rulers throughout Europe. It is interesting that selection was placed at such a high level of importance.

Historical approaches to selection

Assessing people for occupational purposes is not new. The earliest recorded example is said to be from 2200 BC. The Chinese Emperor examined his top officials or mandarins every three years and decided whether to retain them or have them dismissed. Such processes of assessment went on for hundreds of years, building and maintaining a top class civil service to serve the empire. Between 200 BC and 200 AD written exams in law, military affairs, agriculture, revenue and geography were held for entry to the Emperor's service. It is no coincidence that the Chinese empire was the most powerful and long-lasting in human history.

The French in 1791 and the British in 1833 were among the pioneers of open competitive exams for their civil services. The United States followed the British example in the 1860s. The American system from the 1880s onwards used forms of job sample tests, biographical information and a probationary period to decide who would gain permanent appointments.

In a selection system it is very important to ensure the accuracy and fairness of procedures. Some of the procedures used in the early years are remarkably similar to what is done to this day. For example, they included making sure that the characteristics of successful job-holders were the same as those assessed by the exams. That is, the exams were indeed assessing the relevant characteristics for success in the job. They endeavoured to make sure that the administrators of the selection process had minimal opportunity to favour one candidate over another. Standardised administration procedures, using exam numbers so that candidates could not be identified by markers, were developed to prevent this abuse. The actual exam answers had to be assessed in such a way that the most accurate and fair results were obtained. To achieve this, objective and carefully tested marking procedures, using a point system, were devised and developed (DuBois, 1970). These three steps are equivalent to the modern criteria of validity, fairness and objectivity. Any selection system should have these three characteristics to as great an extent as possible. Their obverses which are invalidity, bias and subjectivity, make for a very poor selection system if they are present to any extent.

Interest in selection

Our interest lies mainly in the techniques of selection and the psychological contribution in this area. In this there have been distinct phases in the study and application of selection methods. An early peak occurred in the first two decades of the twentieth century, as Munsterberg and others were pioneering the subject. At this time, a high level of optimism was generated by the possibilities of applying psychology to industry. Methods had recently been developed by means of which jobs could be analysed and people's physical strengths and skills could be assessed. It was felt that the two aspects could be used together with the result that productivity could be maximised.

Another peak of interest was shown in the 1930s to 1940s as government organisations were growing and as the War and mechanisation presented many new problems. By the 1950s faith in selection methods was in relative decline, as was its interest as an academic subject. Studies had suggested that the validities of the selection tests and other processes were low. That is, they did not predict job-related outcomes with the degree of accuracy that they claimed. Interest moved on to broader attempts at improving productivity within the organisation, such as staff development and enhancing motivation. Another aspect of the post-War period which affected the use of selection methods was that in many occupations shortage of skilled staff was a problem and employers were happy to take who they could get, i.e. there was little role for selection as such.

The current position

Recently there has been a growth in interest in selection, as organisations have again taken the subject seriously. The change of attitude has been brought about by a number of social and economic pressures. The emphasis on productivity has been further intensified by the climate of international competition. Labour costs have become a proportionately much higher element in the overall cost structure of companies. Employees have become much more expensive to service and maintain than in previous decades. They can no longer be hired and fired as easily. Legislation relating to dismissal of people makes it all the more important to get the right people. Equality legislation and antidiscrimination laws have made selection a bit of a minefield for employers. The task of sifting through hundreds of application forms for even a few vacancies has focused attention on more sophisticated selection and screening techniques.

In 1995 some British universities at the behest of their Vice-Chancellors began piloting 'employability tests' with a view to using them in due course if they fulfil their expectations. Undergraduates at the end of their courses would take tests to measure their knowledge of business, their communication skills and their ability to work in a team. This is said to be in order to help employers select suitable recruits. According to the secretary of the Association of Graduate Recruiters, employers wanted graduates who could offer more than a degree. Or perhaps less than a degree?

The external environment has had a great influence on selection and recruitment, due to the exceptionally high rates of unemployment and the uncertainties of trading in the global market. This has led to an increasing number of firms seeking to be flexible in their manpower needs (Gunnigle and Flood, 1990). Firms are reluctant to take on permanent workers, with all the attendant commitments and instead they seek to recruit temporary or part-time staff, and in many cases both.

Selection costs

Although psychology may be our main interest, we cannot ignore the fact that selection is a business cost and a very expensive one in many cases. The whole process is expensive to run and the cost of making a mistake may be huge. There are considerable costs in appointing someone who then leaves the company soon after, but these costs do not appear directly on the balance sheet. Most human resource managers think of selection costs as operating costs out of the current annual budget whereas looking at selection costs as a capital investment, which earns a return over a longer period, is more beneficial. This would allow personnel to compete more effectively for investment money, rather than in terms of current operating costs (Cronshaw and Alexander, 1985).

An example from the insurance world illustrates the point. Turnover of insurance agents ranges from 44 per cent to over 60 per cent in the first year (Lombardi *et al.*, 1985). This is very costly, as each of these people had to be inducted into the organisation, supported and trained. There would also be costs in relation to rent, clerical support, financing and disruption. Departing agents are mainly (74 per cent of them) below the median in sales productivity. That is, most of them do not produce enough business to justify employing them anyway. Only a limited number of people are really successful in the insurance industry as sales agents, and the companies' demands for staff are unfillable. Clearly great advantage would accrue to insurance companies if they did not appoint short-tenure people in the first place, and if those appointed were highly productive. Is there a system which will guarantee this result?

Sales staff training costs about half their annual salary, while field support costs two-thirds of salary; to this must be added the cost of recruiting and finally the costs of lost sales if a bad appointment is made. A bad selection decision can cost a company between two and three times the salary of the salesperson (Kerley, 1985).

UK and Irish employment legislation

British and Irish legislation in this area is similar. The main enactments are the Employment Equality Act 1977, Unfair Dismissals 1977, Health, Safety and Welfare and finally Terms and Conditions of Employment. Generally the law is based on the notions of equity and fair dealing. People may not be abused, discriminated against, or subject to unreasonable conditions of work.

Legislation and court cases have probably had an implicit effect in drawing attention to the methods of selection utilised by companies. In the United States the Employment Equality Guidelines state

> The use of any test which adversely affects hiring, promotion, transfer or any other employment or membership opportunity constitutes discrimination unless the test has been validated and shows a high degree of utility, and the person using the test can demonstrate that alternative suitable means of hiring etc. are not available.

Many private sector employers abandoned testing programmes in the 1970s following this guideline, while in the public sector there was more testing, as they had to be seen to be fair and to be able to demonstrate fairness.

There is a relative lack of European research and a lack of interest from the trade unions and employers' groups in the effects of selection methods, something which is surprising on the face of it. UK and Irish Employment legislation has not placed much specific emphasis on the subject (Shimmin, 1989). In some European countries there is legislation. Italy has not permitted tests in selection since the 1970s and Belgium is seeking to pass laws in this area. In Sweden and Holland, the applicant has the right to see test results before the employer and to withdraw the application and have the results destroyed. Recently (1996), the trade union Unison has expressed concern and interest in the use of tests in selection and we can expect to see this focus of attention increasing in the next few years.

Commercial practice in selection

Recruitment and selection

Selection of staff is obviously crucial to the success of any business. Recruitment is the phase in which applicants are sought. Selection takes place after a pool of suitable applicants has been gathered together from the various sources of recruitment. Placement refers to the stage where the choice of candidates has been made and they have to be placed in specific jobs, departments or teams. This may also refer to existing staff who are being moved or retrained, etc.

Human resource planning

Selection is closely related to Human Resource Planning, a term which has acquired rather negative connotations through its being associated, not wrongly, with redundancy and downsizing of organisations. Human resource planning involves forecasting the employment needs of the company and being able at short notice to fill these. Information from job analysis, specifying job requirements, and existing staff member's skills and training can be entered into human resource planning programmes, enabling decisions to be made about how to fill vacancies and remedy skill shortages.

Labour shortages can be filled either by training, external recruitment or internal recruitment. Internal recruitment means finding an existing staff member who could fill the role. It may involve retraining or a redistribution of responsibilities among a team of workers. Both forms of recruitment require a set of knowledge about skills, availability and employment markets. The information required concerns the skills which the job demands, where they can be found and how much it is likely to cost to attract people with these skills. Before any form of selection takes place, some form of human resource planning must be carried out, even if it is a pure guess based on experience, as it will be in most small businesses.

General beliefs

Several surveys into the incidence of use of different methods have been reported in recent years. In the United States, Ryan and Sackett (1989) found great variation among occupational psychologists in terms of preferred method. What people did in selection process seemed to depend on what they liked doing and felt comfortable with. Smith and George (1992) say that some practitioners are seduced by complex procedures which are not very job related. That is, there seems to be an attraction of the mystique aspect of some methods. Robertson (1994) confirms this when he says that there is a considerable gap between research findings and methods used.

Few employers make any check on the validity of their methods; they simply go on using them. There has been a discrepancy between usage and validity, e.g. Dakin and Armstrong (1989) illustrate this in the finding that New Zealand personnel consultants produced a high correlation between their beliefs about the validity of a method and their use of it, but their beliefs were unrelated to the true validity of individual methods. In a practical context, it is amazing that managers of companies, who will critically examine and dissect a new machine or mechanical process, will pass over the inner workings of their selection techniques with a blithe assumption that they are valid.

Incidence of use

Bevan and Fryatt (1988), in a report *Employee Selection in the U.K.*, surveyed by post a total of 750 firms, obtaining a 43 per cent response rate. They found for example that only 16–22 per cent of companies used tests, and that tests were used in the main for higher level jobs. Smith and Abrahamsen's (1992) review of several studies stated that choice of method was not a function of their technical adequacy.

Robertson and Makin (1986) sampled firms in the Times Top 1000 Companies and 304 questionnaires were sent out. A 36 per cent return rate was achieved. They looked at methods used in management appointments. First of all, they showed that a firm would appoint a manager per year in the proportion of just less than 1 per 100 employees. That is, the average firm of 500 employees would appoint 4 new managers or management trainees in an average year. The normal method used was the interview and 90 per cent of interviews involved line managers and also personnel people.

The line manager is generally the next most senior person that the appointee will report to. In most selection panels he or she would be included. The panel interview with two to three interviewers was most commonly used in the companies surveyed. This confirms other similar surveys and seems to be the industry standard. Having more than one interview is also the norm in over 98 per cent of the firms surveyed. While this would certainly be the case for managerial appointments, in the case of operator-level staff one interview would be more usual. However, having said that, it is clear that the more sophisticated multinational firms are putting all staff through a three- or four-part selection process. It was reported that tests are not used at all by 65 per cent of organisations, though 12 per cent used personality tests more often than not and 9 per cent used cognitive tests more often than not. Only 6 per cent used bio-data, but its use was increasing and some firms made it clear that their intention was to use it in future.

A major problem in selection is that many companies appoint relatively few managers in a given year, so that a practice does not develop or get validated. Only the larger companies, who have specialist recruiters working full-time, get the chance to fully develop their techniques.

Porteous and Hodgins (1995), in a countrywide survey, examined the use of selection methods in a representative sample of Irish companies. This study showed that the typical selection programme used in Irish companies consists of an application form or CV to screen the applicants, an interview which forms the basis for the selection decision and reference checks to supposedly validate the procedure.

Large companies were found to be the main test users; 38 per cent of them used cognitive ability tests, while only 2 per cent of the small companies did. Of large companies, 36 per cent said they used personality tests, while 12 per cent of small and medium companies did. In general, large companies use the more sophisticated methods to a greater extent. Of the large companies surveyed 9 per cent used assessment centres compared with 2 per cent of medium and none of the small companies. Similarly, biodata usage is concentrated among large companies (4 per cent). Small companies in particular seemed to know very little about the use of selection methods other than the interview and application form.

In France, Germany, Norway and The Netherlands, interviews are the dominant methods of selection (Smith and Abrahamsen, 1992). When compared with the United States and the United Kingdom, reference checking is less common – 39 per cent of French companies, 23 per cent German and 49 per cent of companies in The Netherlands use this method. Cognitive tests were used by 33 per cent in France, 21 per cent in Germany and 21 per cent in The Netherlands. Personality tests were used in the cases of 38 per cent in France, 6 per cent in Germany and 16 per cent in Norway. Biodata usage was very low, 1 per cent in France, 8 per cent in Germany and 1 per cent in Norway. France differed most from the general international trend. The use of graphology in 52 per cent of vacancies in France is remarkably high. More than 77 per cent of French firms use handwriting analysis to select managers (Shackleton and Newell, 1991). Graphology is more commonly used by small firms.

Stages in the hiring process

There are three phases in the process of hiring staff, namely recruitment, screening and selection. Smith and Robertson (1989) enlarge upon this and specify the various steps in a process which they call the 'selection paradigm'. They say that selection involves the following steps.

Job analysis: outlining what the job involves in terms of tasks, skills and knowledge.

Personnel specification: describing the ideal candidate from the point of view of skills knowledge and other personal attributes such as experience, fitness and personality.

Criterion development: determining how the ideal candidate will be identified in terms of job-related and personal attributes.

Attracting candidates: this is the centre of the recruitment phase and involves getting a good field of possible people to apply for the vacancy.

Choosing the selection method: deciding how to go about the selection phase in terms of tests, interviews, etc.

Avoiding bias in selection: ensuring that the process does not discriminate unfairly against any person or group.

Making a choice: having recruited and assessed, the final point is making a choice between the candidates.

Another perspective on selection is to let a set of principles guide the process. First, selection should be job- or industry-specific. That is, methods and their detailed implementation should be designed for the job in question. Taking 'off-the-shelf' products or methods and expecting them to work for you is unrealistic. The determinants of job performance are specific to the job. Second, selection should be viewed as very much a process of stages which consist of a sequence. Selection at any sophisticated level cannot all be done at once. It is better to take it a step at a time and whittle down the list of possible candidates to a smaller and smaller set. Start off with the more general, most easily ascertainable candidate characteristics and work down to the subjective at the end of the process. At least you will avoid making a glaringly obvious mistake.

Third, choose the methods to fit the criteria, not the other way around. For example, if you want to know about someone's table manners take them to dinner, if you want to know if they can make business decisions, set them a business decision task that you have designed and perfected with your existing managers.

The person specification stage can be approached from two angles. Either take the job first and decide the kind of person who will fit best, or put the primary emphasis on the person who will fit into the environment of the office or company. Companies in fast changing technological sectors of the economy prefer a person first–job later approach, because they need people who are flexible, creative and energetic. Starting from existing job descriptions can restrict choice to a great extent and result in less adaptable people being taken on. The process of applying or seeking descriptors of the person can be seen as functioning along a continuum between the person and the job. The closer we are to the job, the more concrete the descriptors will be, i.e. specific competence will be mentioned, whereas as we move towards the person end, we are getting more abstract and talking in terms of traits (Van Zwanenberg and Wilkinson, 1993). The use of assessment centres has been predicated from a job-first perspective, but this can easily be changed to include more personality and behaviourally diverse exercises.

Consider a really important example for a moment, taken from the world of professional football. One of the most successful club teams in Europe over many years has been Ajax of Amsterdam, and one of their greatest strengths has been their youth development policy. In choosing young boys and girls to enter their coaching schemes and in selecting them for retention afterwards, they have based their appraisal on four areas of skill and aptitude. They look for 'TIPS', which stands for technique, intelligence, personality and speed. So we know what areas of the personnel specification they are looking for. What their standards are and how they assess them is another question. But at least they are getting specific at the initial phases of the recruitment process, after which they believe that they can develop the young athletes into full-grown stars.

Recruitment

Studies of recruitment are not necessarily very psychological. They emphasise issues such as yield per source, where the sources range from internal recruitment (the most common type), employment agencies, headhunters, newspaper advertisements, recommendations and walk-ins. A major issue is the cost per member recruited and this is related to the importance of the position. Methods have been devised to rate the importance of each position so that the recruitment costs are kept at a realistic level. It is evident that not all organisations have heard of this idea, particularly in the public service where there seems to be an inherent obligation to interview all qualified applicants, sometimes at great expense, even for the most low paid jobs. Recruitment costs and methods are also related to other factors such as the demand for labour of a particular type, the size of the available labour market, and the turnover and performance of those eventually hired. Recruitment of applicants has to be approached with caution, as there is the distinct possibility of discrimination against groups of people, depending on how the advertisement is worded and where it appears. We can no longer say, 'strong man wanted'.

Recruitment sources

Taylor and Schmidt (1983) have shown that different recruitment sources are differentially effective because they reach different sectors of the employee market.

There is some proof (Caldwell and Spivey, 1983) that where recruitment is by the informal network of friends and relatives, i.e. employee referrals, this can lead to longer job tenure (US data).

Just how relevant this is in the UK/Irish context is open to examination. Two recent studies refer to this point. The Price Waterhouse Cranfield (PWC) (1992) study showed that internal recruiting in Irish companies applied to over 50 per cent of management jobs; in the case of manual jobs, internal recruiting overall applied to around 30 per cent of jobs and was greater in companies which recognised a trade union and had an established personnel function. Another study in Ireland showed that having a relative on the staff was much more prevalent in a semi-state company than either a private company or a public government organisation. In the semi-state company, over 60 per cent of manual workers had a relative in the company (Hennessy, 1993). Traditionally, access to apprenticeships or junior positions in the company had been primarily available to sons and daughters of existing employees. This may be an acceptable risk in situations where a large main employer dominates a region with a low industrial base.

Realistic job previews

Realistic Job Previews are a direct effort on the part of an organisation to increase the chances that applicants apply for and perhaps accept a job 'with their eyes open'. They consist of a detailed introduction to the company, its structures, policies and history. In theory, at least, they can influence a number of areas of a worker's perception and behaviour. First, studies have shown the main areas affected would be organisational trust and honesty, that is, the perception that the company is up-front about itself and can be trusted by the applicant. Second, volition, that is, a willingness by the applicant to make a commitment and be involved with the company and its goals for the future. Third, organisational caring, where the company is seen to be making an effort towards the applicant and so is perceived as caring. Finally, ambiguity reduction, which means that the applicants are given a clear and factually based perception of the company and the job and so are more at ease in the selection process. By previewing reality, realistic job previews allow the individual to come to the job, or the interview stage, more prepared to cope with eventualities and more knowledgeable about how they themselves may fit into the company and its future plans.

Several studies looking at the effect of realistic job previews on lower level personnel have shown that the effect on turnover, job satisfaction, etc., is negligible. However, recently a study in the US army using several forms of realistic job previews showed some positive effects. Previews worked best in all conditions with the more intelligent and committed army recruit. Previews which combined the effects of dampening optimistic enthusiasm and alleviating some of the negative feelings and fears worked best in effecting retention of the recruits. Those which focused on only one of the latter singly were less effective though not unhelpful. The previews generally increased the feeling among recruits that the army was trustworthy and honest (Meglino *et al.*, 1988).

Positive results have been found in the area of more complex jobs, where the detailed realistic job preview has some effect, according to McEvoy and Cascio (1985) and Reilly *et al.* (1981). It seems logical that realistic job previews should be an effective but strong intervening factor which affects the situation is the job market for the skills involved in the job.

Selecting people for jobs really only becomes meaningful when there are more applicants than positions available. In the present economic situation this is inevitable and has reached an almost unmanageable state in certain cases. For example, over 5000 people queued for application forms when Marks and Spencer opened a new store in Cork in 1988; mind you at the same time, a recent job for a traffic warden only attracted around 50 applicants despite there being over 20000 people without work in the city. One consequence of the unemployment situation is that we now have unusually low voluntary turnover, therefore the people hired have to be flexible, because they are liable to be given different jobs in a firm over time.

General introduction to methods used

There is a wide variety of methods used to make choices among the applicants for jobs. Given the specification and the list of candidates, it is the task of the selector to devise or choose a fair and valid way of assessing the candidates so that the best come to the top. The following is an overview of the prevalent methods each of which will be considered in detail in later chapters.

Application forms

Application forms are almost universally used and in many situations are advisable for legal reasons, e.g. racial and religious monitoring (applicants for jobs in the Northern Ireland Civil Service will be asked their religion, for example). Research on the nature of application forms shows that there is little common ground apart from name, address, date of birth and reason for leaving last job. Most application forms ask for information which is of little or no relevance to the job, such as what school the applicant attended.

Curriculum vitae

In the present employment situation, many people send in their curriculum vitae (CV) to any number of firms in the hope of being noticed. Unfortunately the ruling practice is to file the CVs in a drawer and rarely are they referred to again. The CV is meant to represent a brief (two pages is best) summary of the individual's experience and knowledge.

Interviews

Employment interviews concentrate particularly on education and job experience which match up to job requirements, even in the presence of other strong applicant characteristics. Interviews have many formats depending on their number (serial interviews), the number of interviewers (panels) and the degree of structure imposed on the process. There are also stress interviews, but these should only be used in situations where the job involved is likely to require coping with stress of a similar kind. The interview is all about giving and forming an impression. This is important at the interview and is no less important at the CV stage. Impression Management is an interpersonal influence process where the influencer tries to control the flow of information in terms of content and effects. It is this that the interviewer or CV reader makes a judgement on.

References

This is a method with a built-in bias, i.e. the writer is bound to favour the applicant. In the commercial setting, many such references are by telephone and used for final checking of an applicant who is well considered. References have been shown to have almost no predictive value in relation to job performance. Their validity is very low, at around 0.14. It is possible to improve them slightly by getting references from people who have been in a position to see the applicant working and so can evaluate a person's job-related behaviour. A specially constructed reference form which asks specific job-related questions should be used. Over 90 per cent of Irish firms collect reference reports, most frequently in the case of clerical and administrative jobs. It should not be forgotten that child abusers who get jobs as athletic coaches or child-care workers can invariably come with glowing references from previous employers or priests. The best thing that can be done with a reference is to ignore it and this is increasingly what companies are doing, unless it is negative.

Beware too of ambiguity: an office worker who created absolute chaos in her office due to her inefficiency and tendency to paranoia and resentment put her employer's name down as a referee. Among the glowing tributes paid to her in the reference were, 'Miss Smith will certainly be missed around here . . . ' and 'Her organisational skills were remarkable'.

Biographical information

Biographical information includes information about a person's past life and work experience and is usually gathered via the application form. More sophisticated ways of using this kind of information are called 'bio-data' and 'Weighted Application Blanks'. Each of these methods takes information and assigns a value to it in different ways. The values are then totalled into a score and candidates are ranked according to the level of their scores. Both of these methods benefit from fairly large samples of applicants and bio-data requires statistical expertise and analysis using computers. Their effectiveness is significantly greater than any form of applicant sifting by hand.

Work samples

Work sample tests consist of parts of the actual job which the applicant has to carry out. Their performance is rated according to various criteria. For example, wiring a plug is quite common and typing tests are also widely used. Such tests can have a high degree of validity as might be expected, e.g. for mechanics, electronic technicians, etc., but they are time consuming to construct, administer and score and would only be used at the final selection stage. There is a danger in thinking that just getting 'someone to do something' constitutes a test. Unless care is taken in the process of designing and administering the test piece, the results could be worse than useless. A common application is in selecting people to go on training courses.

Psychometric tests

Guion classified the kinds of tests used as general intellectual ability, specific intellectual abilities, motivational and personality. Aptitude tests are most often used and are mainly in the specific abilities category. They are intended as tests of what people can do and also of what they might be able to learn to do. A common aptitude test would be numerical reasoning. People who scored high on this might be more suitable for jobs involving calculation or estimation than those scoring low. High scorers might also be more trainable in, say, accountancy if they do well on this kind of test. There is a wide range of possible aptitude tests, including physical and manual aptitudes. As we shall see, the use of tests is increasing and there are problems in relation to the proper use of tests by companies.

Situational exercises

There is a wide range of possible assessments that can be categorised under this heading. They include leaderless group discussions, in-basket exercises and physical strength tests. Thinking them up and designing them is cumbersome, but much more difficult is the task of scoring and validating them. There is often a large element of subjective judgement in the scoring part and different judges often disagree on what score to award each applicant.

Assessment centres

Assessment centres are testing situations in which a variety of tests and exercises including all or any of the above are given to a group of applicants over the course of a day or several days, usually at a particular site. A number of trained judges and selectors are involved and applicants are put through a number of 'hoops' designed to detect their strengths and weaknesses. Finkle (1976) defined assessment centres as 'group oriented standardised series of activities which provide a basis for judgements or predictions of human behaviours believed or known to be relevant to work performed'.

Example

Recruitment and selection at the new Toyota plant at Burnaston, Derbyshire (*The Guardian*, 17 December 1992). Workers in this new factory producing the Toyota Carina are to be called team workers and their selection was very different from the usual methods ruling in such factories. The applicants were first of all required to complete a large bio-data questionnaire; this was followed by aptitude tests of ability to learn and of numerical ability. There was then a targeted behavioural interview lasting 75 minutes. Those who were selected were subjected to 6 hours of simulated production-line activity. After this there was a final interview and a medical examination.

Job analysis

Selection should be preceded by job analysis which involves specifying the nature of the job to be done and outlining the skills needed to do it. McCormick and Ilgen (1987, p. 39) say 'relevant job information is of major consequence on individuals and also on the effectiveness with which personnel related functions are carried out in organisations'. Despite this obvious point, it is surprising how many people are doing jobs which have never been specified for them. In some cases, the employer has never been clear about what the person has to do and simply works off the cuff and hopes for or insists on cooperation by means of threats or inducements. Many industrial problems arise from this careless use of human resources.

Uses to which job analysis can be put

1. It forms the basis of most personnel selection; in particular it aids in preparing a more job-relevant interview and in preparing a realistic job preview.
2. It serves as an important plank in promotion schemes.
3. It is useful to the organisation in job realignment strategies. For example, it can lead to more flexible work scheduling, e.g. part-time work, and to improvements in job design.
4. It may be needed in legal disputes and may be useful in labour–management relations.
5. It forms a basis of performance appraisal schemes.
6. It may be of assistance in career development.

7. It is central in establishing training needs and permits the establishment of training performance objectives, which are fitted closely to job requirements.

8. Job analysis may also serve to focus on the changing skills component of particular jobs. For example, when a job has changed due to technological progress, the new requirements for the job-holder will become evident after a job analysis.

9. Skill banking. The results of job analysis will show, if assembled appropriately, exactly what sorts of skills are involved in the operation of the business and increase the company appreciation of the kind of workforce required.

10. It is helpful in the forming of Job Families (Pearlman, 1980). This allows employers to use the same selection tests, e.g. aptitude tests for similar jobs, and to construct more job-specific aptitude tests.

11. It can help identify hazardous working conditions.

Jobs tend to be analysed for some specific reason, for example, where legal action is threatened, where performance deficiencies are a problem or where changes are known or alleged to have occurred. The process may involve unfair discrimination in the workplace. It is often lower ranked jobs which will be more closely scrutinised, leaving managerial jobs untouched.

Job analysis procedures can be threatening and can be problematic in a company. To reduce this it is recommended that the management should specify the goals of the programme to the workers, who will be involved and what will be done.

Information required for job analysis

Job analysts have to consider sources, method and plan. Sources may already exist which will provide information about jobs. Job analysis has possibly been carried out recently for similar jobs by other companies. Job analysts must decide on the best method of obtaining first-hand information about the job and a systematic plan is required which will meet the specific objectives of the particular job analysis.

The kinds of information required in job analysis are as follows:

1. Description of the work performed and supervision given or required.

2. Degree of responsibility for the work of others, for materials, safety, public relations, etc.

3. The specific experience, knowledge and training required, worker characteristics required for success on the job or in parts of the job. How one gets promoted in or out of the job.

4. Mental qualities: alertness, quickness, judgement, adaptability, initiative required to predict events.

5. Equipment and material employed; working conditions and physical demands; number employed in the job.

6. Standards of production for the job and how they are devised; how the job relates to other jobs; how the job can be subdivided and combined with others.

7. How workers are usually recruited and also the availability or scarcity of workers; what the normal screening procedures are.

Approaches to collecting job information

The most common way of acquiring the information is to interview employees, superiors and previous holders of the job in question. This has been shown in research to be problematic, as there are often discrepancies between incumbents and supervisors. There is often a lack of communication skills on the part of informants. They may fail to appreciate the real significance of a job in the overall structure or may tend to exaggerate the job, depending on who is collecting the information. There is often a difference between what is done and what should be done, which leads to conflict between worker and supervisor.

Observation of workers is rather limited to manual jobs and is not welcomed by them, as it is intrusive and puts them under pressure. In some situations, job analysts can perform the job themselves but this would only apply to jobs with limited training requirements.

Questionnaires are sometimes used as a means of collecting information. A well-known one is the Position Analysis Questionnaire, which is worker–behaviour orientated in the main and contains items related to job content and attributes required. The Position Analysis Questionnaire contains 194 items such as 'using machines, tools or equipment'. A profile of dimension scores for each job along a number of (45) dimensions is the result. This is a general approach, allowing jobs to be compared across organisations. The results have been combined with various aptitude test scores, making it usable in a selection context. It is however rather abstract and fails to give an idea of a job's purpose. It is also expensive, as the questionnaires and scoring services have to be purchased from a consultancy who market it. The questions relate to six information areas: job context, work output, mental processes, information input, relations with people and other aspects of the work situation. The Position Analysis Questionnaire has been said to be more suitable for mechanical and technical jobs rather than those in the managerial or professional categories, as many items are concerned with manipulating machinery, etc. (McCormick et al., 1972).

A task inventory consists of a long list of tasks obtained from adding together all the tasks involved in a particular area or set of jobs. These are most useful in compiling job descriptions. Each task is rated for each job in terms of variables, such as the amount of time spent on it and its overall importance for the job performance. This method is job orientated rather than worker orientated and is restricted in use to organisations with computing and statistical back-up. According to Harvey et al. (1988) the use of such inventories has become very popular, but the high level of verbal ability required limits the range of situations for which they are suited.

Saville and Holdsworth, who are the leading British Occupational Selection Company, have a work profiling system. Information is collected on job tasks and job context, using a card-sorting method. The system produces job specifications for selection interviewing. It is computer scored and covers three levels of jobs, managerial/professional, service/administration and manual/technical.

Functional job analysis looks at what people do in their jobs in relation to people, data and things. A task is defined as 'fundamental stable work element involving a behaviour and a result'. Work is seen as consisting of some relationship to people, data and things across the job spectrum. Job information is collected by means of open interview and observation, with an emphasis on looking at tasks and their importance in the job.

Some additional methods and sources of information include studying the training procedures and contents of training. Debriefing people who are leaving a job will give quite a different perspective. Time and motion study is carried out by industrial engineers or ergonomists, mainly in the case of machine-paced or tool-using jobs to investigate the most efficient arrangements for doing the job and the normative rate of working.

The Critical Incident Technique can be used in job analysis in an attempt to describe the concrete and specific behaviours necessary for successful job performance (Latham and Wexley, 1981). The method consists of eliciting a large number of effective or ineffective job performance behaviours. The result is that each job is specified in terms of job behaviours. This method has direct applications in performance, as well as being directly useful in devising training programmes.

Results of job analysis research

When the evidence available on the validity of job analysis is reviewed, it becomes clear that validation studies have been few and far between. That is to say, do we actually know if the information collected by the various methods of job analysis truly represent the jobs in question? The lack of research might be because people believe that a direct and comprehensive assessment will invariably yield an adequate description (Fleishman and Mumford, 1991). However, this can be questioned due to the complex nature of job activities and the influence of organisational climate.

Research on the reliability of job analysis has shown that some training is necessary to give accurate results in job analysis, regardless of the method used. However, improvement in quality is not proportional to the amount of training. Accuracy is improved by having more than one rater, and/or approaching several sources for the data. Results have been shown to vary, depending on the experience of the people asked for the data.

Various researchers over the years have tried to reduce the number of dimensions across which jobs vary, according to job analysis requirements. By statistically examining the relations between all the different possible job tasks by means of factor analysis, they come up with a small number of dimensions which encapsulate the differences between jobs; that is, if all jobs were given a score on the dimensions. For example, dimensions that have arisen are as follows:

1. Education and mental ability

2. Precision-operating requirement

3. Bodily agility

4. Artistic aesthetic ability

5. Manual artistic skill

6. Personal skills requirement

7. Extent of physical labour

Such a set of dimensions can be used to describe any job – try it.

Wherever there are jobs there will be job analysis, whether it is formal and reliable or just ad hoc and approximate. As jobs are constantly evolving, so should job analysis be carried out.

Summary

When we look at history, we find that concern over selection has been long-standing. Legal and ethical standards are of the utmost importance in this area. There is a wide range of selection methods used by professionals, but their choice is not always based on logic. The popularity of various methods varies across the European Union, but interviews are at the top of the list in all countries, though psychometric test use is increasing generally. Hiring employees has a number of clear stages of which selection is probably the most vital. Job analysis, which consists of gathering important information concerning jobs, is a crucial stage in recruiting staff and in many other areas.

Activities

1. **In an organisation of your choice, find out from older and younger employees how selection methods have changed over the last 30–40 years.**

2. **Carry out a detailed job analysis, first, of your own job and then of someone else's.**

3. **Consider a list of different jobs and decide if different selection techniques would suit some jobs more than others.**

Further reading

Clifford, J.P. (1994) Job analysis: why do it and how should it be done? *Public Personnel Management*, 23(2), 321–40.

Herriot, P. (1989) *Assessment and Selection in Organizations*. (Chichester, Wiley).

Porteous, M.A. and Hodgins, J. (1995) A survey of selection practices in Irish organisations. *Irish Journal of Psychology*, 16(4), 397–408.

Robertson, I.T. and Makin, P.J. (1986) Management selection in Great Britain: a survey and critique. *Journal of Occupational Psychology*, 59, 45–57.

Schuler, H., Farr, J.L. and Smith, M. (1993) *Personnel Selection and Assessment*. (Hillsdale, NJ LEA).

Shackleton, V. and Newell, S. (1991) Management selection: a comparative survey of methods used in top British and French companies. *Journal of Occupational Psychology*, 64, 45–57.

Smith, J.M. and Abrahamsen, M. (1992) Patterns of selection in six countries. *The Psychologist*, 5, 205–7.

Smith, M. and George, D. (1992) Selection methods. *International Review of Industrial and Organizational Psychology*, 7, 55–97.

Interviewing

Focus questions

Why is interviewing the most widely used form of selection?

How valid has interviewing been regarded by psychometricians?

Are there ways of improving the validity of interviewing?

How can you perform better as a candidate at an interview?

What different options are available for designing interviews?

What are the major stumbling blocks to effective interviewing?

Interviews are the most widely used form of selection method and deserve very close attention. Because they are so familiar, however, they tend to be taken for granted. There are a number of very interesting questions which can be posed in relation to interviewing and there are also provably better ways to perform them than the traditional method.

The basics of interviewing

An interview can be usefully defined as 'a social exchange in which information is elicited by question and observation, an impression is formed and a judgement or decision made'. The fact that it is a 'social' situation is important. There are two parties involved: the interviewee and the interviewer, and while they are having what looks like a conversation, it is really more like a duel. The interviewer seeks information, not only facts which are usually on the application form anyway, but indications about the work potential, the attitudes, the temperament and the availability of the applicant. Having elicited or observed these many pieces of data, the interviewer is faced with the task of assembling them into a meaningful whole and making a judgement. The whole process is truly of such psychological complexity, it is little wonder that it is rarely performed very effectively.

An interviewer's job has been defined as 'to develop accurate perceptions of candidate and to evaluate these in the light of job requirements'. The interviewer has three judgements to make. The first one concerns the applicant's characteristics, the second is whether to recommend the candidate as suitable. This involves the side-by-side comparison of the requirements of the job with the characteristics of the candidate. Third comes the judgement whether to hire or not. That is, taking all the candidates whose personal characteristics show a good match with the person specification or job requirements, which of them is preferred.

Many interviews are of an unstructured 'dynamic' type, in which questions asked are dependent on the social process and not strictly job related. That is to say, the situation actually does devolve into a conversation in which the interviewee manages to side-track the process and talk about some personal aspect which is not relevant to the situation. Favourite topics would be sporting achievements and aspects of social life, such as where they went on holiday, would also be a common trap. At the other extreme, we can have structured job-related interviews. The loosely structured interview has been shown to be the most problematic, in particular to be prone to sex bias where the job is seen as traditionally more of a male preserve (Herriot, 1989). In favour of interviews, it should be pointed out that they are almost the only selection method which is reactive. That is, the interviewee is tested in a situation calling for immediate reaction to a stimulus. The interview situation is unpredictable and creative. The skilled interviewer can take the applicant down the road he or she does not want to go by using various verbal tactics, expressions of disbelief, feigned interest, etc. In the interview, people can be contradicted in a way which no other selection method can imitate. They can be aroused to anger or stressed by continual in-depth questioning and their reaction observed and assessed. Such tactics should not be part of the normal run of events and only used in suitable situations.

Usage in the practical context

A recent survey of management selection methods showed the interview to be the most widely used method. Of UK organisation's surveyed 81 per cent always used interviews and only one never used them (Robertson and Makin, 1986). In America, interviewing ranks above all other methods in frequency of use, according to the US Bureau of National Affairs (1983), second in popularity only to reference checks. From the academic perspective, research on interviewing has waned due to scepticism about interview validity. A common recommendation to improve interview validity is to standardise criteria for evaluation, question sequence, interview length, etc. But situational factors affect these. For example, responsibility for the decision and the risk factors in the appointment have a significant bearing on how the interview is carried out. The after-effects of a bad selection may come back to haunt and embarrass a recruiter.

Popularity

There are many reasons for interviews being the preferred method of selection in the organisational setting. They can be carried out spontaneously, i.e. no preparation, training or special material is required. Almost anyone feels capable of interviewing. In fact the less they know about the problems of valid interviewing, the more capable they tend to imagine they are. Interviews allow people to delude themselves that their judgement of people is of a high order. In-depth checking of interview ratings is a rare occurrence, so people never really get to know just how right or wrong they were.

The interview method appears to have some advantages for the company. They are (superficially) cheap to organise and they allow information about the job and the company to be communicated to all the candidates. Information given in application forms can be clarified or corrected. They help to eliminate candidates who look odd, dress strangely or speak indistinctly. They give an idea of which candidates have good interpersonal skills and whether they will fit in to the organisation. They also allow the direct application of race or gender bias and personal favouritism. Not only that, but they permit these factors to be covered up as the basis of interview decisions are not examinable in most cases.

Elements of the interview

The interview process can be seen as consisting of several parts together with their interaction, that is, the way they combine together, affect each other and produce a result. First, applicant characteristics have the most direct bearing on the process. These include appearance, sex, age, personal characteristics, mannerisms, work experience. The applicant also comes with an expectation, usually about what will be asked but also about how they are going to be treated. Second, we have the interview setting which is a complex environmental issue, including the physical setting and the purpose of the interview. Also relevant here is the preparation of the candidate and how the setting might intimidate the less confident candidate. Third, the characteristics of the interviewer or interviewers have a strong influence. Some of these would be the same as the applicant characteristics, but would also include training and experience as important determinants of interview behaviour. The mood and general pleasantness or otherwise of the interviewer has a distinct bearing. From personal experience of observing many interviewers at work, it is clear that their mood and enthusiasm wanes as the day wears on. Sometimes the first post-lunch interview can be the most daunting of all (for the applicant). Finally, the process itself really consists of the interaction of the previous three aspects, thus leading into the discourse and the judgement.

Interview content

Interviews are found to add very little to the information gained from application forms and psychometric testing, i.e. incremental validity is low. They tend to go over ground that is familiar or to dwell in safe areas of common interest. Studies on interview content have shown that about one-quarter of the information is already on record and only about one-third is directly useful in the process of forming a judgement about the candidate. Around 15 per cent concerns facts on the job and the company and around 12 per cent consists of advice and suggestions (Bass and Barrett, 1981). Interviewers are often in disagreement about what topics should be covered and due to the dynamic flow of some interviews important questions can be left out (Taylor and Sniezek, 1984).

For certain highly technical jobs with specific skills, interview methods have been shown to improve the level of prediction of subsequent performance. In such situations 'hard' questions can be asked and also questions of the situational type are most useful. Despite this, it is surprising how little effort is made in practice to ensure that people know anything. From experience of selection in the chemical industry, I know that candidates would not be asked to describe a process, etc. It is assumed that because they have a relevant degree and experience that they know their stuff, or that they are trainable into meeting the company's requirements.

Interview format

Panel interviews are what we are mainly used to. They consist of a group of interviewers. They allow extreme views to be averaged out. The way in which the ratings of the individual interviewers are averaged or combined could make significant difference to the final rating. Methods include a consensus, where after discussion the chairperson arrives at an agreed decision or rating. Also possible is a straight average of the ratings of individual interviewers. This is liable to lead to very similar ratings for many candidates, as the extremes cancel each other out. A preferable method is for each interviewer to standardise their ratings across all candidates and then the standardised ratings are averaged across interviewers. In Serial interviews the applicant is passed from one person to another for separate interviews about different aspects of the job. One interviewer may ask about job requirements and conditions of work, another might investigate competence and a third might evaluate the candidate from the perspective of personality factors. The interviewers then gather together and discuss their separate conclusions and then come to a final decision. Nowadays, most selection for management jobs or skilled jobs involves more than one interview, though this is more like a repeated panel interview rather than an actual serial format.

Length of selection interviews

The length of selection interviews has been found, in several studies, to be more dependent on the amount of the interviewer's talk. That is, paradoxically, the length was not related to the amount of information the candidate was giving, which we might expect to be the more useful event. It is commonly believed that the higher quality applicants get the longer interview; this has been confirmed in research. This is also a function of the fact that a preliminary decision has been made to hire the applicant and the panel wish to prolong the interview to get a fuller impression. A consistent ratio has been found between length of question and length of answer. Where there is a long question and a short answer, listeners perceive discordance because it is out of expectation.

In a study of 115 employment interviews in the Canadian Army by six personnel officers, it was found that where the interviewer does more talking and there is less silence, there is a greater chance of the interviewee being hired. It was also true but not statistically significant that both applicant time and total time were less in the case of rejected applicants (Anderson, 1960). An interview allows a judgement to be made; where there is less information on which to reject someone there is a greater chance of them being hired.

Process dynamics

The interview is a complex social psychological process and a number of obvious variables can be examined and related to interview outcomes. Process dynamics have been examined in terms of a concept called relational control (Tullar, 1989). In the social exchange, the relation between the interviewee and the interviewer(s) can be described in terms of who is in charge, psychologically. According to Tullar, relational control can be dominant, equivalent or submissive.

Dominant relational control means that attempts are made to restrict the behavioural options of the interviewer. The high dominant interviewee tends to be perceived as self-assured, the equivalent perceived as less motivated. Those at either extreme of dominance or submissiveness can be perceived as sociable.

Relational control in interaction is a perception of behaviour which is difficult to fake and difficult to perceive. It is at an unconscious level. Talk sharing, an antecedent of the above, has been studied quite extensively by social psychologists. One aspect of this is how politicians gain control or otherwise of the interviewer on television and frequently manage not to answer a single question, while at the same time appearing helpful and considerate.

Impression forming

A number of researchers have shown that interview impressions are established quite early on and so determined final ratings quite strongly. Webster (1964, 1982) showed early impressions established a bias which was resistant to correction. Pre-interview information sets up expectancies and can lead to quite different interviewer evaluation (Dipboye *et al.*, 1984), though McDonald and Haekel (1985) modify this to suggest that first impressions are only used for rating if there is no other information available, i.e. if all information is elicited during the interview, then first impressions are more likely to be important. Unstructured interviews lead to decisions being taken early in the interview (Balinsky, 1978).

Negative information tends to outweigh positive information, especially if it comes first or is unusual (Peters and Terborg, 1975). Early studies showed that only one piece of negative information was used as a reason for rejection in over 90 per cent of cases (Bolster and Springbett, 1961). It is also the case that interviewers find it difficult to say why an accepted candidate will succeed than it is to say why a rejected applicant will fail. This seems to establish the point that negative information is more salient than positive in making sense of the judgement process (Hollman, 1972). Initial impressions are usually based on appearance, CV, voice and mannerisms and they have a strong effect on the final judgement. In fact, it has been found that the suitability of the candidate was mainly predicted by three factors; in order of importance these were attraction, gender similarity and interview impression. The latter consisted of perceived ability to express ideas, job knowledge, appearance and drive (Kinicki *et al.*, 1990).

Impression management

Effective Impression Management is an interpersonal influence process where the influencer endeavours to control the flow of information, its content and effects. It is a valuable skill which successful people invariably possess; in some cases you might wonder is it their only skill! It is clearly vital in interviewing where the main basis on which judgement is to be made is an impression. Interviewers should also be aware of impression management skills and discount these to some extent when forming their own final impression.

Recommended tactics for successful impression management include presenting a positive self-description. This involves the obvious basics of appearance and speech, but also includes tactics for turning dialogue towards areas where achievements and successes have occurred. The candidate should try to conform to the opinions or goals of the interviewer or the company. These goals may not be stated and may have to be worked out – doing some homework on a company can often pay dividends in this area. The interviewee should claim positive involvement in positive results. Finally, the interviewee should favourably evaluate events or accomplishments of the interviewer, group or company. Impression management may backfire if it is too intensive or if the situation emphasises authenticity (Baron, 1986; Gardner and Martinko, 1988).

Doing well at interviews

It is very important for all of us to discover how to perform well at interviews. Training people in this black art has become quite a big industry, from the media consultants who train our politicians not to tell us anything, down to the career teachers who will take you through a mock interview. Various researchers have shown that higher interview ratings are related to certain behaviours by the interviewee. It is advisable for an interviewee to respond concisely while, at the same time, answering questions fully. Sticking to the subject is important, as it shows an ability to focus and it avoids the interviewer having to drag the process back from far away. Waffling is a very negatively rated behaviour unless, of course, the interviewer is also a prize waffler. The applicant should only give personal opinions where relevant, in order to avoid looking too big headed (Parsons and Liden, 1984; Rasmussen, 1984).

It is advisable to smile a bit, but not to grin inanely at everyone. Smiling and laughing politely are signs of good social skills and that is something that can be rated at an interview so if a positive rating is given for this, it is likely to spread as per the halo effect to other aspects. Dress should be conservative but appropriate. The interview suit is sometimes rather obvious and people can look quite out of place in it; at the same time open-toed sandals are not clever unless the job is for a lifeguard at the beach. Do not give negative opinions about yourself even in jest; be modest without being self-deprecating. Interviewers will later remember the negative and forget the jest. Ask a question about the company which shows that you have found out something about it, i.e. 'Do you often get visits from the parent company in Waterville, Maine?'. If the job is technical, try and ask a technical question (which people can answer). Try to make the panel identify with you by showing that your interests and aspirations are similar to theirs at your age.

Applicant view

The interview process has also been looked at from the point of view of the applicant. Many interviews leave the applicant with a negative view of the company or with a feeling of discomfort. This is not in any company's best interest, especially if they are recruiting from a local community and are relying on cooperation from the community. Applicants expect the interviewer to say more about the organisation than the interviewer often does. The greater the number of job-related questions that are asked, the more positive the interviewee feels to the organisation (Dipboye, 1992). Interviewers expect the applicants to offer more about themselves than they do (Herriot and Rothwell, 1983). It seems that the decision on whether to accept a job offer also turns on the behaviour of the interviewer (Harn and Thornton, 1985).

Discrimination/expensive questions

Interviews are potentially dangerous situations for an organisation, as panel members can ask the wrong thing at times. For example, recently a woman was asked at an interview whether she would be able to cope with her children's needs as well as the job of school principal. She made a formal complaint and was awarded £300 compensation for distress caused by the discriminatory question (*Equality News*, 1988). In the American context, Arvey (1979) an interview researcher, lists the following information as out of bounds unless they can be shown to be job related: arrest information, citizenship, spouse's salary, child-care arrangements, general health questions, marital status, military discharge information, pregnancy information and home ownership status. To this list we can now add sexual preference and HIV test information.

   More recent developments are interesting and should be considered. Until recently in discrimination cases, the interview has been treated differently from tests for example because it was considered 'subjective' and had no formal scoring method. It was therefore in the company's interest to keep the interview vague and informal and if they treated people differently it was very difficult to prove. This has now changed. The move to more formally scored interviews has been forced on companies; if they are accused of adverse impact they can go about establishing that their interview has some validity for the job. People score differently on it irrespective of race or gender, just as they have had to do with tests in the past. You can imagine the consequences of this decision (Watson vs Fort Worth Bank, 1988).

Validity

The most frequently made point about interviews, which has been shown in numerous studies, is that they are not useful for predicting job success. Mayfield (1964) reviewed eighty studies in the 1960s and came to this conclusion. Reilly and Chao's (1982) review of selection devices found the interview to be among the lowest in validity terms. The situational interview is a possible exception to this. Recently the validity of the situational interview has been shown to be reasonable (0.38) in the case of predicting future performance in administrative jobs (Robertson *et al.*, 1990).

Not all the research has been so gloomy and in the last few years a ray of light has appeared to make interviewers more positive. One study reviewing a number of studies produced a corrected validity coefficient of 0.47 for the interview, with structured interviews being given a very acceptable 0.62 and unstructured 0.31 when all the results were combined (Weisner and Cronshaw, 1988). Certainly where interviews are designed to include a rating recording form, the validity is vastly improved. That is not evidence that the interview is really effective, though the correlations between the interview form ratings and the job performance ratings may both emerge in some way from similar processes, neither of which are particularly accurate.

Interviews get a lot of criticism, though it has to be said that there are so many flaws in using the method that it is unfair to criticise the method; rather it is the inefficient use of it which is at fault. For example, most interviews are carried out by untrained staff who have not decided what they want or how they will recognise what they want when it appears in front of them. They are often nervous and seek release of tension and social confirmation. Very rarely are steps taken to order the process of information, to collect comparable data on each subject. We also tend to regard interviews as the be-all and end-all of selection. They should certainly be part of the process, but only one used for what they are good at, while other methods should assess other things that the interview cannot.

Specific errors in the process

As has been said, interviews are invalid generally, but they can be improved. There are a number of avoidable errors, most of which can be corrected before the interviewer opens their mouth. In some interviews, the interviewer initially likes the applicant based on first impression, then consciously or unconsciously proceeds to bias questions which enable the applicant to show traits which conform to this personal stereotype. Stereotyping also refers to the idea that the interviewer has a preconceived notion of the ideal worker and searches for ways that the applicant either fits or does not fit in with this, depending on whether they liked them in the first place. Interviewers develop their own stereotype of the ideal candidate (independently of others on the panel or perhaps of job requirements) and then accept as suitable applicants those who most closely match that stereotype (Webster, 1964). This would have great potential for producing disagreement between panel members if it was openly discussed initially. Instead what goes on is a sort of tacit psychological tug of war between panel members when it comes to the decision stage. Phillips and Dipboye (1989) confirm previous work and conclude that the processing of information during the interview seems to be biased towards confirming the initial impression.

Some interviewers are insecure in themselves and seek to elicit rapid confirmation of their own lifestyle and identity. To do this they tend to look for 'similar to me' characteristics in the interviewee. This kind of interviewer may talk as much about themselves as about the candidate. An even worse offence is 'self-stroking' where the interviewee manages to praise and admire the interviewer who then 'laps up' the positive response given and more or less agrees with it.

Contrast errors inadvertently occur when interviewers compare candidates with others coming previously or next. It is very difficult to avoid, especially if the contrast between candidates is extreme. The halo effect is most prevalent in interviews where judgement is occurring all the time, a basic good or bad impression made early on colours other judgements. Important information coming after an impression has been formed can have an effect, but negative information is then more powerful than positive (Bolster and Springbett, 1961).

Information received in interviews is often inaccurate and this is particularly so in cases where the information cannot be verified. Distortion at interview has been shown to be quite high; specifically exaggerations are made about previous experience, educational qualifications, pay and success. Over the years, several cases of unqualified 'doctors' have been uncovered in the National Health Service for example. Fortunately, most of them have done a pretty good job. Some have had extensive nursing or first-aid experience and have managed to impress the interview panel on medical issues. Add to this a few fake references and a fictional CV and a hard-pressed Health Authority in an unattractive area makes an appointment. An example of exactly this type was discovered recently in the North of England after the 'doctor' in question had performed over 200 operations.

Judgements

The most pervasive problem in the interview which leads to its low accuracy is that people try to make judgements about traits which cannot be observed. Some characteristics permit more reliable rating than others. Leadership is generally more reliably rated in terms of interjudge agreement than is motivation. Studies of the differences between judges in rating behavioural items in an interview setting have shown that there tends to be better agreement in rating more concrete behaviour and interpersonal behaviour, and less agreement where the behaviour was more abstract, e.g. 'showing responsibility' or in some way future orientated (Arvey and Campion, 1982). In general, the research has shown that interviews are best able to assess two broad characteristics, personal relationships and good citizenship. That is, whether the candidate can speak well, smile, respond naturally to conversation and has the capacity for a social life which involves relating to people. Good citizenship would involve traits such as being kind, doing things for others, having a degree of dependability and conscientiousness (Arvey *et al.*, 1987). Now, these aspects are very important in many jobs and if people have them, then it is possible that suitable job training could equip them to perform well on the job. In the case of some jobs, job knowledge can also be assessed. However, unless the knowledge is very basic, there are better ways of gauging it than an interview, e.g. a test or a job sample.

Judgements and cognitive complexity

As noted in the section on performance appraisal ratings, raters who are more cognitively complex are able to handle more concepts and make more reliable and valid ratings. In many cases, people only use two broad constructs to rate their fellow workers. For example, these usually boil down to likeable and energetic, or to put it another way, sociable and task orientated. We can judge if someone is reasonably sociable and likeable, tends to smile, responds normally and takes part in some social activities, also if they seem to be relatively keen on working and getting things done. Some researchers have tried to extend the range of concepts available by specifically structuring interviews and questions to cover a wider range of areas (Grove, 1981). For example, some success was found where questions were designed to bear on five areas: stamina, willingness to work hard, ability to work with others, ability to learn and initiative.

Situational variables affect judgement through interaction with the interviewer's cognitive characteristics, and again are difficult to control. These include task clarity – more distractions lead to more extreme and inconsistent judgements; the more complex the job the more difficult it is to rely on job-related information and questions; decision-making responsibility – whether the individual is solely responsible or if there is a team or board involved affects the processing of information. People are willing to work very hard during a panel interview, then have their mind made up by one small fact emphasised by a powerful member of the committee. Some managers are masters at 'dropping the bomb' at the right time and then having their choice of candidate imposed on the meeting. Sometimes telling a downright lie about a candidate is the best method, especially as it is done after the candidates have gone home and people are too tired to argue.

Another factor is decision risk. In the real world, much hangs on the decision of an interview panel. The generalisability of studies of the research-only type where no responsibility is required of those making judgements should be questioned. Many studies are of the laboratory type with no relation to the real-life situation.

Research

Interview research, which has looked at all of these aspects, can concentrate on small details of the process, such as how attractiveness affects ratings, or how the speed of speaking affects the judgement of the candidate's intelligence. This is called a Micro-analytic approach. On the other hand, the Macro-analytic approach refers to the study of the broader effects and implications of interviewing. For example, the validity of interview ratings in predicting job tenure; or the extent of interjudge agreement in different interview formats might be examined. A change in research emphasis has been suggested and that is to look more at the interview from the perspective of social psychology, e.g. to focus on the attitudes and intentions of the participants and to build more explicit behaviour models (Harris, 1989).

Unfortunately many interview researchers can only work through simulations of real situations. It is ethically unacceptable to investigate many aspects of interviewing in real-life settings, e.g. manipulation of interviewer or interviewee behaviour, video recording, etc., would be unfair if they varied between candidates for real jobs. We would naturally wonder whether simulation results would be generalisable to the real world. A review of a number of studies concluded that student interviewers tend to be more lenient in making judgements, but that otherwise no important aspects would seem to limit generalisation of results (Bernstein *et al.*, 1975).

Theories in interview research

Although there are no strong contenders for a theory of interviewing, a number of psychological interpretations are relevant to the interview situation. This is particularly the case with Implicit Personality Theory, which suggests that each interviewer has a system for understanding personality. This may have no relationship to reality or to the other interviewers, but it is 'his theory and he is sticking to it'. What is implied is that an observed/observable attribute in a subject is assumed to correlate with or be indicative of hidden attributes, according to the interviewer's own implicit personality theory. Implicit personality theory enables interviewers who are familiar with each other to predict each others' styles, and decision behaviours. It also explains why differences in judgement occur despite identical information.

Cognitive Information Processing Theory focuses on cognitive processing, as the name implies. This includes information acquisition, encoding and storing, memory retrieval and errors. Thus it provides a good basis on which interview research may be carried out. Its connection with the reality of interviewing is yet to be established on a firm footing, though it is promising.

Attribution theory is becoming more important in researchers' specification of models of how interview judgements come about. Dipboye describes a model in several phases. Prior to the interview, the interviewer has some knowledge of the job and the required characteristics. This knowledge is set in the framework of the interviewer's knowledge of the company and its structures, the other people on the panel and the effect of decisions for example. Information about the applicant is available and may be shared or private. All this information sets up a structure of knowledge on which to base or make attributions about what the candidate does and says at the interview. The interview then takes place and, as we have said, the process is affected by the behaviour of the applicant and also by the behaviour of the interviewer, which in turn is biased strongly by pre-interview impressions. The final phase after the interview, includes the process of evaluating the relevant aspects of the candidate and comparing these aspects (KSAs) with the job specification (Dipboye, 1992).

Improvements

Interviews will continue to be used. Therefore we must attempt to improve them as far as possible. Several initiatives are possible including training interviewers, being much more specific in the questions asked and looking at the information received in a more focused way. Alternatives to the basic panel interview are also possible and worthwhile.

Training

Carlson (1967) found that interviewers' experience did not lead to a significant increase in agreement between interviewers, due to the fact that repeated interviews did not have the conditions necessary for a training effect to take place. That is, it is of no help just to do it over and over again. In fact the reverse is likely to be true. Experience leads to complacency and it is easy to relearn your old mistakes until you think you are perfect. In fact you may just be perfectly useless!

Training involves trial, feedback and retrial. If we are going to train people in interviewing, we must be quite deliberate about the conditions we establish for training, i.e. it is no use just doing it over and over again. Training for interviewers must include feedback and the chance to practise new skills repeatedly. Dissecting the interview in front of a video of the process is useful. The interaction of the interview needs to be examined in terms of the kinds of questions, etc., using a technique such as Interaction Process Analysis (Bales, 1950). Behaviour modelling, discussed in Chapter 6, has a particular relevance to interview training.

Some companies have gone as far as training people to be interviewers and having them certified as such. The effectiveness of certified interviewers is much higher than average, e.g. 45 per cent less turnover for new recruits than normal (Daum, 1983). Although training can help to reduce the more gross errors, Webster (1982) points out that it is unreasonable to think that people would change their deeply ingrained habits in people perception after a training course of only a few days or hours. And even more so, it is unreasonable to expect that a person's judgement processes would change significantly. The average interview training course lasts a day at most and is insufficient. Longer courses spreading over five days have been found to be quite effective, however. They concentrate on questioning techniques, listening skills, establishing a supportive environment and paying close attention to the interaction.

The following elements are representative of prevailing opinion on how to organise general purpose interviews.

1. Restrict the use of information to knowledge, skills and abilities that interviews can assess most effectively, i.e. personal relations characteristics (sociability, verbal fluency), good citizenship (dependability, career motivation) and possibly job knowledge. Initial establishment of rapport is vital and may include general conversational topics. But after that phase, the interview should proceed in a planned and structured way.

2. Incorporate more structure in the interview format; make sure all relevant information is gained from the candidate. Use situational questions which allow the candidate to demonstrate some of the behaviours, and possibly traits, that are relevant for the job.

3. Use job-related questions, which obtain detailed specific information about knowledge, skills and abilities required on the job. Prior to the interview, be fully aware of the job-analysis information, or discuss the job with a supervisor, who will probably be on the panel anyway.

4. Devise a formal scoring method. This not only aids recall and comparisons and ensures that important areas are all covered, it also assists several interviewers to focus their attention on the same things.

5. Use team interviews. This relieves one individual of the heavy responsibility load and improves the accuracy of information receipt. Planning is crucial to the success of a team interview; it is not simply a matter of getting more bodies around the table. They should each have a script and a specific objective.

6. Train interviewers in the main skills which are accurate receipt of information, critical evaluation of information received and regulation of their own behaviour in asking questions.

Structure

Evidence clearly confirms that if interviews are structured, they generate information which leads to interviewer agreement (i.e. reliability). The same frame of reference is being applied to all the candidates (Latham and Saari, 1984). Structure is defined, as a 'series of job related questions with predetermined answers that are consistently applied across all interviews for a particular job' (Pursell *et al.*, 1980).

Structured interviews usually contain four types of questions:

1. Situational questions: The applicant is asked how they would respond to various situations which are described in the questions.

2. Job knowledge questions: The applicant needs to demonstrate the basic knowledge necessary to perform the job.

3. Job sample simulation: Includes understanding of terminology, and being able to deal with mock-ups of the job.

4. Worker requirement: Asks workers about their willingness to perform roles under certain conditions, such as shift work, travel abroad, opinions about trade unions.

The Situational interview (Latham *et al.*, 1980) takes critical incident type data from job analysis and reformats these into questions. That is, the central task and environmental features of the job are specified in the job analysis and questions are based on these. Answers can be rated independently by more than one qualified person and some objectivity can be introduced into the scoring.

Latham and Saari (1984) showed that interviews of this type have some provable validity, in that what was said at interview was demonstrated on the job. A recent innovation in the structured interview is the Patterned Behaviour Description Interview (Orpen, 1985). Here the questions are of the type 'how did you respond to X situation in the past', where X is an important job-related event which occurred previously and is likely to occur again. The interviewer does not just seek a straight answer, but uses the response for further teasing out of knowledge, motives and depth of understanding, i.e. they might follow up with, 'Why did you do that? How did the customer react? How did you feel the whole thing went? What did you learn from it that helped you in later situations?'. This has shown some promise.

An extensive series of studies carried out by Motowidlo *et al.* (1992), shows how the process of Structured Behavioural Interviewing is carried out. A number of separate companies in the telecommunications industry took part in a range of experiments involving training and validation of structured behavioural interviewing when they were recruiting managers and marketing people. Critical incident workshops were held with 78 job holders and 61 supervisors to explore aspects of successful and unsuccessful job behaviours focusing on the interpersonal, problem-solving and communication aspects of performance. From this, some 1200 critical job behaviours were identified. These were categorised into four interpersonal dimensions and four problem-solving dimensions.

Interpersonal	Problem-solving
Leadership	Organisation
Assertiveness	Thoroughness
Flexibility	Resourcefulness
Sensitivity	Drive

Questions were developed which related to past situations in which the interviewees could demonstrate the way they behaved with respect to these dimensions, and a rating format was devised for recording answers, e.g. 'Tell me about a time when . . .', was a typical question stem. Following training, interjudge reliability was 0.64 and criterion validity was 0.22, on average (without adjusting for restriction of range, etc.). Thus the performance of the interview method was reasonably satisfactory and above the usual level for interviews.

Recall

Recall of information from interviews has in general been shown to be very variable. Carlson *et al.* (1971) reported an experiment involving forty managers, looking at a twenty minute video of an interview. On twenty factual questions asked, the average number recalled wrongly by the managers was ten. Those who followed a guide and took notes had the best recall. Yet we tend to advise against taking notes during interviews for reasons to do with the candidate, e.g. not to make them too nervous. A compromise is to record immediately after the interview and in accordance with some predesigned data-collecting form.

Example of interview research

The following research took place in a government organisation in the United States (Pulakos *et al.*, 1996). It illustrates a number of points which have been made above.

A pervasive problem with the interview is its validity, which is usually assessed by correlating interviewer ratings with job performance. Of course this brings with it the dilemma of how can we assess job performance and if, as is usual, we have a number of interviewers, how can we account for the individual differences in their skills as interviewers?

The study in question began with an extensive job analysis involving over 1000 people including workers and supervisors. From this data, a structured interview and a job-performance criterion rating scale were developed. An effective total of 62 interviewers in panels of three in a number of separate locations across the country interviewed 515 employees.

The interview attempted to measure eight 'critical skills', seven by questions and one by observation. The eight skill areas were planning, organising and prioritising; relating effectively with others; evaluating information and making decisions; demonstrating initiative and motivation; adapting to changing situations; physical requirements; demonstrating integrity and communicating orally.

The interview questions were 'past-orientated', aimed at getting the respondents to talk about their experience in behaviour relevant to the dimensions. For each dimension, a behaviourally anchored rating scale was developed with a seven point rating, categorised as Low (1 or 2), Moderate (3, 4 or 5) and High (6 or 7).

The interviewers were trained on a day-long course. The training consisted of a lecture on administering the interview, how to probe for information and how to evaluate the effectiveness of the answers. Two video tapes of interviews were observed and trial ratings were made by the participants. Ratings were discussed and feedback was given about the correct rating to apply in particular cases. The job-performance dimensions which candidates' supervisors used to rate them were as follows: recording information; making oral presentations; gathering evidence; reviewing and analysing information; planning, coordinating and organising; attending to detail; working in dangerous situations; developing constructive relations with others; demonstrating effort and initiative; and maintaining a positive image.

Interviewers' ratings averages were from 4.8 to 5.8, showing a small degree of difference in overall severity, but the range of individual interviewer's ratings as measured by their standard deviations was considerable, with standard deviations of 0.36–1.31. This confirms that some people are very tight in their ratings and others use a much wider spread of judgements.

Three methods of combining ratings were used and the resulting rating for each candidate were correlated with their job-performance rating. The methods were consensus (general agreement of three interviewers per candidate), average of raw ratings and average of standardised ratings. Correlations of 0.35, 0.32 and 0.32 were obtained for the respective methods.

Overall then, it seems to have made little difference which method of combining ratings was used, though the whole process was so thorough and training was used for interviewers, so that a good deal of interviewer error in rating was probably eliminated at the beginning. The study illustrates dimensions of behaviour rated at interview and in jobs, as well as the different ways that we can use to combine ratings. A secondary study of the dimensions underlying the interview ratings and the job performance ratings gave the interesting result that one dimension in each case was sufficient to account for the differences between candidates. This suggests that no matter how sophisticated our procedures for making judgements are in this field, the differences between people come down to only one or two dimensions in practice.

Summary

Interviews are and will remain the most popular form of selection method. Interviewing is as much an art as a science and is an underrated activity which actually requires great skill to practise successfully at the higher levels. Interviews vary mainly in the away they are structured and in the degree of planning which goes before. The interview process is a complex social interaction and is subject to many errors of judgement and procedure. Interviews can be very effective if properly structured and planned. More research in the real world is required before interviewing is established in the position it deserves.

Activities

1. Interview a number of people in both structured and unstructured ways about job-related and personal matters. Compare your recall with a recording, if possible.

2. Develop indirect interview questions which would reveal to some extent if someone was 'sociable', 'dominant' or 'task centred'.

3. Find out from some experienced business people just how good they think they are at interviewing (research shows that most if not all think they are). Then investigate their training and their validity procedures.

Further reading

Dipboye, R.L. (1992) *Selection Interviews: Process Perspectives*. (Cincinnati, South Western).

Harris, M.M. (1989) Reconsidering the employment interview: a review of recent literature and suggestions for further research. *Personnel Psychology*, 42, 691–726.

Pulakos, E.D., Schmitt, N., Whitney, D. and Smith, M. (1996) Individual differences in interviewer ratings: the impact of standardization, consensus discussion, and sampling error on the validity of a structured interview. *Personnel Psychology*, 49, 85–102.

Robertson, I.T., Gratton, L. and Rout, U. (1990) The validation of situational interviews for administrative jobs. *Journal of Organizational Behaviour*, 11, 69–76.

Use of psychological tests in selection

10

Focus questions

What makes psychological tests different from other forms of selection method?

Should we be concerned about ethical and legal issues in the use of tests?

What kinds of tests are available?

What is the level of validity of tests?

What do aptitude and ability tests measure?

What are personality tests?

Are there any problems concerning the abuse of personality tests?

A test is generally defined as 'a standardised measure of aptitude, knowledge, ability, personality or performance with fixed rules for administration and scoring' (Reilly and Chao, 1982).

Ghiselli in reviewing the use of tests in selection between 1920 and 1970, found that for every job category there were several tests significantly related to both training and job performance. There are today, literally thousands of tests ranging through ability tests, aptitude tests, work sample tests, personality tests, attitude scales, etc. At the last count, there existed over 80 000 occupationally relevant testing procedures (Furnham, 1992).

Recent surveys on test usage in industry have suggested that the use of ability and aptitude tests has remained fairly stable in the 1980s with about 60 per cent of companies using them to some extent for managerial and technical jobs and under 10 per cent using them for clerical and manual jobs. In the United States,

> There has been a resurgence of testing; testing to screen out applicants who are bad risks (drug testing, lie detector testing, honesty testing, health projections) and to a lesser extent ability and knowledge testing to identify the better prospects. (Hartigan and Wigdor, 1989, p. 17).

The main issues for occupational psychology are, as usual, validity and reliability, but there are also ethical and legal issues to consider as well as appropriateness. In the last few years in Britain, many new testing courses for business people have been set up under the British Psychological Society's scheme for certification in test competency. This was partly to deal with abuses in test use by trying to control more strictly those who could use tests as the market-led demand for occupational testing expanded considerably in the 1990s. Another motive is that, if almost anyone with the proper sales techniques and resources can persuade company directors to use the tests which they are marketing, then psychologists who might be very inadequate salesmen will be left out of the competition. This would be a serious result, not only for the psychologists. Job applicants would be at risk of being assessed less accurately if incompetent people with inadequate tests were allowed free rein. The public deserves to be treated carefully and well in this area. Good tests are not self-evident to the untrained eye and often a lot of work has to go into proving that a test is good. It is not something that can be established with sales patter or a 'road test'.

Features of psychological tests

Psychological tests have three features which distinguish them from other methods of selection:

Standard form:	each applicant is treated in exactly the same way, the test being the same for everyone
Measure a construct:	tests measure something specific which has been defined and established
Normative criteria:	test results are compared to some pre-existing standard usually derived from a sample similar to the applicants

The standard form is delivered via the test booklet containing the questions. Administration instructions including the practice items, and the scoring and interpretation of the score will be included in a Test Manual, in which detailed information concerning test construction, validity and reliability is contained.

Tests measure 'constructs'. These are defined representations of some aspects of human behaviour, temperament and capability. The test maker attempts to compile a measure of the construct and compares the results to other measures of the same or related constructs.

Normative information consists of collected data on previous samples of applicants or other people on the test in question. It enables the test results of any individual to be viewed relative to other people; i.e. relative to other applicants, relative to previously successful workers, relative to people in other groups, e.g. college students, training course graduates, etc.

Using tests confers a number of clear advantages to the company or the test user, though there are also disadvantages (Furnham, 1992). Tests normally result in information which is in the form of numbers and this makes comparisons easier. These may be 'raw scores', percentiles, stens, deviations from means, etc. Numbers of any kind enable a database of results to be maintained, and future progress of people at work can be compared with their relative standings on tests given at entry. This is more or less impossible with interviews as the data from them is usually subjective and verbal rather than numerical. In any case, it is not normally retained in any usable form. Test results are usually explicit and specific, as opposed to the sometimes vague and subjective opinions resulting from interviews. Tests help to eliminate corruption and unfairness, as they are usually objective and provide hard evidence of performance. Tests have a scientific basis, which enables them to be evaluated and improved in a progressive way over time. Psychometrics, which is what most tests are based on, is a recognised discipline in psychology with a number of high-ranking academic journals devoted to it. Tests are said to help people who use them to think in a more behavioural and rational way about assessment. This comes about because tests require people to think in a specific way about what it is they are trying to assess.

There are disadvantages to using tests, some of which are as follows. Tests can be faked to some degree by the applicants. In areas such as personality, motivation and attitudes, people can answer untruthfully or in a planned direction. Many tests contain within them a sort of detection device for such answering. However, in the hands of the less sophisticated test user, faking behaviour may escape detection. Of course one might say that interviews are even more prone to faking and CV and references are hardly monuments to truth and frankness either. It is said that some people lack self-insight or verbal ability and so find tests of the paper and pencil variety difficult to respond to in a consistent way. Test anxiety and other factors can inhibit performance. Some people who would make perfectly good employees are just test-shy. Perhaps they have been out of school for some time or did not fare too well in the classroom. Not all tests are valid and sometimes publishers make too much in the way of claims for their test. Many tests are imported, either into the country or into the firm without proper experiments to test their 'transportability'. Tests can be coached for and can be challenged. This is why we should keep tests secret and constantly updated. They should also be revised frequently and their effectiveness monitored within user companies. Many commercially produced tests have had the same format and content for years and are well known. One aptitude test used in banking circles has been widely pirated for years and probably has now almost negligible validity, yet it is being used at this moment for screening applicants for bank clerk positions. People offer courses in the tests used in the selection for certain professional groups. This tends to reduce the effectiveness of the tests and is also unfair on those who cannot gain access to such courses. Large organisations which use tests for selection should have a test construction specialist on their staff whose full-time work is the assembly, maintenance and validation of testing instruments, but few do.

Important considerations in the use of tests

Ethics

Tests are closely scrutinised by various sectors of the community for their ethical standards, even though there is far less room for unethical behaviour in testing than there is in interviewing, for example. Tests should never be used without a good justification. If a company is going to use tests, it should ensure that the test has some provable relevance to the job or position. This means that people's scores on the test should be compared with aspects of their job performance. Courts of law may now insist on this standard being met. A reasonable idea is to validate the test internally as well as externally. This can be achieved to some extent, by giving the test under genuine test conditions to existing employees in the grade being recruited to.

Other factors which should be included in any ethical testing programme are the applicant's rights to privacy. Test results must never be placed in files that are generally accessible, but kept in a locked file in the Managing Director's office. The test results of people who are not selected should be destroyed or retained without identifying names.

Applicants also have a right to expect a considerate feedback on their performance on tests and an explanation of why they were not selected. Failing to get through a job interview can be rationalised. People can simply tell themselves that they were not feeling good on the day, or that the interviewer did not like them or that the interviewer was a narrow-minded fool. In that way they would not feel too bad, but when they are turned down because they 'failed a test', that is often taken to mean there is something more fundamental at fault in them.

Valid and up-to-date tests should be used. Tests are a little bit like fruit, they have a shelf life of only so long. Even tests of basic cognitive aptitudes can become outdated, due to their form, i.e. they begin to look old fashioned. There are other factors affecting the usability of tests, for example the changing school syllabus may affect people's ability to tackle particular kinds of problems; the changing job requirements may call for a different range of abilities; changes in the pool of recruits due to labour market fluctuations may make the test too easy or too hard.

It should be ensured that everyone has a reasonable chance of performing at their best by setting good conditions for testing and giving adequate practice to all candidates. This applies in all testing situations, but is even more strongly required where the applicants for jobs have been many years out of school and have lost their confidence, if they ever had any, in test-taking situations. In the selection testing for some positions in the British Post Office, applicants are given clear and detailed descriptions of the tests which they will have to take, as well as some practice examples from the tests. There is even some provision for anyone having difficulty understanding the test samples to get some help in preparing for the assessment by phoning an advice hot-line.

In respect of some professions, college entrance and career situations, independent entrepreneurs have set up test coaching services where individuals who are going forward for the selection can be given practice in the tests employed. There is a certain point at which this process either becomes unfair, i.e. less wealthy applicants are not able to afford coaching, or it invalidates the test as a predictor. This would happen if everyone became so well coached that there was insufficient difference in their levels of performance on the test to show any worthwhile correlation with their performance in the training school or on the job.

Some people are liable to associate with the testing process more power than it really possesses and so when they are rejected their feelings of personal worth are deeply affected. The most negative reactions appear to be to intelligence-type tests, whereas people feel better about being rejected after taking job sample tests and other tests which involve them in some kind of activity (Cascio and Phillips, 1979; Robertson and Kandola, 1982).

The British Psychological Society, which oversees the profession of psychology in all its various forms in Britain, has recently instituted a very formal system of qualification of people who wish to use psychological tests in an organisational or occupational context. This requires users to take training courses in the basics of psychometrics and test use. This system is intended to control and monitor test use so as to eliminate the abuses that may arise if tests are used willy-nilly by people with little basic knowledge. The training courses are provided by consultants, test publishers and academic institutions.

Legal

Legal issues arise in relation to discrimination in employment opportunity. Tests must be shown to be job related and to predict job performance. If a test cannot be shown to be related in some way to job performance, then it really should not be used, as it is simply a source of possible discrimination. Ruling people out because their reading is a bit slow or because they are not very good at doing vocabulary tests, when reading and vocabulary have nothing to do with the job, is simply denying access to employment for no good reason.

In 1990, eight guards at Paddington Station, with the support of the Commission for Racial Equality, took British Rail to court after they had failed the train driver assessment process. The process included the taking of a range of published psychometric tests. These included aptitude tests, vigilance and attention tests, a personality test and an interview. On examination, it was clear that the verbal test in particular resulted in Adverse Impact. That is, the minority group applicants had a lower average score and so were less likely to be selected. An out-of-court settlement was agreed and a British Rail Occupational Psychology Centre was formed to review driver assessment. It is interesting in the light of this case that the Commission for Racial Equality in the United Kingdom could report, in 1993 that few firms appear to carry out any racial monitoring of the effects of selection methods.

Adverse impact

Adverse impact is established when if, for example, equal numbers of men and women apply for a job, significantly fewer women than men are appointed. The critical level of difference would be around 80 per cent. This is also relevant in situations where applicants can be categorised into substantial racial or religious groups. If the selection process is for some reason more difficult for members of one group than those of another, then there is something wrong and evidence of adverse impact is apparent. This problem has been especially severe in America where test usage has been less strongly promoted than in the past, though it is still a fairly common practice. US Federal Guidelines have encouraged less reliance on tests because of their allegedly discriminatory character. However, tests can also serve to reduce or eliminate direct personal prejudice if used properly. People's test-taking attitude and experience may significantly interfere with their performance and must be taken into account. On the widely used VG-GATB test, the norms for semi-skilled jobs showed the average White 50th percentile raw score would be at the 84th percentile in the Black-only distribution. The United States Employment Service decided to use group-based norm tables and to refer people to employers accordingly. However, the same test has now been withdrawn from use (see p. 166).

People have recently taken to using the term 'negative impact', which simply means that for some people the testing process was unpleasant or made them react negatively.

Types of tests

Tests can be broadly divided into aptitude tests and personality tests. As far as actual test usage in the job-selection field is concerned, aptitude tests are by far the most frequently used. An aptitude should really relate to the potential that a person has to learn to do something. Having an aptitude is partly based on your biological inheritance, but also on the opportunities you have had at school and the experience you have had. Also of great importance is whether you have benefited by education and experience as opposed to 'dogging off' or failing to do your homework.

Aptitude/ability tests

It has never been possible for psychologists to agree fully upon a definition of intelligence; nor can they agree on the respective roles of biology (inheritance) and experience in making people more or less intelligent. Most intelligence tests require the test taker to infer connections between concepts and supply or recognise relevant associations with given information. They are using their 'working memory', holding and comparing concepts and understanding the relation between them. People who do well on tests such as these also do well on school exams. Thus intelligence predicts success at academic work. At the same time, the kind of questions in intelligence tests are based on the kind of operations that children practise in the school classroom.

In the occupational setting, such tests usually employ verbal concepts and ask the subjects to carry out various kinds of reasoning tasks. Sometimes these activities depend on having a good vocabulary or level of general knowledge, though the job relevance of the latter is doubtful. Non-verbal measures of intelligence use reasoning tasks with numbers, figures and diagrams, abstract series, etc. These may be less discriminatory and less easily coachable.

General cognitive ability (intelligence) has relevance in predicting success in many occupations. According to Hunter, if only one test was allowed in selection, it would save millions of pounds annually if people could be selected using a general ability test appropriate for the job in question. Many people will find the following hard to believe. It is very difficult, if not impossible, to tell the intelligence level of an adult at an interview or in a face-to-face meeting of a normal social kind.

Our social behaviour is not based on abstract concepts or making inferences from given knowledge in the area of words and numbers. We manage to relate socially by simple everyday words, by smiles and gestures, by agreeing with others. In many conversations people are only half listening to the other person and a lot of their mental effort is devoted to what they want to say. We do not critically analyse the depth of responses, etc. People without very much ability are able to get university degrees and get good jobs; on the other hand many quite clever people can appear quite dull if they do not talk out very much. For years deaf people were seen as being intellectually dull, whereas they have the same range of intelligence as the general population. Many capable people fail in interviews and in education because they do not have the social skills, the perseverance and the tolerance to boredom which the successful person has. This is why Hunter's finding is so valid.

Evidence of intelligence test validity for selection

There have been numerous studies correlating supervisor ratings of job performance with cognitive test scores. They have shown moderate correlations (Nathan and Alexander, 1988). In the case of managerial jobs, most selection tests emphasise verbal skills and reasoning. One of the most popular ones is actually called a 'critical reasoning test' and it asks the subject to read a passage of complicated prose and then decide whether a selection of conclusions can be reasonably drawn from the information given.

The relationship between intelligence and managerial performance was established long ago in the work of Edwin Ghiselli. In 1966, Ghiselli showed that intelligence test results were the best predictors of the performance of foremen, administrators and executives. In the 1971 study of managerial talent, there were reported correlations of 0.28–0.45 between intelligence and the performance of managers and personnel officers. Klimoski and Strickland (1981) found that paper and pencil tests of intelligence predicted future managerial performance ratings better than assessment centres did. Several studies show that intelligence tests predict behavioural ratings in jobs or assessment centres (Wolfson, 1985).

However, intelligence on its own will not make a good manager; in some cases too much intelligence may even be a disadvantage. Most people in managerial positions in large companies are fairly intelligent anyway. Some people, e.g. Wagner and Sternberg (1985), have taken a different look at intelligent functioning in managers. They have introduced and developed the idea of 'tacit knowledge' which is related to intelligence but is also independent from it to an extent. It involves an intelligence of how to proceed in any field, the 'streetwise' aspects of business. This is related to the idea of managerial competencies which we will see more and more of in the future (Spencer and Spencer, 1993). Managerial competencies include such aspects of functioning as knowledge (i.e. of the business), physical and intellectual ability, personality types, need states and motivation and the relevant self-image.

Competencies

The competency concept is not yet completely clear and when people speak of it they may be addressing different issues. There are three main perspectives: managerial (knowledge, skills and attitudes), behavioural (behaviour repertoires relevant to a job role) and organisational (strategies and corporate survival skills) (Sparrow, 1995). Brilliant managers can be identified and the core competencies which they possess and which others do not can be sought, and if found they can be trained in others or selected for. This is obviously a sound idea, but as yet it has to gather a substantial following in occupational psychology.

It has been suggested that intelligence tests tend to predict training performance better than actual job performance (Ghiselli and Brown, 1955), but more recent information is quite positive about the validity of these tests. Schmidt and Hunter (1977) suggest that the true validity coefficient is at least 0.37 and Hunter and Hunter in 1984 conclude that if general cognitive ability alone were used, the average validity across all jobs would be 0.54 for training and 0.45 for job proficiency. However, no one is claiming that cognitive ability tests can measure other than some of the attributes that contribute to successful job performance. We should also bear in mind, when faced with the proliferation of tests and test batteries, that Hunter's studies have suggested two factors relevant to job-performance validity, general cognitive ability and psychomotor ability. The third factor 'perceptual' was almost perfectly predictable from the other two. It is generally true of many multiple aptitude batteries that the tests contained in them are quite highly correlated with each other and the amount of variance predicted by one test over another is so small as to be not worth considering. Again, the tendency of publishers of tests is to sell a comprehensive and complex package, usually with an obligatory training course for a thousand pounds and an annual licensing fee of several hundred pounds. Most of this is for commercial rather than strictly psychological reasons. Although the British Psychological Society test competency action referred to earlier is to be welcomed, it is ironic that it is almost easier to buy a handgun in the United Kingdom than a verbal reasoning test.

An experiment carried out in the context of the salesforce of the Philip Morris Tobacco Company involved constructing a simple job sample/aptitude test based on a job analysis of the mathematical elements (arithmetic) in salesforce jobs. The results across a wide range of sales people correlated with supervisors' ratings of the sales person's performance in the math elements of their jobs. This illustrates a sort of additive validity, or what is called incremental validity. The relevance of this test is only for part of the job and there are other factors to be taken into account. But that part might be crucial. In selection we do not need a super-duper test for everything; if we can validly assess even some aspects of the job requirements, then we are improving the situation over ground zero (Diamanti, 1993).

A second major category of ability/aptitude tests is that of Spatial Ability. This would also take in various attempts at mechanical reasoning tests and more specific perception tests. There is clear evidence that people have a spatial ability factor to different degrees. This is seen, for example, in their ability to manipulate a mental image of three-dimensional shapes. Another instance is how good we are at following directions on a map and being able to report how different views will look from different perspectives. Although I consider myself very intelligent, I can still be unsure when driving where some of the small twisty roads in my small town lead to. There are some jobs where this may be a relevant attribute, e.g. van delivery or motorbike courier.

Mechanical reasoning tests ask people to look at pictures of gears, pulleys, etc. and to predict what is going to happen on the basis of the laws of physics. These are often found in some aptitude batteries. It is doubtful that this is really a separate ability from general cognitive ability and spatial, but mechanical tests have been particularly used in the selection of mechanical apprentices. They have job relevance and correlate with training performance to a small extent. It is likely that people can learn the skills involved fairly well after brief exposure to training.

Tests of perceptual speed and accuracy are often included under the heading in the test catalogue, 'Clerical Speed and Accuracy'. For obvious reasons, these tests have been used in the selection of clerical workers in government services. Such tests probably bear only a small relationship to performance and any differences in performance would be better predicted by a general ability test. They do have the advantage of face validity and are less likely to be accused of bias as they appear to be so job relevant.

Aptitude Test Batteries contain all of the above types of tests. The most widely used up till recently has been the General Aptitude Test Battery (GATB) published by the United States Employment Service. This purports to measure nine aptitudes by means of twelve tests, four of these involve apparatus and the remainder are pencil and paper tests. Many studies support the predictive validity of the GATB, but this is due to the fact that it is a good and diffuse measure of general ability, rather than to its measuring specific aptitudes as it pretends to do. The GATB has however been withdrawn from service for the time being and is undergoing a radical review (Wigdor and Sackett, 1993).

The nine areas which the GATB measured were general ability, verbal aptitude, numerical aptitude, spatial aptitude, form perception, clerical aptitude, motor coordination, finger dexterity and manual dexterity. The test was first published in 1947, revised in 1970 and revised again recently. Watts and Everitt (1980) analysed the test intercorrelations and found that only three factors were required to explain them. These were a Symbolic, a Psychomotor and a Perceptual factor. A large Irish data sample was analysed and only four factors were present. These were Symbolic (verbal and numerical) and Perceptual (three-dimensional space and tool matching). The two other factors were heavily correlated with the apparatus tests and were of the Psychomotor type (Hammond, 1984).

Other test batteries include the British version of the Differential Aptitude Test and the NFER test of general ability, which is suited for apprentice and training course entrants and includes verbal, non-verbal, numerical and spatial tests of thinking. The Modern Occupational Skills Test is the most recent contender on the market of this kind of instrument.

The SRA Computer Aptitude Battery (1985) for programmers is an example of a multiaptitude battery for a specific occupational category. It includes verbal meaning, reasoning, letter series, number ability and diagramming. It is said to predict performance in training and in job performance with correlations of 0.30–0.71 and 0.20–0.61, respectively, across a number of studies. The best individual predictor tests were diagramming and reasoning (Neuman and Nomoto, 1990). Another job-specific example is the CRT Skills Test (1989), supposedly suitable for data entry clerks. This has three timed parts: speed and accuracy in data entry, speed and accuracy in numeric data only and speed and accuracy in retrieving customer files and identifying information. Such tests measure job-relevant skills, unlike the previous types of tests which measure psychological constructs in the abstract. If we move one step further on down the ladder of abstraction, we reach job sample tests.

People also differ in their physical abilities or what is often called Motor abilities. Psychomotor ability tests measure physical ability, e.g. agility, strength, reaction time, two-hand coordination. These correlate well with physically demanding jobs. Also included in some situations are tests of physical fitness. Their use has been shown to be associated with a reduction in heart attacks, accidents and absence if physical examination of job holders is regularised. A study of 4480 California Highway Patrol Officers indicated that 'on-the-job' injuries rose in relation to body fat. A fitness programme, reducing body fat, brought about a reduction in accidents and in medical referrals. A similar finding in an English police force found much higher incidence of the above problems in unfit policeman. Testing staff regularly for fitness levels would have a good effect, but the costs would probably outweigh the benefits and some people might feel pressurised or discriminated against, especially if they were partial to cream cakes or beer.

Manual dexterity

Many companies use manual dexterity tests, most of which involve putting small objects into holes on a board as quickly as possible. Some tests involve the use of a pair of tweezers. Such tests are specially useful in screening people for assembly type jobs, as it rapidly eliminates the small minority of the population who have very poor motor control or poor hand–eye coordination.

Personality tests

There are numerous definitions of personality (Pervin, 1980). In selection tests, the trait approach is more prevalent. In this, personality is viewed as a set of traits which individuals show in their behaviour and which are fairly consistent from situation to situation. Measures of these traits can therefore be used to predict an individual's reactions to new situations.

Personality is an abstraction from behaviour; it develops as we grow up and becomes more and more complex as the number of situations in our lives increases. We can be more or less consistent from situation to situation, but within the same situation we should be even more consistent. People with very limited life experiences may have correspondingly one-dimensional personalities, though there are obvious exceptions to this rule.

In 1968, Walter Mischel published a book which for a time took some of the stuffing out of the personalists. It showed that personality tests not only had relatively low validity, something that was already known, but that they failed to predict with any significant degree of accuracy how people would behave in a particular situation. He emphasised the point that from one situation to another the personality of people in fact seemed to be different, rather than the same, as had been claimed. It was suggested that personality is in fact an illusion. Mischel said that personality test exponents committed the fundamental attribution error by attributing behaviour to personality rather than to the situation. Epstein, on the other hand, has countered this by saying that Mischel falls into the trap of deducing general findings from small samples. In fact, personality tests do predict behaviour well in more general terms and across a number of situations. Predicting just one specific behaviour is just too much to expect. There is also a large accumulation of evidence that suggests that our personalities are fairly stable throughout our life, that is, we do not really change much, except for a few unusual exceptions. A longitudinal study carried out in Los Angeles showed that people's behaviour changes little over the years from childhood and adolescence through to old age. A group of people were followed through for forty years and periodically assessed and the major features of their personalities were seen to be relatively unchanged (Block, 1971). It seems, perhaps unfortunately, that our personalities are fairly fixed and unchangeable.

Magaro and Ashbrook (1985) proposed that 'personality serves as the organising force within the individual that guides interactions with the environment so that discrete elements of the person and situation are arranged in a meaningful whole that is manifested in behaviour'. We not only are our personalities, but we interpret the world through them, e.g. if we are paranoid, we not only act secretively and suspiciously, we also view the outside world with a suspicious interpretative framework.

Our personalities are partly dependent on our physiological makeup, principally our endocrine system and our nervous system. Personality is also partly learned. It is also an input variable to learning situations, in that it is a determinant of behaviour and of how people cope in situations. Our personality is thus related to our habits as learners and workers. For example, it might be relevant whether we give up easily. Personality and the way we view ourselves are closely linked to our attitudes and our motivation.

Personality and work

There are many ways in which personality and work are practically linked. This is particularly true in the area of career achievement and progress. Is there a 'successful personality', an ideal personality of a salesman, a policeman, etc.? In the training area, we might ask, How can we take personality or learning style into account in designing training? How do people tackle problems? Can some people function better in a cooperative learning situation rather than a competitive one? How should feedback be given and should everyone receive it in the same way? In respect of motivation at work, are there self-starters? How would you recognise one? What is the effect on personality of long-term unemployment? In personnel selection and team building, do certain personalities blend together better than other combinations?

Personality tests are generally of the questionnaire type and have been widely used in selection situations, though again, as with all tests, the predictive validity is actually quite small, though positive. There are certain situations where particular personality profiles are thought to be especially relevant for the job, e.g. selling.

However, in this area, Wedderburn and others have shown that the personality profile recommended by some test producers for insurance salespersons is actually the opposite of that found in those salespersons who produce the best results. The theory is that the best will be dominant persistent and good at closing sales. In fact, quiet persuasive people with a strong interest in people do better. A more complex reality is that different kinds of salespersons are required to service different populations of customers.

Personality tests can be used in two main ways, rationally and empirically. In a rational application, the management team may discuss the position and perhaps think about previous occupants of the post. From this, they determine a personnel specification, which includes a description of the kind of personality characteristics the ideal candidate might show. They then set an ideal profile, which they try to identify using a personality test. As we see above with the salesperson example, a rational approach can in reality be quite wide of the mark. On the other hand, it can be perfectly adequate. The empirical approach really calls on the expertise of an occupational psychologist with good abilities in statistics. One approach is to take the workers in the area where the vacancy exists and divide them into successful and unsuccessful in broad terms. They are given the personality test used by the selectors and the results are examined with the question, Are there any differences between the two groups on the dimensions of the test? A discriminant function can be calculated and if it successfully separates out the successful from the unsuccessful, then the same mathematical equation can be used to separate the applicants into those who are more like the succeeders and those who are more like the failures. There will of course be a significant bunch in the middle most of the time. This is empirical. It is not based on thinking about the job or the people in the job. It is based only on seeing if there is some aspect of the test results which discriminates among the workers, and then using it.

The functions are called specification equations. They are usually cross-validated on similar samples to make sure they are effective and that the results obtained are not due to chance. An example of this is found in the chemical industry, where it is important to have careful steady people with a strong conscientiousness factor in their personality. Studies by Peter Edmunds have shown that better and safer chemical plant operators have a personality profile of reserved, serious, shy, conscientious, controlled and self-critical. Such a person would not shine very well at an interview. So the traditional means of selection would pass him or her over

(Handyside, 1988). These results have been confirmed by other studies, so they are not chance occurrences.

Empirical keying of personality tests offers a better likelihood of success in this area. This involves finding out which ways certain groups answer the questions on personality tests and combining these questions together to form an empirical scale which will then point out, in a fresh sample usually of job applicants, people who answer the questions in the same way. There are two scales of the California Psychological Inventory which are claimed to predict managerial potential or worker motivation. These have been developed by Gough (1984). It should be noted that these types of specialised subscales of large tests are developed mainly on an empirical basis in particular settings. Hence, because of the question of transportability, they would need to be further validated before being used in this country.

Management team building

Personality tests such as the 16PF, but also many others, have been used in the practice of management team building. This has become even more popular, as management hierarchies are tending to be flattened and more people are given autonomous roles in teams. A common approach is that of Belbin (1981). Following on from years of ad hoc research and an accumulation of experience at a college which trained managers (Henley), Belbin assembled a list of complementary managerial roles and also a method for assigning people to the role they would work best in. This method is the Team Role Inventory, though a personality test may also be used for assigning people to roles which they would likely be comfortable in. Very little in-depth validation of these assignments has been carried out. Belbin's report is largely anecdotal and not strictly controlled in the methodological sense.

The team roles include negotiators, manager–workers, intellectuals and leaders. Leaders, for example, tend to be characterised by higher scores on anxiety and dominance. Intellectuals are the ideas people. They tend to be quieter, intolerant of sameness and always questing for unusual approaches to problems. The concept of team building has not been fully accepted. Furnham et al. (1993) have strongly criticised the Team Role Inventory, which was one of Belbin's instruments, and he does not recommend its use. The distinctive team roles do not seem to exist when data is properly analysed and there is considerable overlap and people often occupy multiple roles, which is theoretically damaging to the whole idea. In reply to the criticism, Belbin said that it was unfair and the method was misused and anyway he now has a new method called 'interplace' which works much better. It must be remembered that there is quite a sizeable amount of money to be made in this field and managers may not be very sophisticated in the psychological area. Some may be more open to being persuaded about a psychological method than they would be about a machine tool or a marketing plan. Academics like to take a much purer scientific view and when these tests and claims are examined in the cold light of day, they rarely live up to all of their promises. Nevertheless, they have an important role to play in bringing about a deeper awareness of people's characteristics.

One instrument which is respectable in its own right, whatever uses to which it might be put, is the 16PF (Cattell *et al.*, 1970). This is a widely used personality questionnaire, so-called because it gives a measure of sixteen factors which the author claims cover the whole of the human personality. The scores on sixteen factors can be reduced to four second-order factors: extraversion, anxiety, toughness and independence. A recent revision of the test includes an additional fifth factor, control. This test was originally developed by Raymond Cattell and has been rigorously researched over a period of almost fifty years. Its author is one of the most respected scientists in the world of psychology. The study quoted above by Edmunds is one of many that have been carried out with the 16PF. Its psychometric properties are excellent and its validity in occupational selection is reasonable.

Another widely used test is the OPQ which was developed in the 1980s by Peter Saville and Roger Holdsworth. From small beginnings, these two people have built a substantial company with branches or agencies in over twenty countries, marketing psychological assessment methods. The OPQ has various formats and is sold on a highly commercialised basis. In reality, it has not been as widely researched by independent examiners as for example the 16PF, but it is one of the biggest selling items in the catalogue of Saville and Holdsworth Ltd. Robertson and Kinder (1993) reported a comprehensive validation study of the OPQ. Validity coefficients from over twenty studies were examined. The best level of prediction arrived at was by combining a number of scales and was 0.33. Some criteria were found not to be able to be predicted as claimed, e.g. adaptability, planning, organising ability and inter-personal skills. Most recently, another study of one of the OPQ versions suggested that it had acceptable psychometric properties for the most part, but that about a one-quarter of its scales were inadequate and that the measurement model on which it was based probably needed more development (Barrett *et al.*, 1996).

There are other models for personality assessment which do not need to contain this type of structure, but they are not usually used in selection contexts. In some manage-ment selection situations, the candidates may even be asked to take the Minnesota Multiphasic Personality Inventory (MMPI) (Hathaway and McKinley, 1967), which is essentially a test used by clinical psychologists to formulate personality diagnoses in relation to mental illness or personality disorders. This instrument was not designed for use in job selection, having been formed and validated largely in the population of mental hospital patients. In the hands of a qualified psychologist, it might be useful in ruling out people with possible mental disorders from higher management positions.

Not quite a test

One form of personality test not uncommon in the commercial world, but somewhat frowned upon by psychologists, takes the form of sets of four adjectives from which the subject chooses two most like and two most unlike him/herself. These tests give scores on four factors: dominance, influence, steadiness and compliance and claim that, for example, the most effective insurance salespersons are characterised by a pattern inclusive of high 'I' and some other details. There are some twenty-four published varieties of this kind of test; the best of them stress that the test should not be used in any exclusive sense as a selection device but only as a guide to interview content and probing. However, human nature being what it is, that warning is probably more ignored than heeded.

These types of tests have been referred to as 'pseudotests' (Cook, 1993), though this is rather scathing and fails to consider the whole picture. Landy refers to the ways of promoting pseudo-psychological tests in airline magazines and glossy management and business journals. Managers need to be cautious in relation to personality assessment and demand to see concrete evidence rather than promises of wondrous results.

Misleading use of personality tests

A recent article in *Nature* by Blinkhorn and Johnson (1990), pointed to the expanding use of personality tests in the context of selection and warned that such tests had very low validity, but that it was easy to pull the wool over the eyes of the 'punters'. The article was written in a rather condescending tone, yet it gained considerable attention and from it has followed a number of television programmes and claims against companies who have apparently rejected applicants for jobs on the basis of personality test results. However, there were some factual aspects which are worth responding to.

In summary, the main points made were as follows. There are too many dimensions in personality tests giving a pseudo-comprehensiveness, which is really a myth. This is for the most part true. Most tests will condense down to from 3 to 5 strong dimensions on analysis. They said that the profiles of real people are rarely used to validate test-derived profiles or types. Again this is mainly true, though many of us who use such tests regularly see confirmed before our eyes 'real' people personality profiles when we see the people at interviews or subsequently on the job. Of course there is a strong risk of self-delusion here or what is called the 'Barnum' effect, after the circus proprietor. This means that we can be easily duped into seeing what we want to see and in the case of personality interpretations (and horoscopes), we ignore the inconsistencies and focus in on the consistencies in the story, convincing ourselves that it is true. In a more statistical vein, they say that some people use hypothesis testing in an inappropriate way. This is no doubt true, though the same accusation could be made in many areas. Another critique was that proven and cross-validated relationships between personality test results and job performance are almost non-existent. This depends what they mean by 'proven', etc.

A number of replies to this article have defended personality test use and criticised the content and manner of the article, e.g. Fletcher (1991). In summing up the situation, we should remember that personality tests are only conveniences. They allow large numbers of questions about behaviour and preferences to be asked in a short period of time. These questions are collated into sets and scores accumulated depending on the subject's answers. Thus people broadly describe themselves and they can be given a place along several dimensions.

There are three questions of relevance. First, is the place on the dimension that is given approximately correct? For example, is the candidate really more extroverted than 80 per cent of his or her peers? Second, if this is true, is it of proven relevance to the job? Third, when the candidate is being interviewed will someone take up the subject of personality and give him or her a chance to defend or disagree with the test results?

Considerations in using personality tests

In any application of personality tests, it should also be ensured that the questions are not unnecessarily intrusive of people's privacy and that the results are kept closely confidential. Tests should not be used for job selection unless they have been shown to have a proven relevance for the job or for the company in question, i.e. use should be based on research not on claims or conjectures. Tests should only be used as a piece of back-up evidence or as a lead into further and more face-to-face investigations. Questionnaire tests of personality are subject to 'faking'. People can make an intelligent guess as to the kind of personality that is being sought by the employer. Some tests have built-in scales to discover people who are exaggerating their sociability and lack of neurotic tendencies, but ultimately if you are smart enough you can project a false image to a questionnaire.

Personality test scales should, apart from reliability and validity referred to elsewhere, have properties such as unidimensionality. That is – they each should measure one thing and they should be statistically independent of the other scales in the instrument. Analysis of their results across different samples of subjects should consistently show the existence of these scales in a statistical sense.

Ng and Smith (1991) carried out a meta-analysis of studies from 1953 to 1990 and suggest an overall validity of 0.25 for personality tests. They say that non-work-related personality tests used as selection tools are poor predictors of job success and if used should be treated with caution. Schmitt *et al.* (1984) reported a validity coefficient derived from many separate studies, using a range of personality tests, of 0.149. This is not very impressive, though there are so many problems in studies of this kind that this result is only suggestive at best. First, serious problems exist in criteria definition and measurement, i.e. what are the test results being compared with as performance criteria? Second, most such studies suffer from considerable leakage from the sample for many reasons, so that ultimately the range of performance and personality measures is much smaller than is required to give reasonable correlations.

Objective and projective personality tests

Two other approaches to the assessment of personality are not common in occupational selection, but we can expect them to be increasingly seen in future years. These are 'Objective' tests and 'Projective' tests. In objective personality assessment, people are given tasks to do and the manner of their approach to the tasks is observed and rated. It might be observed whether they are persevering in the face of obstacles, or if they show confidence or frustration, or if they are aware of all the elements in the situation or are overfocused on a detail, etc.

Projective tests are such as Word Association Tests or Sentence Completion Tests. They originate in child psychology or in clinical psychology if we include the Rorschach ink-blot test, which is familiar to many people from its appearance in various Hollywood epics of girls with multiple personalities. Projective tests are difficult and time consuming to score, but they are not easily fakeable and can produce unexpected insights into people's makeup in a way no other test can.

The five factor model

The five factor model is the result of an accumulation of research in personality assessment by questionnaire and suggests that five factors are sufficient to describe personality. These factors are Extroversion, Emotional Stability, Agreeableness, Conscientiousness and Openness to Experience. Barrick and Mount (1991) outline the use of the five factor model and show that factors of personality have relationships to job performance across a range of occupations, though the relationships are not very strong. The main test which assesses the five factors at present is the NEO (Costa and McCrae,1988). This model has yet to make a significant impact in occupational psychology, but it will feature in future developments without any doubt. Not everyone has found the five factor model complete enough as it stands. It has been suggested that the extroversion factor should be further subdivided into Sociability-group orientated and Assertiveness-dominance factors (Hogan, 1982). In a practical context, when we interpret extroversion we tend to think of it as consisting of combinations of factors like the above, rather than as a blanket all-in-one factor anyway. Hough *et al.* (1990) have further suggested that the six factors need to be increased to nine to include some apparently worthwhile additions such as masculinity–femininity, locus of control and achievement scales. Hough's conclusion is that the five factor model is an over-simplification (Hough, 1992).

The above personality tests are based on trait models and they are constructed using item analysis and factor analysis. Other tests, which are less frequently seen but still used by their devotees, are based on 'Need' theory (Murray, 1938), which has a surface relevance to the work situation and relates closely to motivation and other aspects of workplace behaviour, perhaps more directly than the trait approach. These include the Personality Research Form, the Edwards Personal Preference Inventory and the Gordon Personal Profile.

Yet another approach to personality assessment is based on the identification of Types. There are several 'type' tests which combine questionnaire-type items with adjective checklists in the one instrument thus, they would say, improving the range of assessment methods. The most well-known instrument in this class is the Myers–Briggs Type Inventory (Myers and McCauley, 1985). The result of using this is that the applicant is classified into one of sixteen possible types. In theory, either rationally (probably) or from empirical research, there should be one or two 'types' who will fill the role required by a particular job and if the applicant fits any of these types, they will be shortlisted for further investigation.

Objective assessments of typological approaches have found them to be wanting in comparison to the trait model discussed above. It is a question of whether people vary along a number of dimensions (traits) or can be put into a number of boxes (types). Not only that, but will they stay in the boxes? And if not, what box will they jump into? York and John (1992) have provided evidence in a study of mature women that boundaries between types can be 'fuzzy' as opposed to the alternative view that types are discrete. They would maintain that people are more or less representative of a type, and not necessarily exactly of the type in question. Schneider and Hough (1995) conclude that the evidence for the existence of distinct and meaningful type categories, which would affect our interpretation of personality, is not strong and that further research is required to establish this conceptualisation. There is also a risk that in thinking of people as 'types', we have great difficulty explaining their behaviour when they fail to act according to type, as they are bound to do.

Personality and its assessment is a fascinating subject with many applications to work. We can expect to see its influence growing in the future. There is enormous scope for much more probing and detailed assessment to be made using computers, which can ask more and more questions and analyse patterns of responses as they are being made. However, we need a good working model of personality for this to happen.

Summary

This chapter has looked at the kinds of psychological tests which are available and has considered some of the practical and ethical questions which must be kept in mind by test users. Tests are widely used and it is vital that ethics, validity and reliability are always ensured. Tests measure specific aspects of the person and so can be very useful, but they are also coachable, fakeable and people have different degrees of familiarity with tests and this can affect their performance. The assumption that tests can be used in different settings has to be carefully examined. Aptitude tests are strong, as tests go, and personality tests are weak. Personality tests are useful but should not be used on their own for any decision concerning a person's livelihood and welfare. 'Competency' is a new concept which blends testing with performance assessment and will become more important in time.

Activities

1. **Discuss different kinds of jobs and consider whether there are any kinds of tests that would be useful in the selection process for them.**

2. **Ask people if they think their personalities could be assessed by paper and pencil tests or are if they think they are too variable and inconsistent for this approach.**

3. **Find out about the providers of testing services in your locality and how they are qualified and trained to carry out their function.**

Further reading

Barrick, M.R. and Mount, M.K. (1991) The big five personality dimensions and job performance: a meta-analysis. *Personnel Psychology*, 41, 1–26.

Blinkhorn, S. and Johnson, C. (1990) The insignificance of personality testing. *Nature*, 348, 671–2.

Fletcher, C. (1991) Personality tests the great debate. *Personnel Management*, September, 38–42.

Hartigan, J.A. and Wigdor, A.K. (1989) (eds) *Fairness in Employment Testing*. (Washington, DC, National Academy Press).

Hough, L.M., Eaton, N.K., Kamp, J.D. and McLoy, R.A. (1990) Criterion related validities of personality constructs and the effect of response distortion on those validities. *Journal of Applied Psychology Monograph*, 75(5), 581–95.

Kwiatkowski, R. (1994) Testing in the workplace. *The Psychologist*, Special Issue, 7(1), 10–32, (BPS, Leicester).

Schneider, R.J. and Hough, L.M. (1995) Personality and industrial/organisational psychology. *International Review of Industrial and Organizational Psychology*, 10, 75–129.

Miscellaneous selection techniques

11

Focus questions

How should you fill in an application form?

What makes a good CV?

How can employers use our past behaviour and experience in selection?

What is an assessment centre?

What is the significance of honesty testing?

Application forms

In almost all job selections, the applicants are required to complete some kind of application form. This asks for basic personal data and previous work experience and relevant qualifications.

Application forms have several basic advantages for the firm:

1. Comparisons between applicants are easily made because everyone has had to offer the same set of information, whereas when people are allowed to send their own CV, information is widely varied.

2. Firms can also code and store the information more easily and can in fact use it later in research on the validation of their methods of selection, as we shall see later.

3. The firm can retain a record of a legally binding statement made by the applicant which could form the basis for subsequent dismissal if the information given proved to be seriously inaccurate, for example, claiming experience or qualifications which were false.

Application forms are very susceptible to falsification. There are various ways of doing this including exaggeration or, quite commonly, straightforward lies. An interesting study examined the accuracy of information which was given in the cases of 111 applications for posts as nurse's aides, by comparing what was said with what previous employers said about the candidate, her tenure and level of wages (Schmitt, 1976). It was found that 15 per cent of the people who the applicant had claimed to be previous employers said the applicant had in fact never worked for them. There was disagreement on the stated reasons for termination in 25 per cent of cases. Over half the previous employers disagreed on the length of previous employment and over 70 per cent disagreed on the level of previous salary earned.

As said earlier, much of the information on application forms is rarely verified. For example, about 10 per cent of Irish firms never verify information on application forms, and over 60 per cent only verify some information, such as education and previous employment record. The remainder claimed that they verified all information, according to a report by Garavan (1990).

Application form information can be used almost like a psychological test to predict job criteria such as turnover. This is called the Weighted Application Blank method and it will be discussed below. The basic initial process of application sifting or shortlisting has become a major task in selection as the numbers applying for posts has increased. Apart from the laborious and boring job which it entails, it is also an area where major difficulties can be introduced. Evidence from the United States would suggest that it is very prone to bias and, in general, females are discriminated against. In terms of process, application forms are not well designed or well read and it is generally surface characteristics of the application which are used as grounds for rejection in the first place. There is tendency to look for reasons to leave people out, rather than to look for positive aspects to include them in. Such things as bad writing, too many job changes and an address on the wrong side of town can cause applications to be discarded at the outset. Later, job-relevant experiences and hobbies are important as are relevant job skills and education (Wingrove *et al.*, 1984). If an individual's personality shines through from an application form with interesting or unusual activities, their chance of at least being further considered has been shown to be greater.

A recent study shows another unwitting discrimination in the use of application forms. The Institute of Manpower Studies has shown that illiterates are seen to suffer disproportionately in job seeking because they cannot read and fill in the forms. About one in six people are thought to be at risk in this way (*The Guardian*, 7 October 1991).

Curriculum vitae

The CV or resumé is an important component of the selection process; in many cases it forms one-third of the process and in almost all cases it represents the initial hurdle at which the majority of applicants good, bad and indifferent will fall. In the light of its significance, it is not surprising that there is an abundance of advice from practitioners and teachers on how to assemble resumés. There are even software packages dedicated to the production of attractive resumés. There is general agreement that the two most important sections are education and previous job experience. In terms of information presented, it is preferable to say what you were doing rather than where you were at. It is important to emphasise skills acquired and accomplishments achieved.

The CV reader or sifter may use these sections to make highly subjective and inaccurate estimates of the applicant's standing on a number of crucial attributes. The application sifter attempts to match the applicant's accomplishments to job requirements, especially relevant training and experience in activities connected to the job. The fact that the person may be a sad failure in these activities is not apparent from the application form. The applicant's competence and social standing is judged from the school or college's reputation and the level of qualification obtained. Again, this is a characteristic of an institution and a very dubious one at that; it says very little about the person. However, if you have been to Eton or Benenden, it is useful. Motivation and persistence are judged from such things as length of time spent in a given activity or previous job, consistency of goal direction and reasons for changing jobs (Pibal, 1985).

Another aspect of resumé or CV screening features the idea of attribution, which is becoming more relevant in selection in recent years. When people read CVs, they attribute relevance and power to various elements and it has been found that the attribution depends on the job in question. Recruiters use an implicit (in their head and not specified formally) job requirements model. If an attribute is thought more relevant for the job, it will be rated more highly and if the job is different, the ratings change. Biographical items are generally seen by recruiters to indicate ability and almost all are thought to indicate motivation in some way. Items which are thought to represent motivation most are thought to be the most useful (Brown and Campion, 1994). One thing you may conclude from this is that sending round the same old CV from place to place is not going to get you very far. Try to make your CV job specific!

Weighted Application Blanks and biographical data

Several trends in psychological theory have given us the idea that 'the best predictor of future behaviour is relevant past behaviour'. Many influences and research results have all suggested that people are fairly consistent in their behaviour and in the main they do not change very much, even from childhood on. For example, we could cite longitudinal evidence in developmental psychology, the relative ineffectiveness of psychotherapy and the limited effects of schemes to rehabilitate criminals as supporting the idea that people's habits are very difficult to change unless their environments also change radically.

The idea of behavioural ecology is useful here (Lerner, 1991). People function in 'embedded contexts'. We both shape and are shaped by our environments. Developmentally, we learn the contexts in which we have to operate and we adapt our behaviour to suit these, in accordance with the basic traits and abilities that we have. As more or less arrogant human beings, we think we have freedom of choice, but in fact our choices are first of all constrained by where we are situated, then secondly, significantly influenced by the details of that environment.

In selection situations, the information that people want more than anything is the history of the person's recent work performance. They have learned through bitter experience that leopards really do not change their spots. Much of this information is gathered by phone calls to previous employers, but they are not always free to speak openly about people. Sometimes an employer is desperate to get rid of a member of staff and will not feel too upset if someone else takes over the problem of a poor worker.

There is a distinction between application forms, weighted application blanks and biographical data questionnaires. Application forms ask for factual history of applicant's work history, qualifications and experience. The weighted application blank surveys a broader set of similar data concerning previous experience, education, etc. The information is usually directly job related and factual. When it comes to scoring the form, each item is given an empirical weight derived from percentage methods on the existing workforce, e.g. horizontal percentage method is a relatively simple method and is commonly used. Bio-data forms ask an even broader range of questions and are more like a personality test, in parts. They may ask about attitudes to work and preferences for different activities. They require a higher level of statistical sophistication at the scoring and interpretation stage.

Horizontal percentage method

Personnel files are examined to identify successful and unsuccessful employees according to various criteria as turnover or absenteeism and a particular criterion measure is chosen, such as job tenure. Although you may think that this is not relevant in today's employment situation, it still is, for example in a recently opened leisure centre (which I attend), one-third of the staff appointed left for various reasons of dissatisfaction inside the first twelve months of operation. Next, the personnel files are searched to identify two groups of workers those who left and those who remained. The application form information from the personnel files is then examined to pick out questions and answers (variables) that differentiate the two groups. We could divide the workers and ex-workers into graduate and non-graduate as shown in the table below.

Item	Groups	Stayed	Left	Total	%	Weight
Qualification	Degree	20	20	40	50	50
	No degree	45	15	60	75	75

Individual items from the application form are then weighted, according to the extent that members of the successful and unsuccessful groups possess them. Weights vary, reflecting the importance of particular answers in apparently accounting for success. For example in the above case, non-graduates tended to have a higher prevalence of staying with the company. Applicants' answers over a number of questions are converted into numbers and multiplied by weights to produce a total score. This score can be cross-validated on another sample or, as is often the case, on a part of the workforce who were left out of the original exercise. The question being, does the weighted score derived from the application form predict success in another group just as it did in the first group?

Bio-data

The use of bio-data goes back quite along way; for example, Siegel was constructing biographical questionnaires in 1956 for use with student samples. The bio-data questionnaire method seeks more personal information about previous history, opinions, family background, preferences, hobbies, etc. The format employed is usually multiple choice-type questions. Some of this kind of information cannot be verified. Data is often classified into 'soft' and 'hard', the latter being verifiable. In fact, studies have shown that both soft and hard items perform equally well as discriminators, so it is not a point to worry about except in relation to the question of falsification.

Owens and Schoenfeldt (1979) initiated a study of student types, which was later carried on longitudinally by others. Students were categorised on the basis of their bio-data questionnaire into a number of distinct behavioural types. When the students were returned to in adult life, the type categorisations proved to have stood the test of time, in the sense that their career outcomes were very much in line with their original type. For example, one of the types for females was 'Cognitively Complex Achievers', and they went far in their career and tended to be least likely to have families. A high percentage of predictions based on the types were found to be reasonably accurate.

One of the leading researchers into bio-data, defines it as follows: 'biodata permits the respondent to describe himself in terms of demographic, experiential and attitudinal variables presumed or demonstrated to be related to personality structure, personal adjustment or success' (Owens, 1976). Or in other words, it is the aim of bio-data questionnaires to provide a description of an individual's life history by means of a retrospective self-report, in an objectively scorable format.

Fleishman in 1988 referred to bio-data as one of the new frontiers in the area of performance prediction. In a world where employers have been taken to court for discriminatory selection on the grounds of age, sex, race and even looks, it is not surprising that they would use a method which can at least be proved to be fair, provided the questions are tested for bias and provided the results can be shown to be job related. The latter two tasks are usually manageable.

Weighted application blanks or bio-data were being used by 11 per cent of US companies in 1983 and the number is growing. In Britain their penetration has been significantly less, around 5 per cent according to Robertson and Makin (1986). Smith and Abrahamsen (1992) found 4 per cent of companies in Britain and up to 8 per cent in Germany stated that they used bio-data methods. In Ireland, their use is almost negligible around 3 per cent.

There will always be a natural ceiling on the use of bio-data methods, as they need large samples of recruits, regular large recruiting cohorts, and some statistical expertise and an investment in the method, which is not easy for many managers to understand. They tend to be used in the forces, police, insurance sales forces and banks.

Reservations in the use of biographical methods

Although the increasing popularity of this method is partly due to the employment equality and antidiscrimination legislation, an opportunity for discrimination still exists in bio-data, particularly on social class lines. Differences have been shown between the sexes, but the racial discrimination issue is less problematic.

Provided questions are job relevant, it is much harder to be accused of unfair practice with this method than with any other. However with bio-data, the questions are not all job related in the sense of content, though they may be statistically. Often questions are about attitudes to work and supervision, interests and hobbies, economic beliefs and early life experiences and choices. Such topics are like a red rag to a bull in certain quarters. Some people would like to have us believe that there is no difference between people and everyone is the same. In which case, why have selection at all? Certainly they do not want performance measurement and psychological testing, as it reminds them of discrimination. It has to be emphasised that choosing between people is a blatant act of discrimination and nothing more. The important point is whether the grounds of discrimination are realistic, fair and relevant.

- *Realistic*: Do all the applicants have a reasonable chance of displaying the criteria in some degree?
- *Fair*: Given what they display, are people treated on the merits of this and not on some hidden variable of influence?
- *Relevant*: Are the criteria that people are being asked for of proven or arguable relevance to the job or company?

Of course bio-data results should not be used to determine who gets a job. They should be used as a first stage in a screening process which leads into relevant aptitude testing, interviewing, then job sample tests and final interview.

Biographical data taken directly from CVs or resumés can be used in a job-relevant way by recruiters. Most resumés can be divided into three general sections, education/work experience/interests, activities and honours, and they tend to be fairly similar in the information they cover. Biographical information can be assessed as an indicator of attributes which are thought to be desirable for the job. Those which are more desirable are rated more highly. Studies of how recruiters respond to different kinds of bio-data items have been carried out. Most studies have been done in the United States in the area of college recruitment.

Most research on bio-data has focused on empirical studies of criterion validity from highly structured, bio-data questionnaires and less on the resumé type of bio-data information. Brown and Campion (1994) studied how recruiters could use resumé information directly. They constructed twenty-two categories of items from resumés and from interviewing recruiters in a variety of companies. Many items were judged to represent abilities and almost all items were judged to represent motivation. Attributes used were language, mathematics, physical, interpersonal, leadership and motivation. Each item was judged for overall use for making judgements of a person's standing on these attributes. Items which were thought to reflect motivation were also rated as the most useful.

A second study by Mael (1991) showed that recruiters use a job requirements concept implicitly, as item use varied by job; bio-data items were used to judge abilities, but more than that perceptions of what bio-data items indicate showed consistency among recruiters. Certain items were perceived as more useful than others for forming impressions.

Approaches to constructing items

Items for bio-data questionnaires can be deliberately constructed beforehand by several methods, e.g. the biographical essay method was used by Russell *et al.*, (1990), in a study which constructed a bio-data questionnaire in the US Navy. Other approaches use job-related concepts, and get supervisors to talk in general about the background and interests of successful employees. Drakeley *et al.* (1988) suggest distinguishing between items which ask about achievement, motivation and background. This probably helps to get a clearer conceptual basis to items and ensures a good coverage of the possible areas. In a rational approach, the constructor conceives of the ideal candidate for the job and imagines what that person might be like in terms of interests and background. Of course he or she might be entirely mistaken, but only time will tell. There is very much a trial and error aspect to the business of questionnaire item writing.

Methodological problems

Transportability refers to the question of whether a bio-data questionnaire and its accompanying scoring cut-offs can be used in a different company or even country. This is a problem which must be answered empirically. Recent evidence suggests that they can be used in other cultures, provided the cultural differences are small. It is back to the question of the ecological influences on behaviour. Shrinkage of validity over time has been thought to be a problem, but there is now evidence recently that this may not be such a problem. It is more likely to be a problem where samples are small and the validity was due to chance in the first place. In relation to bio-data, falsification involves giving answers to bio-data questions which the applicant thinks the employer is looking for. It is vital to protect the answer keys, or else the method becomes totally useless in no time. Practically all bio-data questionnaires will be sent by post to the applicant's home. It is therefore possible and in some cases inevitable that the applicant's mother will complete it for her idle son. Having them completed again, perhaps in short form when the candidate comes for interview, is the only way around this problem.

Bio-data leans heavily on psychometric methods, such as item analysis and cluster analysis, to establish meaningful groups of items, just as in the case of personality questionnaires. Questionnaires can be validated later by the use of factor analysis and discriminant function analysis.

Childs and Klimoski (1986) carried out a factor analysis of a seventy-two item bio-data questionnaire and they found five factors: social orientation, economic stability, work ethic, educational achievement and interpersonal confidence. In a general sense, such variables can have considerable face validity to the job situation and can be further strengthened in their validity after the selection has been carried out by correlating them with certain performance criteria.

Empiricism versus theoretical rationale

The charge of raw empiricism against theoretical rationale is often levelled at the bio-data approach. People tend to be prejudiced against it because of the uncertainty, i.e. it does not seem to make a lot of sense. In the empirical case, it is only what correlates with what, and these correlations may only arise by chance, unless there has been a replication study. The rational method makes more sense, but the rationale may be wrong. In a comparison between empirical and rational methods of using bio-data, Mitchell and Klimoski (1982) stated that the rational approach was not so good at prediction, but showed less shrinkage.

Validity

An important approach to validating these methods is cross-validation. This usually includes establishing prediction equations on one sample and then examining if these equations are similarly effective on a second sample. This can also apply within one sample which is divided into a developmental group and a 'hold out' group, the latter being used to test the equations developed using the data of the first group. This is the main way of validating bio-data within an organisation.

A number of large-scale reviews of validity have been carried out since Dunnette in 1972, the latest being by Mumford and Stokes in 1992. Average validities are quite high, from 0.25 to 0.38. In Reilly and Chao's comparison of the validity of many techniques over a large number of separate studies, the criterion-related validity for bio-data ranged from 0.32 to 0.46, which is a respectable level.

Hunter and Hunter (1984) in their review of alternative predictors of job performance, say that only bio-data reaches anywhere near the levels of cognitive tests. Bio-data methodology is almost as valid as cognitive tests and it offers a different perspective independent of the cognitive test (Stokes and Reddy, 1992).

It has been suggested that the reason for the apparent high validity of bio-data is the correspondence between bio-data and criterion data (point-to-point correspondence) (Asher and Sciarrino, 1974), or 'success breeds success'. That is, the behaviours that score well on bio-data are the same or similar to those shown at work, which raters of performance unconsciously pick up on when making ratings. Somewhat in support of this is the finding that bio-data questionnaires are good predictors of ratings, but less good at predicting objective measures of achievement (Drakeley, 1989). The reliability of bio-data questionnaires is usually quite high, figures around the 0.8–0.9 mark for factors, though less for individual items have been reported.

A recent meta-analysis carried out by Rothstein et al. (1990) looked at 79 American organisations and 11 000 supervisor jobs, and found a mean prediction of job performance of 0.33. These findings related to a particular instrument commercially used in the United States, the 'Supervisory Profile Record' (Richardson et al., 1981). Another meta-analytic review by Bliesener (1991) showed a much wider range of validities from –0.05 to 0.62, depending on samples studied and criteria used the figures varied widely. Hough (1984) has used an 'accomplishment record method' which correlate highly with job performance. In a study of 329 lawyers, she concluded that the method worked, was fair and was not discriminatory against women or minorities. Cascio (1976), using a weighted application blank method, has shown that quite accurate predictions of job tenure are obtainable. Cascio states that when proper procedures are used, the personal history data method gives very good predictions of future work behaviour.

It could also be very economic in use. For example, in predicting performance effectiveness within seven Navy occupational groups, just four life history items yielded cross-validated Multiple R of 0.33 in 7932 men and women (Hoiberg and Pugh 1978). Vineberg and Joyner (1982) review a number of military applications of bio-data and conclude that validity coefficients of predicting job performance are around 0.20–0.29. Drakeley *et al.* (1988) say that bio-data proved to be a highly valid predictor of job performance and turnover in a study of 700 Royal Navy officers. Scores were weighted on a per cent method in relation to training course grades as a criterion. Predictors of withdrawal, for example, included orientation to science rather than arts, stable home background and membership in uniformed organisations as a youth. A couple of examples of bio-data items the first given by Cureton in study of predicting success in flight training is that the item 'did you make model aeroplanes as a child' was as good a predictor as the whole Air Force test battery in World War II. Also, 'attendance at a circus while a child' was a good predictor of door-to-door salesperson's success (Appel and Fineberg, 1969).

Assessment centres

Assessment centres are a relatively recent innovation in personnel selection. They are particularly useful in management selection. They owe their origins to organisations such as the Army and Navy and to the large American corporations. They are now frequently used in organisations such as the Police and the Post Office. Apart from their efficacy, which has been well established, they also have the appearance of thoroughness and, usually, fairness.

The basics of an assessment centre are that individuals are brought together in a particular location where specialists have set up situations, mainly of a problem-solving kind, and where trained raters are standing by with predetermined rating methods to rate the applicants. The tasks and situations have generally been devised on the basis of job analysis (Byham, 1980). In fact, it is recommended that there is a specific relation between job analysis and job sample-type exercises in the assessment centre. Though it should be noted that not all assessment centres need to be specifically job related. If they are going to be used in a selection/promotion context as opposed to a personal development context, then they certainly need to contain a high degree of job relatedness in their exercises in order for them to be effective. Centres process from six to twelve people at a time; the ratio of assessors to subjects varies from 3:1 to 1:1. It has been noted that assessment centre validity is improved if they are well organised and there is careful quality control (Smith and George, 1992). The raters need to be carefully nurtured through good quality training, regular feedback sessions and monitoring of ratings.

Origins

Assessment Centres were first used in industry by the American Telephone and Telegraph Company in order to generate information for use in employee development and in promotional decisions. They were also used quite early on by the War Office Selection Boards in Britain and by the OSS in the United States to recruit and train spies. An example of an exercise was that each individual had to devise a cover story and stick to it under all sorts of pressure.

What is assessed?

Getting people together with their peers for extended time periods is obviously going to give a much better opportunity for observing a wide range of behaviours which cannot normally be seen at an interview or assessed by a test. In particular, how people interact, deal with conflict and settle arguments or approach problems can be judged. How they actually set about work can be observed, i.e. whether they work in bursts or steadily throughout a period, whether they are planful or impulsive, etc. Characteristics often assessed for managerial and executive jobs are work motivation, leadership ability, interpersonal skills, administrative skills, career orientation and ability to perform under stress (Jewell and Siegall, 1985).

As an example, the following are the dimensions assessed in a British assessment centre: problem investigation, problem solving, planning and organising, interpersonal sensitivity, influencing skills, assertiveness, oral communication, written communication and flexibility (Crawley *et al.*, 1990). The emphasis here is on problem solving and interpersonal behaviour. Much of managerial work is basically problem solving and then communicating and supervising the solution to problems by staff, so assessment centres ought to be pretty useful in selecting managers if they are properly conducted.

Applications

As well as being used in selection, assessment centres also have considerable applicability for other purposes, such as stimulating self-development and more effective career planning through heightened self-knowledge. There are also applications in which assessment centre reports are combined with in-house training schemes. This gives the opportunity to capitalise on up-to-date knowledge of the employees and on their motivation to change. They are also useful in personnel resource planning. Large organisations can use the results to find and develop suitable staff from within their present complement. In other less direct ways, the payoff for the firm is likely to be worth the expense. There is the considerable saving in cost in avoiding wrong decisions. This is particularly true in the appointment of managers and trainee managers, where a great deal of money is often invested in training and developing the successful candidates. A recent utility analysis of the Home Office selection for police promotion concluded that the savings were in the order of £0.5million when compared with interview selection, for example. There are also individual payoffs in terms of self-development and career planning, which are considerable though difficult to quantify. Assessment centres have several spin-off effects which have nothing to do with their original primary purpose. For example, managers who are trained as assessors for the purpose of an assessment centre benefit in various interpersonal judgement and communication skills applicable to situations outside of the assessment centre. That is, the effect of taking part as judges heightens their own interpersonal sensitivity and perhaps their knowledge of human behaviour (Lorenzo, 1984). This is similar to the effect of introducing psychometric tests to a firm, discussed previously. People are made to think more about what they are looking for in staff and this has the effect of improving their ability to recognise these characteristics and develop them in themselves and others.

The reliability of assessment centres has been shown to be quite high overall. Substantial increases in reliability have been achieved where there is significant training of observers. Companies which have full-time assessment centres or specialist firms which run them have the best record, as far as reliability is concerned. Interrater reliability is the extent to which different raters agree on their rating of an individual on a characteristic and this is the main focus of assessment centre reliability. But just because people agree does not necessarily mean they are right, nor does it mean that the assessment centre is doing a useful job. We also need to have validity.

Ritchie and Moses (1983) showed that the assessment centres ratings of 1097 women managers were significantly associated with career progress seven years later. This is of course an indication of predictive validity. The conclusion of Cascio and Sibley (1979) was that there was sufficient evidence for the criterion-related validity of assessment centres to warrant further research and usage of them. Gaugler *et al.* (1987) reported the results of putting together a large number of validity studies on assessment centres (meta-analysis) and found a mean validity coefficient of 0.47 which is very high. In this case, some reservations are necessary, as the range and quality of the assessment centres was considerable and assumptions about methodological control, etc., are difficult to justify. So perhaps this result is not so impressive as it seems.

The crucial aspect of an assessment centre is the rating process. Efforts have been focused on how this can be improved in terms of accuracy and consistency. There is little evidence to suggest, for example, that psychologists make better raters than specifically trained managers. Assessment centres benefit, like training, by being job- and company-specific. Where people know the jobs, and work with existing staff, they have a better grounding for making the right judgements when it comes to the assessment centre. But how do people make judgements? A major issue which is common to all situations where people make judgements on others is the question, what are the judgements based on? It has been shown that assessors can be judging people on different criteria and also are often using only one or two criteria. A factor analysis of the judgements of raters showed that they used only two underlying dimensions, one of which was a global positive versus negative view and the second, which was less important, was a task-orientated judgement. That is, how well was the person going about the set task? It is not uncommon in judgement situations to find that the 'complexity' of judgement boils down to one or two dimensions and no more (Russell, 1985).

It has been established that using too many dimensions puts too great a strain on assessors (Gaugler and Thornton, 1989). So dimensions should be limited in number and carefully chosen. Emphasis should be on performance dimensions rather than on personal style, for example. Behaviour checklists have been recommended by Reilly *et al.* (1990). These enable people to cover all the relevant areas. They also afford consistency from one time to another and they can be modified and improved, just as psychometric tests can. For example, if there was an area where raters were found over time to disagree more often average, then that area could be further developed to afford more clarity. Or it could be dispensed with and replaced by a more assessable aspect.

Example of an assessment centre

In the Home Office Extended Interview Scheme, variations of which have been running for many years for the promotion of senior police officers, groups of five to six candidates are assessed by three assessors, a chairman, a police officer and a non-police person (e.g. psychologist). The candidates are put through a leaderless group discussion, a committee exercise with a rotating chairperson, a written appreciation of a file of documents and a letter-drafting test in response to a hypothetical situation. They also have to complete some intelligence and job knowledge tests. They are then interviewed twice by panel and by psychologist, and peer nominations from within their assessment group are also considered. Finally, an overall assessment rating is agreed by the panel (Feltham, 1988). In the typical situation, candidates are classified into 40:40:20 suitable, questionable, reject.

Two aspects often predicted from assessment centre ratings are promotion and performance. Some findings suggest that there is higher success in predicting promotion. In the case of the Home Office system, validity was shown with supervisor ratings only and not with rank attained or with training performance.

To a certain extent the success of assessment centres has been questioned and accused of being partly illusory. It has been said that the assessment centre method has a certain headstart in being valid, because behaviours which impress raters and lead to good ratings are the same behaviours which later lead to promotion. Good ratings on the personnel file have a future weight in determining subsequent promotion, that is, people who previously impressed with good performance at the assessment centre's stage are given more favourable treatment when it comes to promotion. This is called 'criterion contamination'. However, the consensus of opinion (Kraut and Scott, 1972; Howard, 1974) says that this effect is minimal and unlikely to operate at the later stages of careers anyway.

Another aspect of contamination is called 'policy capturing'. Assessors may have an unconscious or indeed conscious notion of which qualities are associated with success in the organisation. In their ratings of candidates, they may favour those who show these qualities. They tend to rate more highly people who resemble themselves and who share their own management philosophy or style.

In all selection situations, we need to be aware of the effect the process has on individuals. People can be considerably affected by their participation in assessment centres. Some participants have reported that the effects last for many months and lead to loss of self-confidence and disillusionment with the organisation. It is normally a very stressful process, and there needs to be careful handling of people, especially if they are liable to be rejected. Forward-looking organisations are now putting a lot of resources into sensitive debriefing and counselling. Research has shown that assessment centre failures have lowered self-esteem for some time afterwards (Bourgeois et al., 1975; MacKinnon, 1975). This arises because of the much greater degree of arousal engendered by the process compared to any other. People become much more involved, they have to relate to others, they are trying their best, then they fail. Sometimes the failure is very public in front of their colleagues, who they then see getting promoted above them. No wonder they feel shattered. An interesting study compared candidates' self-ratings both before and after the assessment centre. Participants' self-ratings bore no relation to the assessment centre ratings. Does this mean they do not know themselves very well or perhaps the ratings are invalid? Could it be that training or experience in the sort of things the assessment centre is looking for would improve the level of agreement as we have seen with other applications of the rating method? Well after the assessment centre, the successful candidates' self-ratings improved in that they now agreed far more with the ratings given by the assessment centre. The unsuccessful candidates' self-ratings level of agreement did not improve. They clearly rated themselves fairly positively, whereas the judges thought otherwise (Fletcher and Kerslake, 1992).

It is interesting in this context to understand just how much pressure can be generated in these artificial situations. Experiments in social psychology have shown that people given various roles to play (e.g. prisoners and guards) will become dangerously overinvolved, with harmful effects on some of the participants. Assessment centres can also generate a hothouse atmosphere and people can 'go over the top' or feel they are being dissected and laid bare. They may then have to go into work the following week and face their 'torturers' again.

Integrity tests

Sackett and Harris (1984) in reviewing integrity (honesty) tests concluded that evidence of their usefulness has yet to be produced. In an update in 1989, they state that two approaches have emerged, one being overt integrity tests, one part of which deals with attitudes to theft and dishonesty and the second to admissions of behaviours of theft, etc. The second type of approach is indirect and empirical, in that personality tests have been keyed specifically against known theft criteria in work populations. Absenteeism, turnover and sabotage have been added to theft as criteria. Slora stated that 'findings suggest that 30% to 44% of all employees engage in some kind of theft in the workplace'. That statement is based on an accumulation of findings in various covert observations and admissions after being found out, etc., and also from anonymous staff questionnaires in the United States.

Honesty scales examine employees' attitudes to theft and counter-productivity, also their 'integrity'. Integrity would cover an individual's general attitudes and behaviour in respect of dishonesty. For example:

1. If your best friend cheated in an exam would you report them to the lecturer?

2. If a student obtained a copy of the exam paper would you seek to get a copy for yourself from them?

3. If a lecturer accidentally left this year's exam paper on their desk and had to leave the room for a minute, would you take a peek?

The typical student who is not a paragon of virtue would probably answer NO, YES, YES to these three questions. We could write many similar questions, all varying in the degree of dishonesty, the degree of effort involved in carrying out the behaviour, the number of people affected, the extent of the advantage taken, etc., and come up with a pretty realistic student integrity test. We could then compare its results against actual behaviour in experimental situations and against actual student cheating, obtained perhaps from an anonymous questionnaire about actual dishonest behaviours.

Very few people are really completely honest and have never cheated or borrowed something without putting it back. A good practical test of honesty is to ask someone have they ever stolen anything no matter how small; only really dishonest people will say no.

Integrity tests are designed to predict an employee's resistance to engage in theft and counter-productivity in the workplace. They may also relate to an employee's standing on other behaviours, including drug avoidance, non-violence, safety attitudes and record. These facets of workplace behaviour are, as we have seen, becoming increasingly important to companies.

The validity of integrity tests is high and makes them worth using in many situations. One study compared the honesty test scores of 1073 people who had been hired and subsequently dismissed for various breaches of honesty, sabotage or counter-productivity, with the normative scores of the whole population of similar workers. This found that 23 per cent of the population of people hired for general positions scored below the cut-off standard, but in comparison, 44 per cent of the counter-productive employees did (Jones *et al.*, 1991). In the general validation sample of such tests, 43 per cent of those scoring below the standard on the honesty scale actually admit prior theft, while 4 per cent of those scoring above the standard admit theft. According to Jones 'most employee thefts are never detected, in fact research suggests that only 3% to 5% of dishonest employees are ever detected' (Jones *et al.*, 1990).

In an anonymous survey, a cross-section of employees in 234 supermarkets of 6 companies, 43 per cent admitted some theft of cash and property; the respondents admitted average per head theft of $44 per year and estimated that the average (other) employee steals $1200 per year (Slora and Boye, 1989a). The trade association of the US supermarket industry in a survey announced in 1989 that 52.9 per cent of all supermarket theft was carried out by employees. The average known value of stolen merchandise per incident of theft was $104 derived from an average of 3 known instances of employee theft per store (Slora and Boye, 1989b).

In the above survey, 30 per cent of the companies used integrity testing before taking on staff. The general penetration of honesty tests in Europe is much less than this. Their effectiveness is quite considerable however; for example, a comparison was made between the employees of companies who used tests for honesty with those who did not. The method used a long questionnaire about work behaviour which included only a few questions on theft to disguise the central purpose of the survey. One employee per store was selected at random and the response was anonymous. Results suggested that companies using tests had less than half the reported estimated amount stolen compared to the non-test companies.

A recent survey in Ireland of small businesses revealed that over 60 per cent admitted to having been victims of fraud. One in five were discovered by accident and less than one in ten had been spotted by the companies' auditors. The average cost of these frauds was £3000 each. In only 10 per cent of cases did the firm resort to prosecution. Banks and building societies literally have money walking out the door, from time to time, but they will never prosecute because the harmful effect on customer confidence is too great. Our European laws on mobility of employment have given the professional fraudster a playground of opportunity. Banks of course will rarely employ people from other countries. This is another reason why they favour settled family men and women for their senior jobs.

Common techniques of the professional fraudster or 'white collar' criminal include keeping two sets of accounts, 'now you see it, now you don't'. A company that trusts one individual only to do all the accounting is leaving themselves wide open to being ripped off. The photocopier has become a great boon to the fraudster; copies of invoices and orders can be changed and then recopied. The phoney copy is then filed or sent out and the balance of money or stock is quietly removed by the thief. False companies are set up which then start to order and pay regularly. The goods themselves can be recirculated in the company being frauded and sold again. At a crucial point when trust has been established, a giant order is placed and never paid for. The false company is never heard from again. This is one of the commonest ways in which small businesses are put out of business by robbers. The embarrassment and waste of time involved added to the difficulty of getting a conviction persuade many firms to just write off the loss. Of course you and I and the other honest customers pay in the end. All prices have an inbuilt margin to allow for loss. A survey of British firms in 1992 found that firms were more at risk from managers than from shopfloor workers. Another survey of large Irish firms showed that over 56 per cent of frauds were carried out by employees (Fitzgerald, 1995).

Computer- and video-based testing

Modern technology can assist in the assessment of applicants to a considerable extent. Many tests are now computerised and this is becoming the method of choice in larger assessment situations where many thousands of applicants may have to be processed (Bartram, 1994). The basic principles of computerised testing are the same as far as test construction, validity, reliability and utility are concerned, only the method of implementation is different. But computerised testing has advantages not available to the paper and pencil situation. For example, in-house norms, i.e. standards for the specific company using the test, can be quickly assembled. Weak items can be quickly identified and eliminated. Sophisticated item-writing technology can be used to generate new items based on the established principles of construction. Tests themselves can be individually tailored to the applicant while the test is going on, making testing less tedious and more reliable. Very precise timing can be made of responses and question presentations.

The video camera is now taking a place in assessment. Recruits can be shown video films of situations in jobs and asked to comment on particular aspects of the situation. Medical students are assessed in this way for their clinical abilities. This means that they all get the same question, i.e. patient presented in the same way.

In a research study, newly appointed insurance agents were shown a video of an agent interacting with a client. They then had to respond, in a multiple choice format, to questions about the best strategy to take at points in the interactions. Scores were strongly related to agent turnover and productivity (Dalessio, 1994). The video session was used again after the applicants had had some job experience and gained some familiarity with the situations. One question which this result raises is whether it would work prior to hiring, and this has not been tried (Dalessio, personal communication).

Graphology

Graphology is the attempt to evaluate people's characters from specimens of their handwriting. Formerly this was a kind of game, but now it has become big business. It has even been resorted to by companies to try to predict managerial ability. It has been imported from the continent where it has been popular for years and there are now some English and Irish experts offering a service in this field. Robertson and Makin's survey suggested that some 8 per cent of UK companies took handwriting into account in some situations. The validity of graphology is very low indeed and probably non-existent. Ben-Shakhar *et al.* (1986) compared the analyses of graphologists to those of a psychologist and lay people given the same content-laden piece of writing and found them to be very inaccurate, with validities of around 0.14–0.19. Graphologists and clinical psychologists rated the biographical scripts of a number of bank employees on a list of psychological traits. Both sets of ratings were then compared with the employees' supervisors, people who knew them at firsthand. There was a small level of agreement between both sets of experts and the supervisors. However, before concluding that there is some validity in graphology, read on. When the basic factual information was extracted from the scripts and put into a mechanical formula to predict success at work, the predictions were superior to those of the experts. A further study gave graphologists eight employment categories and the scripts of forty successful professionals and asked them to predict who was in which occupation. Results were no better than would have been obtained by pure random arrangement.

Rafaeli and Klimoski (1983) studied twenty graphologists and found that they tended to agree with each others' assessments to a certain extent, but that their assessments did not agree with some external criteria such as supervisors' ratings of employee behaviour, self-ratings and sales productivity.

Handwriting is an example of a complex psychomotor skill which is fairly consistent in most individuals. If it was a valid predictor of anything useful, it would not be very difficult to fake it. If writing backward sloping does mean you are shy and introverted, if writing really small means you are miserly and anxious, then when we fill in a job application we can all deliberately write big and forward sloping for the occasion. It really has to be said that any company using graphology is plumbing the ultimate depths of self-delusional hocus-pocus and is wasting their shareholders' money. But that will not stop them using it.

Recently, a graphology expert gave the following insights which you might like to examine for validity. In relation to the line on the page, the writing above the line refers to your intellectual aspects, those on the line to your stomach and those below the line to your sexual organs! If 'g', 'y' and 'i' are curved in, you need to be protected. Alienated people have large spaces between their 'I' and the next letter in the sentence. In signatures, if the first letter is huge and the rest of the letters are covered by it, this represents someone who is saying 'don't interfere with me'. If there is a large space between the first and second name, the person may be experiencing problems with their family. If someone writes a note with tiny writing ending with a large signature this is saying 'what I say is of no importance but look at me' (*The Irish Times*, March 1996).

Work and job sample tests

These are used mainly in trade selection. These involve putting the applicant through a realistic job problem or task and assessing, usually by observation, how this was carried out. The most common is the Typing test, but this is only suitable for some jobs. The situational interview mentioned previously attempts to replicate the process verbally.

Role-playing tests are very effective though difficult to arrange and sometimes unfair, as people have different degrees of experience. They have been used in assessing the potential of candidates for telemarketing sales jobs. This is a job in which the representative makes unarranged ('cold') calls to small businesses to persuade them to sample products and services. The work is performed entirely by telephone and clearly calls for a special set of skills and a suitable personality.

In one experiment, the ratees were rated on three scales, which each had behavioural anchors. The scales were called communication, sales ability and social sensitivity. Raters were suitably trained and rehearsed in the scripts used. Job performance criteria against which the ratings were compared included customer service, sales skills, sales results and administrative efficiency. The ratings were combined and correlated with the job performance criteria in a study of the concurrent validity of the method, using existing telemarketers. Validity criteria ranged from 0.24 to 0.44 for the composite criterion (Squires *et al.*, 1991).

In-basket tests

An adaptation of the job sample test in management selection is the In-basket or In-tray test, which again has been shown to be of some use. Fredericksen (1962) is the main originator of the idea. He describes the content of the tray as letters, memos, notes of telephone calls and other material. The subject is given details of the background of the company and their assumed position and is then required to act by producing a suitable response to the information. Assessment of the results produced is normally in relation to job criteria, though what we might call an empirical assessment is possible and has been reported by Lopez (1966), who took the responses of managers and trainees to the same material and found differences. Trainees were more wordy, less aware of the importance of issues, saw fewer implications for the rest of the organisation and tended to resort to complete delegation without retaining some measure of control. Turnage and Muchinsky (1984) found in-basket measures predicted career potential ratings, but not job performance appraisals.

Simulation

Job samples, assessment centres and in-basket tests are all forms of simulation. That is, they are situations where there is a direct physical resemblance to the work setting and tasks. Those which are more directly similar are sometimes called 'high fidelity' simulations because they bear a close resemblance to jobs. We can also have 'low fidelity' simulation which would include job-related questions, situational or theoretical questions asked at interview or by questionnaire, i.e. low fidelity are written or spoken presentations, high fidelity are more like the real thing.

In the area of supervisory personnel selection, early examples of low fidelity simulations include the 'How Supervise' questionnaire introduced in the 1940s (File, 1945). This was quite widely used for a long time. It included a list of supervisory practices and opinions, and examples of company policies. Subjects indicated if they thought the policies were desirable or not and if they agreed with the opinions and practices. A later example is the Supervisory Practices Test (Bruce and Learner, 1958) which consisted of fifty items such as:

> If I make an error assigning work to a group, I would:
>
> > ask for suggestions to correct the mistake
> >
> > explain the mistake so that employees would not lose their respect for me
> >
> > correct the error as soon as it was detected.

Motowidlo *et al.* (1990) recently experimented with a similar instrument. The simulation questionnaire was developed through job analysis, then was successively passed before a number of supervisors and managers in several companies. A fifty-eight item simulation questionnaire emerged from the process. Respondents were given five options for each situation and asked to indicate their most likely and least likely behaviour choice. They scored plus points if their mosts and leasts coincided with those choices of the construction sample. They scored minus if they indicated a most likely where the preferred choice was a least likely, etc.

Results were correlated with a number of performance criteria of an interpersonal and a problem-solving kind as well as overall effectiveness as a supervisor, based on ratings from managers across several companies. Satisfactory predictions were achieved with the instrument. Instruments of this kind have a number of benefits in the selection situation. First, they are clearly job-related and they have shown predictive validity in the job situation. Second, they have convincing face validity for applicants and are not personally intrusive. Third, to date at least they have not shown adverse impact between minority groups or genders. They should therefore be quite usable in selection for reducing applicant pools to manageable proportions. One difficulty is that to construct them properly takes considerable time and effort, as well as cooperation from a lot of busy people. To get this, you need the active support of the top management in the companies concerned.

Projective tests

Projective tests are quite common in clinical psychology. In them, a number of vague or ambiguous stimuli are presented to a subject and they have to complete or react to the stimuli one by one. The stimuli are usually pictures and sometimes words. A projective test used in management selection is the Miner Sentence Completion Test which claims to identify people who reach higher levels in managerial hierarchies by measuring their level of motivation (Berman and Miner, 1985). Though measuring motivation by a test is rather difficult, it may be possible to assess its source rather than its strength or consistency.

Summary

There are many possibilities in selection, giving the human imagination a broad field to to work on, and new methods are being produced all the time. Curricula Vitae are most widely used and perhaps present the greatest opportunity for unfairness to operate. Bio-data and weighted application forms represent cheap and efficient ways of screening out unsuitable people from large samples of applicants. Their validity has been shown to be fairly high. Integrity testing is a growing area with many dangers attached to it. However, dishonesty in the workplace is probably growing at an enormous rate, though the figures are difficult to come by to justify this assertion. Assessment centres are highly effective though expensive, and in some cases their validity may be an illusion.

Activities

1. Discuss the extent to which your behaviour is consistent from situation to situation. Does this have any relevance for your job behaviour and preferences?

2. Get hold of a number of application forms from various companies and compare them, with a view to seeing 'what they are getting at'.

3. Construct a Student Honesty Test and see how your friends respond. Can you differentiate between them using their answers?

Further reading

Drakeley, R.J., Herriot, P. and Jones, A. (1988) Biographical data, training success and turnover. *Journal of Occupational Psychology*, 61, 145–52.

Fletcher, C. (1991a) Candidate's reactions to assessment centres and their outcomes: a longitudinal study. *Journal of Occupational Psychology*, 64(2), 117–28.

Owens, W.A. (1976) Background data. In M.D. Dunnette (ed.) *Handbook of Industrial and Organizational Psychology*. (Chicago, Rand-McNally).

Peterson, N.G. (1990) Specifying domains of biographical data and outlining new areas for selection tests. *Personnel Psychology*, 43, 247–76.

Pibal, D.C. (1985) Criteria for effective resumes as perceived by personnel directors. *Personnel Administrator*, 30(5), 119–23.

Sackett, P.R. and Harris, M.M. (1984) Honesty selection for personnel selection: a review and critique. *Personnel Psychology*, 37, 221–46.

Sackett, P.R., Burns, L.R. and Callahan, C. (1989) Integrity testing for personnel selection: an update. *Personnel Psychology*, 43, 491–529.

Santy, P.A. (1994) *Choosing The 'Right Stuff': The Psychological Selection of Astronauts and Cosmonauts*. (Westport, CT, Praeger).

Psychological factors and unemployment

Focus questions

Why study unemployment in a book about work?

How do people react generally and over time to being unemployed?

Are there any benefits for anybody from unemployment?

What are the financial and health effects?

How does unemployment affect lifestyle and self-esteem?

What should we be aware of from a methodological point of view if we should wish to study unemployment?

Unemployment and redundancy can be studied from various perspectives. There is the actual numerical incidence and the relationship with economic factors; there is the impact on individuals and communities, which include economic, psychological and health effects; there are the responses made to unemployment such as retraining, early retirement and job-finding strategies. All of these involve human behaviour so they all have a more or less psychological component.

Significance of unemployment

It is also reasonable that the psychology of work should pay some attention to the Psychology of Unemployment. Unemployment and work are closely interleaved and in many respects are what we might call codependent on each other. One of the major variables used in evaluating jobs, both by employers and employees, is security. Security is a major job benefit, in exchange for which people are often willing to accept lower wages. Decisions about accepting job offers are highly dependent on the individual's perception of the security of the job weighed against the opportunities offered. For the potential employee, this is essentially a judgement about the chances of becoming unemployed from the given job. In the case of young people, this is less of a consideration than it is with the middle-aged.

Policies in recruitment depend to a large extent on the availability of labour and this includes the unemployed and also those workers who may expect better conditions in another job should they change. Costs of recruiting new staff are affected by the number of people available. If people have to be hunted and seduced from existing employers, this can put upward pressure on the costs of employing staff, e.g. through having to offer higher wage rates and better conditions.

Most working lives will include periods of unemployment or 'rest'. For example, during the 1980s, Denmark experienced one of its highest rates of unemployment, averaging 10 per cent. One in four wage earners experienced a period of unemployment at least once per year. This fact reflects not just the availability of employment, but also its security. People were able to find work, but were soon unemployed again (Iversen and Sarboe, 1988). This illustrates a common problem in most unemployment studies which is that the 'pool' of unemployed people is constantly changing, as people move in and out of work. When we study the unemployed, the members of the group are never the same from one time to the next, unless we are studying the 'chronic' or long-term unemployed, who present a totally different psychological picture.

All those who work will have to consider the prospect of retirement and many will have to accept the fact of redundancy. For many people, work will never be the nine-to-five arrangement with the pension at the end of the road after forty-five years or so of service. There are many alternative ways of 'doing work' and we should consider how these arrangements affect the individuals involved. People can be temporary or part-time. They can be in job-sharing arrangements, can work from home or can be on the road 90 per cent of the time, calling in to a workplace or office once a week or so. There are psychological considerations surrounding all these different formats of working life.

Unemployment, viewed as a problem affecting society as a whole, together with the government responses to alleviate its effects, goes a long way back in history, even to the Pyramids. The provision of work schemes to give employment and income to the poor has a long history (Garatty, 1978). The Pyramids in Egypt may have been one of the first examples of 'workfare'. Certainly the Famine Walls in Ireland and many Highland roadways in Scotland were means of providing work for the poor and unemployed citizens. In those far off days, it was thought 'morally harmful' to give people charity without them doing something in return. Quite often, in Victorian workhouses in particular, the 'something' was often arduous and unpleasant. Moral leaders of the day thought that people would decline into sloth, indolence and depravity if they were not strenuously discouraged from a life of idleness and beggary. Recently in various European countries thoughts of this kind have been re-emerging quite strongly.

Consequences of unemployment

The psychological consequences of unemployment are very significant to the individuals and their families and those responsible for employment and job creation should be fully aware of the effects. Many of us will experience periods of unemployment in our own lives. We should learn to take a positive approach wherever possible and an awareness of the pitfalls may be helpful. The time may come when except for a small minority of key workers, everyone else in the population will either be unemployed or providing a social service to the unemployed. The difference between being at one side or the other of the benefit counter may be an accident of fate in many cases. We may also have a choice to make at various times in our lives which can affect the rate of unemployment. Elections are an obvious example but there are others. We may be in a position to create a job, or share a job or reduce overtime or working hours. We may have to decide between machinery and labour.

In many communities, there are people like the 'Iron Lady', a small business woman, who as the name implies 'irons'. She irons shirts all day long, saving many people from doing a boring household job and she has made a job for herself. There are many people like her who have responded to the demands of the labour market by offering the skills which they have or have learned while working, setting up consultancies of many kinds and providing essential services.

Facts and figures

Unemployment is at a higher level than ever before in most Western countries. At the same time, the number of people in work is greater than ever before. There are changes in the composition of the employed labour force. Many more women are now working and the jobs traditionally done by men with little skill or education have considerably declined in number due to intense mechanisation of farming and construction. In the near future there will be more women than men in the workforce. Earlier retirement and longer education periods have also affected the participation rates. Many people's working lives are shorter than in former years and certainly much shorter than was the case for their parents.

In most European countries, around one-third of the unemployed will have been more than one year out of work and around one-fifth to one-quarter are more than two years without work. At the same time, substantial numbers of unemployed people are between jobs for one reason or another. There are various ways of defining the term 'long-term unemployed', but usually this has been defined as being out of work for twenty-seven weeks or more on a continuous basis. The more insoluble problems of unemployment are usually presented by this group of people and their families. It has been said that unemployment becomes 'a way of life'. Self-esteem declines, motivation to find work declines and acceptance of a very low but liveable form of existence is common.

Unemployment is also rather selective as to who it affects; there have always been considerable variations in its impact. For unskilled non-agricultural workers, the rate has only fallen below 25 per cent in one census since 1926 and for the upper middle classes it has only gone above 3 per cent on one occasion (Breen, 1990). Thus the actual incidence of unemployment is moderated by a number of social variables. Young people are more likely to be unemployed than older people. In Australia, for example, higher rates have been found among young women, aborigines, those from minority ethnic backgrounds, the disabled and those living in working-class suburbs (Daley, 1983). Similar patterns are found throughout Britain and Europe.

The children of people with lower skills and income have greatly reduced opportunities to gain employment. In the real world, where vacancies occur in companies, those working there already are the first to know about them. They go home and tell their relatives and friends and probably try to put in a word for somebody with the personnel department. Thus whether someone belongs to an employed or an unemployed community or family will have an effect on determining their chances of finding a job.

In many societies, what has been called a 'welfare trap' exists, particularly for lower paid people who fall out of work. The Replacement ratio is the extent to which Social welfare payments replace average industrial earnings, i.e. the ratio of welfare benefits over average pay. If a man is married with two children, the ratio is around 70 per cent and it rises to 100 per cent where there are four children. Moves are now in train to alter these balances to the eventual disadvantage of the non-working population. Another way to look at the economic benefits is to consider the extent to which unemployment pay replaces previous wages averaged across all recipients. This ranges from 64 per cent in Denmark to under 10 per cent in Italy. In most countries this replacement percentage has increased from the 1970s to the 1990s, with the exception of Britain, Germany and Belgium. The greatest improvement is shown by Portugal. The Irish figure rose from around 20 to 30 per cent in the same period (*The Economist*, 25 May 1996).

There is a wide range of 'apparent' advantages to being unemployed, such as fuel allowances, rent rebates, cheap tickets for certain events, free medical treatment, travel concessions, etc., but the long-term effect is poverty and all that this entails. The advantages are to some extent illusory and the process which people have to go through to obtain them can be tedious and drawn out, almost as if they were designed to make the applicant give up. Life on welfare demands the development of a mind-set containing dogged determination and the ability to withstand treatment which most of us would find humiliating. It is no coincidence that the use of alcohol and mind-altering substances is high in the communities at the bottom of the employment ladder.

People who are most likely to suffer unemployment, i.e. the unskilled and poorly qualified, tend to have larger families. The welfare rules and their implementation may even indirectly encourage them to have larger families. The children concerned will have poorer educational opportunities and a dangerous cycle is set going. The answer to that dilemma in social policy terms is to vastly improve the educational and housing facilities of the population, but in the last few decades relative differences in educational opportunity and access to housing have widened in many European countries.

What tends to be happening, psychologically, is that our attitudes to the unemployed are being changed so that we can feel OK about blaming them. They are stigmatised in effect. Being unemployed and deciding not to work is a sensible economic decision for many people. We should not blame people for making it, rather the fault, if any, lies with our social system which has set the conditions in which such a decision can be made.

General reactions to unemployment

One of the earliest studies of unemployment to use a psychological type of approach was published in Germany in 1933, and finally published in English in the United States and England in 1971 (Jahoda et al., 1971). This has been a very influential volume, cited many thousands of times, and used as an inspirational source by many workers in the field. Data was collected by a number of different methods but all pointing to the same target. This has become known, methodologically, as 'triangulation'. Psychologists have recognised that the form of a question often determines the content of an answer. Similarly the way data is collected, e.g. by face-to-face interview, by paper and pencil questionnaire, by observation, by examination of documents, e.g. letters, or by participating in some event, determines the kind of answer obtained to the research question. In Marienthal all of these methods and more were employed. The effects of unemployment were found to be many and various. Negative, positive and ambivalent states coexisted. Many of the findings are the same as those of today's investigations. Unemployment was found to be associated with many negative psychological reactions, such as demoralisation, apathy, depression, disorientated time structure, reduced activity levels and a decline in psychological well-being, which were followed by the experience of extreme poverty. The results were not welcomed by the German Government of the time and many copies of the book were consigned to the flames (Fryer, 1992).

In 1981, British Steel closed its plant in Workington with the loss of 3000 jobs. In an average year, deaths among the steel workers past and present would have amounted to two or three, mostly of retired men. But eighteen months after the closure there were 98 deaths, all of people under 65, and 2 were young people who committed suicide. The unemployment arising from plant closures may be temporary, depending on the setting. Greater problems are experienced where the affected workforce is less skilled and older. The geographical isolation of the community and the sources of alternative work are major factors in the impact of closures (*The Guardian*, March 1992).

Meaning of work

The impact of unemployment varies considerably with the way people perceive work and with the differences in what they get out of their work. These factors may vary from individual to individual, as with Warr's description (see below), or at a more global level across groups. The sociological perspective maintains that the effects of unemployment will vary with the way in which different occupational groups experience work (Ashton, 1986). The effects of unemployment can be mitigated by the individual's family and social environment, including the extent to which unemployment is shared by others. Whether there is a contrast effect of people living next door earning good money and being apparently much better off, is also a factor. Personal vulnerability is also important in whether the person will rise above the crisis. If the experience of unemployment is common in the family background of the individual, then they may not feel particularly unusual.

Benefits of work

Work contributes a number of benefits to the individual, some of which are psychological rather than physical and also less apparent. These benefits have been called 'vitamins' (Warr, 1987) and are as follows:

1. Opportunity for control
2. Opportunity for skill use
3. Externally generated goals
4. Variety
5. Environmental clarity
6. Availability of money
7. Physical security
8. Opportunity for interpersonal contact
9. Valued social position.

The effects of unemployment include the loss of these benefits, depending on whether the job had them in the first place of course. Loss of work is more than just an economic event; its effects impinge on the individual's overall well-being. According to Jahoda, a lifelong contributor to this topic, it is the loss of the latent functions of work which cause the psychological deterioration rather than the loss of pay itself. Jahoda's view would include the concept that our reaction to loss of work is tied in with our own view of the purpose of work; i.e. money, activity, variety, temporal structure, social contacts and personal identity. Research in the area shows that, if a person's identity is very much tied up with their job, then they suffer greatly at its loss, whereas if the job was just a means of adding to an already adequate family income, the loss can be easily accepted (Jahoda, 1982).

The people most seriously affected by unemployment are usually those in the middle-age range. They are used to fairly high levels of employment, they have high feelings of job commitment and they have dependants who are still at school or college. Young people, especially if they are still living at home, are least affected. They tend to have an active social network, a sharing of problems, plenty of diversion and sometimes enough money for at least some form of social life (Breakwell *et al.*, 1984). Numerically though, the age group 15–24 experiences unemployment rates almost double those of older workers in Europe, Australia and the United States (Winefield *et al.*, 1993). They have also not developed a pattern of working and have managed to live without the 'vitamins' of work or they get them elsewhere. The older age group whose families have grown up may be somewhat less vulnerable. They can view unemployment as a form of early retirement and accept it provided they have no financial strain.

In general, across the broad sweep of the population, there are several main consequences following from the state of unemployment. These include a feeling of material loss due to the lack of money, combined with the effects of living in a consumerist society. Then there is the reduction in the range of social contacts caused by the restricted social network of the unemployed compared to employed people. The person's self-concept may change and the other people's reactions to the person can be affected by the social stereotyping of the unemployed (Archer and Rhodes, 1993). Many studies document the association of unemployment with a lack of feelings of psychological well-being and with mental and physical disorders, lack of self-esteem and social isolation. There is a lot of autobiographical and case history evidence which backs up the observation that there is 'the gradual but cumulative erosion of life through unemployment' (Whelan *et al.*, 1991).

Paradoxical benefits of unemployment

It is perhaps an odd fact that in certain ways, although unemployment is a social evil and is generally to be avoided, it can bring some kind of benefits to some people. The opposite of unemployment, which is growing and booming employment, brings with it various social and personal problems. In times of boom, more money becomes available and people spend more on drinking alcohol. This can lead to its abuse and other socially negative behaviours such as crime, marital problems and accidents. Car accidents increase significantly as the roads become busier with commuters and people are in more of a hurry to get places. Work accidents inevitably increase as there is more work and more pressurised work going on (Dooley and Catalano, 1988). Industrial toxic waste and hazards of various physical kinds increase. So in a broader context, society has a cost to bear for high employment. This is a point that is rarely referred to in the search for employment opportunities for the workforce. It is of course tied up with the environmental movement, associated politically with the Greens.

A group of people who benefit economically from high unemployment are those on fixed incomes, such as pensioners. Inflation is their biggest enemy, eroding their savings and the buying power of their pensions. Unemployment slows the rate of inflation and so helps them maintain their standard of living.

Some studies have also shown that mothers who work actually feel better once they can no longer work due to a recession, but have to stay at home and become more involved in the homemaker role. Such women are often in low-paid jobs with poor levels of satisfaction anyway. They manage to adjust to the lower income and often get more out of staying at home than they do fighting their way through traffic, leaving children at minders and doing a possibly boring or stressful job.

The idea that some people find unemployment liberating has been suggested and in order to examine this question Fryer and Payne (1984) carried out a study which attempted to identify positive reactions to unemployment. After much searching in a large industrial town, they found eleven unemployed people who reported that they found unemployment liberating. Each of them was involved in voluntary work on a regular time schedule and all were relatively well-qualified and educated people. They were not unskilled or blue-collar workers, for whom unemployment is more sudden and more likely. The difficulty they had tracking down such people may speak volumes for the negative effects that unemployment has on people's lives.

Phase model

The phase model of the impact of unemployment dates from the 1930s and has not been much developed since. It is in fact the kind of model which is found in various transaction-type situations, such as disasters and bereavements. In the case of the redundant worker, they may not have the beneficial effects of group support, etc., which people in other situations of loss often have. The model says that the unemployed would normally go through the phases of shock, optimism, pessimism, and finally acceptance or fatalism (Eisenberg and Lazarsfeld, 1938).

However there is a lack of direct confirmation for a stage theory of bereavement, just as there is for a stage process of adjustment to employment loss. Archer and Rhodes (1987) concluded that the stage theory was not widely supported by evidence in a consistent way. The stages tended to be seen in data after the event, and that in ongoing longitudinal studies they have not been so evident. The best that could be said was that 'the empirical data on reaction to unemployment can be viewed to some extent as a broad pattern of change from shock, disbelief, optimism to some form of realisation and acceptance'. Such explanations tend to overlook the effect of individual differences in reactions to situations. We could not expect everyone to react in the same way. It would be useful to know what determines individuals' reactions.

Financial effects

One of the more obvious effects of unemployment is usually that it drastically reduces the income of those affected. We would expect that this would have follow-on effects which would be quite significant. However, an examination of the research shows that the situation is not as simple as that.

Ullah (1990) studied the level of income among unemployed youths and related it to their feelings of well-being. The findings suggested that it was not the actual reduction in the level of pay that was important but rather the level of financial strain felt by the subjects, i.e. not how poor they were, but how poor they felt. Rowley and Feather (1987) showed how increased financial strain is a major factor. Such strain imposes limits on the person's opportunities to shop, travel or purchase entertainment. These effects are themselves related to poorer time structuring in normal day-to-day activities. Time structuring is in effect having something definite to do at a given time on a regular basis. People do not realise how structured their day is until something dramatic happens to show them. Several other studies, including several by Warr's team, seem to confirm this broad conclusion that the actual amount of money available is not directly associated with deterioration in a person's health or well-being, but that it often has an intermediary effect.

However, another set of studies from another perspective does show that the shortage of money is a factor. Looking at the long-term unemployed in a community blighted by unemployment, Whelan et al. (1991) paint a vivid picture of the grinding effect of poverty. In this report they describe how the unemployed gradually become deprived of even the basic necessities, e.g. having only one serviceable pair of shoes. They are eventually unable to provide children with the basic necessities for school, they have to queue and sometimes beg for things, they get resentful at 'unnecessary' spending, finally they give up the struggle and let the effects of poverty do their worst. The life expectancy of the long-term unemployed declines, as does their health and sometimes the effects are seen in the disturbed behaviour of children. The middle-class community sees the rising tide of crime which is generated and respond by blaming and punishing the disadvantaged.

The effects are correspondingly greater where social support is less. The impact of economic stress on mental health increases where there is less support. Separated women with children are among the most seriously affected. Their rates of mental illness and self-harmful behaviour are considerably elevated, as are those for single men. Many of the latter take to serious alcohol and substance abuse and sometimes have to support themselves by crime and drug selling. The rate of suicide increase among young men in their twenties is higher than for any other group in society and in some areas is reaching very worrying levels. For example, taking data from hospital discharges in Scotland between the periods 1981–1983 and 1991–1993, cases of self-poisoning, e.g. taking overdoses, which had rapidly increased during the 1960s and flattened out again in the 1970s, showed a marked increase. The fall in the rate of increase was particularly sharp in the case of young women. But, for the period covered by the study, 1980s–1990s, self-poisoning in men had increased by almost 60 per cent in the ages 15–19 and 20–24 and by 40 per cent in the group 25–29. For women, the increase showed a different pattern, almost 60 per cent in the age group 15–19, but only 26 per cent in the group 20–24 and 4 per cent in the next age grouping. Teenagers of both genders are getting increasingly depressed; and in males this continues, but for women it tails off, perhaps when they start to have babies, and obtain a broader social identity not open to unemployed men (McLoone and Crombie, 1996).

Effects on health

Many studies on the effects of unemployment are cross-sectional. This means that they study a cross-section of the population at a single point in time and compare the results across groups within the sample. The groups in question might be the employed versus the unemployed, or employed professional versus unemployed professional. Differences between the groups are then used to base inferences applied to the wider population.

Many studies show that there is poorer health generally among the unemployed. Health data is always a little suspect, however. It is often the marginally employed and so perhaps the not so healthy who are the first to be laid off. Studies quoting health statistics may be relying on data from an 'abnormal' group. We need to be careful in jumping to conclusions about the consequences that being in a particular group has on something else. It might be the 'something else' which determined the person's belonging to the group in the first place.

There have been many studies of the psychological well-being of cross-sections of the population. For example, Banks and Jackson (1982) administered the General Health Questionnaire (Goldberg, 1978) to 1000 school-leavers at the point of leaving school and again two years later. They found the scores of those who had not found work to have moved in the poor health direction, while those who had found work showed no change in well-being. Finlay-Jones and Eckhardt (1984) noted that 43 per cent of unemployed young people reported depressive symptoms. They found a zero correlation between income and General Health Questionnaire scores. That is, the amount of money available, on its own, was not related to feelings of well-being.

The most recent study of this kind took place in the West of Scotland as part of a longitudinal study on physical and mental health in young people (West and Sweeting, 1996). A 'longitudinal' study is one in which the same people are followed up some time later and the measurements or observations are repeated. Cross-sectional studies done at different times may suggest that while unemployment figures rise, mental health problems increase, but a longitudinal study provides stronger evidence, because the real change in people is observable. Recent evidence has indeed suggested that mental health in young people in general has deteriorated. General indicators of problem experiencing, such as incidence of crime, alcohol and drug abuse, depression, eating disorders and suicidal behaviour, have all increased substantially in the recent decade (Rutter and Smith, 1995). West and Sweeting's study reported quite high levels of general health and mental health problems in young people, contrary to popular views that youth are healthy and happy. Their sample consisted of over a 1000 young people who were interviewed at ages, 15, 18 and again at 21 years. This study allowed the level of health concerns, etc., at the earlier age level to be allowed for when looking at the effects of unemployment on health at the later age levels. Findings were that for almost all measures of well-being, the unemployed young people were significantly worse off than those in work or in higher education. For example, from 7 to 9 per cent of the unemployed people reported making some form of attempt at suicide, compared to 2–4 per cent in the other groups. As the number of unemployment experiences the young person had increased, so did the extent of their mental and physical health problems.

Wider social effects

Evidence has been provided from epidemiological studies. These take incidence figures for any behaviours, diseases or sets of symptoms and contrast them across populations at different times or places or between people in different subcategories. Barling and Handal (1980) found 27.6 per cent of first-time patients in mental hospitals were unemployed, compared to a rate of unemployment of 6 per cent in the community as a whole at the time. This might suggest that unemployment precipitates mental problems. While it certainly does in some cases, not all the unemployed first-time mental patients can put their problems down to being out of work.

Following the recession of 1973–1974, Brenner (1983), and Brenner and Mooney (1983), reported on the broader social consequences of unemployment. Indications were that economic downturn led to a number of consequences which were quantifiable. For example, total mortality increased by 2.3 per cent, suicide by 1 per cent and mental hospital admissions by 6 per cent. Total arrests also increased by 6 per cent. It was concluded that for every 1 per cent increase in unemployment in the United States, there were statistically significant increases in suicide, mental hospital admission, homicides, and stress-related illnesses. These kind of figures are aggregates from a wide range of data collected by different people in different ways. They should be interpreted with caution. Many other factors may be affecting the final figures and the figures themselves are often culled from various State statistics, some of which use different definitions to others.

However, it appears that as unemployment increases so does the mortality rate. There is not a simple cause-and-effect relationship. For example, women who are married to unemployed men also show higher mortality rates (Moser *et al.*, 1984).

Shepherd and Barraclough (1980) investigated seventy-five suicides and found that the person's mental health precipitated work loss in many cases and then the work loss increased their mental problems. A thought provoking point from Platt and Krietman (1984) is the finding that when unemployment is low, the relative risk of parasuicide among the unemployed is high, but it declines when unemployment increases. Platt (1984), in a review of over twenty studies of a time-series type since the 1960s, noted that the majority showed that the rates of unemployment and suicide were closely associated with each other. In a general sense, there is little doubt that a society inflicted with high levels of unemployment, where formerly they were low, will show increased instances of self-harm. Platt (1986) reported that the rate of suicide increases, especially after one month and again after twelve months of unemployment, suggesting a phase effect on mental well-being.

In the Economic and Social Research Institute Reports of 1989 and 1991, the unemployed were five times more likely to suffer psychological distress than those who were employed. Some percentages of those showing psychological distress in various categories were: women 19 per cent, men 15 per cent, widowed 26 per cent and separated or divorced 37 per cent. As a comparison, in Northern Ireland a study by Cairns and Wilson (1984) reported that 26 per cent of the general population were above the threshold for psychological distress, as were 67 per cent of widows of people killed in sectarian violence.

Comparing the employed with the unemployed is not comparing like with like, as there are many prior reasons for being unemployed in the first place which also affect psychological health, so considerable confounding is possible (Bartley, 1988). Some studies have avoided or reduced this autoselection problem by various means. Even when unemployment rates are excessive and many normally regular working people are put out of work, the health differences remain. A Dutch study controlling for prior health problems, still showed a difference in mental health. A telling fact is that many studies have shown that people make rapid gains in psychological well-being when they regain employment.

A study in Denmark compared 1153 men, who worked at the Helsigor shipyard in 1982 and which later closed down, with 441 men, at the Danneborg shipyard which remained open. This showed a pronounced relation between General Health Questionnaire scores and employment status. Also relevant was a feeling of concern about losing a job and this was related to the General Health Questionnaire score (Iversen and Sarboe, 1988).

Psychological effects

Lifestyles

Unemployment is inevitably associated with changes in lifestyle and many of these changes are in the direction of 'bad health'. Many authors have commented on the loss of time structure as one of the most severe results of unemployment. Previous arrangements, lifestyles and habits which may have been ruled by the clock to a large extent are no longer necessary. People have too much spare time and one day is very much like another.

According to some writers on the subject, there emerges a clear life pattern in the case of the long-term unemployed. This consists of a long lie in bed until late morning or early afternoon, staying up late into the night, and avoiding certain places where the employed will be. A kind of self-imposed 'apartheid' attitude develops. Warr (1987) describes alcoholism as an effect of unemployment; the unemployed person was found to drink faster and to drink more at a sitting than equivalent employed people.

Warr and Payne (1983) reported that unemployed people spend more time in social contact with friends, though they have more time in the first place. Unemployed men from the middle classes were more likely to have wives in work than men from working-class backgrounds. So working-class families are likely to experience a greater burden when the main earner becomes unemployed.

Trew and Kilpatrick's (1985) study of lifestyles and psychological well-being among unemployed men in Northern Ireland found that those who had experienced reductions in entertainment and social activities had significantly poorer scores on psychological well-being, as measured by the General Health Questionnaire.

A study by the Economic and Social Research Institute in 1991 took a 10 per cent random sample of the unemployed in Tallaght, a vast suburb of Dublin. Of the sample, 40 per cent had been unemployed for one to three years. The principal problems highlighted were boredom, exclusion from the normal social life of peers and financial hardship. A high level of pessimism was seen, with 34 per cent saying they saw little prospect of obtaining work in the next two years. Set alongside this report, in an almost ironic contrast, was the more or less simultaneous publicity given to one of the main employers in the Tallaght area, which had experienced years of labour–management turmoil. The management had asked, not for the first time in ten years, for the workers to vote on a restructuring plan involving further redundancies and new work arrangements. The workers voted against the scheme, and the company lost its major contract. The workers cited bad and insensitive management as the cause of the factory's problems and they were not prepared to be treated in what they perceived as an unjust way. One year on (April, 1996) the firm announced that it was closing down and 800 people are to be added to the dole queue. In a sense, the workers have been put in the position of voting themselves out of a job. It could be that they have been manipulated so that the plant closure can be seen as 'their fault'. On the other hand, in an area of mass unemployment, probably approaching 70 per cent in some sections, a major employer and a workforce apparently cannot find a compromise to save jobs.

Unemployment leads gradually to poverty and this leads to deprivation of normal lifestyle. Relative to those in their community who are in work, the unemployed have less and less of the things that other people have. Living with such deprivations over a long period of time produces the deterioration in health and mental well-being. Choice is eliminated, safety valves are lost, improvements in circumstances are unlikely, depression sets in, self-care is neglected and diet is poor (Whelan, 1992). According to Whelan's analysis, unemployment, leading to loss of income and to poverty, has its effects on mental health mediated through its effects on lifestyle. Primary lifestyle deprivation includes lack of sufficient heat, lack of variety and nourishment in food, build-up of arrears in bills, having to buy second-hand clothes, etc. Secondary lifestyle deprivation is represented by not being able to save, not having a daily paper, losing the telephone, giving up hobbies, and not being able to buy presents for people in the family. The higher levels of lifestyle deprivation relate most to the higher General Health Questionnaire scores in both the unemployed and their spouses. An observable consequence of such situations is that it is generally the poorest members of the community who are the most avid lottery players. The lottery offers at least a fantasy of release from the bondage of poverty and a fantasy is better than nothing (actually it is often better than the real thing).

Self-esteem

Kelvin and Jarrett (1985) maintained that people think less positively about the unemployed. Glyptis (1989) says that society at large tends to share the politician's ambivalence towards the unemployed. It has been noted that 'being left on the scrapheap' or the feeling of being abandoned is one of the most common phrases used to describe their situation by unemployed people. The unemployed form an identifiable social outgroup who can be relatively easily stigmatised and lumped together as dole scroungers, etc., when in reality only a minority start off that way and most would prefer not to be living off the taxpayer. Numerous studies report that the unemployed have less social self-esteem than employed people (Miles, 1983).

Tiggemann and Winefield (1989) showed that the person's future status in relation to employment could be predicted to some extent while they were still at school. Prior to their leaving school, they got several thousand teenagers to complete questionnaires giving background variables, academic intentions, personality variables, attitude to work and intentions for the future. Future status in terms of being employed, being a student or being unemployed was related to higher levels of achievement motivation, external locus of control and higher self-esteem. The highest scores were those of the employed people and the lowest those of the unemployed. A person's rating of the importance of getting a job also was a good predictor of whether they ended up in the employed group or not. Unemployment was also predicted by a student's ethnic origin, social class background and whether there was unemployment in the family. The strongest associations in the study were with the group who ended up in further education, that is, easiest to predict, based on academic intentions and potential. Findings in this area have been mixed and it is not possible to say that unemployment is directly related to personality, potential or attitudes, as the variables are interactive and affected by other social factors, which in turn affect employment. If your dad is going to get you an apprenticeship or your mum owns a shop, you should have a fairly positive attitude about your future, which in turn will boost your self-esteem, etc.

Dooley and Prause (1995) using data from the United States longitudinal study of youth provided evidence showing that self-esteem (as measured by a short questionnaire) rose in general after the students had left school. However, much higher rises were shown in those who were employed in satisfying jobs. Those who were unemployed had very small rises in self-esteem. This shows that being in work is an essential point of transition from adolescence to adulthood and those who are denied this opportunity have a relatively much poorer view of their own self-worth.

In another study in France and Italy, which is somewhat parallel to the above, Fraccaroli *et al.* (1994) used the idea of a person's Social Self-Description, which was derived from the person's rating of themselves compared to others in terms of availability of money, opportunity for social contacts and psychological well-being, etc. They indicated that youth unemployment is an extremely heterogeneous and varied phenomenon. That is, it is not just one experience, the same for everyone and capable of being simply labelled and put away. Unemployment can be seen as part of a process model in which the young person has to maintain an acceptable social identity as part of the process of growing up. Depending on the existing stage of the individual's identity formation and the environment in which he or she is growing up, unemployment will have different effects on that identity. Alternative identities are required where the work identity is denied due to unemployment. People have to do something to preserve their self-esteem. Pretending they do not want or need a job could be one of them. Or as unemployed actors tend to say when they are not working, they are 'resting'.

Coping

Brenner and Starrin (1988) identified coping orientation and style based on attitudes of mastery and control as a significant moderating factor influencing the ability of unemployment to cause stress, both physical and emotional. That is, there were intervening factors which they discovered in people's attitudes which could reduce the damaging effects on unemployment on morale and self-esteem. They also point out, in an idea derived from Karl Marx, that unemployment can often be associated with high levels of overtime working, and that it is associated with the intensification of labour. From the perspective of the capitalist, unemployment concentrates the mind of the worker, who feels more insecure and so works better. It also allows more output from a smaller workforce. It relieves the upward pressure on wages, reduces inflation, as we have already pointed out and allows our European countries some chance in the almost unfair competition with the child labour economies of the East.

Methodological issues in unemployment research

In reading any longitudinal research studies in this area, we must be aware of possible problems which may affect the validity of the findings. There is bound to be very high wastage because very few people are actually unemployed for more than a year continuously out of any general sample of unemployed people. From time to time most people find at least part-time or temporary positions. Those who do not may have special reasons for being unemployed, i.e. they are musicians, or they are not unemployed at all but working 'on the black', or they may be completely unemployable due to mental or physical problems. There are great differences in vulnerability to long-term unemployment, and gender differences in the acceptability of unemployment have also been demonstrated.

Aggregate time-series studies are weak for several reasons, though they are also useful for other reasons. First, the units of analysis are gross, e.g. years, states and regions, and so they lump together a lot of individually varying figures into one. Second, data is collected from such a wide variety of sources and put together, e.g. hospital admissions come from private and public hospitals, data-collecting methods across different sites are not identical, admissions differ, e.g. first, repeated, chronic, etc. Proper control variables are often not available. So aggregation tends to lump together varied experiences and may produce an unrealistic average, which may not truly represent anything.

There is an effect called 'the ecological fallacy' named by Robinson (1950). When we average out the behaviour occurrences and their supposed causes in a group or community, then make the assumption that the apparent resulting relationship applies to individuals in the group, we can be committing an illogical and spurious presumption.

For example, if we take the case of suicide rates and unemployment, there are many possible explanations and reservations, of which the following are only examples.

1. The suicide figures may be inflated by cases of relatives of the unemployed who are indirectly affected.

2. There may be quite a number of borderline cases who may have been on the verge of suicide, but in the negative atmosphere combined with the prevalent talk of unemployment are pushed over the edge.

3. Other factors which are partly affected by economic recession, such as extent of health and social service provisions may leave vulnerable people more exposed than normal.

These and many other smaller factors will act separately and cumulatively to impact on the suicide rate. But that is a long way from concluding that being made unemployed leads to suicide for a particular individual or for a certain specific group of people.

There is also the fallacy of reverse causation. People with high levels of personal or social problems have an increased likelihood of being unemployed or being made redundant. They are also more vulnerable to psychological disturbance, which may precede a suicide attempt.

Marie Jahoda has been a central figure in the research on unemployment for almost fifty years. She points out that the methods used in this research are usually not the best if we want to find truly valid results. Most studies use questionnaires which are sent out to people. A slight improvement in this is the face-to-face interview using a structured questionnaire with follow-up questions. Both these methods only get at an approximation of reality. People's responses to questions and interviewers are determined by the situation and may not represent their real feelings and behaviour. Yet that is all we have to go on most of the time. There are alternatives which would give a clearer picture, but they are not often implemented. These methods include triangulation and unobtrusive measures.

In the final analysis, 'resigned adaptation' is how most people cope with long-term unemployment. This involves eventual withdrawal from job seeking, limited routines of behaviour and avoiding new situations which may be threatening or potentially expensive. In sum, 'By wanting less, long-term unemployed people achieve less, and they become less' (Whelan *et al.*, 1991).

Summary

Unemployment, retirement or redundancy will affect us all and we need to adopt a strategy early on so that we are in control of the situation and not the reverse. People have reactions to unemployment which are dependent on many different factors. These factors include their surrounding social environment as well as their previous levels of health and mental well-being. Unemployment is generally not good for people, whereas retirement usually is. Despite this, there are some beneficial side-effects of unemployment for a few individuals and for society, though the total effect is undoubtedly on the negative side of the balance sheet. How we view ourselves, what our jobs are and how important they are to us, and our position in a community or family are crucial intermediaries in our reactions to unemployment. Governments and social and business organisations can be more proactive in dealing with unemployed and redundant workers.

Activities

1. Consider the unemployment situation in your area. What is the response of the community and the agencies? How serious is the problem?

2. Ask a person who has been unemployed for a long time how it affects their lifestyle and the opportunities of their family.

3.   **Talk to a selection of different people who have experienced unemployment and are now at work. How do they compare their situations before and after, in terms of some of the things mentioned in this chapter?**

Further reading

Feather, N.T. (1990) *The Psychological Impact of Unemployment*. (New York, Springer-Verlag).
O'Brien, G. (1986) *Psychology of Work and Unemployment*. (Chichester, Wiley).
Warr, P.B. (1987) *Work, Unemployment and Mental Health*. (Oxford, Clarendon Press).
Winefield, A.H. (1995) Unemployment: its psychological cost. *International Review of Industrial and Organisational Psychology*, 10, 170–212.

Stress at work

CHAPTER 13

Focus questions

What is meant by stress at work?

Are you likely to get 'stressed out' and if so is there anything you can do to avoid it?

Are some occupations or people more vulnerable than others?

How can we measure stress?

Can we promote good health and resistance to stress?

What do companies do to help employees cope?

Working to death in Japan

According to a correspondent in Tokyo, the Japanese Ministry of Labour has admitted the danger of a disease called 'karoshi' which is said to be killing up to 10 000 people in the prime of life. This is death by exhaustion, hitherto denied or swept under the carpet. In Japan, the working hours per year are on average longer than in Europe (2150 Japan, 1989 UK, 1957 USA, 1638 Germany). There have been several legal cases and in one of them a bank clerk calculated that in the mid 1980s about 40 per cent of the employees of Fuji Bank got home after midnight (*The Guardian* 26 August 1992).

This is the sort of report that regularly appears in the press. It gives credence to the idea that work is stressful and getting more so as the 'pace of life' increases, foreign competition gets stronger and technology becomes more complex and demanding. At the other end of the scale, however, we are taking more holidays than ever before. The leisure industry is booming. Golf courses, leisure centres and health clubs are springing up all around us. Are we really so stressed or are we having a great time?

The 'stress' concept has been emphasised over the past twenty years by a small group of academics. The result of this effort has been the breathing of life into a flimsy concept, so that not a week goes by in which we do not hear the term being used. On the other hand, but less well publicised, is the opposite or nearly opposite view of some academics, which is that our characterisation of stress is a serious case of mistaken identity. A wide collection of different symptoms and problems have been subsumed by a neat umbrella concept, probably because the concept is short and easy to digest, as opposed to having any validity. The whole idea of stress at work has a high level of public credibility and acceptability; it is also meat and drink for journalists.

There are many alternative explanations for stress. Depression and personality disorder would come top of most lists. Tiredness and inability or unwillingness to work can be helped by various self-inflicted causes such as alcohol and drugs, excessive smoking and excessive proportions of carbohydrates and fats in the diet. Stress can be a cover up for some of these poisons. Numerous environmental problems, many of which have seemingly grown in the last few decades, may have reduced people's overall motivation to work or stick at an unappealing job. These include family problems, housing difficulties, having to travel long distances to work and the effect of seeing neighbours and friends who may be retired, unemployed or disabled, surviving fairly well without the necessity of turning up at a place of work every day for ever and ever.

Stress

Whether we like the concept of stress or not, we are certainly stuck with it for the time being and it will help to get some idea of what it involves. In an article about stress, Fletcher (1988) makes the following observation, 'Mental health is not so much a freedom from specific frustrations as it is an overall balanced relationship to the world'. That is, we will not do away with stress or mental ill-health by a kind of sanitisation process which rids us of all difficulties. We must learn to live with our difficulties and get them into perspective.

Stressors, difficulties and strains are all around us and are part of life. And as has been said, 'The vast majority of people who are exposed to stressful life events do not develop emotional disorder' (Kessler *et al.*, 1985). While this statement may be true, we can well believe that such people get pretty fed up, especially if they keep being exposed to such events with little hope of relief. As with most human conditions, ranging from cancer to work stress, people are different in the extent to which their bodies provide an initially receptive environment for the problem. Thereafter, the conditions in the hosting environment must be right for the formation and growth of the problem. Many people are physically and psychologically immune to problems up to a certain level, while others succumb relatively quickly. While evidence does not lead to straightforward conclusions regarding work and illness or work and strain, general indications are that different types of work (i.e. occupational classi-fications) are associated with different degrees of illness and strain. But strain and emotional negativism are apparently reported less as we move up the social class scale (leaving occupation out).

Work itself has many positive effects on health, as we have seen in the case of the different effects that unemployment has in sections of the population. Within a given profession, e.g. dentists, nurses, teachers or car workers, the differences in the job demands, goals and supports have been shown to be related to stress.

Origins

Hans Selye (1956) was the main originator of the concept that we now call stress. In his thesis, stress was a physiological response of the body which was part of its natural adaptation to threat. Thus stress is not bad but is actually necessary. As his work was about physiological responses to physical stimuli, there is no reason to assume that many of the psychological constructs mentioned in association with stress have anything to do with the original conception of Seyle.

The social and psychological focus on stress in recent years has moved away from the original idea. In fact, stress and the feelings of anxiety which usually accompany it are up to a point seen as beneficial in many endeavours. In performance or competition, a certain amount of 'precompetitive anxiety' is necessary to bring out the best in the performer. From athletes to opera singers, admissions of anxiety or even fear before a performance are quite common. Anxiety helps them to reach their peak.

Stress has become a major focus of interest across a number of areas of work. The actual incidence of stress is thought to be high, though accurate estimates are really impossible to come by. A survey in United States estimated 11 million workers felt their exposure to mental stress endangered their health. Half the respondents felt they had experienced moderate levels of stress in the two weeks prior to the inter-view. These figures are very subjective and are derived from a more general health survey (Silverman *et al.*, 1987).

The word 'stress' has many meanings and is very difficult to define in a consistent way (Briner and Reynolds, 1993). It refers to a concept which on its own explains very little. Does it add to our understanding to label a workgroup or an individual as 'stressed' just because we observe a collection of particular symptoms? Much attention is paid to the construct, despite difficulties with measurement and definition. In the modern approaches to job design, quality circles, etc., there is a focus on reducing stress and increasing satisfaction by increasing the individual's control over work and inputs to decision making.

At the extreme end, job stress and low work satisfaction are thought to be responsible for a phenomenon known as Mass Psychogenic Illness. This is mostly associated with repetitive jobs and situations where there are poor industrial relations. This condition includes symptoms such as headaches and dizziness. Within a given work grouping, the symptoms have an epidemic-like spread but have no real physical basis (Colligan and Murphy, 1979). The results are increases in absence and in other problems such as errors, wastage and accidents.

Stress has been hypothesised as underlying or being related to a wide and varied range of symptoms and phenomena. There are research findings which will confirm the relationship between stress, as measured in various ways, with lack of motivation, absenteeism, high cholesterol levels, anxiety, prolonged strikes, organisational climate, etc.

Physiology and stress

In the physiological area, stress-related hormones are found to be higher in administrators and scientists, yet at lower levels in assembly workers. In one study, cholesterol levels within the staff were found to be higher in upper levels of the workforce. Uric acid levels, which lead to gout, kidney stones and joint problems have been found to be higher in executive classes and also in people who are more ambitious. These and many other chemicals are produced in our bodies when we are anxious, or fatigued or when our immune system is fighting an invader. The fact that they are associated with reported stress and with job stressors at least shows there is something there and that all stress is not a product of the imagination.

The physiological assessment of stress at work uses a variety of indicators including the cardiovascular, the biochemical and the physical. Cardiovascular includes heart rate and blood pressure. Biochemical includes uric acid, blood sugar and most of all cholesterol. A physical sign is the presence of a gastrointestinal problem, for example peptic ulcers (Fried, 1988). Often when we are faced with physiological measures, we tend to think that they are more accurate than psychological ones. After all they come from medicine and they are done with very sophisticated equipment. However, workers in this area readily admit that measurement issues are far from clear cut. There are a number of reasons for this: levels of chemicals fluctuate very rapidly in the body even from hour to hour, there are seasonal variations in cholesterol and there are almost immediate variations in response to diet. There are many as yet unknown genetic differences: blood pressure is not a stable entity, and multiple assessments are needed for accuracy; there are race and sex differences and finally there are definitional and measurement differences from study to study.

There are now fairly firm indications that our psychological state has a bearing on the physiological. There are fundamental links between the central nervous system (brain, spinal chord, etc.) and the immune system, which determines our susceptibility to infection (Ader and Cohen, 1985). The cardiovascular and the immune systems have been shown to be conditionable, so in a sense they form an integrated behavioural system (Engel, 1986). Psychological factors have been linked to infectious diseases, cancer and heart disease and the biochemical system has been shown to be related to psychosomatic factors (Ruff *et al.*, 1985). A strong intervening factor, especially in relation to heart disease, is that other risk factors like smoking, diet and poorer genetic inheritances are much more prevalent in the lower socio-economic classes. For example, 30 per cent of all the hypertension cases in the United States occur among the black population. It can be concluded that there is in fact an inverse relation between occupational level and coronary risk. Another way of thinking about this is to say that, work stress would have to get many hundred times worse before its effects on the occurrence of heart disease were equal to the effects of smoking, diet and inheritance. In fact, the effects of inheritance in bringing about most life-threatening conditions would be greater, across the population as a whole, than the combined effects of all other factors.

Consider for example that 10 per cent of smokers die of lung cancer, and 10 per cent of lung cancer deaths are non-smokers. With Coronary Heart Disease, 40 per cent show no evidence of significant risk factors (Eysenck, 1984). Cohen and Williamson (1991) reviewed studies in the area relating stress and illness and concluded that the evidence points to the link being no more than suggestive at best. So stress has an undeniable physical repercussion, more in some people than in others. But compared with many other factors, it is only responsible for a slight effect and it is also difficult to separate out in its actual effects.

Health and well-being

General lifestyle and health pattern are connected. Lifestyle can be defined as

> The sum of decisions by individuals that affect their health and that can to some extent be controlled by them; decisions that affect health negatively then create self-imposed risks; and in that sense individuals contribute to their own illness or health. (Lalonde, 1975).

We have already thought about lifestyle in relation to the unemployed. It crops up again here in relation to whether people will be more or less vulnerable to the effects of stressors in the work environment.

Smoking, consuming animal fat, taking exercise and consuming alcohol are all related to health outcomes. They are to some extent controllable by the individual. People are seeking more control over their health and well-being. Taking exercise and keeping the mind active have been shown to have positive effects on the immune system, slowing the ageing process and helping to protect against illness and deterioration. However, there is not a simple linear relationship: many exercisers have CHD and many lazy people who drink and smoke live a long time (Ivancevich and Matteson, 1988).

Type A personality

People with Type A personalities are thought to experience stress more and to report stressors more frequently. The Type A behaviour pattern was originally observed in Coronary Heart Disease patients; it includes a prevalence of behaviours such as fast and emphatic speech, a tendency to interrupt other people and easily aroused irritabilities (Friedman and Rosenman, 1959). Two key elements were a struggle with time and with other people (hostility). Matthews *et al.* (1977) identified time urgency, hostility and proneness to anger as significant in CHD occurrence. The relationship to work of this set of behaviours is beginning to be documented. The traditional striving ambitious person, often a man at least up to now, rises quickly and then drops dead of a heart attack. Components of the concept are anxiety, impatience and irritability and striving for status.

Seven physical health patterns have been found to be specifically correlated with physical health (Belloc and Breslow, 1972).

1.   Sleeping 7–8 hours a day.
2.   Eating a good breakfast every day.
3.   Never or rarely eating between meals.
4.   Maintaining appropriate weight.
5.   Never smoking cigarettes.
6.   Moderate use of alcohol.
7.   Regular physical activity.

Men who followed all seven practices had 28 per cent of the mortality rate of men, at equivalent ages, who followed three or less. The comparable difference for women is 43 per cent. Many companies now include health programmes and the monitoring of people's fitness levels in their employee welfare remit. Some companies even include health club subscriptions for their staff and encourage physical exercise sessions after work. Evidence suggests that this is a good way to relieve the effects of work stress. However it also reduces repetitive motion injuries (see below).

These programmes date from the 1970s when the effects of sedentary occupations, the demise of walking and the high levels of fat in the diet were associated with alarming increases in heart disease in the United States. Business organisations in America promoted health education to try to decrease health costs including stress, absenteeism and injuries. They also sought to improve employee health generally and to improve productivity by having fitter workers and reducing job turnover. Programmes are seen as operating at three levels. At the first level, programmes are educative and encouraging, trying to generate interest and awareness of the issues involved in healthy lifestyles. At the second level, programmes for fitness and modifying behaviour are introduced. The third level programmes incorporate facilities at the worksite and a health-promoting environment all through the organisation, affecting such areas as the food in the canteen, the banning of smoking, etc.

The evidence is fairly strong that such interventions are successful. People's health improves for the time of the programme at least. Absences and sick days are reduced quite significantly, e.g. around 20 per cent and there are positive changes in employee attitudes. Programmes can be expensive, especially at the third level and the financial payback to the company may not cover the costs. However that is a difficult question to decide, as the long-term effects can never be estimated. On the whole companies are positive about the programmes (Gebhart and Crump, 1990).

One problem with fitness programmes is that they are difficult to maintain and most people who enter them give up after only a short time unless they are continuously encouraged. The role of self-efficacy has been found to be central to effective programmes in health maintenance. Self-efficacy involves the belief that one's self is effective and developing, that one is having a positive influence on events and that the environment is under some degree of self-control.

The constituents of a programme which enables self-efficacy to grow in any application seeking behaviour change have been outlined as follows (Mahoney, 1975).

Self-monitoring	Keep a record, outlining what was done and the progress noted
Analyse	Each sequence of critical behaviour should be laid out in detail showing how it relates to other things
Goal setting and contracting	Outline a precise schedule of goals and the consequences of attaining them and give dates and details
Feedback	Get indications of progress from others
Reinforcement	Develop a self-reward system
Modelling	Arrange opportunities to observe correct behaviour in others
Cognitive processes	Use imagery to visualise consequences

Studying stressors and stress

Many environments including work contain stressors, which in their turn cause stress. When strain or stress becomes intense, unremitting people respond emotionally and appear to be 'stressed out'. However, observed relationships between work stressors and stress reactions tend to be small when looked at in an epidemio-logical way, that is, across a broad representative sample of widely varying people. There are several reasons for this:

- Work is only one of several factors contributing to stress.
- Using medical/disease based measures of stress is often not practicable.
- Adjustment to stress takes place over a prolonged period, and snapshot studies may miss crucial changes.
- Small relationships across a sample may hide very significant associations occur-ring in parts of the sample (i.e. high stressed Ss).

Studies in occupational stress, at least those carried out by psychologists, are often of the self-report type where questionnaires are given out and returned by a sample of willing participants. The studies are often cross-sectional, in which com-parisons are made simultaneously across two or more groups in their answers to a questionnaire. The groups are often such that one would be expected to be more under strain than the other and they know it. Having analysed the answers to the questionnaires it is difficult to know for certain whether any observed differences are due to expectation effects, political pressures or to actual job factors producing stress. There is often a confusing set of constructs being measured ranging from distress, negative affectivity, stressors and strains. Mackay *et al.* (1978), using a self-report measure (the Stress Arousal Checklist (SACL)), investigated stress and arousal in repetitive work situations. They argued that their results indicated that a marked discrepancy between actual and expected arousal can lead to compensatory behaviour, which in turn gives rise to negative feelings and so higher stress is reported. So it is the effect of the expectation which leads indirectly to the stress report, just one example of where a situation can be manipulated to give a result which could be interpreted in several different ways.

Job stressors are the situational aspects of work which give rise to stress, such as workload, role conflict and lack of autonomy. Any job will contain a number of stressors at various levels, and of course these will interact with the individual in his or her situation. One individual may be more vulnerable because, for example, they are new to a job; someone else may be more vulnerable because they are constantly concerned about the health of their child. Factors implicated as stressors and on which research has been done include overload/underload, mobility and work changes, responsibility and support from the boss. While it is mostly job-related factors that are used to explain stress, it is instructive to consider the individual's emotional (affective) response to stress and their perception of it. As we have said, it is rather difficult to define so it is hardly surprising to find that people have their own idea of what it is, as has been said, 'certain people will remain unhappy and dissatis-fied no matter how the job is designed' (Firth-Cozens, 1992).

Stress can arise from the role conflict between family and work. Studies have re-ported at least quite high figures for this conflict, e.g. 38 per cent of men and 45 per cent of married women with children reported that job and family life conflicted (Quinn and Staines, 1979). Negative Affectivity is likely to complicate the issue even further. People have suggested that we all have a tendency to experience a general level of feeling (also known as 'affect') and this affect may be positive or negative. If you are of the negative affectivity class, then you are liable to report stress and strain more than others. It is like optimists and pessimists, or what we tend to call 'begrudgers'.

Effects of stress on others

Occupational stress affects the spouses of workers to some extent. They share illness patterns and stress-related complaints. One explanation is that work moulds cognitive structure, which in turn affects the domestic environment that the partners inhabit. Because they share an environment and interact cognitively, they will have a lot in common as far as psychological stressors are concerned. Added to this must be the fact that there is a degree of self-selection for occupations. People go into roles which are in line with their personalities and attitudes (e.g. salesperson, insurance clerk, police). Husbands and wives choose each other on a basis of compatibility, so predetermined shared proneness exists and is maintained. Many marriage partnerships are formed at work also.

Barling and Rosenbaum (1986) claimed that stressful work events showed an association with wife abuse at home, though they did admit this may be simply a rationalisation on the part of the abuser. Male police officers under work stress, for example, show more anger, less involvement in family affairs and are more likely to have unsatisfactory marriages (Jackson and Maslach, 1982).

Burnout

Burnout is a relatively new concept which is closely related to the experiencing of stress. The feeling is characterised for many burned-out workers that, 'a job is a job is a job'. Or else it is, after however many months or years of stagnation, frustration and apathy, no job at all. Burnout has been defined as one of the responses to long, persistent and unremitting work stress. Its most general manifestation is that workers become more and more emotionally detached from their jobs finding neither pleasure nore pain in them. The three most common symptoms are emotional exhaustion, depersonalisation and low personal accomplishment. Cherniss (1980) has argued that there is strong overlap with the concept of depression.

Burnout is often measured by questionnaires which attempt to measure its frequency and intensity. The Maslach Burnout Inventory (1981) is one of the most frequently quoted and contains three subscales to measure emotional exhaustion, depersonalisation and personal accomplishment. Twenty-two items are rated on a six-point scale and are both positive and negative, e.g. 'I feel very energetic', 'Working with people directly puts too much stress on me' (Maslach and Jackson, 1980, 1981).

Concern has been expressed recently at the excessive working hours that some people are now working. At the other end of the scale, we are also concerned at the excessive numbers of people who are not working any hours! The rich are getting richer and the poor are getting poorer. Some people with jobs are working more and more while more people are not working at all. One of the outcomes of burnout can be occupational stress, where lack of productivity due to burnout is compensated for by working longer hours (Freudenberger, 1974). This leads to the behaviour of the workaholic, though Machlowitz (1980) defines workaholism as a total devotion to one's occupation or cause, where all available time is devoted to serve this purpose. There are also situational factors leading to excessive working. It may be better to use the term 'work orientation' (Nagy, 1985) and view people as having higher or lower standing on this attitudinal variable. Nagy surveyed 251 university secretaries but only 153 returned their forms. There was a high level of burnout among those who returned forms. No one knows if those who did not return their forms were so burned out that they just could not be bothered to fill them in.

Burnout and copout

Some people have attempted to distinguish burnout from the more common 'copout'. This can be important as the concept burnout is now being entered for excuse of the year, as so many people are using it to excuse bad performance. Meier (1984) differentiates burnout from dissatisfaction to the extent that burnout implies exhaustion or lack of energy for work, 'burn-out is psychological strain resulting from occupational stress'. To be facetious for a moment, the three terms in this quote could be arranged in any order and the sentence would still make sense. What does this tell you?

There are generally five stages in burnout. First, there is initial enthusiasm and commitment to the job, next, stagnation resulting from insoluble organisational problems, then frustration when things remain untreated, which is followed by total apathy towards the organisation and finally disinterest and detachment are so extreme that outside intervention is needed to help.

Burnout is job related and is not related to problems at home. Those most likely to suffer are the young, enthusiastic and idealistic workers. Burnout can be distinguished from stress, as stress is generally short term and specific.

Copout is finding excuses for poor performance and involves malingering and feeling bad, blaming external factors and acting the part of the perpetual victim to make life easy. Common excuses for copout are age, security, money, family, attitude and personal life. Burnout is job related, but copout represents more of a personality problem.

Professions and burnout

Teaching is a stressful occupation and there is a relationship between teaching and burnout. Factors which have been identified in studies relating to teacher burnout have included, administrative practices, such as lack of support, personality and environmental factors, role conflict and ambiguity. Burned-out teachers give significantly less information, less praise, less acceptance of their students' ideas and interact less frequently with them.

A study in 1991 looked at teachers' responses to the Maslach Burnout Inventory at three times during the school year and found it tended to be increasing then decreasing, reaching a peak in February. But there was no overall consistency in the patterns over time shown by different teachers, though slightly more showed an increase than showed a decrease over the year (Capel, 1991).

Firth and Britton (1989) studied a sample of nurses over a two-year period, and related absences and job turnover to burnout, role ambiguity and perceived support from superiors. Lack of support (perceived) and emotional exhaustion predicted absences of four days; feelings of depersonalisation predicted job turnover.

Dentists are another occupation said to be high in stress. A survey (Cooper *et al.*, 1988) of a large sample of British dentists in general practice, found that the dentists showed lower levels of well-being than the general population. Major stressors associated with mental ill-health were 'time scheduling demands' and 'negative patient perceptions'. Males appeared to experience more stress and dissatisfaction than females and the time in the profession was related to mental ill-health problems. Dentists are second only to farmers in the rate at which they take their own lives.

The job of police officer is both prone to burnout and stress. The job itself is significantly affected by the results of burnout. Police work consists of assembling information by question and observation, making decisions quickly and safely, keeping cool when others are shocked, enraged or scared, and interacting with people who may be mad, dangerous or just plain irritating. All these functions are affected by burnout.

Problems which appear to lead to burnout in the police force are the bureaucratic nature of the job; legal loopholes in the criminal justice system, life-threatening aspects and internal competitiveness in the promotion stakes. Goodman (1990) developed two reasonably effective predictors of burnout in the police force. One equation used trait anxiety and number of days of sick leave per year in previous job. The second equation employed predictors derived from the current job situation, sick days, loss of work due to family problems, few social outlets and bad court decisions. When officers scored highly in these characteristics, they were more likely to be found in the burnout high scores also.

Sources of stress in blue-collar workers

Many blue-collar jobs contain the following elements which have been associated with work stress. Some jobs which contain all three can be thought of as the most stressful, unless other alleviating factors are introduced.

1. Heavy work and arduous physical conditions
2. Monotonous, paced, speeded work
3. Tasks which are cognitively complex and performed under time constraints.

Managerial stress

Studies of management have identified a large number (forty) of interacting factors which can be identified with higher levels of stress. These can be grouped into seven major categories (Cooper and Marshall, 1988):

1. Intrinsic to the job: pacing, overload, working conditions
2. Organisational role: responsibility, ambiguity, conflict
3. Relationships at work
4. Career development
5. Organisational structure and climate
6. Sources outside the organisation, such as family problems, financial
7. Individual differences, personality, Type A behaviour patterns.

Both the manager and the personnel department can be proactive in dealing with these issues. Most problems associated with stress factors are very gradual in their build-up, tackling the causes or associated factors early and continually can bring major benefits. Stress in the workplace can be effectively controlled if the will is there.

Stress in computer-based work

A great deal of attention has been focused on sources of stress in computer-based work since the PC became such a dominant feature of office and business life. A range of musculoskeletal problems have been reported and they are prevalent in workers who use computers for long periods of time, such as data entry clerks. It would be intriguing to know why Repetitive Strain Injury (RSI) became a prevalent problem in keyboard workers in the 1980s and 1990s while three or four generations of typists in typing pools throughout the world appear to have survived without resort to this concept. Though such problems were heard of then, they were not as serious. Typists took breaks to do other things, they moved about more to deliver or to collect work and so on. Are the problems to do with gender, or a lack of training in proper posture and build-up of the relevant tendons which girls on secretarial courses benefited from? Reasons given by the Occupational Health and Safety Administration include, inadequate work stations, longer periods without breaks and greater awareness on the part of workers of the symptoms. One response to this at the Xerox corporation in Webster, New York, is the daily stretching and bending exercises which the workers are encouraged to do.

A number of sources of stress in computer-based work have been identified. They have been categorised as originating in the design of the equipment (work-station layout, video display and keyboard design, software characteristics), the changed nature of the work (increased mental load, less opportunity for control and planning of work), the response of the organisation (training and user support, job design, lack of planning and long-term strategies), and finally when all else fails, the operator can be blamed (low stress tolerance, inappropriate cognitive skills, computerphobia and the like). Other factors of a psycho-social kind have now been recognised as relating to health problems, such as isolation and concerns over job security.

The International Standards Organisation has published requirements for office work with visual display units and software (ISO9241, 1992). This provides a set of standards which enable such set-ups to be evaluated and deemed suitable or otherwise for the task. It also directs the attention of manufacturers towards acceptable ways of designing their products. The long-term effects should be a reduction in stress-related problems in this area of work.

Many studies have found high levels of eyestrain/visual fatigue in prolonged VDU use, but this is not due to the features of the VDU itself. Bad positioning of equipment, poor levels of surrounding light and other environmental issues are to blame, though VDU workers are advised to have their eyes checked regularly. Earlier fears that there were special risks for women in relation to pregnancy and fertility have not been confirmed. So far, the belief held by researchers is that some effects which had been noted were 'statistical' events and detailed studies trying to confirm them have not succeeded (Bramwell and Cooper, 1995). Overall, we are looking at a job design problem. Computers have taken their place at work with the virulence of a virus and we have not had time to make appropriate adjustments to their presence.

Ways of coping

We will all be stressed out from time to time; we might even be burned out. It would be nice to know of ways of dealing with the situation. This seems at first sight to be a little fatuous, since by definition if you feel bad enough to be burned out, you will probably not feel positive enough to take sensible recuperative actions.

Environmental stressors affect individuals differently; people have varied coping strategies and individual reactions to stress. Coping is multidimensional and dependent on many situational factors and particularly the appraisal of the situation by the individual. People do not have a uniform coping style for every situation except in the minority of cases. That is, coping is not a personality trait.

Billings and Moos (1981) outline a number of generalised methods of coping:

1. *Active–cognitive*: the subject manages the appraisal of the stressful event. That is, by seeing the event differently, changing the emphasis of one's perceptions, etc., the situation can be ameliorated.

2.   *Active–behavioural*: the subject deals directly with the situation. Actual steps are taken to change the situation for the benefit of the individual. The issue is addressed, aspects are changed, support is gathered from colleagues, etc.

3.   *Avoidance*: confrontation is avoided. This is also a behaviour, but not one bringing about change in perception or the situation. The stressors are still present but are ignored or avoided. Sometimes this is the only alternative, but sometimes there is no alternative.

Some approaches distinguish between problem-focused coping, in which the person directly alters the situation or their appraisal of it, and emotion-focused coping, where the person attempts to regulate emotional reactions to the situation.

There are a number of approaches to assessing how people cope. Albert Bandura, (1982) has written about 'self-efficacy', a construct which has many diverse applications. In relation to coping, it can help us understand why some people are better copers than others. Learning to be more self-efficacious or effective is possible and can improve people's coping abilities. The 'Ways of Coping Checklist' was developed by Folkman and Lazarus (1985) and is intended to distinguish between problem- and emotion-focused approaches and describes specific coping methods. Spivack and co-workers have developed a comprehensive approach to coping which they call a 'Problem-solving Approach'. Leading on from this over the years have come the many cognitive–behavioural approaches, which are currently the most common approach and possibly the most practical.

Coping attempts typically employ several simultaneous strategies and attack or deal with different parts of the situation at different times. Here are some of the ways suggested for coping.

Reward substitution

Stop regarding your current activity or work in that case as a source of reward. Line up your other activities and see what rewards they bring you. Try to maximise these rewards, either by getting more of them or even pretending you like them more than you really do. Your dull, boring, repetitive and unrewarding job will not seem so vital after all and you will feel better, especially as five o'clock approaches.

Positive comparison

This involves comparing your current situation, which you find unpleasant, with an earlier situation which in various important ways was even worse, or if that is not possible, then you make comparisons with other people you know who are definitely worse off than you. This might be called the 'at least I have a job' scenario.

Optimistic action

This refers to the worker's efforts to actually bring about a change in the less pleasant aspects of the working environment. Specifically, some therapists recommend making a list of the bad things about your situation. Divide each thing up into its smallest affectable components, then list the components in order of their seriousness. Starting at the bottom of the list, the least serious, think of a way to change it and do that, now!

Selective ignoring

Look for some positive aspect in every negative situation. Try to pay less attention to the bad bits and accentuate your interest in the good bits.

This advice might work in some situations, but in a large study of workers in Chicago, Pearlin and Schooler (1978) concluded that, because our occupational roles are much more impersonally organised, the scope for these therapeutic manoeuvres may be considerably reduced. In addition, they pointed out that the person's ability to put together and operate an effective coping strategy is likely to be very dependent in most cases on the quality of the 'resources' at the person's disposal.

Workplace interventions for stress reduction and prevention

There are three main kinds of intervention in the workplace: employee assistance programmes, stress management training and stress reduction strategies; the first two target the employee and the third the environment (Murphy, 1988).

Employee assistance programmes

Employee assistance programmes developed from the employee welfare aspect of personnel work. In larger organisations, a nurse or a social worker was assigned responsibility for various aspects of staff social and physical well-being. Macey's department store in New York is said to be the first company to introduce a programme of this kind in 1917 (Carty, 1990). The ESB were one of the first companies in Ireland to explicitly introduce such a service. Their main concern was the level of alcohol abuse in full-time permanent staff. Since 1974, they have employed psychology graduates in the capacity of counsellors to deal with this problem.

According to Gerstein and Bayer (1990) employee assistance programmes were originally colonised by recovering alcohol abusers and industrial nurse/social worker people. Consequently employee assistance programmes developed a ring-fence against psychologists and psychiatrists in order to preserve a territory. They say that employee assistance programme people were threatened, but this is a thing of the past and developments are possible with a more professional approach. On the other hand, some think that since the programmes moved away from dealing with explicit substance abuse to broader family and welfare problems, they have lost their ability to deal with their (possibly) primary function.

The problems of alcoholics at work are considerable and companies need to take serious steps to limit their negative impact and to try to rehabilitate sufferers. Recent statistics in this area suggest that 10 per cent of the workforce experience alcohol-related problems; alcoholics take four times as many days off, they are three times as likely to have accidents, and at least 20 per cent of accidents at work involve intoxicated people (*Personnel Management Factsheet*, No. 20, August 1989). Drug abuse is another issue, involving as it does the question of compulsory drug testing which is now in place in some parts of the United States, particularly in government service jobs and those in sensitive areas.

An employee with a serious personal problem cannot be giving their full attention to work and is thus a possible liability on the company if not an actual source of loss (Steddon, 1990). Companies can be held responsible for the behaviour of their workforce; the company can be sued if that behaviour is damaging to the public or to its clients. Although employee assistance programmes have a humanitarian orientation, the main reason for their survival and proliferation is a business one. The new Health, Safety and Welfare at Work Acts which have been introduced in most European countries impose obligations on employers to identify risks in the workplace and to nominate a staff member to be responsible in this area.

Another environmental pressure has encouraged the growth of employee assistance programmes and that is the cyclical nature of production in the last two decades, as the world economy has lurched from one minicrisis to another. Firms have had to make people redundant and rehire them a short while later. The companies with the best reputations for caring for workers in these eventualities are the ones which get the better staff more readily when demand picks up. As with Robert Owen, there are good commercial reasons for providing welfare services for staff.

Employee assistance programmes generally work through prevention and/or confrontation. Prevention works through the concept of wellness and is basically educational and encouraging. They offer health screening and fitness programmes, social activities and try to build increased personal awareness regarding physical and mental well-being. Confrontational approaches are constructive and focus on the problem employee, offering assistance and advice where appropriate, but also providing much closer supervision and guidance to eliminate problems or eventually the worker. Such an approach, by focusing on the problem worker, tends to overlook the fact that the work environment may be mainly at fault in creating stress and negativism.

An example of a confrontational approach was practised by the personnel manager of a food processing company in Cork. He was a former union official and knew workers' behaviour from both sides of the union/management divide. The perennial problem of absenteeism was substantially reduced to negligible proportions in this company. The personnel manager (Donal) knew that most absences were due to too much drink the night before and sleeping late. In sunny weather, people tended to opt for the beach rather than the factory. Donal's policy was to call around to the house of the absent staff member on receiving the phone call that they were ill. If the individual was at home, then sympathetic concern was expressed about their health and arrangements made about their return to work. Casual absence very quickly fell away when this policy was introduced. Of course if the worker was not at home when allegedly off sick, he or she was put on a warning, which could mean more serious consequences.

Essential ingredients of employee assistance programmes include a commitment from top management and clear policies. On the staff side, union cooperation and supervisor training in problem identification and awareness are necessary. There needs to be a continuum of care in the community and liaison with medical and social services. Confidentiality, good record keeping and service evaluation reports complete the picture from the management side.

Stress management training

Stress management training makes people more aware of stressors and their effects. Techniques of stress reduction are taught to try to decrease the individual's personal vulnerability to stressors. These techniques include relaxation, meditation and various methods with a cognitive focus, which get the person to appraise their environment in a different way.

Research on the effectiveness of this training is inconclusive. Some show positive results, others little or none; it seems to partly depend on the research focus. So there is no clear answer but stress management training is increasing in popularity. Companies think it is a good thing even though objective proof is lacking. A major obstacle to research in this area is that participants are self-selected in the first place. The methods are unique to each programme and very dependent on the personality and style of the coordinator. Outcomes are not easily specified in a measurable format and outside influences on outcomes will always interfere with the interpretation of programme results.

Summary

The concept of stress is important in its own right and also as a component in much employment change. Awareness of the harmful effects of work is increasing and various measures are being employed to counteract them. Psychology needs to work at putting together reliable and effective ways of measuring stress and intervening in stressful work situations. At present the subject is in a developmental phase. Ways of dealing with stress range from the individual changing ways of thinking or perceiving of work or modifying their personalities, to environmental campaigns within the work site.

Activities

1. Make a catalogue of the sources of stress in your or your partner's life and
    examine them from the point of view of controllability and coping mechanisms
    which are appropriate.

2. Discuss a number of different jobs and try to outline the stress aspects of each.
    Then follow up your hypotheses by putting them to a person in the actual jobs.

3. How could copout be applied to college and universities? Looking at people you
    know who have dropped out or have contemplated it, consider if a stress ex-
    planation would fit their situation. If possible, without being too intrusive, ask
    them.

Further reading

Cohen and Williamson (1991) Stress and infectious disease in humans. *Psychological Bulletin*,
     109, 5–24.
Cooper, C.L. and Payne, R. (eds) (1988) *Causes and Consequences of Coping With Stress at Work.*
     (Chichester, Wiley).
Cox, T. (1993) *Stress Research and Stress Management: Putting Theory to Work.* (Sudbury, HSE
     Books).
Griffiths, A. (1996) The benefits of employee exercise programmes: a review. *Work & Stress*,
     10(1), 5–23.

CHAPTER 14

Age, gender and discrimination

Focus questions

What are your attitudes towards older working people that you meet in the course of your day?

Why do some people want to keep working as long as possible and others seek to retire as soon as they can?

How can employers use retired workers more effectively and what is the point of them doing so?

Are there any differences between women and men in terms of their management skills and abilities?

What is the significance and meaning of 'sexual harassment'?

Why do women find it more difficult to go to the top in companies?

People become 'out of work' for structural reasons, i.e. their factory closes or no one wants horses shod anymore. They also lose their jobs because of age. We shall consider some of the relations of age and work in this section. The relationship of age and performance has a long history. James McEwan, a weaver in Perth, in giving his evidence to the Select Committee on Handloom Weavers in 1834, was asked to comment on their weekly earnings. He replied, 'I have classified them here. Weavers under 16 years of age 5s 9d (five shillings and nine pence, i.e. about 27p in decimal money), deducting 1 shilling (5p) for the loom, making 4s and 9d. Above 16 and under 55, 8 shillings and 9 pence, above 55, 6 shillings deducting the same'.

The older weaver was regarded in the strict and ever-so-real economy of the 1830s as worth about 25 per cent less than the worker in the prime of age between 16 and 55. Presumably the older workers were in fact less productive, for one reason or another. In the modern economy the same issue is again present in various forms. For example, the main issues now being examined are age discrimination in selection and promotion, the question whether there are genuine differences in performance between young and old, the stereotypes of the older worker and how they affect recruitment and careers, the question of retirement age and people's right to work after a mandatory retirement.

In Tom Paine's *Rights of Man* (1792), the same theme is echoed.

> At 50 though the mental faculties of man are in full vigour and his judgement better than at any preceding date, the bodily powers for laborious life are on the decline. He cannot bear the same quantity of fatigue as at an earlier period. He begins to earn less and is less capable of enduring wind and weather; and in those more retired employments where much sight is required, he fails apace, and sees himself like an old horse, beginning to be turned adrift.

Ageing and work

Participation in the labour force

The extent to which a particular social grouping is employed is referred to as their Labour Force Participation Rate. The participation rates of older men have fallen considerably in the last thirty years, along with the decline in manufacturing and agricultural employment. The rate was fairly steady from the 1890s until the 1950s when the decline set in. Women's participation rates have risen, but they started from a much lower baseline. Even in the case of women, the participation of older workers is being affected by increasing prosperity, provision of welfare benefits and pensions schemes. In many countries, older workers can be found congregating in a limited range of occupations such as mining, textiles and railways. Younger workers with superior education gain employment in more technologically advanced industries.

Problems of the older worker

Research into occupational aspects of ageing, known as industrial gerontology, is concerned with the employment and retirement problems of older workers. It is a subject which is rapidly developing in occupational psychology, since workers become more vulnerable to changes in the labour market as they get older. Difficulties which are age related begin to appear in the 40s and increase in the 50s. These problems include adapting to new and developing technology, and keeping up with the pace of fellow workers or machines. The older workers may have difficulty in gaining access to training programmes and so as their skills become outdated, they have more difficulty keeping up to date.

Older workers who become unemployed are much less likely to obtain new employment and when they do, they are usually faced with a reduction in wages and conditions. Voluntary withdrawal from the workforce is common and self-imposed retirement in an implicit sense is accepted. Braddy and Gray (1987) suggest that between 25 and 75 per cent of the workforce (USA) would prefer some alternative to full-time retirement. They carried out a controlled experiment with elderly people, some in a job club and some given a job-finding manual. Much higher success in finding people some form of work was achieved for those in the job club, which are groups of people who are looking for jobs and who meet regularly, pool information and usually use facilities in a centre to produce CVs and support each other in their job searches. They have shown better than average success in getting people of all ages placed in work.

Age discrimination

Age discrimination is quite active in recruitment and older people are often ruled out after a certain age from the shortlist. Employers often hold negative stereotypes of the older worker and in any case they prefer to take on younger people, as they are usually less expensive, more flexible and quicker to pick up new skills. Managers also have been shown to hold negative stereotypes of older workers. They tend to be viewed as less employable, particularly for more demanding jobs. They are seen as having less adaptability, lower performance capacity and potential difficulties in coping with new technology. They are however regarded as being more stable, reliable and honest (Rosen and Jerdee, 1988).

Many job vacancies are either tacitly or blatantly age limited. In a practical context, one of the first factors used in sifting through application forms is the applicant's age. This might not be openly admitted to, but it is certainly the case. On a more public front, a British study looking at advertisements of 16000 job vacancies, found that one-quarter had age limits stated. The majority of limited positions set their limits at or below forty years. Professional jobs were less limited in age (Jolly *et al.*, 1980). Legal complaints of age discrimination are very much on the increase in the United States (Snyder and Barrett, 1988).

Ageing workers and society

There have been general changes in the age of the population and in the social environment which findings in this subject need to be set against. The population is getting older in Western society, so in some situations shortages of labour must be met by extending the working life of suitable employees. In some countries, steps have been taken to eliminate mandatory retirement in certain situations, e.g. United States. Age discrimination is now recognised as one of the jeopardies of hiring and promoting staff and in the United States there has been an Age Discrimination Act since 1967, amended in 1978. Other countries have not gone this far, but the same sentiments have been expressed through the process of common law in specific cases.

Some writers have suggested that society and individuals are too age conscious, and that we tend to mark our progress against the scale of chronological age to a large extent. If we have not reached a certain position or achieved a certain goal by a certain age, then we tend to take a negative evaluation of our career progress. In some cases, people are inclined to give up after a certain age and 'go mouldy' in effect. The expectations of workers in relation to age may, in fact, be more dependent on their perceptions of their parents' experience rather than perceptions of the current labour market.

Company policy for older workers

It has been recommended that companies develop specific policies for older workers and be proactive in how they treat them (McLaughlin, 1989). Those with potential should be encouraged to stay. Various incentives such as increasing the flexibility of their hours or increasing the choice in tasks they carry out might help to convince them to stay on. Where otherwise good employees have obsolete skills, every effort should be made to retrain them to adapt to new requirements. Loyal workers who are good time-keepers and who contribute to the company in many subtle ways are worth retaining. Close examination should be carried out of older workers, many of whom are on unrewarding career plateaux which they do not enjoy, but cannot change. More effective career paths can be redrawn for such workers to the benefit of the company.

Confidence in their ability to learn new skills is a big factor in participation of older workers in retraining programmes. Coberly (1985) described how older workers at GEC were retrained rather than recruiting new workers. This led to considerable financial savings.

Downgrading is another alternative for older workers and is attractive to 70 per cent of senior managers when given as an alternative over retirement (Hall and Isabella, 1985). This involves them remaining with the company, but in a less pressurised job at a lower salary level. In some organisations this is a deliberate preretirement policy. The workload is gradually reduced and the areas of responsibility are given over progressively to younger workers. This benefits the company by the passing on of skills and knowledge from one generation to the next.

Retirement

Since the 1960s, early retirement has become accepted and even popular. Numerous public and private schemes have been introduced into most industrial countries. Men in their late fifties are increasingly likely to have left full-time participation in the labour force, particularly where the economic development and modernisation are gaining pace. The declines in agricultural and in heavy industrial employment have left a considerable number of unskilled and semi-skilled men with no possibilities of gainful employment. The population as a whole is ageing in most developed countries and social security benefits have until now been improving.

'Retired' people are getting younger and they are no longer a homogeneous population as far as age is concerned. People are now retiring at various ages, as young as 50 in some cases.

Atchley (1982) has said there are three phases to the retirement process and it should be looked at as a sociological transition phenomena.

Phase	Contents
Preretirement phase	Developing attitudes and making plans
Retirement transition	Surveying the situation and relating to the factors which impinge on the decision
Post-retirement phase	Physical, social and mental effects of the decision

Retirement plans are mainly dependent on opportunity and pension. While people may have the intention, they still need the appropriate circumstances to bring it into fruition. People with negative feelings to their work (alienation, disinterest), are more likely to plan to retire early. Although various factors are thought to lead people into the retirement decision, there is no consistently effective predictor of retirement which would apply either individually or to groups. Some factors are found to have some effect in some populations, such as length of time in the workforce, e.g. teachers tend to retire after a certain number of years if possible. Having the opportunity to interact with others may help people to retire. Data for men and women tell a different story however (Talaga and Beehr, 1989).

Retirement has been viewed as a way of reducing unemployment and helping younger people into work. Labour force participation rates in the United States of men aged 62–64 dropped by 30 per cent between 1963 and 1983 (Rones, 1985). There has been a considerable mental shift in recent years towards viewing retirement as a positive step. There are flexible schemes such as partial retirement, retaining retirees as consultants and call-back arrangements for busy times.

The Swedish system of retirement offers a range of options and is very flexible. Partial retirement is available and encouraged and is a lead into normal retirement. This phased scheme has been around since 1976. The partial pension option is especially popular with blue-collar workers. Recipients show better health and lower absenteeism. It has also had the effect of lowering the numbers opting for full-time early retirement (Ginsburg, 1985).

Consequences of retirement

In general, individuals report high levels of satisfaction. Physical health and financial security are the crucial factors moderating individual reaction. The most important determinant of retirement by choice has been the individual's financial situation. In some cases, poor health also motivates the decision to leave early (Braddy and Gray, 1987). It has been found that academics tend to work longer than they have to because of a failure to appreciate the financial trade-offs and also because of the relatively high levels of job satisfaction. They are more inclined than other professions to postpone retirement if possible (Palmore *et al.*, 1984).

Career plateau

The 'Career Plateau' is a term for a stage in career development which 'represents a point beyond which the probability of promotion is quite low' (Ference *et al.*, 1977). The extent of career plateauing is dependent on the business cycle and the nature of the organisation. Corporate strategy has a significant effect. A company operating in a relatively fixed business environment had considerably more plateaued workers than one in a high growth segment (Slocum *et al.*, 1985). Likewise in many bureaucratic government or local authority jobs people may arrive at a career plateau in their early thirties and remain there until retirement. These people are often experiencing a kind of hidden distress which they would be reluctant to admit to.

Approaches to moving people off career plateaux by providing challenge and incentives have proved successful. 'Intrapreneurship' and special projects, as well as a change of stereotyped attitudes held by management all help. Special roles can be created for people within an organisation which add to the value they provide to their colleagues. Experimental centres or informal groups are set up, which encourage people to do something that may not have immediate business relevance, but has the effect of forming a team and possibly generating ideas for application in other areas. Many plateaued employees have a wealth of experience and insights which, in the normal run of events, are left to stagnate.

Ference *et al.* (1977) divided workers into four categories depending whether they had high or low performance and whether they had a high or low likelihood of promotion.

Current performance	Likelihood of future promotion	
	Low	High
High	Solid citizens	Stars
Low	Deadwood	Learners

Solid citizens can be organisationally plateaued by reason of age, inability to compete or because of organisational needs superseding their own, i.e. they may be the only person available, willing and able to do a certain range of tasks, so that to promote them from their current position would cost the organisation far more than the resulting benefit. This is at least one of the illusory compensations of many middle-aged workers who have established a niche and view themselves as indispensable.

Deadwood may arise from a number of managerial failures. Appraisals may have been inaccurate or not reacted to properly. Marginal or poor performance may have been ignored for too long. Opportunities for skills upgrading, retraining and development may not have been provided. Evidence shows that the longer people are with an organisation, the more likely they are to stay with it. They are in effect, a long-term asset of the company. The company should recognise that they need to service their assets regularly and not leave them to deteriorate psychologically and become useless.

Career paths need to be developed in the context of an individual's total life situation. Attitudes and aspirations of individual managers need to be monitored. Promoting individuals beyond their current level of ability is a classic way of creating deadwood. What is needed in most companies is a proactive human resource policy where people are regarded as dynamic and constantly improvable, rather than static and to be tolerated. People need to be regarded 'from a psychological' point of view. That is, they can be developed and their contribution to the organisation improved. If they are neglected, they may change for the worse. The early industrial psychologists tended to regard people as mere adjuncts to machines. But unlike machines, people are capable of learning and growing and can manage surprising feats if suitably treated. Deadwood can be kept to a minimum without necessarily digging it up.

Workers may also be personally plateaued due to lack of technical skills or a lack of career skills. The latter is a form of organisational naivety where the individual has failed to play a good game of organisational politics or has failed to perceive opportunities and competitors at the right time. They may lack sufficient drive or have decided to be inactive in the career progression stakes and concentrate on extramural interests such as gardening or golf.

Obsolescence

Obsolescence is related to specific knowledge and skills, which the changing nature of the job causes to become redundant. It comes about when the assets of the person are no longer congruent with those required for the job. The duties and responsibilities of the job may have changed due to a variety of market, technological or structural developments. The individual who was previously able to match the job requirements falls behind what is needed. However, while actual speed of operation may decline with age, broad abilities to meet job requirements do not (Fossum *et al.*, 1986). Skills obsolescence is determined by interactions involving the individual, the employer and the external market. Initially obsolescence was viewed as a deficiency, due to out of date knowledge of an individual relative to others currently practising in the same field. In these terms, an individual could evade obsolescence by emigrating to a more technically backward region where the lack of current knowledge would not be so evident.

Age and job performance

A comprehensive review of the relation between age and work was published by Rhodes (1983). She reviewed a number of studies in the area of age and performance. Results were fairly evenly divided across all possible outcomes. That is, it depends on the job, the situation and factors such as the individual's level of skill or experience whether there will be noticeable decrements in performance. Results were not consistent in any direction regarding the changes in performance with age. Rhodes reported eight positive relationships, nine negative, eight inverted U and nine nonsignificant. Where studies controlled for experience, two-thirds yielded no significant correlations between age and performance. In general, the effect that age had on performance was very slight.

Other studies have reached similar conclusions. Stagner (1985) concluded that 'the most distressing conclusion from studies of job performance changes with age is that they are ambiguous'. The major cause of the inconsistencies is the type of work performed according to Waldman and Avolio (1993), though McEvoy and Cascio (1989) did not agree with the latter statement. They reviewed ninety-six studies of age and performance over a twenty-two year period and found that with the exception of the very young employee, age and job performance are positively correlated. That is, where there are objective measures of job performance, the older worker performs better than the younger. However, where supervisor ratings are concerned, older workers tend to receive less favourable reviews by supervisors. Clearly we might be looking at the effects of stereotyping here, where the generally negative perception of the older person is affecting the rating. Much of the longitudinal research in the age/performance area has been with academic or research workers.

For many skilled and semi-skilled manual jobs, an inverted U relationship tends to be observed. Performance peaks in the thirties or forties and then gradually declines. However, in a direct comparison between older and younger workers, the older tend to out-perform their younger colleagues. Another problem in the area is that experience is a very relevant contributor to work performance and while experience and age are often correlated, this is not always the case. Some older workers may not have long experience of the job they are currently doing. Thus there can be confounding of the two variables in research, with the effects of either confused together (Schmidt et al., 1988).

In some areas of academic endeavour such as theoretical physics, the peak performance tends to be in the late twenties or early thirties, whereas in philosophy, literature or theology for example, it may take many years to develop mature insights and breadth of knowledge.

Declining physical ability

There are various declines in physical abilities which act to the disadvantage of the older worker. Sensory performance, physical strength and agility and speed of response all decline with age, and in jobs where they are important the older worker is at a disadvantage (Verillo and Verillo, 1985). Older workers also do less well on aptitude tests. In older industries and traditional companies with a 'family atmosphere', older workers can be placed in posts where their age would not be a handicap, e.g. transfer to lighter work.

Age differences should not be overstated, as older workers can often compensate for declining ability with greater use of patience and general know-how. With longer practice periods, they can often pick up skills as well as the young. Older workers may also be more committed to the company as they are less distracted by family concerns. Their attendance and job commitment are also likely to be at least as good as younger employees. Turnover and turnover intention are very much lower as age increases. The same is true for avoidable absence, but not so for unavoidable absence. This means older people are far less inclined to take time off when they feel like it, but are more likely to fall ill with a more serious illness which prevents them working. The incidence of work-related accidents has been found to decline with age in most studies, though not in all (Rhodes, 1983).

It has been proposed that the value of different motivators changes with age. Job challenge, task variety and characteristics and feedback are more important to the younger worker. At older age levels, the motivating effect of these tends to decline and autonomy, achievement and recognition are more important.

Gender issues

Sex stereotyping occurs when an employee is judged according to traditional images and expectations based on gender. For example, a female with short hair, no makeup and a tendency to use coarse language is not fitting into the feminine model. Denying her promotion or a job, on the grounds that her non-traditional behaviour pattern is not acceptable or comfortable to live with, amounts to discrimination.

A court case taken against Price Waterhouse has become quite well known in the United States. Ann Hopkins was a leading exponent in her field of investment consultancy and, based on her performance, was well ahead of many of her male rivals for a partnership in the company. However, she was turned down on two occasions, and felt her progress was being barred by gender discrimination, based on what she had been told and heard from senior partners. She resigned, set up her own consultancy and lodged a claim for constructive dismissal. Her feelings were that the company treated her unfairly because she failed to fulfil their image of a female, and that because of this they effectively put her out to dry in terms of her career. After much litigation over nine years and appeals up to the Supreme Court, Hopkins won her case and was granted over $300000 in back pay and a partnership in the company. New legislation in 1991 has added that punitive damages may be claimed in such cases, making it even more important for male company executives to rid their minds of prejudicial stereotypes of females and judge all people equally on their merits. This of course means that HR people must develop more effective and valid ways to profile people's performance.

Attractiveness in females is taken as an indicator of femininity and to the extent that jobs are stereotyped as masculine, e.g. managerial jobs, attractiveness is not always an asset for females, though it is for males. This affects selection, promotion and performance evaluation. Women going for management jobs find it more difficult to penetrate above a certain level and attractive women, while finding the going easy early on, find their progress slowing up as they near the top.

Women

Of top managerial positions in the United States, 4.8 per cent were held by women in 1992, compared to 2.9 per cent in 1986 (*Fortune*, 21 September 1992, pp. 44–56). Yet, set this against the possibly depressing statistic that, according to Maol (1993) in the *Irish Times*, three out of four Irish women see the primary role of women as being motherhood and providing for their family. Although equality in access to employment is the aim of the European Union and of most business organisations, it is not a simple black and white issue. Employing a woman is not the same as employing a man. In a general way, both genders have their advantages and disadvantages in psychological and behavioural terms. Even economically, some people maintain there is a difference, with women regarded as more expensive to employ than men, because of their counter-productive expectations and perceptions of the workplace and their attention to child rearing (Schwartz, 1989).

Male workers' and executives' stereotypical resistance to female bosses is quite evident. However, even the most chauvinistic man cannot hold off the progress of women forever. In United States retailing, women initially found that resistance to women managers dropped after the first few women became managers, but re-emerged again stronger than ever when the 15 per cent level was reached. It looked like a case of 'so far but no further', as the male power caucus began to feel really threatened by the increasing posse of female bosses swooping in at them. It is however just another barrier to be overcome by women in the struggle for equality of treatment in promotion.

A term 'the glass ceiling' has been coined to denote the barrier to women proceeding to the top of management hierarchies. The situation is improving, however as the number of women in organisations increases, a 'critical mass' will eventually develop and traditional barriers will be broken. Three reasons put forward for the differential progress of women include first, that they have different capabilities from men. Because of their socialisation, they tend not to have the same qualifications or behaviour patterns which would lead to rapid promotion. A second view concerns the prejudice of male organisations, or perhaps of shareholders. Stereotypes of women are inimical to business dynamism and therefore because these exist at the back of people's minds they inhibit the success of women. Perhaps even the women themselves unconsciously act in accordance with those stereotypes. A third view is that of the power and politics of organisational cultures. With women being in the minority and being in positions of lesser power, they are excluded from many of the rituals and tactical discussions which might take place among coteries of men in men's places (Burke and McKeen, 1992).

A study of female executives showed that women need to possess the same skills as men to succeed, but also need that little bit extra and have to take a tactically aware position on their careers and the men in their organisations. They had to perform that little bit better, have excellent relations with people at work, look for help from senior managers and be supportive of the men they worked with and for. They had to clearly separate their business and home lives and be hard-headed and clearly ambitious (Morrison *et al.*, 1987).

A charming story is told by Julienne Hanson in a totally unrelated context (Hanson, 1995), but it is so relevant to gender and work that it is worth studying and reflecting on. It concerns the role of males and females in primitive societies. In these societies there is a simple division of labour based on gender, which is that the males hunt and the females gather, i.e. leaves, seeds, crops, fruit, etc. Hunting is a high-status prestige activity. It normally contributes little to the diet of the tribe, accounting for only around one-quarter of the food actually consumed. Gathering is time consuming and onerous, but it is highly productive. It has been estimated that the productivity per man-hour for hunting is around 800 calories and for gathering around 2000 calories. Remember that we need about 2000 calories a day to live and you will see the relevance. The probability of hunters 'bringing home the bacon' on any given expedition is less than 1 per cent. There are some men who have killed scarcely a single large animal during their entire lives. Hunters are notorious for leaving camp with a great flourish of activity only to squat down again out of sight of their wives and gamble away their weapons! Hunting and gathering differ in status, risk and outcome. There is often much ritual and attention paid to hunters both before and after the hunt. Celebrations, dancing, magic and special costumes are related to the hunt, while the gathering is of no account. Perhaps there are some parallels between this and gender differences in job roles in management?

At the same time, we must not imagine that men and women in general are identical; there are many behaviour differences. Whether you like to think of them as socio-cultural conditioning is beside the point, although it can be the subject of a very fascinating discussion. The following study illustrates this point to some extent. Male and female shop assistants were observed discreetly in their interaction with customers; other variables taken into consideration were whether they were wearing their smocks and name badges and whether there was another salesperson in attendance. Results showed that females gave significantly more emotional signals to clients than males. Male customers received more frequent positive emotional signals from both genders of sales assistants. The assistants tended to be more expressive when they had their uniform on than when dressed in ordinary clothes. They were less positive when other assistants were around and also when a queue had formed for attention. Emotional expression is central to roles which involve serving others and it differs by gender (Rafaeli, 1989). Male midwives are unusual and women prefer the midwife to be female though in an emergency situation they are happy to compromise. Women find work more stressful than men. When it comes to balancing the family and the career, it is usually the women on whom the major responsibilities lie, even in the so-called dual career families where the man might appear to be sharing the burden. It is also the women who have to be more flexible and give up more opportunities in non-work fields in order to cope with the broad array of demands on their time.

Gender bias in job evaluation

Unfairness in job evaluation should also be mentioned. This concerns the fact that it is often the jobs of lower grade workers, and particularly women workers, which are subject to more rigorous evaluation in an effort to limit wage increases. This was illustrated recently (1995) when a Manchester car dealer was found guilty of breaching the equal pay laws by discriminating against women employees in clerical and administrative jobs compared to men working on the shopfloor. This was probably the first time in Britain that the conduct of job evaluation studies had been critically examined from a legal point of view. The women's claim was based on the argument that their jobs and shopfloor jobs had not been compared in terms of the demands made on them by the work; instead the jobs were looked at as a whole and ranked according to what members of an assessment panel felt they were worth. This approach tended to undervalue jobs, especially those done by women. If the jobs had been properly and fairly assessed under some appropriate headings as outlined in Chapter 4 (see 'Job evaluation', pp. 60–62), they could have had no complaint.

Sexual harassment 'They just don't get it'

This is another area of behaviour at work which has risen to prominence in our consciousness over the last two decades and which continues to expand its effects and consequences in business as our understanding grows and as case law develops. In a survey, 46 per cent of men said that women are flattered by flirting, whereas only 5 per cent of women agreed that women would be flattered.

Gender as a basis for discrimination was added at the last minute to the US Civil Rights Act of 1964 by the opponents of the Bill. They judged that they would be able to block the legislation which had been primarily aimed at securing equality of treatment for ethnic minorities by introducing the gender issue. The plan backfired and the Bill was passed in its expanded form. The legislators had put into law an Act which had been intended to protect minorities but it was now, in some ways, protecting a majority. The behaviour which it was opposed to in the gender area was ill-defined and unclear and it is still expanding as our understanding of harassment grows.

For example, the concept of a harassing environment is one of the latest additions. Pornographic pictures of females in the workplace are harassing (*Robinson* vs

Jacksonville Shipyards, 1991). An environment in which sexual power of one gender over another is openly flaunted is harassing. Harassment is about touching, gestures or making suggestions which are unwelcome. It is about promising or withholding rewards or promotions for some sexual favour. These are the more blatant examples. There are more subtle examples.

Organisational romance

Social-sexual behaviour at work is a widespread occurrence. It is more participated in by men who use sexual talk to express their feelings and are more overtly sexual in their behaviour, at the same time it is women who are more offended and hurt by sexual behaviours (Gutek, 1985). Much of this behaviour has negative connotations as in the above examples of harassment, but an increasing concern of organisations is the romantic side which may have no deliberate negative implications. In a local authority office a few miles from here a man and a woman are in love. They have been in love for ten years at least. They pass notes to each other and have their sandwiches together. Their colleagues find their behaviour straining and continually wonder if an emotional bomb is about to explode. The feeling of the office manager, who is my informant, is that their work is affected. The man is married.

The organisational romance is an increasing phenomenon, judging by the number of discussions in journals. This is partly due to the increased participation of women in offices and in higher levels of management and to the fact that they are much more involved in promotion, competition and organisational politics. Organisations require to have a policy towards such relationships. The culture has to forbid or condone. They need to decide if they are going to separate the partners by allocating them to different duties or offices or to allow liaisons to occur freely and accept the consequences. Knowingly condoning a romance which subsequently has a consequential damage, e.g. a divorce or a failure to give a proper service, may expose the company to litigation.

Published literature on the subject reviewed by Maniero (1986), shows that approaches to studying and understanding the topic can be divided into a number of sections. First is the question of the antecedent conditions for the romance: are there any obvious signs to look for or precautions to take? Proximity seems to be the main determinant and the intensity of the work relationship is also important. Where work involves emotional commitment and where joint success is experienced, then mutual arousal levels are heightened. Deeper appreciation of the partner occurs and may be resolved in sexual interaction.

Second, what are the main decision factors in organisational romance? The principal risk factors involved are to career prospects in some cases. For the higher status partner, the main risk is loss of respect, while the lower status partner has to balance the risk of loss of self-esteem. However, both aspects seem relevant to both partners. Risks to home and family are relevant concerns to the married participant. The main reasons given for deciding to develop an involvement are, in order of importance, love, job, ego and power.

Another issue concerns the extent to which the company may be exposed to risk due to the change in internal work relationship dynamics. These include role conflict and the conflict between loyalty to the organisation versus loyalty to the relationship. Damage may also be done through effects on the other members of the work group. The main finding here is that negative effects are more encountered than positive. These include hostility, lower output and distorted communication.

Finally, what managerial approaches are possible and most effective? In some cases there is a definite policy such as married couples not being allowed to work together. It has been said that organisational romance represents an inevitable conflict of interest, in which the company will lose out at all stages of the romantic process. Organisations need policies to subvert such entanglements or to react appropriately when they are known to exist. Objective work performance has been put forward as the deciding issue. If it is not affected, does the romance matter?

The last two decades have seen a major increase in the proportion of women in the workforce; they now represent roughly 40 per cent. Over the years, organisations having been largely designed by men for men have not taken advantage of the special talents of the woman worker and have tended, by dint of their structure and attitudes, to make it more difficult for women than for men to progress in career terms.

Summary

Age and job performance are not directly related in the majority of jobs, and in some roles older people perform better than their younger colleagues. Age stereotypes are very strongly held. There have been great changes in the participation in the workforce of older people. Society and companies will need to be more receptive to the idea of keeping and using older workers to the maximum effect. The shape of peoples' careers is also changing as they get older and we need to be prepared for greater levels of adjustment on both sides to accommodate older workers and also to train and mentor the young apprentices. Stereotyping also affects the female employee. Women's career progress is often not smooth and steady and reaching the upper floors of management is often difficult, due to the imposition of artificial and unseen barriers, stemming from people's attitudes. Social-sexual behaviour includes sexual harassment and organisational affairs. Both are being increasingly reported and made the subject of expensive law cases. Management needs to be proactive in relation to many issues concerned with gender, rather than waiting for problems to happen.

Activities

1. **Follow up some retired workers and analyse their views on the effects of retirement.**

2. **Examine the view that academics do not know how or when to retire with some of your older lecturers.**

3. **Find some women managers and discuss the 'glass ceiling' effect with them. Do they perceive it or is it just an excuse?**

Further reading

Belbin, R.M. (1969) Industrial gerontology: origins, issues and applications in Europe. *Industrial Gerontology*, 1, 12–25.

Birren, J.E., Robinson, P.K and Livingston, S.E. (1986) *Age, Health and Employment*. (Englewood Cliffs, NJ, Prentice Hall).

Burke, R.J. and McKeen, C.A. (1992) Women in management. *International Review of Industrial and Organizational Psychology*, 7, 245–83.

Collinson, M. and Collinson, D. (1996) 'Its only Dick': the sexual harassment of women managers in insurance sales. *Work, Employment and Society*, 10(1), 29–56.

Gutek, B.A. (1985) Sex and the workplace: the impact of sexual behaviour and harassment on women, men and the organization. (San Francisco, Jossey-Bass).

Maule, A.J., Cliff, D.R. and Taylor, R. (1996) Early retirement decisions and how they affect later quality of life. *Ageing and Society*, 16, 177–204.

Emerging issues

Focus questions

Should a business be concerned about right and wrong?

How responsible is an individual worker for what their company does to the environment and to people?

Should affirmative action be encouraged or is it a form of discrimination?

What is the significance of AIDS in the workplace?

What is the correct response to the employee or job applicant with AIDS?

Is work becoming more, and not less, dangerous despite all the regulations?

What should be done about violence at work?

Will there be any jobs left in the future?

What kind of work will there be?

Ethics in business

A topic which is growing in interest is the ethics of business. What can people be expected to do for the firm? How many lies can a man tell? If a company is setting up a plant in a third-world country and is avoiding expensive safety precautions which they would be required to install in the country of origin, is their staff morally bound to refuse to work or morally bound to work? One issue is whether the ethics of the origin country are the important ones or whether the standards of the host country are the relevant ones. Two thousand people were killed and many others severely poisoned a few years ago when an American-owned plant in India exploded and poisoned the surrounding population. Claims are still being processed and fought over.

According to Shepard *et al.* (1991), Adam Smith's *Wealth of Nations* was interpreted so as to give support for the predatory selfish economic urge of the nineteenth century. Smith however said that self-interest could never be an end in itself and that a social system of moral justice based in fairness was crucial. Nowadays they maintain that 'our current economic ideology fails to reflect important distinctions for a vocabulary of ethics and since we seem as a society to be disturbed about the unethical behaviour running rampant in business today there is an urgent need for an injection of a vocabulary of ethics into our teaching of economic ideology'.

Some people might believe that ethics has nothing to do with business and that 'business ethics' is a contradiction in terms. Others might feel that good ethics is good business. Business ethics has its roots in moral philosophy, for example the philosophical theories of Kant, Bentham (Utilitarianism) and John Stuart Mill. Ethics was originally discussed in a somewhat abstract way, but it became increasingly relevant in all areas where humans have to make choices about others. For example R.S. Peters in the context of education opened up a large-scale debate into children's and parents' rights, teacher's behaviour and government obligations. Medical ethics has always had a role in medical training, but in recent years has come to prominence with the debates over abortion, euthanasia and assisted suicide.

Given the dynamic environment in which businesses must operate today, the traditional view of ethics is too static to be useful. Does a consensus really exist? Changes in the nature of the business environment have included the growth of conflicting interest groups (shareholders, employees, community). There has been a great increase in the use of legal criteria when problems of an ethical kind arise. Sometimes the conclusion is that 'if it's legal it's ethical', and the lawyer's sanction has replaced that of the religious person of days gone by.

Ethics is concerned with clarifying what constitutes human welfare and the kind of conduct necessary to promote it (Powers and Vogel, 1980). Ethical behaviour is not governed by hard-and-fast rules; rather it adapts and changes in response to social norms. It represents a 'continuous adjustment of interests'. What was considered ethical in the 1950s and 1960s, for example management prescriptions of standard of dress, employees not allowed to access files, would be considered improper today.

The last few years have witnessed a dramatic growth in interest for ethics in the workplace. New journals, e.g. *Journal of Business Ethics*; *Employee Rights and Responsibilities*, have been founded. One of the principal reasons why this interest has arisen is that widely publicised corporate scandals have exacted high costs and fines in recent times. Public confidence in the reputation of the company and low employee morale result. The public are much more alert to what is going on. Recently Shell had to back down very rapidly on their decision to tow a disused oil platform and sink it in the ocean. Their petrol sales had plummeted to such dangerously low levels within days of the publicity that they were forced to rescind their decision.

Responsibility

Business ethics at the societal level focuses on the role of business in society at large, e.g. the proper relationship between corporation and state. What are the moral responsibilities of companies to the communities in which they operate and to society at large? Friedman (1970) claimed that companies have only one social responsibility and that is to increase their profits. He does not advocate a total disregard of morality. He says that the drive for profit is required to conform to the law and 'ethical custom'. Businesses may seek to do good, provided they do so in order to serve the goal of profit maximisation. It is all right, for example, for a company to provide a local community with amenities if this is done to encourage recruitment, or to generate useful goodwill. He calls it 'hypocritical window-dressing', but it is acceptable because it is in accordance with his profit-maximising criteria. As 'artificial persons', corporations could not have responsibilities; these can only be held by people. This is a subject of debate in business ethics. The basic premise of the case against is that we cannot attribute responsibilities to corporations, because they do not act on the basis of intentions as people do. A business corporation is not merely a collection of individuals, but a highly organised hierarchical structure which is engaged in the systematic direction of human activity towards a common end. This embodies the complex interrelationships of a mass of individual intentions, giving them meaning and direction. The whole is greater than the sum of the parts, so corporations are accountable. But only particular individuals provide corporations with their intentions, i.e. the policy-makers.

Moral responsibility is mostly about accountability. How can we punish corporations? They cannot suffer physical harm, they can only suffer financial harm via fines and boycotts. But it is obviously people, in the shape of shareholders, employees, customers and the like, who will be harmed. Their dividends will be reduced and their employment prospects damaged. There is no way of punishing corporations, it is in reality the punishment of people. A court in 1995 awarded punitive damages of 6 million dollars against a prominent American legal firm, one of whose top executives had spent ten years systematically sexually harassing female staff under him in a childish way, for example, by dropping paper clips down their blouses and then trying to pull them out. The partners knew what was going on, as there had been complaints, but they chose to overlook them as the man was a valuable asset in a business sense.

Ethical questions can also focus on the relationships between the key groups that have a stake in the company, customers, financiers, communities and employees. Ethical questions, such as the proper level of returns to stockholders, fairness in dealing with suppliers, appropriate level of commitment to the community, etc., are important in the daily management of organisations. Stakeholder questions are not independent of societal questions. If the purpose of the business is to maximise returns to shareholders, as Friedman claims, then there are obvious implications for how other stakeholder relationships are managed. Williamson (1984) stated that it is rational that only shareholders and their representatives sit on governing boards of corporations. He argues that other stakeholder groups have effective contractual arrangements that better safeguard their interests than does board membership. But what about the larger social role of the corporation? Goodpaster (1984) defends the position that corporations can have a conscience and should be moral agents that are held no more or less accountable than human agents. Some issues include insider trading, multi-million pound payoffs, locker-room tips and bluffing in the firm–supplier relationship. Carr (1968) likens bluffing on price negotiations to a game where both parties know the rules, 'The ethics of a business are not those of society, but rather those of the poker game'.

Some attention has been given to the firm–customer relationship. The 1980s saw a whole new emphasis being given to the concept of customer service (Peters and Waterman, 1982). Here we are dealing with such issues as marketing and consumer affairs. Research on the ethics of advertising raises issues such as, what is truth and, how much information is enough? Other issues in the public eye include the effects on communities of plants closing, and the issues of pollution and environmental damage.

Employees have a special place in the network of stakeholder relationships. Issues include, drug testing, privacy, employee rights, etc. Landy (1989) outlines some areas specific to Testing and Evaluation for consideration. He says that evaluation and assessment of people presents 'one of the most significant tests of ethical behaviour'. Practitioners must be aware of the most recent advances in the field, staying abreast of new tests and testing procedures and ways of measuring work performance and recent developments in theory on intellectual abilities, work motivation, accident prevention, etc. Also, there is a responsibility to individual workers and people applying for employment.

Ethical standards which should be observed include the following:

1. The employer must guard against the invasion of privacy, e.g. should not use a questionnaire for personal information of a sensitive nature if there is no clear reason for collecting that information.

2. The employer must guarantee confidentiality, with no casual discussion of test scores of individuals.

3. They should be prepared to provide feedback about evaluation and present information in such a way that the individual understands what the score means.

4. An individual who has been evaluated has the right to know how the information will be used. Similarly a person who evaluates another, e.g. supervisor rating a subordinate, has a right to know what the data will be used for.

5. Data should not be kept for too long. It can become stale. It would be unethical to use pre-employment test scores of individuals collected twenty years ago to assist in making a promotion decision today. It does not accurately represent the person today.

Employee policy

Ewing (1977) stated that employees should not be asked to give up the basic political rights of freedom of speech, privacy, etc., which liberal society grants them in life outside the organisation. Many of his suggestions have been implemented, e.g. 'open-door' policies and codes of conduct. Employees are more aware of these issues and are willing to take legal action when they believe that their privacy rights have been violated by employers. Between 1985 and 1987 there were nearly 100 jury verdicts, averaging $316000 in favour of employees. In 1979 to 1980, there was none. Privacy cases most often involved drug testing, computer monitoring and dismissal charges. Davidson (1988) claims that drug testing violates the employee's right to privacy and without serious and compelling reason it is not justified. In the United States, drug testing is more than ever becoming a condition of employment and many organisations are carrying out random tests.

In view of the legal requirements surrounding personal privacy, employers should know the legislation and plan necessary changes in the management of personnel information. In most European countries, Data Protection Acts have been passed which regulate the collection, processing, keeping, use and disclosure of personal information that is processed by automated means. Such laws do not apply to data which is held in manual files. The act gives a right to every individual to establish the existence of personal data, to have access to such data and to have inaccurate data rectified or erased.

Affirmative action/reverse discrimination

In order to achieve greater equality for disadvantaged workers, some philosophers and employers advocate a policy of 'affirmative action'. This involves the recognition that certain groups have been disadvantaged in the past and seeks to implement deliberate measures to compensate for this. This may involve policies of 'positive discrimination', sometimes called 'reverse discrimination'. Examples include setting quotas for disadvantaged groups, or allowing an applicant's gender or race to influence the decision to hire.

Nagel (1988) defends affirmative action based on the social need 'to remove the stubborn residues of racial caste'. It is needed to redress past discrimination against minorities and women. However, affirmative action policies are controversial. Treating sex or gender as a reason for putting someone at an advantage is unfair and the point is to try and achieve fairness. Richards (1980) in *The Sceptical Feminist* points out that affirmative action can only be used as a short-term measure for specific purposes relating to the status of women.

The statement 'good ethics is good business' cannot be true without qualification. Take for example, British tea companies paying low wages to Third World plantation workers. For one company to generously increase wages would be disastrous for it in commercial terms. Their product would be at a price disadvantage relative to the rivals who did not increase wages and their profits would decline. Therefore, there is a limit to the degree to which ethics and commercial self-interest can converge. Being ethical imposes limits, perhaps cost. But, on balance, benefits (company reputation, public esteem, employee loyalty and trust of other companies) outweigh the costs, so 'ethics pays'. In general, most companies contain their drive for profit within broad legal and moral limits.

Drummond and Bain (1994) predict that ethics will become a very important area for managers in the future. A major influence is perceived changes in society's values. Companies need to empower employees at all levels to identify the shifts and act accordingly. Employees need to be aware of the corporate values and standards so that their actions support and add to the corporate ethos.

Interventions

In the future, awareness programmes, special ethical training programmes, selection procedures (hiring individuals possessing high ethical standards), group seminars on issues (peer influence is important) and codes of ethics (statements of the norms and beliefs of the organisation), will all become important.

Example

Zeebrugge Car Ferry Disaster – 'Herald of Free Enterprise' 1987

This disaster was occasioned by the failure to close the bow doors properly. Mr. X who usually closed them was asleep during a public address call. But it was not a simple case of one person's error, as there was no effective system for ensuring the doors were closed. Mr. X's superior, who was responsible for ensuring that they were closed, also had to be on the bridge during 'harbour stations' call. From here, neither he nor the captain could see if the doors were closed. In 1985, a captain had written to notify the company's chief superintendent and suggested indicator lights. Directors had also been alerted to other problems, e.g. shortcomings in arrangements for counting passengers, and the question of the stability of the open car deck.

The Court of Formal Inquiry decided that the blame rested not only on the three principal crew members involved but also with the company, which was ordered to pay £350 000 costs. Following this, a coroner's jury returned a verdict of unlawful killing. This led to criminal charges being brought against the company and its workers. In 1990, the trial judge directed the jury to 'withdraw from consideration' the charges against the company and five of the seven individuals. The prosecution decided that it was not in the public interest to continue the case. Reasons given for dropping the case were that it could not be proven that there was gross negligence required for manslaughter. It had sailed under its defective arrangements before, so the risk of an accident was not 'obvious'. The company evaded the criminal law, but suffered costs in damages and bad publicity. Today the issue of the basically unsafe nature of roll on–roll off ferries is still in the public arena.

AIDS in the workplace

The prevalence and spread of AIDS has dramatically affected all of our lifestyles at the end of the twentieth century. It has had no less effect in the context of the workplace. Our awareness of AIDS and models of reaction to AIDS at work have both developed on American experience. AIDS is one of the top three concerns of American employers according to a survey in *Fortune* magazine (1988). An estimate by the US insurance company AllState said that the cost of AIDS to business in terms of lost productivity, recruitment and training cost would be somewhere in the region of $55 billion dollars, or in other words almost the total profit of the 100 top companies. As well as such costs being a significant attention grabber, legal issues are arising. These range from suits from infected workers who claim discrimination to suits from affected customers of organisations with an AIDS-affected employee.

There is much fear and misapprehension about AIDS at work. This obliges management to implement policies, both educational and managerial, to help people come to terms with the social effects of the disease. Workers in the healthcare frontline are most likely to be exposed to AIDS, though even for them the incidence of contracting the illness has been small. A strong public fear is of contracting AIDS through food products, but this is virtually impossible and no cases have been shown to exist. It is nevertheless a fear and has forced food producing companies to be extra vigilant and to react to staff with cuts and abrasions. AIDS screening has become an issue, with some companies introducing it for new staff. Tests for HIV are however not 100 per cent reliable and the virus takes several weeks after infection before it shows up in test samples.

Being HIV positive would not initially make someone any less effective in their job than they were before. An employee cannot be dismissed for being HIV positive or for being an AIDS sufferer, though some companies have used non-disclosure of information as an excuse to implement dismissal. The risks of transmission in most situations are minute, yet many people have had to leave jobs because of social pressure from colleagues. Very strong negative attitudes have been shown in the population in general towards infected people. Even a Christian organisation equated AIDS with homosexual behaviour and led on from this to argue that civil rights protection need not extend to gay people. Strangely, a not inconsiderable proportion of the workforce, including many of the senior executives of this organisation, is either latently or overtly gay themselves. This hopefully illustrates the moral confusion which exists in this area.

Violence and accidents at work

The reduction of violence at work is another area where the design of work and the workplace can have a significant impact. According to Landy, instances of violence at work are increasing in the United States. In Northern Ireland an RUC man, apparently suffering from the effects of cumulative job stress, decided to make his own contribution to the security situation and shot dead three Sinn Fein members in Belfast on 4 February 1992. Workers from two different shifts in a bacon factory had a serious physical fracas in the carpark at changeover time over productivity issues. In this case, their enthusiasm or work commitment appeared to overheat, (they were currently under a competitive incentive plan put in by a consultant), and spilled over into a dispute between the groups.

During 1992 in the United States slightly more than 6000 workers lost their lives due to injuries and accidents received while at work. Five deaths occur for every 100000 people employed. For every fatality involving a female there are nine involving a male. Those categories of worker with the relatively higher risk factor are males, those over 65 and those working in farming, transport, mining and construction.

Highway vehicle accidents were the largest cause of death for male workers; for females the highest cause of death was workplace homicide! In 1992 in the United States, 1004 people were actually murdered while at their work. That figure includes 822 shootings and 82 stabbings. Of deaths at work, 3 per cent were due to self-inflicted injuries, i.e. suicide. Falls at work accounted for a sizeable number of deaths, 590 (10 per cent) and electrocutions for 334 (5 per cent). A significantly higher risk was also evident in the self-employed family business area, which accounted for 20 per cent of fatalities, though it only represents 9 per cent of registered employed people (Toscano and Windau, 1993).

It seems that the United States Postal Service is particularly unfortunate, with over thirty fatal attacks per annum. The phrase 'going postal' has now entered the language to indicate a loss of self-control with dangerous consequences. Postal workers seem to be under great pressure at work and this is thought to be one of the causes of the inordinate amount of incidents.

European legislation in the area of Health and Safety at Work is aimed at reducing the hazards in the workplace. Included among these are psycho-social hazards which may give rise to violence. The major focus is in reducing the incidence of violence, i.e. prevention by suitable control measures and design of environments. Also relevant is the aetiology of violent acts. An effective response to violence requires a detailed understanding of its origins. A difficulty found in this and related topics is that the recording of violent acts is very inconsistent. In many situations, the admission that a violent act has taken place is an admission of defeat and managers often prefer to deal with the situation in their own way and not make a report of an incident. The culture of reporting and exaggerating violent acts varies from time to time, depending on the media's chosen point of focus.

Estimates are that up to five times as many incidents of violent crime occur than are reported (Hough and Mayhew, 1983). A survey of violent acts occurring in UK public houses found that only around one in seven were ever reported by managers to outside authorities (Cox *et al.*, 1988). A manager would prefer to avoid getting a reputation as one who cannot cope with difficult customers. Also once the act has occurred, there is an attitude of 'it's happened and there is no need to make a fuss over it'. Managers may have limited faith that there is ever going to be any useful response to reporting the act anyway and in this they are probably right.

Workers who are most prone to being on the receiving end of violence at work are those providing a service which the recipients have, or think they have, an 'entitlement' to. The recipients themselves are often poor, vulnerable people who are under emotional or financial stress and if their entitlements are refused or reduced, perhaps without apparent reason, this forms a stimulus for violence. Social workers, nurses, housing and social security staff are vulnerable to this spillover violence resulting from frustration. Police and prison officers meet their customers in very trying circumstances and violence is ever-present in the job. Those working in the entertainment industry, especially where alcohol or drugs are supplied, such as in bars and clubs, are victims of a more aimless violence arising from lack of control and the flare-ups of petty disputes.

Responses to violence

Responses to violence in the workplace need to be informed with the facts and their analysis. Most violence arises through an escalation process, which when examined after the event is reasonably evident. Staff are trained to recognise the process in its formation and progress and to withdraw or behave in a placatory manner before things get out of control. Much violence can be avoided if the staff are well trained in recognising the warning signs and respond appropriately.

Working environments can be better designed so that violence is less likely and, if it occurs, can be more easily responded to, for example controlling crowds, being informative about queue times, providing appropriate numbers of staff and support people at peak times, preventing clients massing, providing good lighting, avoiding having essential paths (to toilets, exits, pay-counters) and crossing areas of potential disturbance, are some of the obvious steps which are taken.

Violence can usefully be viewed as a behavioural sequence in a context. Aspects of context and the behaviour of others provide a stimulus, while people's response provides a source of maintenance or escalation. Cox and Leather (1994) suggest using a control cycle model to respond in a preventative way to violence-prone areas of work. This consists of a sequence which is repeated.

> Identify problem
>
> Design response strategies
>
> Plan and implement strategies
>
> Monitor their success
>
> Feedback results into redesign

Future work

Globalisation of production

The extent to which production has been internationalised in the last decade is really enormous; for example there are now 80 000 foreign joint ventures currently operating in China, while ten years ago there were a mere handful. Similar expansions are occurring in Eastern Europe and the states which were formerly part of the Soviet Union. An example of the globalisation of production is given by Robert Reich (1991). The constituents of a $10 000 General Motors car consists of over 60 per cent foreign-sourced materials and labour.

$3000	South Korea	Assembly and labour
$1750	Japan	Advanced components
$750	West Germany	Styling and design engineering
$400	Taiwan, Singapore	Small components
$250	Britain	Advertising and marketing
$50	Ireland	Data processing

These figures are probably quite out of date as we write. Globalisation will have taken a further step.

Changing job roles

Work roles or occupations have increasingly proliferated over the years. Descartes in the seventeenth century counted two to three dozen disciplines in which an individual might pursue a career. Today that number is well over 20000. In 1930, the US Department of Labor enumerated 80 different kinds of work; today the number is over 800 and rising. The future of work is thus of an ever-increasing number of jobs in ever more specialised areas. This has vast implications for people at work as they may be over-specialised and they may have to retrain regularly. It also puts an onus on job designers and companies to use existing skills in new ways and to build in the opportunity for people to adapt without having to move root and branch via a training course to a new location. Jobs need to be truly organic and grow with the person, not static with a limited lifecycle.

The internal labour market in companies is breaking down. Loyalty and self-development are not necessarily being rewarded, as they once were, with security, promotion and more pay. Increased competition, declining union power and changing philosophy and policies of governments and employers have essentially turned the clock back to the labour market arrangements of the late 1800s and early 1900s resulting in subcontracting, contingent pay, performance pay and more employee and managerial discretion (Capelli, 1995). Those people with rare and valuable skills and experience can charge what they like and the more the better, while those relatively unskilled have to fend for themselves or become long-term unemployed. It is possible of course, that in a few years this situation will reverse itself and companies will again realise the value of cohesive and committed workforces, etc.

Roessner (1985) maintains that one-quarter to one-third of all clerical jobs will be gone by the year 2000. They will be replaced by the gradual use and development of voice recognition, optical character recognition and expert systems. Management changes will elicit more production from fewer and less expensive workers. These changes include the use of quality circles, more home and flexible working and cafeteria fringe benefits, giving workers better rewards for better performance or for not working.

Responses to the withering away of jobs

Our European Union governments and most importantly we ourselves must develop policy options to deal with these kind of issues. How are we going to react and how are we going to vote? Are there ways which might be considered to maintain employment? A number of responses are possible. We might vastly increase the development of environmental infrastructure, e.g. roads, railways, ports, etc. Pumping investment into these areas is highly labour-intensive and also usually good for the community. It is difficult to globalise building a road, though my civil engineering colleagues predict that road surfaces will eventually be bought in and laid down in a sort of prefabricated manner. We will almost certainly expand the ratio of providers to clients, e.g. nurses, social workers, teachers and counsellors. This seems to be happening, and then it is not happening. Governments seeking to save money prefer to make nurses unemployed than to stop making weapon systems of mass destruction. (Of course, war is in itself a very good creator of employment in all ways, both during and after. Unfortunately it leaves the countries involved with enormous debts to pay back.) A number of changes to the fiscal system are thought likely. Tax systems will be changed to give optimum reward to innovation and business, overtime and excessive pay may be taxed more severely, making the employment of more people a better option.

There are other options which will lead to large increases in labour requirements. We can reduce the working week to 30 hours or 4 days, but this is not popular. Recently the European Court insisted that a 48 hour working week would be the maximum allowed in the Union. In the future, we can expect that workers will be given more sabbatical leave for education and training. Early retirement will be widespread and the age level will decline. Child allowance/care subsidies will be given in increasing numbers to facilitate people with families. National service corps may be introduced to 'soak up' the increasing numbers of unemployable young men, particularly those who are becoming an increasing burden on the communities due to vandalism and petty crime. Free higher education is more or less available and will also include a greater number of mature students, though the scope here is less than it was, as many of the eligible and motivated people are already through the system. Most of the participants in adult education are and have always been women in any case (Shostak, 1993).

Flexible firms

The flexible firm is a concept introduced by Atkinson (1984) from the UK Institute of Manpower Studies. Companies seek to increase their ability to adapt to the demands of the market and at the same time, keep their cost profile under control. These efforts have great implications for the workforce. The principal sources of greater flexibility are in the selection, training and placement of the workforce. For example, multiskilling replaced traditional craft demarcation lines (Aer Lingus). There has been a very large increase in subcontracting to fulfil parts of the work requirements, e.g. recruitment consultants and accountants. Companies are also forcing down payments, taking advantage of the large pool in labour, e.g. bank assistant grade. In the legal area, trainees are taken on and paid minimum salaries until they are qualified and then they are let go. Even in surgery, the future trend is going to be that certain operations which are routine and depend largely on high-technology equipment could be and one day will be performed by technicians rather than surgeons.

New work arrangements include the idea of flexibility, i.e. anyone can do anything, free-floating working day, part-time work and home-working. In the 1990s these have been the characteristics of situations which have given rise to increases in employment as opposed to the traditional arrangements, which have experienced declines. Examples of flexible work include consultancy, contracting, self-employment, seasonal work and undeclared work. Many organisations find such arrangements attractive and suitable for their requirements for staff. Temporary workers, for example, represent the most common form of part-time work, as managers can respond instantly to the needs of the market in an uncertain environment. Temporary workers can be viewed as a kind of security ringfence around the hard core of permanent staff. Layoffs and casualties are absorbed by the temps, while the permanents sail on. This is creating a class-stratified workforce in a particularly unpleasant way.

Part-time work

Women are in part-time work much more frequently than men, the ratio is between 20:1 in Austria and Germany to around 4:1 in Denmark and The Netherlands. In Ireland, 18 per cent of females and 4 per cent of males who are in employment are part-timers, while the figures for Britain are 44 per cent and 6 per cent. The European Union is attempting to secure more employment rights for part-time workers, but many countries and especially employers are opposed to this. Surveys have suggested that many women prefer part-time work and that employers seeing part-time work as gender-based have structured work around this fact, i.e. making both the work itself and the shift system and hours of work suitable for the part-time female model of employee. Increased flexibility and lower wage and benefit costs are the main attraction for employers (Zeytinoglu, 1992).

Women's increasing presence in the workforce has coincided with an increase in the proportion of part-time jobs. Contingent workers, as they are sometimes called, have been a feature of many labour markets for a long time. Home-workers, migrant workers, seasonal workers and subcontractors have been accepted as normal in some industries such as agriculture and tourism. Nowadays, the incidence of part-time work is not restricted, but has spread into almost all sectors of industry and even education. In many colleges and universities the people who have the most significant contact with students are often part-time or temporary, for example, postgraduates, language assistants and tutors.

Part-time workers have been regarded less favourably in terms of their work commitment and other attitudes to work. This is partly a reflection of society's views of contingent-type workers, such as migrant workers, and the organisation's stance on the expendability of part-time workers, i.e 'because we don't think you are very significant you won't think we are very significant either'. This is a function of attributions and not necessarily a true reflection of reality. Studies of part-time workers show mixed results, but they often perceive their treatment in the workplace as less favourable, though their commitment to work is not any different from full-time workers. In some cases, i.e. professional women, their feelings are often more positive to work, especially in professions where men tend to be dominant in numbers. Part-time women workers' level of satisfaction with home and work life has been found to be higher than in the case of full-time female employees (Barker, 1993). It is not only women who are seeking part-time work; this is becoming increasingly attractive to men too. A survey at Du Pont company of over 100 000 workers found the number of men interested in part-time work had increased from 18 per cent in 1985 to 33 per cent in 1988 (Kantrowitz et al., 1989).

Workforces have become very diverse in recent years and this diversity will increase. The majority of the workforce in most countries are now not the traditional male breadwinner with a family at home. There are single mothers, divorced people, dual career families, double jobbers and so on. There is much greater potential for conflict, as the workers try to balance their family demands and responsibilities with those of work. That these conflicts give rise to stress has already been discussed, but what can firms do about it? In order to survive and compete for this increasingly diverse workforce, companies need to think about family supportive policies. These will include building in some of the following to the company personnel system: child care at work, facilities for those looking after elderly relatives, more flexitime and job sharing, information and referral services for the care of sick children, family leave and so on. Thus workers' dependencies and outside work responsibilities will have to be catered for (Thomas and Ganster, 1995).

Women, particularly in the 'developing' countries, are relatively low paid, yet their domestic duties are still there to be done after work. In the future, there is going to be a steady increase in the number of dependent elderly parents to be looked after; again this has been traditionally 'women's work' (Moore, 1995).

The forms of work in modern industrial society are, according to Moore, waged work (what we tend to think of as 'jobs'), unwaged productive work (e.g. Asian family enterprises in the garment industry), domestic work (cleaning, cooking), welfare work (looking after the weak, elderly, relatives), emotion work (caring for and bonding people in the family and social group) and human capital work (bearing and caring for children). As can be seen, many of these forms of work are traditionally 'women's work' rather than men's.

Job sharing

Job sharing became popular in the 1980s and was seen as an advantageous arrangement for married women wanting to return to the workforce. Less turnover is experienced, but disadvantages are found in the loss of tacit job knowledge and of the political dimensions of the working environment and in relationships with fellow workers. This may all be summed up in the phrase 'weakened job commitment'.

Teleworking

Robert Reich in his book *The Work of Nations* states that the foot-soldiers of the worldwide data-based economies are now the data processors sitting at banks of terminals in Third World countries linked to worldwide networks. The Caribbean, the Philippines and to a lesser extent Ireland have become the centres of large data-processing operations, often for companies in the United States and other developed areas. Workers in these places are very much cheaper than in the United States, equally skilful, but most importantly have job turnover rates as low as 2 per cent, while in the United States the turnover figure in these occupations is as high as 35 per cent. According to the United Nations, Jamaican 'digiport' workers earn less than 10 per cent per hour of the United States job rates. The European Commission has put some effort into supporting teleworking. This is motivated partly by a desire to breathe economic life into remote rural areas. A major initial advantage to the teleworker is the reduction in commuting time and effort compared to the office job. More general questions have to be addressed in the long term concerning workers' satisfaction, management styles, the effect on organisational culture and the fact that teleworking jobs may often be more cognitively demanding because of the lack of support in decision making. Such supports have to be designed into the system more explicitly than in regular jobs.

In the mid 1980s it was estimated that 7 per cent of the UK workforce worked from home; today the figure is much greater. In these situations the worker can easily become or feel exploited. Less control is able to be exercised over work demands which come continually down the line and the boundaries of work and home life become obscured, with the possible effects on the relationship with partners and children.

Management practices have to adjust too. Some managers have difficulty coping with the teleworker because he or she is out of sight. Much decision making may have to be devolved to the worker and a more specific approach to work objectives taken. It is not a case of leaving people on their own at the end of a telephone line; communication and feedback are vital, perhaps even more so than when the worker is physically present (Dooley, 1996). In any case, communication is not the same if it takes place by e-mail, phone, video conferencing or face to face. People still prefer face to face for emotionally laden dialogues or where they need to persuade or argue. E-mail leads to stilted dialogues where nuances are not developed and facts are the centre of the communication.

These are some of the important issues which occupational psychology will have to become deeply involved in. They will change much of what has gone before in this book, as the changing patterns of work make the old theories and perspectives out of date. Your contribution to this process is eagerly anticipated!

Summary

This chapter raised a number of different issues which will make an impact on most of our working lives. There are important moral and ethical dilemmas ahead as our communities get richer and the less fortunate get poorer. Many of these issues impinge on the workforce and certainly in our role as consumers of the products of the workforce. Even though we may not be directly affected, we are duty bound to be informed and to hold a view about ethical issues, immigration, low-wage economies, and exploitation of part-time workers. We can vote for higher taxes and job creation or we can vote for unfettered capitalism, or we can work out a compromise where the rights of workers and the right of people to work can be balanced against a fair distribution of resources, so that almost everyone is comfortable with their life and their moral position.

Activities

1. **Discuss what you think work will look like in 100 years.**

2. **Ask older people about the changes they have seen in their work and that of others over their lifespan.**

3. **In your college or company, find out about the ethical committee. Who decides what is right or wrong? Can you identify instances where people have to make finely balanced ethical choices?**

Further reading

Capelli, P. (1995) Re-thinking employment. *British Journal of Industrial Relations*, 33(4), 563–602.

Chapman, A.J., Sheehy, N.P., Heywood, S., Dooley, B. and Collins, S.C. (1995) The organizational implications of teleworking. *International Review of Industrial and Organizational Psychology*, 10, 229–48.

Guest, D.E. (1994) Organisational psychology and human resource management. *European Work and Organizational Psychologist*, 4, 251–70.

Robertson, J. (1985) *Future Work*. (Aldershot, Gower).

The organisational context

Focus questions

Why do people join unions?

Is there such a person as a born leader?

How can organisational communication be improved?

What is a work team?

Are organisations more than just the people in them?

So far we have taken a mainly 'micro-level' view of occupational psychology. That is, we have looked at the problems at the level of the individual as the primary focus. Many texts usually called 'organisational psychology', focus on issues at a group or organisational level. In the first chapter we briefly referred to them under the heading 'social psychology' as it was social psychologists who first presented them for large-scale public consumption before the industrial/organisational psychologists took them over and adapted them for their own purposes. We will now take a brief look at some of these issues, starting with union–management relations and the psychology of trade union membership.

Unions and management

Since the early 1980s, the declining power of the trade unions has been an item on the agenda wherever organisational politics or psychology are discussed. A very large consideration in any organisation used to be what the trade union view would be of 'this', where 'this' meant anything from performance appraisal, to selection testing to antidiscrimination policies. In general, it is regrettable to have to say that the trade union view in many places was 'we don't like it', but we might get to like it provided you recognise that you are asking us to alter the working conditions of our members and pay us accordingly for cooperating with your proposed change. Economic changes referred to in earlier chapters, such as the growth in unemployment, globalisation of competition from low-wage economies, increasing proportions of part-time workers and in women members in the workforce have forced fundamental changes in the behaviour of management and unions. The industrial power of the large unions was greatly reduced by the significant decline in several major British industries such as coal and shipbuilding and the privatisation of others such as the public utilities. At the latest count (Milner, 1995), no union is recognised in 47 per cent of British plants with over twenty-five workers, in stark contrast to the situation only a few decades ago.

     One of the major transformations has been the considerable reduction in the use of the 'strike' as a means of pursuing industrial objectives. Apart from a change in trade union ethos, which has moved them away from the obstructionist posture of the past, there has also been legislation which has affected the procedures for arranging strikes. This includes cooling-off periods, compulsory ballots and restrictions on secondary picketing, all of which have had a role to play in downgrading the strike weapon. Although strikes still occur, they are usually short-lived and sporadic. A great change has taken place in the attitudes of both sides of industry. In many cases, the perception is that 'we are all in this together', all on the one side. Although less is heard about trade unions in the media, they are still fulfilling vital roles in the economy. Technical, professional and service unions have grown and replaced the traditional 'cloth cap and steel toe-cap' brigade. Attitudes to negotiations and to objectives for workers have changed substantially. The unions are now led by more qualified and skilled people, who have no inferiority complex to play down or hide by a show of muscle, as in former days.

Psychological influence on the industrial relations scene has not been lacking over the last two decades, though it cannot be said to have been very prominent either. The kinds of issues considered have been widely varying. Of principal interest has been the process of negotiation. As this is largely a communication and influencing process, it is very amenable to the interpretations of psychology. A second area is that of the development, both in its increase and in its decline, of commitment to a trade union. We have noted interest in work commitment earlier on, but there is also a considerable interest in how people gain and lose their commitment to a trade union. Some of the leading trade union figures over the years have been very talented people who could have been successful and wealthy in many areas, but chose to work for the union. They are often fired with a social conscience or with a strong political commitment to the working classes.

Another fascinating area of study is the strike. How does this destructive piece of group behaviour emerge and how can it be prevented? How can the entrenched and sometimes bitter positions of the opposing parties be unfrozen and resolved? Numerous psychological theories have been applied towards explaining the occurrence and maintenance of strike behaviour. These range from the familiar 'frustration–aggression' hypothesis, to social interactionist theories, e.g. 'mob rule', and recently to cognitive theories, e.g. relative deprivation (Bluen, 1994).

The Works Council, supposedly a cooperative group of workers and management, is one of the suggested alternatives to the trade union. Many multinational companies setting up on this side of the Atlantic seek 'no-union' agreements, but are prepared to go along with the idea of a Works Council and its subsidiary committees. How do such Councils function and how does the experience of worker directors change their attitudes and their relations with their fellow workers? This is another useful and growing set of study topics for psychologists. Recruitment to unions is another area of study which is vital from the trade union point of view. People are now free to join or not to join a union and many have seemingly opted not to. Is this due to apathy or just meanness or is there some deeper reason?

According to Hartley and Kelly (1986), we need to define industrial relations in terms of both individual and collective behaviour. One point of view will not encompass the complexity of the subject. Earlier research in this subject has tended to focus more on the collectivist angle, topics such as the growth and development of the group, leadership, the dynamics of communication, the environmental effects, etc. However, industrial relations is essentially about 'control over work relations' (Hyman, 1975), and this control can be exercised by the individual as well as by the group. Ultimately, as we have seen, the individual has the choice of whether to cooperate or not, to accept a solution or not or to resist a change or not. In the final analysis, the individual can even leave the job and seek another and in some cases does precisely that. The changing nature of work can be seen as responsible for this shift in the psychology of industrial relations. The heavy emphasis on qualifications, technological competencies and individualisation of the production process within the context of teams, is all leading the individual worker to becoming a decision-maker, a builder of their own career. Because there is no longer a job for life, there is no longer a worker–management relationship for life either. We have to learn to adapt in this area, as in any other.

Another view of industrial relations contrasts the traditional somewhat 'masculine' topics, such as power, conflict, winning and struggling, with the more 'feminine' and more modern topics, such as developing cooperation, learning to accommodate others, and working out harmonious living arrangements between the various human elements in the production process (Walker, 1979). The growth of these new topics may be partly the result of the increasing presence of women in the workplace and of the increasing numbers of female managers, particularly in the personnel sector.

Union participation

This topic has been of greater interest since the decline of the large union power blocks, such as the miners. New 'techno' unions have taken this issue more seriously, as the workers now have the choice not to be in a union and often exercise it. It is of great interest to the union if they can determine motives for participation. The lifeblood of any union, whether progressive or traditionalist, has been numbers.

As far as we know to date, joining a union has largely been a matter of availability and opportunity. Studies of individual factors such as gender or age, or of job-related factors, such as skill or occupational level, have not produced consistent relations with union-joining behaviour (Guest and Dewe, 1988).

Trade union activity is in most instances an occasional behaviour. In many companies or organisations, most of the time there is not much apparent need for union activity. Participation in voting, e.g. for a shop steward or in actual decision making, is generally very low. It takes a cause of some kind or another to bring people out, and even then they can be quite apathetic until they are threatened personally. People are content to belong, partly for insurance reasons, as long as they do not have to do much. Our own local university branch of the lecturers' union has over 200 members, but annual meetings can usually be held around a dining-room table. The organisational or industrial setting is important in heightening or lessening the perceived advantages of belonging to a union. In many settings it can be observed that workers are loyal to their craft, i.e. a fitter will not do the work of an electrician and vice versa. This is a loyalty that is paramount over that to the more abstract concept of the union. The union serves as a source of support in many ways, but it is the workgroup or craft group that welds the workers together and serves to initiate actions which may later be taken up by one or more unions.

Commitment to the union or to the company ('dual commitment') has been looked at by many researchers. Union commitment has been shown to increase if there is industrial unrest, culminating in a strike. People's perceptions are substantially altered during and after a strike. Comparing striking workers to non-strikers shows that the strikers change their evaluation of working conditions downward during the strike and evaluate post-strike packages more positively than do the others. In a scenario of decline in union membership, those who remain are more committed. Strikes bring about greater cohesion in the workforce, more support for militant action and higher evaluations of union leaders than previously. These effects are even enhanced if the strike brings about a degree of hardship (Mellor, 1990).

A scale frequently used to measure union commitment, developed by Gordon *et al.* (1980) has four factors underlying strength of union commitment. These are union loyalty, responsibility to the union, willingness to work for the union and belief in unionism. Early socialisation experiences at work and with union members are the best predictors of high scores on the first two factors, with past and present activity predicting the third and fourth factors. Job satisfaction correlates positively with the first factor, but not with the other three. Some items from this scale are as follows:

> I feel a sense of pride being a part of the union.
>
> The union's problems are my problems.
>
> If asked I would run for elected office in this union.
>
> My values and the union's values are not very similar.
>
> As long as I am doing the kind of work I enjoy, it doesn't matter if I belong to a union.

Leadership

Of all the topics in the occupational psychology literature, leadership is probably the one which captures the public imagination and which speaks more directly to management in organisations than any other. It is not difficult to see why. Anyone with a little ambition wants to be the 'boss' and most of us in the groups that we work in sometimes think that we could do a far better job if we were in charge. We ask ourselves, do I have what it takes to be the leader or am I better off just 'towing the line' and doing a good job as a number two? Is there something in all of us which determines whether we will be the leader or not? Do I show the right kind of behaviours and decisions which might get me noticed and promoted? Or do I have no chance in this organisation, because leaders come from a different social sector, or occupational sector, and so on? These four questions originate in the three main approaches to studying leadership.

Trait Approach:	Some people have personality characteristics which suit them for leadership roles more than others.
Behavioural Approach:	Leaders are people who in the situation behave differently from others. They have habits and styles of behaviour which make them suitable for the role.
Organisational/Situational Approach:	Settings construct their own leaders; whether through politics or tradition certain people are groomed for success and emerge as the leader in terms of the requirement of the organisation.

Trait approaches

Research which asks group members to nominate leaders and then examines the characteristic traits which distinguish leaders from the rest has come up with some consistent results. In such situations, the leaders are stronger in traits of intelligence, dominance and masculinity (Lord *et al.*, 1984).

Being seen as a leader in a group is not the same as being able to successfully perform the role of leader. The most important person is usually the chief executive and below them, the leaders of the crucial sections of the enterprise. Findings have suggested that there are again some consistencies in the kinds of general traits that effective managers need to possess. Again intelligence is the most important. In terms of the 'Big Five' personality factors mentioned earlier, people who are high on conscientiousness and extroversion are likely to perform more effectively in managerial roles. These findings vary from study to study, suggesting that in certain managerial situations personality traits make a bigger difference than in others. Extroversion includes being enthusiastic, liking the company of others, being sociable, high seeking for stimulation and change. The highly conscientious person is concerned with doing things right, getting things finished, looking after details, having a vision of perfection and having ideals (Tett and Jackson, 1991).

Various combinations in the individual of power and achievement needs have been shown to be associated with success in leaders in different kinds of organisations. A high need for achievement accompanied by high power needs is only suitable in situations where dominance and driving force can be tolerated. Independent entrepreneurs in their own business or salespeople in strongly competitive situations may succeed with this kind of combination, but in more orderly settings they will not be accepted. Here the need to be able to play down the strength of power needs, combined with a strong will to win is necessary. This has been called 'high power inhibition', which allows the need for power to be more socialised.

McClelland and Boyzatis (1982) carried out a longitudinal study in an American telephone company; those recruits who were high on the leadership motive pattern had substantially enhanced their career progression compared to others at eight and sixteen years after recruitment. This, however, was only true to any significant extent for those in non-technical specialities; it did not apply to the technical people. A similar result was found in officers in the Navy. Leadership motive pattern was derived from codings of stories from the Thematic Apperception Test (TAT) (Murray, 1938), according to three dimensions: need for power, need for affiliation and self-control. The TAT is a form of projective test, in which people are presented with a number of black and white pictures and are asked to tell a story based on the scene. They say,

> Power is important because it shows that the person is interested in the 'influence game', in having effects on others; lower Affiliation needs enables the manager to make difficult decisions without fear of being disliked; high self-control is important because it means the person is likely to be concerned with maintaining organisational systems and following procedures. (McClelland and Boyzatis, 1982)

Cognitive resource theory

This is one of several formulations which are beginning to put together the trait and the environmental moderator of trait expression as a viable explanation for differential leadership effectiveness. Suitable traits must interact with suitable environments, as has been suggested above. Where the group is strongly supportive of the leader and where the aims of the group are identified with very strongly, a less dominant kind of leader can be very effective, provided the trait of high intelligence is present. Someone who is able to lead by the power of their diagnostic ability and their skill at identifying opportunities, for example, can be very effective in a group which is committed strongly to the group goals. Such leaders are likely to be found in scientific or research environments where the outright power needs of the business developer might be quite unacceptable. The Cognitive Resource theory is still in its development stages. Fiedler and Garcia (1987) incorporate the variables of leader intelligence, technical competence and experience. While those who recruit managers seek to identify strengths in these three areas with a view to effective selection, Fiedler and Garcia maintain that the leader's cognitive resources will only affect group performance under certain definable conditions. A number of testable hypothesis have followed from this theory.

- *Leader under stress*: intelligence will be diverted from the task and so intelligence and competence may not correlate with group performance.
- *Leader is directive*: there will be higher correlations of intelligence with performance.
- *Group is supportive*: correlation of intelligence with performance will be enhanced.
- *Group supportive and leader non-directive*: intelligence of group members will show enhanced correlation with performance.
- *Task is intellectually demanding*: leader's intelligence and performance will correlate.
- *Leader under stress*: job-relevant experience will correlate more with performance than intelligence.

Vecchio's view is that the original trait theory view has been largely discredited by empirical evidence. It has a simplistic approach of relating traits directly to performance (Vecchio, 1990). However, our traits are what may influence our behaviour at choice points. Choices are also influenced by environmental situation, so a direct link between traits and performance is unlikely in an individual case, but over large groups of individuals in similar environments or with the same individual over a large number of occasions, the consistency of their traits must bring about behavioural choices of a consistent kind.

Vecchio studied Cognitive Response theory in a sample of United States Air Force recruits, giving them various laboratory-type exercises, having measured their intelligence and various leader-type variables. They were assigned randomly to different workgroups. The tasks involved such as the 'moon problem', where they had to decide on the rank order of usefulness of a range of objects to a moon expedition. The recruits were given a small reward for their participation. Another study by Zaccaro *et al.* (1991) took 108 Florida University undergraduates and asked them to assemble moon tents out of folded paper. They were assigned to various groups with different leaders and partners. They filled in questionnaires about themselves and their partners' leadership qualities and the performances of the groups were assessed over a two-day period. The students received $5. Before doing the experiment, they were assessed and told about the leadership dimensions which were of interest. While results of these types of experiments show some confirmation of the theoretical position, they are fairly weak and the measurement of variations in group performances is not surprisingly slight. Whether such experimental achievements with such unrepresentative members of the population would cut much ice in the real world is for you to judge.

Behavioural approaches

Leaders behave differently, or so the theory goes, otherwise they would not be the leader. What is it about their behaviour that makes them suitable to lead? Early studies, around fifty years ago, identified the democratic–autocratic styles of leader behaviour. A little later in the 1950s, this was moderated to the employee-orientated behaviour and the task-orientated behaviour styles, suggesting that this dimension and its two extremes spanned the possibilities of leadership behaviour.

A more complex development of this kind of model then suggested that there were two dimensions needed to encapsulate the behaviour patterns of the leader. These were 'initiating structure' and 'consideration' (Stodgill and Coons, 1957). Initiating structure involved being clear, setting agendas, transmitting requirements, getting everyone in place and promoting a strong and consistent attitude; the other dimension involved being friendly and approachable, listening to members' points of view, valuing suggestions and treating everyone the same. The two dimensions were seen as independent and people could be high or low on both. So we could have a highly considerate, high initiator, etc.

Although this combination might be thought to be the most likely to bring about effective leadership, research did not establish this beyond all possible doubt. People have looked at the results in terms of performance and satisfaction, and have found that high initiators of structure get good performance out of their teams, though this is not always the case; whereas the highly considerate are generally consistent high producers of satisfaction in their followers. Blake and Mouton (1964) formalised a two-dimensional theory and described the Managerial Grid, giving rise to the so-called grid theory of leadership. With nine positions possible on two dimensions (task orientation, employee orientation), eighty-one leadership types were feasible.

Organisational setting

Leaders and their followers or subordinates must function in a setting and the leader's traits or behaviours may have little effect if the characteristics of the setting turn out to be a mismatch with what the individual has to offer. A given situation may also bring about a leader who possesses none of the standard recommended attributes, whether of behaviour or trait makeup. Settings consist of the members of the organisation, the tasks which have to be carried out and the external economic or political environment. The overall structure of the organisation is also a major influence. This may vary between a very hierarchical one, with many layers requiring upward and downward transmission and possibly translation of messages to those which are single layered or flat. From research studies, Yukl (1981) draws a number of general conclusions about how the situation moderates the behaviour of leaders. Size of group, hostility of the market, task specificity, distance from leaders to followers and function of leader in the organisation appear to make a difference in general as to how leader behaviours will produce effective actions. In a large organisation with a number of layers, the lower level managers will need to concentrate on technical matters and monitor the actions of their subordinates; the advantage for participative employee-orientated styles is not present. Where the function of the department is productive, and more concrete or technical goals have got be achieved, the autocratic task-orientated style wins the day. In departments dealing with interpretations, emotions or values, the participative style is necessary. So in personnel, legal sections, customer relations and sales teams there is a need to keep the followers positive, in an emotional sense, to maintain their sensitivities to other's needs and so the participative style has to be used. An exception to this is a very autocratic personnel manager that I have done work for. Her situation is that of a flat hierarchy, an excessively production-orientated business, producing components for computers in a very pressurised environment and her role is not only personnel, but also training manager and senior supervisor. Her style is probably ideal for this setting, though she would be a miserable failure unless she adapted in many other settings. Size of the group being led has an effect, in that as the group gets larger, the tendency for the more autocratic style to be necessary increases. The quality of the workforce has an effect also. If this is poor and much checking and correcting is necessary, then the autocratic style wins. Stress in the outside environment, e.g. customer complaints, supplier lateness, poor material sources and so on, mean that the leader's attention has to be on patching-up the situation and again the directive autocrat will be more successful.

The question as to whether the manager or the situation has more effect on the performance of the organisation can be looked at in miniature if we consider the performance of our favourite football team. On many occasions, managers' heads roll when the team performance is in the decline. The new manager comes in and often the situation improves for a short while only. Factors in the players are changed by the appearance of the new manager. The main ones are the threat to their careers. If they do not buck up for the new manager, they are threatened; second, the new regime instils a temporary lift to confidence and belief which can work wonders until reality returns; third, a small change in playing style may bring about slightly more success. In the long run, the changing of managers does not make much difference. A study confirming this observation was carried out on American baseball sides over a period of fifty years, showing that the major factor relating to the team's success was their performance in the previous year, and the change of manager had little consistent effect (Allen *et al.*, 1979). In the business environment, the performance of a company is in many cases determined as much by environmental factors as by management genius.

In many organisations people move up the ladder from supervisor to manager to chief executive. Are we to assume that their leadership style or their traits change as they move up? Surely not, though they must adapt to the new expectations of their new positions and moderate and gradually adjust their previously successful style. In fact, some recent approaches to leadership style have used a cognitive model, saying that leadership is a matter of perceptions of the followers. Once someone is accepted in their minds as an effective leader, they accept that person and then their perceptions of the leader's action are adjusted to fit in with this acceptance. To some extent, it works the other way around too, as the leader has a perception of their followers, and if this is positive in some respects and success ensues, then the perception develops further along a positive dimension. When failure hits these situations, people are rightly 'shattered'; in a way it is the illusion which is shattered, but this is personally very hard to recognise and explanations are sought elsewhere and blame attributed accordingly.

Categorisation theory

Categorisation theory (Rosch and Lloyd, 1978) would suggest that our daily life and in particular our communication with others is made possible to the extent that we form categories and share them with others. Categories group together different stimuli and treat them as equivalent for a purpose, in a context. Spanners, chisels, screwdrivers and files would be in a 'tool' category, though we might find another category containing files, e.g. eyebrow pencils, lipstick, tweezers. Likewise, in another categorisation 'screwdriver' is a cocktail. Categories enable us to process information and communicate.

Categorisation theory applied to leadership views the perceiver as an active processor of information about the leader's behaviour. Observing leader behaviour, or any behaviour for that matter, we will compare it to a set of categorisations which we have in our head about leadership. Among various applications of this theory, three stand out. The main one is the internal structure of leadership categories, followed by how the existence of these categories permits processes surrounding leadership, for example remembering, and finally it attempts to explain leadership perception in terms of categories.

Categories have a structure, horizontally and vertically. Membership is in terms of family resemblances, i.e. shared features. Categories have prototypes, which are their basic stripped-down typical member. Once categories are learned, the individual is equipped to represent the confusing complexities of the world of stimuli into an ordered set of abstract concepts. This being available, the perceiver can then 'make sense' of stimuli, selectively attend and make judgements, store and retrieve information. An application of this theory, in a study involving students' perceptions of leaders, gave the attributes with the strongest validity for the leader category as intelligent, honest, understanding, verbally skilled and determined (Lord *et al.*, 1984).

Leadership has been extensively studied in Japan for over thirty years, following the interest of some American researchers who wished to see if their models had cross-cultural validity. Misumi and Peterson (1985) maintain that Japanese and American interpretations of leadership may differ because the cultures differ intellectually, to the extent that Japan is more inductive and America more deductive in their approach to intellectual problems. So while the Americans have tended to classify and break down, the Japanese tend to open up and build structures. In Japan, a performance–maintenance two-dimensional model has been experimented with. Performance includes planning, pressure, discipline and coordination, while maintenance involves group maintenance, consideration and friendliness. The combination high performance and high maintenance (PM) has ranked first in relation to productivity and attitudinal criteria with the low-end combination, P and M, last; the rankings of P-type and M-type vary. Various combinations of P and M in relation to various specifiable tasks and settings are seen to work.

Examples of questions for each dimension	
Performance dimension	Maintenance dimension
Is your superior strict about regulations?	Can you talk freely with your superior about your work?
To what extent does your superior give you instructions and orders?	Do you think your superior trusts you?

More important than 'what makes a leader different?' which a lot of research seems to be concerned with, is the question, 'what difference does a leader make?'; similar words, but a different issue.

How does leader behaviour impact on the performance or success of the group? Take the subject of creativity in a group, a vital area in many businesses. What leader behaviour will enhance or possibly reduce creativity? There are many environmental aspects which have been indicated as associated with creativity. Of course the artist or writer is generally a solitary individual, at least at the point of production, though not at the point of incubation or generation of the 'masterpiece', for which they often need stimulation and excitement. Environments which are organic and unpredictable, as opposed to mechanistic, will be more positive settings for creative work. If the surrounding environment is perceived as including autonomy, support and trust, then the creative person works better. Isaksen (1983) emphasises the role of the leader in maintaining a supportive environment through behaviour engendering empathy, warmth, trust, genuineness and flexibility. Creativity is predicated by self-efficacy, esteem and confidence. It is also enhanced by increasing the time allowed for production.

A very good example of the above, and incidentally of a very clear reporting style for academic work, is the paper by Redmond, Mumford and Teach (1993). They manipulated three aspects of leader behaviour and observed their effects on the production of creative marketing strategies in groups of students. The self-efficacy condition, in which they generated the latter in the subjects, contributed to quality and originality in the solutions. The goal-orientation condition was one in which they emphasised learning and performance goals and had no effect; the problem construction condition, in which people were either told just to do their best or were given an emphasis towards concentrating on likely problems and were asked to verbalise possible problems in their own terms, had an influence on the quality of solutions, probably through differences in motivation. Although this study used students, it was nevertheless fairly realistic and it showed that leader style, in the terms specified, brought about different solutions to problems in a creative setting, e.g. devising marketing plans for products.

Organisational communication

It is good to talk, but in many organisations it would be good just to know what is going on. Working groups of all kinds are social organisations with consistently observable characteristics and processes. Whether a workgroup functions well is not just a matter of individuals, nor just a matter of selection, training, motivation and so on. The workgroup is more than the sum of its parts.

The organisation has a structure which may be relatively fixed or fluid and members have roles within that structure. Some of these roles are explicit job roles defined by their title, but as well as these they have social roles which are often unconsciously acknowledged by the group members. Members of the group communicate with each other and with other groups, and this communication varies in its effectiveness, content and process.

Communication in organisations sends mainly work-related information. It is not always verbal and it is not always open. Along with every verbal message goes a set of emotional signatures; for the most part these are neutral but sometimes they may imply hostility, envy or anger, i.e. this is your job, why should I have to do it? Communication varies in terms of its path and it has limitations. Many messages are for certain eyes only. There is a formal management structure which determines the communication path and there is an informal structure which waylays the information at times and redistributes it in a transformed form. In any organisation, leaks and rumours abound. Information can mean power and denote privilege. The boundaries of communication represent a message themselves, indicating that some segments of the organisation are not included.

All messages have to be processed and understood, probably shared with others and reacted to. The perceptions of messages is very much dependent on the receiver's culture and experience. Training and longevity in an organisation allow ready understanding of messages which the relative newcomer may fail to perceive.

Information transmission in an organisation is subject to decay as the process extends. Deliberate distortion, brought in by rephrasing or reducing the content of the message as it penetrates the lower ranks, is common. Unconscious alteration of the original sense of messages occurs as they are processed by one perceiver and passed on.

New office design and the advent of telecommunications by networked PCs has recently fundamentally changed the nature of communication in organisations, so as to make previous views and theories redundant. A new grammar of communication has to be learned by people. Electronic messages cannot be taken back, nor can they be given with a knowing look or an 'only joking' tone of voice. Video conferencing or computer conferencing are now becoming commonplace. This, it is hoped, may lead to greater creativity as bright, creative people often tended to be drowned out by the noisier, less talented people in group face-to-face discussion. The function of the chairperson in the past was to ensure that all valuable contributions were heard and people had the opportunity to bounce ideas off each other, but this was a variable skill.

In the process of problem solving, a vital element is the generation of ideas relative to the problem. The idea of 'brainstorming' (Osborn, 1953) is not a new one, but it has stood the test of time, and there are many varieties of it available. People randomly or freely associate to a theme and so stimulate others. Something said sparks off a memory of an experience in one group member and this, recounted, brings a new association from another. The connections may be arbitrary, but by one means or another a serendipitous solution to a problem is arrived at in a way that would be impossible if all the individuals worked on their own.

Individuals working on their own and later pooling their information and ideas are called 'nominal groups'. McGrath (1984) says that in normal circumstances individuals working on their own are more productive of ideas than are individual in groups.

Three hypotheses have been offered to explain the loss of productivity in brainstorming; these are production blocking, evaluation apprehension and free riding (Diehl and Stroebe, 1987).

- *Production blocking*: caused by the effects of other people's contributions, people may lose their 'turn', may forget what they were going to say or may be inhibited because someone said something contrary to their intended contribution.

- *Evaluation apprehension*: social inhibition, perhaps in the face of a more senior person, an individual is afraid of making a fool of themself.

- *Free riding*: there is lack of participation by some who let others do the work, effectively reducing the size of the group in communication terms.

To examine this question, participants were each given an individual terminal connected to everyone else (Networked). This eliminates production blocking and free riding can be eliminated. If productions were unlabelled, it would also eliminate evaluation apprehension. Results showed that larger groups were most productive and that groups of sizes eight to ten outperformed nominal groups (Valacich *et al.*, 1994).

Effective leaders and managers are known for having distinctive communication styles. The best communicators are relaxed in their presentation giving the appearance of warmth and intimacy. Aiding this effect is the ability to maintain good eye-contact and to listen to the other person. In giving a message, the effective communicator is clear and concise, chooses words carefully and uses them economically. Their sentences do not 'close off' options for the other person and they avoid stating things in ways which put other people on the defensive (Klauss and Bass, 1982). Certain styles of language are more effective and also associated with more dominant personalities. Tips to more commanding speech patterns include such as these: avoid conditionals such as 'if', 'but' and 'maybe'; avoid stacking up alternatives in sentences, i.e. do not confuse the listener with a double request or a double argument, give them one at a time; avoid any signs of apology or doubt. Make sure that you start your sentences at the beginning, not half way through finishing them off with the real beginning. Do not give reasons for orders, if they are orders and you are entitled to order, then order. If they are requests, give reasons if really necessary, but be polite and definite.

Teams in organisations

A workgroup or team, is seen by its members and others as a social entity; its members are interdependent in their performances and they also belong to a much larger social system; their task performance affects others. Work teams have become

Example

Stacking boxes: some requests in different styles and their likely consequences.

Stack these boxes!	Yes Ma'am!
I was just thinking these boxes have been in the way for a long while; someone is going to trip over them; could you stack them please?	Three preambles; he's lost interest.
I wonder if you would mind ever so much stacking these boxes for me?	What if he does mind; do you go away?
Peter, you're not doing anything very much at the moment, could you stack these boxes?	You have just accused the guy of being idle.
If these boxes were out of the way, things would be a lot tidier round here.	Oh really, why tell me?
Oh right, yes, that reminds me, these boxes, have you got a minute? Could you maybe make a bit of room round here so I can maybe bring a desk in or something?	No chance.

an area of increasing focus in organisational psychology and business management. Modern organisations are becoming arranged into multifunction teams of ten to twenty people, and into product-centred groups comprising various specialities. People are being forced out of their professional specialisation niches into team contexts where they are expected to make their own contribution and then some more. These moves are in response to competition, the obsolescence of experts and the bureaucratic despond that some large companies, particularly Japanese and American, found themselves sinking into (Reich, 1987). It is vital that we learn the conditions that engender effectiveness in work teams. Autonomous workgroups as they may be called among other things, cover four broad areas of functionality (Campbell and Campbell, 1988).

Advice and involvement	Quality circles, employee involvement groups
Production and service	Production employees getting together to look at their group skills; Volvo was one of the first well-known examples
Projects and developments	Engineers in design, software design particularly
Action and negotiation	Military applications, emergency crews, medicine, e.g. surgery, research

Team development involves structural elements such as norms, which prescribe the limits of what individuals are allowed to do and roles, which outline what their specific functionalities in the structure are. The main focus of teamwork is on cohesiveness and getting the right blend of people to work together. Getting people to learn the basic politics of teamworking can be difficult. Changes in attitudes are required in respect of such things as authority, ownership of ideas and permissions. Teams can be vulnerable and in many situations they have not survived very long unchanged. Members need to be prepared for higher levels of toleration and be willing to participate and work together, despite interpersonal conflicts. This has been identified with the term 'team maturity'. It involves a much less ego-involved style of participation, but a no less enthusiastic one.

Teams are characterised by synergy. The members recognise and appreciate the fact that their coming together and suppressing some of their personal goals leads to the achievement of much greater goal accomplishment than the sum of their individual contributions, working apart, could have achieved. This leads to the development of another necessary team characteristic, commitment (Katzenbach and Smith, 1993). The dissolution of work teams after the end of projects has in some cases led to a kind of bereavement feeling among some members.

Composition of teams is a subject which is examinable in relation to team effectiveness. Effectiveness itself is usually measured by outcomes in terms of products and achievements, not unnaturally, but viability and atmosphere are also signs of group effectiveness. Team size and heterogeneity have been used as variable in the quest for effectiveness predictors. Campion *et al.* (1993) found size was positively related to effectiveness, but heterogeneity was not. Another study over a number of work teams contradicted this and found that heterogeneity was positively associated with group effectiveness, as was size (Magjuka and Baldwin, 1991). Heterogeneity may involve a multiplicity of skills coming together in a team. It may also refer to a combination of gender, age, backgrounds and attitudes. In both definitional senses, studies have tended to show that heterogeneity is a positive force in team makeup. It has also been confirmed that teams of members who are familiar with each other perform more effectively than others. Where familiarity grows over time from a low base, performance generally grows too. This familiarity effect has been shown in various groups.

The above is only a smattering of the enormous volume of work in this field, which has many large volumes devoted to it exclusively. It is a theoretically dense area, whose practical implications may be said to struggle to make a really significant impact in the industrial world.

Summary

Trade union membership and commitment are found to vary in people, just like work commitment, though union-related behaviour is sporadic and intense. Leadership is a very well-worn topic, with many competing theories. No view really predominates in the academic world and few views have found any lasting relevance or popularity in the business world. The area is a very complex one of environment, behaviours and people's characteristics, including their perceptions. Theories from one perspective only are likely to answer only a limited number of questions, if that. Teamworking appears as an increasingly effective way of managing workers, and as a source of ideas and research for psychologists, it is a fruitful area. Again, generalisable findings of real significance are in the minority.

Activities

1. **What teams have you been a member of? How did you choose the leader, and how satisfied were you with his or her performance? What characteristics seemed to make the leader more or less effective?**

2. **Examine how the communication network in your college or organisation is arranged, both formally and informally. Then decide how what you hear and what you are allowed to hear are filtered, corrupted and passed on.**

Further reading

Campbell, J.P. and Campbell, R.J. (1988) *Productivity in Organisations.* (San Francisco, Jossey-Bass).

Guzzo, R.A. and Dickson, M.W. (1996) Teams in organisations: recent research on performance and effectiveness. *Annual Review of Psychology*, 47, 307–38.

Hisrich, R.D. (1990) Entrepreneurship/intrapreneurship. *American Psychologist*, 45(2), 209–22.

Hollander, E.P. and Offermann, L.R. (1990) Power and leadership in organizations. *American Psychologist*, 45(2), 179–89.

Peeters, M. (1994) Production organisation in the clothing sector: analysis of teamwork pioneers in the Netherlands. *European Work and Organizational Psychologist*, 4, 239–50.

References

Adair, J.G. (1984) The Hawthorne Effect: a reconsideration of the methodological artefact. *Journal of Applied Psychology*, 69, 334–45.

Adams, J.S. (1965) Inequity in social exchange. In L. Berkowitz (ed.) *Advances in Experimental Social Psychology*. Vol. 2. (New York, Academic Press).

Ader, R. and Cohen, N. (1985) CNS-immune system interactions: conditioning phenomena. *Behavioural and Brain Sciences*, 8, 379–94.

Albert, T.C., Schriesheim, C.A. and Michael, W.B. (1986) Invariance of the factorial validity of a job performance scale. *Educational and Psychological Measurement*, 46(1), 237–44.

Alderfer, C.P. (1969) An empirical test of a new theory of human needs. *Organisational Behavior and Human Performance*, 4, 142–75.

Allen, M.P., Panian, S.K. and Lotz, R.E. (1979) Managerial succession and organisational performance: a recalcitrant problem re-visited. *Administrative Science Quarterly*, 24, 167–80.

Anderson, C.W. (1960) The relation between speaking times and decision in the employment interview. *Journal of Applied Psychology*, 44(4), 267–8.

Antonioni, D. (1994) The effects of feedback accountability on upward appraisal ratings. *Personnel Psychology*, 47(2), 349–56.

Appel, V. and Fineberg, M.R. (1969) Recruiting door-to-door salesmen. *Journal of Applied Psychology*, 53(5), 362–6.

Archer, J. and Rhodes, V. (1987) Bereavement and reactions to job loss: a comparative review. *British Journal of Social Psychology*, 26, 211–24.

Archer, J. and Rhodes, V. (1993) The grief process and job loss: a cross-sectional study. *British Journal of Psychology*, 84, 395–410.

Arendt, H. (1958) *The Human Condition*. (Chicago, University of Chicago Press).

Arvey, R.D. (1979) Unfair discrimination in the employment interview: legal and psychological aspects. *Psychological Bulletin*, 86, 736–65.

Arvey, R.D., Bouchard, T.J., Segal, N.L. and Abraham, L.M. (1989) Job satisfaction: environmental and genetic components. *Journal of Applied Psychology*, 74(2), 187–92.

Arvey, R.D. and Campion, J.E. (1982) The employment interview: a summary and review of recent research. *Personnel Psychology*, 35, 281–322.

Arvey, R.D. and Falvey, R.H. (1988) *Fairness in Selecting Employees*, 2nd edn. (Reading, MA, Addison-Wesley).

Arvey, R.D., Miller, H.E., Gould, R. and Burch, P. (1987) Interview validity for selecting sales clerks. *Personnel Psychology*, 40, 1–12.

Ash, A. (1994) Participants reactions to appraisal of managers: results of a pilot. *Public Personnel Management*, 23(2), 237–56.

Asher, J.J. and Sciarrino, J.A. (1974) Realistic work samples: a review. *Personnel Psychology*, 27, 519–34.

Ashton, D.N. (1986) *Unemployment Under Capitalism*. (London, Greenwood).

Atchley, R.C. (1982) Retirement as a social institution. *American Review of Sociology*, 8, 263–87.

Atkinson, J. (1984) Manpower strategies for flexible organizations. *Personnel Management*, 16, 28–31.

Bales, R.F. (1950) *Interaction Process Analysis: A Method for the Study of Small Groups*. (Cambridge, MA, Addison-Wesley).

Balinsky, B. (1978) *Improving Personnel Selection Through Effective Interviewing: Essentials for Management*. (New York, Martin Brace).

Bandura, A. (1978) The self-system in reciprocal determinism. *American Psychologist*, 33, 344–58.

Bandura, A. (1982) Self efficacy mechanism in human agency. *American Psychologist*, 37, 122–47.

Banks, M.H. and Jackson, P.R. (1982) Unemployment and the risk of minor psychiatric disorder in young people: cross-sectional and longitudinal evidence. *Psychological Medicine*, 12, 789–98.

Barker, K. (1993) Changing assumptions and contingent solutions: the cost and benefits of women working full and part-time. *Sex Roles*, 28(1/2), 47–71.

Barling, J. and Rosenbaum. A. (1986) Work stressors and wife abuse. *Journal of Applied Psychology*, 71(2), 346–8.

Barling, P.W. and Handal, P.J. (1980) Incidence of the utilization of public mental health facilities as a function of short term economic decline. *American Journal of Community Psychology*, 8, 31–9.

Baron, R.A. (1986) Self presentation in job interviews when there can be too much of a good thing. *Journal of Applied Psychology*, 16, 16–28.

Barrett, P., Kline, P., Paltiel, L. and Eysenck, H.J. (1996) An evaluation of the psychometric properties of the concept 5.2 Occupational Personality Questionnaire. *Journal of Occupational Psychology*, 69, 1–19.

Barrick, M.R. and Mount, M.K. (1991) The big five personality dimensions and job performance: a meta-analysis. *Personnel Psychology*, 41, 1–26.

Bartley, M. (1988) Unemployment and health – selection or causation – a false antithesis. *Sociology of Health*, 10(1), 41–67.

Bartram, D. (1994) Computer based assessment. *International Review of Industrial and Organizational Psychology*, 9, 31–70.

Bass, B.M. and Barrett, G.V. (1981) *People, Work and Organizations*. (Boston, Allyn and Bacon).

Beit-Hallahmi, B. (1979) Personal and social components of the Protestant ethic. *Journal of Social Psychology*, 109, 263–7.

Belbin, E. and Shimmin, S. (1964) Training the middle-aged for inspection work. *Occupational Psychology*, 38, 49–57.

Belbin, R.M. (1969) Industrial gerontology: origins, issues and applications in Europe. *Industrial Gerontology*, 1, 12–25.

Belbin, R.M. (1981) *Management Teams*. (Oxford, Heinemann).

Belloc, N.B. and Breslow, L. (1972) Relationship between physical health status and health practices. *Preventive Medicine*, 1, 409–21.

Ben-Shakhar, G., Bar-Hellel, M., Bilu, Y., Ben-Abba, E. and Flug, A. (1986) Can graphology predict occupational success? Two empirical studies and some methodological ruminations. *Journal of Applied Psychology*, 71, 645–53.

Benson, P.L., Severs, D., Tatgeulorst, J. and Loddengaard, N. (1980) The social costs of obesity: a non-reactive field trial. *Social Behavior and Personality*, 21, 75–87.

Berman, F.E. and Miner, J.B. (1985) Motivation to manage at the top executive level: a test of the hierarchic role-motivation theory. *Personnel Psychology*, 38, 377–91.

Bernardin, H. and Beatty, R. (1984) *Performance Appraisal: Assessing Performance at Work*. (Boston, Kent Press).

Bernstein, V., Hakel, M.D. and Harlan, A. (1975) The college student as interviewer: a threat to generalisability? *Journal of Applied Psychology*, 60, 266–8.

Beutler, L.E., Storm, A., Kirkish, P., Scogin, F. and Gaines, J.A. (1985) Parameters in the prediction of police officer performance. *Professional Psychology: Research and Practice*, 16(2), 324–35.

Bevan, S. and Fryatt, J. (1988) *Employee selection in the U.K.* (Brighton: Institute of Manpower Studies).

Beynon, H. (1984) *Working for Ford*. (Harmondsworth, Penguin).

Billings, A. and Moos, R. (1981) The role of coping responses and social resources in attenuating the stress of life events. *Journal of Behavioral Medicine*, 4 139–57.

Birren, J.E., Robinson, P.K. and Livingston, S.E. (1986) *Age, Health and Employment*. (Englewood Cliffs, NJ, Prentice Hall).

Blake, R.R. and Mouton, J.S. (1964) *The Managerial Grid*. (Houston, Gulf Pub).

Blanz, F. and Ghiselli, E.E. (1972) The mixed standard scale: a new rating system. *Personnel Psychology*, 25, 185–99.

Blau, G.J. (1985) Relationship of extrinsic, intrinsic and demographic predictors to various types of withdrawal behaviours. *Journal of Applied Psychology*, 70, 442–50.

Bliesener, T. (1991) Validity of biographical data for prediction of job success, quoted in W.M.M. Altink (1991). *European Work and Organizational Psychologist*, 1(4), 248.

Blinkhorn, S. and Johnson, C. (1990) The insignificance of personality testing. *Nature*, 348, 671–2.

Block, J. (1971) *Lives Through Time*. (Berkeley, Bancroft Books).

Bluen, S. (1994) The psychology of strikes. *International Review of Industrial and Organizational Psychology*, 9, 113–45.

Blum, M.L. and Naylor, J.C. (1968) *Industrial Psychology, Its Theoretical and Social Foundations*. (New York, Harper Row).

Blumberg, M. and Pringle, C.D. (1982) The missing opportunity in organizational research: some implications for a theory of work performance. *Academy of Management Review*, 7(4), 560–9.

Bolster, B. and Springbett, B. (1961) The reaction of interviewers to favourable and unfavourable information. *Journal of Applied Psychology*, 45, 97–103.

Borman, W.C. (1978) Exploring lower and upper limits in job performance ratings. *Journal of Applied Psychology*, 63, 135–44.

Borman, W.C., White, L.A., Pulakos, E.D. and Oppler, S.H. (1991) Models of supervisory job performance ratings. *Journal of Applied Psychology*, 76, 863–72.

Boudreau, J.W. (1983) Economic considerations in estimating the utility of human resource productivity improvement programs. *Personnel Psychology*, 36, 551–76.

Boudreau, J.W. (1989) Utility analysis: a review and agenda for future research. In M. Smith and I. Robertson (eds) *Advances in Personnel Selection and Assessment*. (London: Wiley).

Bourgeois, R.P., Leim, M.A., Slivinski, L.W., Grant, K.W. (1975) Evaluation of assessment centres in terms of acceptability. *Canadian Personnel and Industrial Relations Journal*, 22, 17–20.

Boyzatis, R.E. (1982) *The Competent Manager*. (New York, Wiley).

Braddy, B.A. and Gray, D.O. (1987) Employment services for older job seekers: a comparison of two client centred approaches. *The Gerontologist*, 27(5), 565–72.

Bramwell, R. and Cooper, C.L. (1995) VDU's in the workplace: psychological and health implications. *International Review of Industrial and Organizational Psychology*, 10, 213–27.

Breakwell, G.M., Collie, A., Harrison, B. and Propper, C. (1984) Attitudes towards the unemployed: effects of threatened identity. *British Journal of Social Psychology*, 23, 87–8.

Breakwell, G.M., Hammond, S. and Fife-Schaw, C.F. (eds) (1995) *Research Methods in Psychology*. (London, Sage).

Breen, R. (1990) *Understanding Contemporary Ireland*. (Dublin, Gill & Macmillan).

Brenner, M.H. (1983) Mortality and economic instability: detailed analysis for Britain and comparative analysis for selected industrialised countries. *International Journal of Health Services*, 13, 563–619.

Brenner, M.H. and Mooney, A. (1983) Unemployment and health in the context of economic change. *Social Science and Medicine*, 17, 1125–38.

Brenner, S.-O. and Starrin, B. (1988) Unemployment and health in Sweden: public issues and private troubles. *Journal of Social Issues*, 44(4). Special issue, *Psychological Effects of Unemployment*, 125–40.

Briner, R. and Reynolds, S. (1993) Bad theory and bad practice in occupational stress. *Occupational Psychologist*, 19, 8–13.

Bronfenbrenner, U. (1961) The changing American child: a speculative analysis. *Journal of Sociological Issues*, 17, 6–17.

Brooke, P.B. and Price, J.L. (1989) The determinants of employee absenteeism: an empirical test of a causal model. *Journal of Occupational Psychology*, 62, 1–19.

Brown, B.K. and Campion, M.A. (1994) Biodata phenomenology: recruiter's perceptions and use of biographical information in resume screening. *Journal of Applied Psychology*, 79(6), 897–908.

Bruce, M.M. and Learner, B.D. (1958) A supervisory practice test. *Personnel Psychology*, 11, 207–16.

Buchholz, R.A. (1978) An empirical study of contemporary beliefs about work in American society. *Journal of Applied Psychology*, 63(2), 219–27.

Bureau of National Affairs (1983) *Employee Selection Procedures, ASPA (45)*. (Washington DC, BNA).

Burke, L., Porteous, M.A. and Watson, J. (1995) *Participant Perceptions of Community Employment*. (Cork, FAS–South West Region).

Burke, R.J. and McKeen, C.A. (1992) Women in management. *International Review of Industrial and Organizational Psychology*, 7, 245–83.

Bycio, P. (1992) Job performance and absenteeism: a review and meta-analysis. *Human Relations*, 45(2), 193–220.

Byham, W. (1980) Starting an assessment centre the correct way. *Personnel Administrator, Personnel Psychology*, 27–32.

Cairns, E. and Wilson, R. (1984) The impact of political violence on mild psychiatric morbidity in Northern Ireland. *British Journal of Psychiatry*, 145, 631–5.

Caldwell, D.F. and Spivey, W.A. (1983) The relationship between recruiting source and employee success: an analysis by race. *Personnel Psychology*, 36(1), 67–72.

Campbell, J.P. (1971) Personnel training and development. *Annual Review of Psychology*, 22, 565–602.

Campbell, J.P. and Campbell, R.J. (1988) *Productivity in Organisations*. (San Francisco, Jossey-Bass).

Campbell, J.P., Dunnette, M.D., Lawler, E.E. III and Weick, K.E. (1970) *Managerial Behaviour, Performance and Effectiveness*. (New York, McGraw-Hill).

Campion, M.A. and McClelland, C.L. (1993) Follow-up and extension of the interdisciplinary examination of the costs and benefits of enlarged jobs. *Journal of Applied Psychology*, 78, 339–51.

Campion, M.A., Medsker, G.J. and Higgs, A.C. (1993) Relations between work group characteristics and effectiveness: implications for designing effective work groups. *Personnel Psychology*, 46, 823–50.

Capel, S.A. (1991) A longitudinal study of burnout in teachers. *British Journal of Educational Psychology*, 61(1), 36–45.

Capelli, P. (1995) Re-thinking employment. *British Journal of Industrial Relations*, 33(4), 563–602.

Carlson, R.E. (1967) Selection interview decisions: the relative influence of factual and written information on an interviewer's final rating. *Journal of Applied Psychology*, 51, 460–8.

Carlson, R.E., Thayer, P.W., Mayfield, E.C. and Peterson, D.A. (1971) Improvements in the selection interview. *Personnel Journal*, 50, 268–75.

Carr, A. (1968) Is business bluffing ethical? *Harvard Business Review*, 46, 143–53.

Carroll, S.J. and Tosi, H.L. (1973) *Management by objectives: applications and research*. (New York, Macmillan).

Carty, P. (1990). Workplace solutions to private problems. *Accountancy U.K.*, 106 (1168), December.

Cascio, W.F. (1976) Turnover, biographical data, and fair employment practice. *Journal of Applied Psychology*, 61, 576–80.

Cascio, W.F. and Phillips, N. (1979) Performance testing: a rose among thorns. *Personnel Psychology*, 32, 751–66.

Cascio, W.F. and Silbey, V. (1979) Utility of the assessment centre as a selection device. *Journal of Applied Psychology*, 64, 107–18.

Cassidy, T. and Lynn, R. (1989) A mutifactorial approach to achievement motivation: the development of a comprehensive measure. *Journal of Occupational Psychology*, 62(4), 301–12.

Cattell, R.B., Eber, H.W. and Tatsuoka, M.M. (1970) *The 16-Factor Personality Questionnaire.* (Champaign, IL, IPAT).

Chapman, A.J., Sheehy, N.P., Heywood, S., Dooley, B. and Collins, S.C. (1995) The organizational implications of teleworking. *International Review of Industrial and Organizational Psychology*, 10, 229–48.

Cherniss, C. (1990) *Professional Burnout in Human Service Organisations.* (New York, Praeger).

Cherrington, D.J. (1980) *The Work Ethic: Working Values and Values That Work.* (New York, Amacom).

Childs, A. and Klimoski, R.J. (1986) Successfully predicting career success: an application of biographical inventory. *Journal of Applied Psychology*, 71, 3–8.

Clarke, A.E. (1996) Job satisfaction in Britain. *British Journal of Industrial Relations*, 34(2), 189–219.

Clegg, C.W. (1983) Psychology of employee lateness, absence and turnover: a methodological critique and empirical study. *Journal of Applied Psychology*, 68, 88–101.

Clifford, J.P. (1994) Job analysis: why do it and how should it be done? *Public Personnel Management*, 23(2), 321–40.

Coberly, S. (1985) Keeping older workers on the job. *Ageing*, 349, 23–36.

Cohen, S. and Williamson, G.M. (1991) Stress and infectious disease in humans. *Psychological Bulletin*, 109, 5–24.

Colligan, M.J. and Murphy, L.R. (1979) Mass psychogenic illness in organisations: an overview. *Journal of Occupational Psychology*, 52, 77–90.

Collinson, M. and Collinson, D. (1996) 'Its only Dick': the sexual harassment of women managers in insurance sales. *Work, Employment and Society*, 10(1), 29–56.

Cook, J.D., Hepworth, S.J., Wall, T.D. and Warr, P.B. (1981) *The Experience of Work.* (London, Academic Press).

Cook, M. (1993) *Personnel Selection and Productivity.* 2nd edn. (Chichester, Wiley).

Cooper, C.L. and Marshall, J. (1988) Sources of managerial and white collar stress. In C.L. Cooper and R. Payne (eds) *Causes and Consequences of Coping With Stress at Work.* (Chichester, Wiley).

Cooper, C.L. and Payne, R. (eds) (1988) *Causes and Consequences of Coping With Stress at Work.* (Chichester, Wiley).

Cooper, C.L., Watts, J., Baglioni, A.J. and Kelly, M. (1988) Occupational stress among general practice dentists. *Journal of Occupational Psychology*, 61(2), 163–74.

Costa, P.T and McCrae, R.R. (1988) *The NEO Personality Inventory Manual.* (Odessa, Psychological Assessment Resources).

Cox, T. and Leather, P. (1994) The prevention of violence at work: application of a cognitive behavioural theory. *International Review of Industrial and Organizational Psychology*, 9, 213–46.

Cox, T. (1993) *Stress Research and Stress Management: Putting Theory to Work.* (Sudbury, HSE Books).

Cox, T., Hillas, S., Higgins, G. and Boot, N. (1988) Nature and control of violence in managed houses. Centre for Organizational Health and Development: University of Nottingham. Cited in T. Cox and P. Leather (eds) (1994) *The Prevention of Violence at Work.*

Crawley, B., Pinder, R. and Herriot, P. (1990) Assessment centre dimensions, personality and aptitudes. *Journal of Occupational Psychology*, 63, 211–16.

Cronbach, L.J. and Gleser, G.C. (1965) *Psychological Tests and Personnel Decisions.* (Urbana IL, University of Illinois Press).

Cronshaw, S.F. Alexander, R.A. (1985) One answer to the demand for accountability: selection utility as an investment decision. *Organisational Behaviour and Human Decision Processes*, 35, 102–18.

Cusack, C.K. (1991) An investigation into the personal profile analysis and the Myers-Briggs type inventory as indications of personality types in the Irish police force. M.A. Thesis, University College Cork.

Dakin, S. and Armstrong, J.S. (1989) Predicting job performance: a comparison of expert opinion and research findings. *International Journal of Forecasting*, 5, 187–94.

Dalessio, A.T. (1994) Predicting insurance agent turnover using a video based situational judgement test. *Journal of Business and Psychology*, 99(1), 23–32.

Daley, M. (1983) Employment, unemployment and young people: a South Australian perspective, in Tiggeman and Winefield (1989), *Journal of Occupational Psychology*, 62, 79–86.

Dalton, D.R., Kratchardt, D.M. and Porter, L.M. (1981) Functional turnover: an empirical assessment. *Journal of Applied Psychology*, 66(6), 716–21.

Dalton, D.R. and Mesch, D.J. (1992) The impact of employee initiated transfer on absenteeism: a four year cohort assessment. *Human Relations*, 45(3), 291–304.

Dalton, D.R. and Perry, J.L. (1981) Absenteeism and the collective bargaining agreement: an empirical test. *Academy of Management Journal*, 24, 425–31.

Daum, J.W. (1983) Interviewer training: the key to an innovative selection process that works. *Training*, 20, 57–9.

Davidson, D. (1988) Employee testing: an ethical perspective. *Journal of Business Ethics*, 7, 211–17.

Davies, D.R., Matthews, G. and Wong, C.S.K. (1991) Ageing and work. *International Review of Industrial and Organizational Psychology*, 6, 149–212.

Department of Education and Employment (1996) *Financial Control of Payments Made Under the Training for Work and Youth Training Programmes in England*. (London, HMSO).

Diamanti, T. (1993) Unitarian validation of a mathematical problem solving exercise for sales occupations. *Journal of Business and Psychology*, 7(4), 383–401.

Diehl, M. and Stroebe, W. (1987) Productivity loss in 'brainstorming' groups: towards the solution of a riddle. *Journal of Personality and Social Psychology*, 53, 497–509.

Dilts, D.A. and Deitsch, C.R. (1986) Absentee workers back on the job: the case of GM. *Business Horizons*, 29(2), 46–51.

Dipboye, R.L. (1992) *Selection Interviews: Process Perspectives*. (Cincinnati, South Western).

Dipboye, R.L., Fontanelle, G.A. and Garner, K. (1984) Effects of previewing the applicant on interview process and outcomes. *Journal of Applied Psychology*, 69, 118–28.

Dooley, B. (1996) At work away from work. *The Psychologist*, 9(4), 155–8.

Dooley, D. and Catalano, R.A. (1988) Recent research of the psychological effects of unemployment. *Journal of Social Issues*, 44, 1–12.

Dooley, D. and Prause, J. (1995) Effects of unemployment on school leaver self-esteem. *Journal of Occupational and Organizational Psychology*, 68, 177–92.

Downs, S. and Roberts, A. (1977) The training of underground train guards: a case study with a field experiment. *Journal of Occupational Psychology*, 50, 11–120.

Drakeley, R. (1989) Biographical data. In P. Herriot (ed.) *Assessment and Selection in Organizations*. (Chichester, Wiley).

Drakeley, R.J., Herriot, P. and Jones, A. (1988) Biographical data, training success and turnover. *Journal of Occupational Psychology*, 61, 145–52.

Driver, R.W. and Watson, C.J. (1989) Construct validity of voluntary and involuntary absenteeism. *Journal of Business and Psychology*, 4, 109–18.

Drummond, J. and Bain, B. (1994) *Managing Business Ethics: A Reader on Business Ethics for Managers and Students*. (London, Butterworth).

DuBois, P. (1970) *A History of Psychological Testing*. (Boston, Allyn and Bacon).

Eichel, E. and Bender, H.E. (1984) *Performance Appraisal*. (New York, American Management Association).

Eisenberg, P. and Lazarsfeld, P.F. (1938) *The Psychological Effects of Unemployment*. (Wakefield, E.P. Publishing).

Elliot, R.H. and Peaton, A.L. (1994) The probationary period in the selection process: a survey of its use at the State level. *Public Personnel Management*, 23(1), 47–59.

Engel, B.T. (1986) An essay on circulation as behaviour. *The Behaviour and Brain Sciences*, 9, 285–318.

England, G.W. (1991). The meaning of working in the U.S.A.: recent changes. *European Work and Organizational Psychologist*, 1(2/3), 111–24.

Ewing, D. (1977) *Freedom Inside the Organisation*. (New York, Dutton).

Eysenck, H.J. (1984) Personality, stress and lung cancer. In S.Rachman (ed.) *Contributions to Medical Psychology*. (Oxford, Pergamon).

Eysenck, H.J. (1994) Meta-analysis and its problems. *British Medical Journal*, 309, 789–92.

Farrell, D. and Stamm, C.L. (1988) Meta-analysis of the correlates of employee absence. *Human Relations*, 41, 211–27.

Feather, N. (1982) Unemployment and its psychological correlates: a study of depressive symptoms, self-esteem, Protestant ethic values, attributional style and apathy. *Australian Journal of Psychology*, 34, 309–23.

Feather, N. (1985) Attitudes values and attributions: explanations for unemployment. *Journal of Personality and Social Psychology*, 48, 876–89.

Feather, N.T. (1990) *The Psychological Impact of Unemployment*. (New York, Springer-Verlag).

Feldman, J. (1986) Instrumentation and training for performance appraisal: a perceptual cognitive viewpoint. In Rowland and Ferris (eds) *Research in Personnel and Human Resource Mangement*. (Greenwich, CT: JAI Press).

Feltham, R. (1988) Validity of a police assessment centre: a 1 to 19 year follow-up. *Journal of Occupational Psychology*, 61, 129–44.

Ference, T.P., Stoner, J.A. and Warren, E.K. (1977) Managing the career plateau. *Academy of Management Review*, 2, 602–12.

Fiedler, F.E. and Garcia, J.E. (1987) *New Approaches to Effective Leadership: Cognitive Resources and Organisational Performance*. (New York, Wiley).

File, Q.W. (1945) The measurement of supervisory quality in industry. *Journal of Applied Psychology*, 29, 323–37.

Fineman, S. (1977) The achievement motive construct. Where are we now? *British Journal of Psychology*, 68, 1–22.

Finkle, R.B. (1976) Managerial assessment centres. In M.D. Dunnette (ed.) *Handbook of Industrial and Organizational Psychology*. (Chicago, Rand-McNally).

Finlay-Jones, R.A. and Eckhardt, B. (1984) A social and psychiatric survey of unemployment among young people. *Australian and New Zealand Journal of Psychiatry*, 18, 135–43.

Finn, R. and Fontaine, P. (1984) Performance appraisal: some dynamics and dilemmas. *Public Personnel Management*, 13, 335–42.

Firth, H. and Britton, P. (1989). 'Burnout', absence and turnover amongst British nursing staff. *Journal of Occupational Psychology*, 62, 55–9.

Firth-Cozens, J. (1992) Why me? A case study of the process of perceived occupational stress. *Human Relations*, 45(2), 131–41.

Fitzgerald, K. (1995) The £225 million fraud bill. *Business and Finance*, 32(7), 7–8.

Flanagan, J.C. (1954) The critical incident technique. *Psychological Bulletin*, 51, 327–58.

Flanagan, R.J., Strauss, G. and Ulman, L. (1974) Worker discontent and workplace behaviour. *Industrial Relations*, 13, 101–23.

Fleishman, E.A. (1988) Some new frontiers in personnel selection research. *Personnel Psychology*, 42, 679–701.

Fleishman, E.A. and Mumford, M.D. (1991) Evaluating classifications of job behaviour: a construct validation of the ability requirements scales. *Personnel Administrator*, 24, 82–92.

Fleishman, E.A. and Quaintance, M.K. (1984) *Taxonomies of Human Performance*. (New York, Academic Press).

Fletcher, C. (1988) The epidemiology of occupational stress. Ch. 1 in Cooper and Payne (eds), *Causes and Consequences of Coping with Stress at Work*. (Chichester, Wiley).

Fletcher, C. (1991a) Candidate's reactions to assessment centres and their outcomes: a longitudinal study. *Journal of Occupational Psychology*, 64(2), 117–28.

Fletcher, C. (1991b) Personality tests: the great debate. *Personnel Management*, September, 38–42.

Fletcher, C. and Kerslake, C. (1992) The impact of assessment centres and their outcomes on participants' self assessments. *Human Relations*, 45(3), 281–9.

Folger, R. and Konovsky, M. (1989) Effects of procedural and distributive justice on reactions to pay raise decisions. *Academy of Management Journal*, 32, 115–30.

Folkman, S. and Lazarus, R.S. (1985) If it changes it must be a process: a study of emotion and coping during three stages of college examinations. *Journal of Personality and Social Psychology*, 48, 150–70.

Ford, J.K. and Kraiger, K. (1995) The application of cognitive constructs and principles to the instructional systems model of training: implications for needs assessment, design and transfer. *International Review of Industrial and Organizational Psychology*, 10, 1–48.

Fossum, J.A., Arvey, R.D., Paradise, C.A. and Robbis, N.E. (1986) Modelling the skills obsolescence process: a psychological/economic integration. *Academy of Management Review*, 11, 362–74.

Foushee, H.C. (1984) Dyads and triads at 35,000ft. *American Psychologist*, 39, 885–93.

Fox, J.B. and Scott, J.R. (1943) *Absenteeism: Management's Problem*. (Boston, Graduate School of Business Managment).

Fraccaroli, F., Le Blanc, A. and Hajjar, V. (1994) Social self-description and affective well being in young unemployed people: a comparative study. *European Work and Organizational Psychologist*, 4(2), 81–100.

Fredericksen, N. (1962) Factors in in-basket performance. *Psychological Monographs*, 76 (541).

Freudenberger, H. (1974) Staff burnout. *Journal of Social Issues*, 30, 159–65.

Fried, Y. (1988) Physiological assessment of stress at work. Ch. 11, in C.L. Cooper and R. Payne (eds) *Causes and Consequences of Coping With Stress at Work*. (Chichester, Wiley).

Fried, Y. and Ferris, G.R. (1986) The dimensionality of job characteristics. *Journal of Applied Psychology*, 71, 419–26.

Friedlander, F. and Greenberg, S. (1971) Effects of job attitudes, training and organizational climate on performance of the hard-core unemployed. *Journal of Applied Psychology*, 55, 287–95.

Friedman, M. (1970) The social responsibility of business is to increase profits. *New York Times Magazine*, 13 September, pp. 32–3.

Friedman, M.G. (1986) 10 steps to objective appraisals. *Personnel Journal*, 66–71.

Friedman, M. and Rosenman, R.H. (1959) Association of specific overt behaviour pattern with blood and cardiovascular findings. *Journal of American Medical Association*, 169, 1286–96.

Fryer, D. (1992) Introduction to Marienthal and beyond. *Journal of Occupational Psychology*, 65, 257–8.

Fryer, D.M. and Payne, R.L. (1984) Proactivity in unemployment. Findings and implications. *Leisure Studies*, 3, 273–95.

Furnham, A. (1984) The protestant work ethic, voting behaviour and attitudes to the trade unions. *Political Studies*, 420–36.

Furnham, A. (1987) Work related beliefs and human values. *Personality and Individual Differences*, 8(5), 627–37.

Furnham, A. (1992) *Personality at Work: The Role of Individual Differences in the Workplace*. (London, Routledge).

Furnham, A., Steele, H. and Pendleton, D. (1993) A psychometric assessment of the Belbin Team-role self-perception inventory. *Journal of Occupational Psychology*, 66(3), 245–58.

Gagne, R.M., Briggs, L.J. (1974) *Principles of Instructional Design*. (New York: Holt, Rinehart and Winston).

Gagne, R.M., Briggs, L.J. and Wager, W.W. (1985) *Principles of Instructional Design* (3rd edn). (New York: Holt, Rinehart and Winston).

Ganster, D.C. and Schaubroeck, J. (1991) Work stress and employee health. *Journal of Management*, 17, 235–71.

Garavan, T.N. (1990) Employment reference checking and the selection process: practices in Irish companies. *Industrial Relations News*, 32, 16–20.

Gardner, W.L. and Martinko, M.J. (1988) Impression management in organisations. *Journal of Management*, 14, 321–38.

Garraty, J.A. (1978) *Unemployment in History, Economic Thought and Public Policy*. (New York, Harper Row).

Garrison, K.R. and Muchinsky, P.M. (1977) Attitudinal and biographical predictors of incidental absenteeism. *Journal of Vocational Behaviour*, 10, 221–30.

Gaugler, B.B., Rosenthal, D. Thornton, G.C. and Bentson, C. (1987) Meta-analysis of assessment centre validity. *Journal of Applied Psychology*, 72, 493–511.

Gaugler, B.B. and Thornton, G.C. (1989) Number of assessment dimensions as a determinant of assessor accuracy. *Journal of Applied Psychology*, 74(4), 611–18.

Gebhart, G.L. and Crump, C.E. (1990) Employee fitness and wellness programs in the workplace. *American Psychologist*, 45(2), 262–72.

Gerstein, L.H. and Bayer, G.A. (1990) Counselling psychology and employee assistance programmes; problems, obstacles and potential contribution. *Journal of Business and Psychology*, 5(1), 101–11.

Gettinger, M. and White, M.A. (1979) Which is the stronger correlate of school learning, time to learn or measured intelligence? *Journal of Educational Psychology*, 71, 405–12.

Ghiselli, E.E. (1966) *The Validity of Occupational Aptitude Tests*. (New York, Wiley).

Ghiselli, E.E. (1973) The validity of aptitude tests in personnel selection. *Personnel Psychology*, 26, 461–77.

Ghiselli, E.E. and Brown, C.W. (1955) *Personnel and Industrial Psychology*. 2nd edn. (New York, McGraw-Hill).

Ginsburg, H. (1985) Flexible and partial retirement for Norwegian and Swedish workers. *Monthly Labor Review*, 108(10), 33–43.

Glaser, R. (1982) Instructional psychology: past, present and future. *American Psychologist*, 37, 292–305.

Glyptis, S. (1989) *Leisure and Unemployment*. (Milton Keynes, Open University).

Goldberg, D. (1978) *Manual for the General Health Questionnaire*. (Windsor, NFER).

Goldstein, A.P. and Sorcher, M. (1974) *Changing Supervisory Behavior*. (New York, Pergamon).

Goldstein, I.L. (1974) *Training: Program development and evaluation*. (Monterey, CA, Brooks/Cole).

Goldstein, I.L. (1986) *Training in Organisations; Needs assessment: development and evaluation*. (Monterey, CA, Brooks-Cole).

Goldstein, I.L. and associates (1989) *Training and Development in Organisations*. (San Francisco, Jossey-Bass).

Goodman, A.M. (1990) A model for police officer burnout. *Journal of Business and Psychology*, 5(1), 85–99.

Goodpaster, K. (1984) The concept of corporate responsibility. In *Just Business*. (Philadelphia, Temple University Press).

Gordon, M.E., Philpot, J.W., Burt, R.E., Thompson, C.A. and Spiller, W.E. (1980) Commitment to the union: development of a measure and an examination of its correlates. *Journal of Applied Psychology*, 65(4), 479–99.

Gough, H.G. (1984) A managerial potential scale for the California psychological inventory. *Journal of Applied Psychology*, 69, 233–40.

Griffiths, A. (1996) The benefits of employee exercise programmes: a review. *Work & Stress*, 10(1), 5–23.

Grove, D.A. (1981) A behavioural consistency approach to decision making on employee selection. *Personnel Psychology*, 34, 55–64.

Guest, D.E. (1994) Organisational psychology and human resource management. *European Work and Organizational Psychologist*, 4, 251–70.

Guest, D.E. and Dewe, P. (1988) Why do workers belong to a trade union? A social and psychological study in the U.K. electronics industry. *British Journal of Industrial Relations*.

Gunnigle, P. and Flood, P.C. (1990) *Personnel Management in Ireland*. (Dublin, Gill & Macmillan).

Gutek, B.A. (1985) *Sex and the Workplace: The Impact of Sexual Behaviour and Harrassment on Women, Men and the Organization*. (San Francisco, Jossey-Bass).

Guzzo, R.A. and Dickson, M.W. (1996) Teams in organisations: recent research on performance and effectiveness. *Annual Review of Psychology*, 47, 307–38.

Hackman, J.R. and Oldham, G.R. (1975) Development of the job diagnostic survey. *Journal of Applied Psychology*, 60, 159–79.

Hackman, J.R. and Oldham, G.R. (1976) Motivation through the design of work: test of a theory. *Organizational Behaviour and Human Performance*, 16, 250–79.

Hall, C.S. and Lindzey, G. (1957) *Theories of Personality*. (New York, Wiley).

Hall, D.T. and Isabella, L.A. (1985) Downward movement and career development. *Organisational Dynamics*, 14, 3–23.

Hammond, S.M. (1984) A investigation into the factor structure of the general aptitude test battery. *Journal of Occupational Psychology*, 57, 43–8.

Handyside, J. (1988) Occupational validity studies in the U.K. In *The Analysis of Personality in Research and Assessment*, pp. 125–30, (London, IARC).

Hanson, J. (1995) Hunters and gatherers among the tribes of academe. *The New Academic*, 4(1), 12–13.

Harn, T.J. and Thornton, G.C. (1985) Recruiter counselling behaviours and applicant impressions, *Journal of Occupational Psychology*, 54, 165–73.

Harris, M.M. (1989) Reconsidering the employment interview. *Personnel Psychology*, 42, 691–726.

Hartigan, J.A. and Wigdor, A.K. (eds) (1989) *Fairness in Employment Testing*. (Washington, National Academy Press).

Hartley, J.F. and Kelly, J. (1986) Psychology and industrial relations: from conflict to cooperation? *Journal of Occupational Psychology*, 59, 161–76.

Harvey, R.J., Friedman, L., Hakel, M.D. and Cornelius, E.T. (1988) Dimensionality of the job element inventory: a simplified worker oriented job analysis questionnaire, *Journal of Applied Psychology*, 73(4), 639–46.

Hathaway, S.R. and McKinley, J.C. (1967) *Manual for the Minnesota Multiphasic Personality Inventory*. (New York, Psychological Corporation).

Heckhausen, H., Schmalt, H.-D. and Schneider, L. (1985) *Achievement Motivation in Perspective*. (Orlando, FL, Academic Press).

Heller, F. (1991) Reassessing the work ethic: a new look at work and other activities. *European Work and Organizational Psychologist*, 1(2/3), 147–60.

Helmreich, R.L. (1984) Cockpit management attitudes. *Human Factors*, 26(5), 583–9.

Heneman, H.G. (1975) Research round-up. *Personnel Administrator*, June, 61.

Hennessy, A.G. (1993) The extent of employee referrals and nepotism in Irish industry. Thesis submitted for M.A. degree in Occupational Psychology, University College Cork.

Herriot, P. (1989) *Assessment and Selection in Organizations*. (Chichester, Wiley).

Herriot, P. and Rothwell, C. (1983) Expectations and impressions in the graduate selection interview. *Journal of Occupational Psychology*, 56, 303–14.

Herzberg, F. (1966) *Work and the Nature of Man*. (Cleveland, World Publishing).

Herzberg, F., Mausner, B. and Snyderman, B. (1959) *The Motivation to Work*. (New York, Wiley).

Hinrichs, J.R. (1976) Personnel Training. In M.D. Dunnett (ed.) *Handbook of Industrial and Organizational Psychology*. (Skokie, IL: Rand McNally).

Hisrich, R.D. (1990) Entrepreneurship/intrapreneurship. *American Psychologist*, 45(2), 209–22.

Hobson, C.J., Mendel, R.M. and Gibson, F.W. (1981) Classifying performance appraisal criteria. *Organisational Behaviour and Human Performance*, 28, 164–88.

Hodson, R. (1991) Workplace behaviours – good soldiers, smooth operators and saboteurs. *Work and Occupations*, 18, 271–90.

Hofstede, G. (1980) *Culture's Consequences: International Differences in Work Related Values*. (Beverly Hills, Sage).

Hogan, R.T. (1982) Socioanalytic theory of personality. In M.M. Page (ed.) *Nebraska Symposium on Motivation: Personality, Current Theory and Research*. (Lincoln: University Nebraska).

Hoiberg, A. and Pugh, W.M. (1978) Predicting Navy effectiveness: expectations, motivation, personality, aptitude and background variables. *Personnel Psychology*, 31, 841–52.

Hollander, E.P. and Offermann, L.R. (1990) Power and leadership in organizations. *American Psychologist*, 45(2), 179–89.

Hollenbeck, J.R. and Klein, H.J. (1987) Goal commitment and the goal setting process: problems, prospects and proposals for future research. *Journal of Applied Psychology*, 72, 212–20.

Hollenbeck, J.R., Williams, C. and Klein, H.J. (1989) An empirical examination of antecedents of commitment to difficult goals. *Journal of Applied Psychology*, 74, 18–23.

Hollman, T. (1972) Employment interviewer's errors in processing positive and negative information. *Journal of Applied Psychology*, 56, 130–4.

Hoppock, R. (1935) *Job Satisfaction*. (New York, Harper Row).

Hough, L.M. (1984) Development and evaluation of the accomplishment record method of selecting and promoting professionals. *Journal of Applied Psychology*, 69, 135–46.

Hough, L.M. (1992) The 'big five' personality variables – construct confusion: description versus prediction. *Human Performance*, 5, 139–55.

Hough, L.M., Eaton, N.K., Kamp, J.D. and McLoy, R.A. (1990) Criterion related validities of personality constructs and the effect of response distortion on those validities. *Journal of Applied Psychology. Monograph*, 75(5), 581–95.

Hough, M. and Mayhew, P. (1983) *The British Crime Survey*. (London, HMSO).

House, R.J. and Wigdor, L.A. (1967) Herzberg's dual factor theory of job satisfaction and motivation: a review of the evidence and criticism. *Personnel Psychology*, 20, 369–89.

House, R.J. (1967) *Management Development: Design, Evaluation and Implementation*. (Ann Arbor, University of Michigan).

Howard, A. (1974) An assessment of assessment centres. *Academy of Management Journal*, 17, 115–34.

Howard, A. and Bray, D.W. (1988) *Managerial Lives in Transition: Advancing Age and Changing Times*. (New York, Guilford Press).

Hull, C.L. (1928) *Aptitude Testing*. (London, Harrop).

Hunter, J. and Hunter, R. (1984) Validity and utility of alternative predictors of job performance. *Psychology Bulletin*, 96, 72–98.

Hyman, R. (1975) *Industrial Relations: A Marxist Introduction*. (London, Macmillan).

Iaffaldano, M.T. and Muchinsky, P.M. (1985) Job satisfaction and job performance: a meta-analysis. *Psychological Bulletin*, 97, 251–73.

ISO (1992) *ISO:9241: Ergonomic Requirements for Office Work With Visual Display Terminals*. (Dublin: International Standards Office).

Isaksen, S.G. (1983) Towards a model for the facilitation of creative problem solving. *Journal of Creative Behaviour*, 17(1), 18–31.

Ivancevich, J.M. (1985) Predicting absenteeism from prior absence and work attitudes. *Academy of Management Journal*, 28, 219–28.

Ivancevich, J.M. and Matteson, M.T. (1988) Promoting the individual's health and well being. In C.L. Cooper and R. Payne (eds) *Causes and Consequences of Coping With Stress at Work*. (Chichester, Wiley).

Iversen, L. and Sarboe, S. (1988) Psychological well-being among unemployed and employed people after a company closedown: a longitudinal study. *Journal of Social Issues*, 44, 141–52.

Jackofsky, E.F. and Peters, L.H. (1983) Job turnover vs company turnover: reassessment of the March Simon participation hypothesis. *Journal of Applied Psychology*, 68(3), 490–5.

Jackson, S.E. (1983) Participation in decison making as a strategy for reducing job related strain. *Journal of Applied Psychology*, 68(1), 3–19.

Jackson, S.E. and Maslach, C. (1982) After-effects of job related stress: families as victims. *Journal of Occupational Behaviour*, 3, 63–77.

Jahoda, M. (1982) *Employment and Unemployment*. (Cambridge, Cambridge University Press).

Jahoda, M., Lazarsfeld, P.F. and Zeisel, H. (1971) *Marienthal: The Sociography of an Unemployed Community*. (New York, Aldine-Atherton).

James, W. (1890) *Principles of Psychology*. (New York, Henry Holt).

Jenkins, J. (1946) Validity for what? *Journal of Consulting Psychology*, 10, 93–8.

Jewell, L.N. and Siegall, M. (1985) *Contemporary Industrial/Organizational Psychology*. (St. Paul, West Publishing Company).

Johns, G. (1978) Attitudinal and non-attitudinal predictors of two forms of absence from work. *Organizational Behaviour and Human Performance*, 22, 431–44.

Jolly, T., Creigh, S. and Mingay, A. (1980) Age as a factor in Employment. *Research Paper 11*. (London, Department of Employment).

Jones, J.W., Joy, D.S., Werner, S.H. and Orban, J.A. (1991) Criterion related validity of a pre-employment integrity inventory: a large scale between groups comparison. *Perceptual Motor Skills*, 72, 131–6.

Jones, J.W., Slora, K.B. and Boye, M.W. (1990) Theft reduction through personnel selection: a control group design in the supermarket industry. *Journal of Business and Psychology*, 5(2), 275–9.

Kantrowitz, B., Wingert, P. and Robins, K. (1989) Advocating a 'mommy track'. *Newsweek*, 113, 45.

Kanungo, R.N. (1982) Measurement of job and work involvement. *Journal of Applied Psychology*, 67(3), 341–9.

Katzell, R.A. and Thompson, D.E. (1990) Work motivation. *American Psychologist*, 45(2), 144–53.

Katzenbach, J.R. and Smith, D.K. (1993) *The Wisdom of Teams: Creating the High Performance Organisation*. (Boston, Harvard Business School).

Keller, R.T. (1983) Predicting absenteeism from prior absenteeism, attitudinal factors, and non attitudinal factors. *Journal of Applied Psychology*, 68, 536–40.

Kelvin, P. and Jarrett, J.E. (1985) *Unemployment: Its Social and Psychological Effects*. (Cambridge, Cambridge University Press).

Kerley, J.W. (1985) New England Life takes steps to ensure its future. *Sales and Marketing Management*, 135, 74–7.

Kessler, R.C., Price, R.H. and Wortman, C.B. (1985) Social factors in psychopathology: stress, social support, and coping processes. *Annual Review of Psychology*, 36, 531–72.

Kimble, G.A. (1996) *Psychology: the Hope of a Science*. (Cambridge, MA, MIT Press).

King, N. (1970) Clarification and evaluation of the two factor theory of job satisfaction. *Psychological Bulletin*, 74(1), 18–31.

Kinicki, A.J., Lockwood, C.A., Horn, P.W. and Griffith, R.W. (1990) Interviewer predictions of applicant qualifications and interviewer validity: aggregate and individual analyses. *Journal of Applied Psychology*, 75, 477–86.

Klauss, R. and Bass, B. (1982) *Interpersonal Communication in Organisations*. (New York, Academic Press).

Klimoski, R. and Brickner, M. (1987) Why do assessment centers work? The puzzle of assessment center validity. *Personnel Psychology*, 40, 243–60.

Klimoski, R. and Strickland, W.J. (1981) A comparative view of assessment centres. In R. Klimoski and M. Brickner (1987). *Personnel Psychology*, 40, 243–60.

Kolb, D. (1976) *Learning Style Inventory*. (Boston: McBer & Co).

Kolb, D.A. (1981) Experiential learning theory and the learning styles inventory: a reply to Freedman and Stumpf. *Academy of Management Review*, 6, 289–96.

Kolb, D. (1985) *Learning Style Inventory*. (Boston: McBer & Co).

Kopelman, R.E. (1985) Job redesign and productivity: a review of the evidence. *National Productivity Review*, 4, 237–55.

Korman, A.K. (1968) The prediction of managerial performance. *Personnel Psychology*, 21, 295–322.

Kraiger, K. and Ford, J. (1985) A meta-analysis of ratee race effects in performance ratings. *Journal of Applied Psychology*, 70(1), 56–65.

Kraut, J.I. and Scott, G.J. (1972) Validity of an operational management assessment program. *Journal of Applied Psychology*, 56, 124–9.

Kwiatkowski, R. (1994) Testing in the Workplace. *The Psychologist*, Special Issue, 7(1), 10–32. (BPS, Leicester).

Lalonde, M. (1975) *A New Perspective on the Health of Canadians*. (Information Canada, Ottawa).

Landy, F.J. (1985) *Psychology of Work Behaviour*. 3rd edn. (Homewood, IL, Dorsey Press).

Landy, F.J. (1989) *Psychology of Work Behaviour*. 4th edn. (Pacific Grove, CA, Brooks-Cole).

Landy, F.J. and Farr, J.L. (1980) Performance rating. *Psychological Bulletin*, 87, 72–107.

Landy, F.J., Farr, J.L. and Jacobs, R.R. (1982) Utility concepts in performance measurement. *Organisational Behaviour and Human Performance*, 30, 15–40.

Landy, F.J. and Trumbo, D.A. (1980) *Psychology of Work Behaviour*. (Homewood, IL, Dorsey Press).

Larkin, J. and Pines, H. (1979) No fat persons need apply. *Sociology of Work and Occupations*. 6, 312–27.

Larsen, H.H. and Bang, S.M. (1993) Development dialogues as an alternative to performance appraisal: a tool for strategic human resource development in Europe. *Research in Personnel and Human Resource Management*, Supplement 3, 171–88.

Latham, G.P. and Frayne, C.A. (1989) Self-management training for increasing job attendance: a follow-up and replication. *Journal of Applied Psychology*, 74(3) 411–16.

Latham, G.P. and Saari, L.M. (1984) Do people do what they say? Further studies on the situation interview. *Journal Of Applied Psychology*, 69, 569–73.

Latham, G.P., Saari, L.M., Pursell, E.D. and Campion, M.A. (1980) The situational interview. *Journal of Applied Psychology*, 65, 422–7.

Latham, G.P. and Wexley, K.N. (1981) *Increasing Productivity Through Performance Appraisal*. (Reading, MA., Addison-Wesley).

Lawrence P.R. and Lorsch, J.W. (1967) *Organization and Environment: Managing Differentiation and integration*. (Boston: Harvard University Graduate School of Business).

Lawshe, C.H. (1975) A quantitative approach to content validity. *Personnel Psychology*, 28, 563–75.

Lerner, R.M. (1991) Changing organism-context relations as the basic process of development: a developmental contextual perspective. *Developmental Psychology*, 27, 27–32.

Locke, E.A. (1970) Job satisfaction and job performance: a theoretical analysis. *Organisational Behaviour and Human Decision Processes*, 5, 484–500.

Locke, E.A. (1976) The nature and causes of job satisfaction. In M.D. Dunnette (ed.) *Handbook of Industrial and Organizational Psychology*. (Skokie, IL, Rand-McNally).

Locke, E.A. (1990) What is job satisfaction? *Organisational Behaviour and Human Performance*, 4, 309–36.

Locke, E.A., Shaw, K., Saari, L. and Latham, G.P. (1981) Goal setting and task performance, 1969–1980. *Psychological Bulletin*, 90, 125–52.

Lombardi, L.J., Boyce, D.P. and Gopalan, R.S. (1985) Investing in new agents: a cost blueprint, in A.T. Dalessio (1994). Prediciting insurance agent turnover using a video based situational judgment test. *Journal of Business and Psychology*, 9(1), 23–32.

Long, P. (1986) *Performance Appraisal Re-visited*. (London: IPM).

Lopez, F.M. (1966) *Evaluating executive decisions making: the in-basket technique*. (New York, American Management Association).

Lord, R.G., Foti, R.J. and Devader, C.L. (1984) A test of leadership categorisation theory: internal structure, information processing, and leadership perceptions. *Organizational Behaviour and Human Performance*, 34, 343–96.

Lorenzo, R.V. (1984) Effects of assessorship on managers' proficiency in acquiring, evaluating, and communicating information about people. *Personnel Psychology*, 37, 617–34.

Mabe, P.A. and West, S.G. (1982) Validity of self-evaluation of ability: a review and meta-analysis. *Journal of Applied Psychology*, 67, 280–96.

Machiavelli (1966) *The Prince*. (New York, Bantam, original work dated 1513).

Machlowitz, M. (1980) *Workaholics: living with them, working with them*. (New York, New American Library).

Mackay, C., Cox, T., Burrows, G. and Lazzerini, T. (1978) Inventory for the measurement of self-reported stress and arousal. *British Journal of Social and Clinical Psychology*, 17(3), 283–4.

MacKinnon, D.W. (1975) *An Overview of an Assessment Centre (No. 1)*. (Greensboro, NC, Centre for Creative Leadership).

Mael, F.A. (1991) A conceptual rationale for the domain and attributes of bio-data. *Personnel Psychology*, 44, 763–92.

Magaro, P.A. and Ashbrook, R.M. (1985) The personality of societal groups. *Journal of Personality and Social Psychology*, 48, 1479–89.

Magjuka, R.J. and Baldwin, T.T. (1991) Team based employee involvement programs: effects of design and administration. *Personnel Psychology*, 44, 793–812.

Mahoney, M.J. (1975) The behavioural treatment of obesity. In A.J. Enelow and J.P. Henderson (eds) *Applying Behavioural Science to Cardiovascular Risk*. pp. 121–32. (Dallas, American Heart Association).

Maniero, L.A. (1986) A review and analysis of power dynamics in organisational romances. *Academy of Management Review*, 11(4), 750–62.

Maol, M.T. (1993) Women's main role is still in the home. Survey. *Irish Times*, 13 February.

Markham, S.E. (1988) Pay for performance dilemma revisited: empirical example of the important group effects. *Journal of Applied Psychology* 73(2), 172–80.

Markham, S.E., Dansereau, F. and Alutto, J.A. (1982) Female versus male absence rates: a temporal analysis. *Personnel Psychology*, 35, 371–82.

Martocchio, J.J. and Harrison, D.A. (1993) To be there or not to be there?: Questions, theories, and methods in absenteeism research. *Research in Personnel and Human Resources Management*, Vol. 11, 259–328.

Maslach, C. and Jackson, S.E. (1980) *Maslach Burnout Inventory*. (Palo Alto, Consulting Psychologist Press).

Maslach, C. and Jackson, S.E. (1981) The measurement of experienced burnout. *Journal of Occupational Behaviour*, 2, 99–113.

Maslow, A.H. (1970) *Motivation and Personality*, 2nd edn. (New York, Harper Row).

Mason, J.W. (1975) A historical view of the stress field. *Journal of Human Stress*, 1, 6–12, and 22–36.

Matthews, K.A., Glass, D.C. and Rosenman, R.H. *et al.*. (1977) Competitive drive, pattern A and coronary heart disease: a further analysis of some data from the Western Collaborative group. *Journal of Chronic Diseases*, 30, 489–98.

Maule, A.J., Cliff, D.R. and Taylor, R. (1996) Early retirement decisions and how they affect later quality of life. *Ageing and Society*, 16, 177–204.

Mayfield, E.C. (1964) The selection interview: a re-evaluation of research. *Personnel Psychology*, 17, 239–60.

McClelland, D.C. (1975) *Power: The Inner Experience*. (New York, Irvington).

McClelland, D.C., Atkinson, J.W., Clark, R.A. and Lowell, E.L. (1953) *The Achievement Motive*. (New York, Appleton Century Crofts).

McClelland, D.C. and Boyzatis, R.E. (1982) Leadership motive pattern and long-term success in management. *Journal of Applied Psychology*, 67(6), 737–43.

McCormick, E.J. (1979) *Job Analysis: Methods and Applications*. (Amacom, New York).

McCormick, E.J. and Ilgen, D. (1987) *Industrial and Organizational Psychology*. (Routledge, London).

McCormick, E.J., Jeanneret, P.R. and Mecham, R.C. (1972) *Technical Manual for the Position Analysis Questionnaire*. (West Lafayette, IN, Purdue Research Foundation).

McDonald, T. and Haekel, M.D. (1985) Effects of applicant race, sex, suitability and answers on interviewer's questioning strategy and ratings. *Personnel Psychology*, 38, 321–34.

McEnery, J. and McEnery, J.M. (1987) Self rating in management training needs assessment: a neglected opportunity? *Journal of Occupational Psychology*, 60, 49–60.

McEvoy, G.M. and Cascio, W.F. (1985) Strategies for reducing employee turnover: a meta-analysis. *Journal of Applied Psychology*, 70, 342–53.

McEvoy, G.M. and Cascio, W.F. (1989) Cumulative evidence of the relationship between employee age and job performance. *Journal of Applied Psychology*, 74(1), 11–17.

McFarland, W.B. (1977) *Manpower Costs and Performance Measurement*. (New York, National Association of Accountants).

McGehee, W. and Thayer, P.W. (1961) *Training in Business and Industry*. (New York, Wiley).

McGrath, J.E. (1984) *Groups: Interaction and Performance*. (Englewood Cliffs, NJ, Prentice Hall).

McGrath, J.E. and Rotchford, N.L. (1983) Time and behaviour in organisations. *Research in Organizational Behaviour*, 5, 57–101.

McGregor, D. (1960) *The Human Side of Enterprise*. (New York, McGraw-Hill).

McHenry, J.J., Hough, L.M, Toquam, J.L., Hanson, M. and Ashworth, S. (1990) Project A validity results: the relation between prediction and criterion domains. *Personnel Psychology* 43, 335–54.

McLaughlin, A. (1989) *Older Worker Taskforce: Key Policy Issues for the Future*. (Washington DC, US Department of Labor).

McLoone, P. and Crombie, I.K. (1996) Hospitalisation for deliberate self poisoning in Scotland: trends in rates and types of drugs used. *British Journal of Psychiatry*, 169, 81–5.

Meehl, P. (1954) *Clinical vs Statistical Prediction*. (Minneapolis, University of Minnesota).

Meglino, B.M., DeNisi, D.S., Youngblood, S.A. and Williams, K.J. (1988) Effects of realistic Job previews: a comparison using an enhancement and a reduction preview. *Journal of Applied Psychology*, 723, 259–66.

Meier, S.T. (1984) The construct validity of burnout. *Journal of Occupational Psychology*, 57, 211–19.

Mellor, S. (1990) The relationship between membership decline and union commitment: a field study of local unions in crisis. *Journal of Applied Psychology*, 75(3), 258–67.

Miles, I. (1983) *Adaptation to Unemployment*. (Science Policy Research Unit, Occasional papers No. 20 University of Sussex).

Milkovich, G.T. and Wigdor, A.K. (1991) *Pay for Performance*. (Washington DC, National Academy Press).

Milner, S. (1995) Where do we go from here? *British Journal of Industrial Relations*, 37(4), 609–15.

Mirels, H. and Garrett, J. (1971) Protestant work ethic as a personality variable. *Journal of Consulting and Clinical Psychology*, 36, 40–4.

Mischel, W. (1968) *Personality and Assessment*. (New York, Wiley).

Misumi, J. and Peterson, M.F. (1985) The performance-maintenance theory of leadership: review of a research program. *Administrative Science Quarterly*, 30, 198–223.

Misumi, J. and Yamori, K. (1991) Values and beyond: training for higher work centrality in Japan. *European Work and Organizational Psychologist*, 1, (2/3), 135–46.

Mitchell, T.W. and Klimoski, R.J. (1982) Is it rational to be empirical? A test of methods for scoring biographical data. *Journal of Applied Psychology*, 67, 411–18.

Mobley, W.H., Horner, S.O. and Hollingsworth, A.T. (1978) An evaluation of precursors of hospital employee turnover. *Journal of Applied Psychology*, 63, 408–14.

Moore, H.L. (1995) The future of work. *British Journal of Industrial Relations*, 33(4), 657–78.

Moore, M.L. and Dutton, P. (1978) Training needs analysis: review and critique. *Academy of Management Review*, 2, 532–45.

Moran, A.P. (1990) Allegiance to the work ethic, achievement motivation and fatalism in Irish and American people. *Irish Journal Psychology*, 11(1), 82–96.

Morishima, M. (1995) Embedding HRM in a social context. *British Journal of Industrial Relations*, 33(4), 617–40.

Morrison, A.M., White, R.P. and VanVelsor, E. (1987) *Breaking the Glass Ceiling*. (Reading, MA, Addison-Wesley).

Moser, K.A., Fox, A.J. and Jones, D.R. (1984) Unemployment and mortality in the OPCS longitudinal study. *Lancet*, 2(8415), 1324–9.

Motowidlo, S.J., Carter, G.W., Dunnette, M.D., Tippins, N., Werner, S., Burnett, J.R. and Vaughan, M.J. (1992) Studies of the structured behavioural interview. *Journal of Applied Psychology*, 77(5), 571–87.

Motowidlo, S.J., Dunnette, M.D. and Carter, G.W. (1990) An alternative selection procedure: the low fidelity simulation. *Journal of Applied Psychology*, 75(6), 640–7.

MOW International Team (1987) *The Meaning of Working*. (New York, Academic Press).

Muchinsky, P.M. (1977) Employee absence: a review of the literature. *Journal of Vocational Behaviour*, 10, 316–40.

Mumford, M.D. and Stokes, G.S. (1992) Developmental determinants of individual action: theory and practice in the application of background data measures. In M.D. Dunnette and L.M. Hough (eds) *Handbook of Industrial and Organizational Psychology*. Vol. III. (Palo Alto, Consulting Psychologists Press).

Munsterberg, H. (1913) (reprint 1973). *Psychology and Industrial Efficiency*. (Easton, Hive Publishing Co).

Murphy, L.R. in Cooper, C.L. and Payne, R. (1988) *Workplace Interventions for Stress Reduction and Prevention*.

Murray, H.A. (1938) *Explorations in Personality*. (New York, Oxford Press).

Myers, I.B. and McCaulley, M.H. (1985) *Manual: A Guide to the Development and Use of the Myers-Briggs Type Indicator*. (Palo Alto, Consulting Psychologists Press).

Nagel, T. (1988) A defence of affirmative action. In T. Beauchamp and N. Bowie (eds) *Ethical Theory and Business*, 3rd edn. (Englewood Cliffs, NJ, Prentice Hall).

Nagy, S. (1985) Burnout and selected variables as components of occupational stress. *Psychology Reports*, 56, 195–200.

Napier, N.K and Latham, G.P. (1986) Outcome expectations of people who conduct performance appraisal. *Personnel Psychology*, 39(4), 827–37.

Nathan, B. and Alexander, R. (1988) A comparison of criteria for test validation: a meta-analytic investigation. *Personnel Psychology*, 41, 517–35.

Naylor, J.C. and Shine, L.C. (1965) A table for determining the mean criterion score obtained by using a selection device. *Journal of Industrial Psychology*, 3, 33–42.

Neuman, G.A. and Nomoto, J.T. (1990) Personnel selection tests for computer professional and support technicians. *Journal of Business and Psychology*, 5(2), 165–77.

Newton, J.J. (1989) Occupational stress and coping with stress. *Human Relations*, 42, 363–82.

Ng, E. and Smith. M.C. (1991) An updated meta-analysis on the validity of personality tests for personnel selection. Cited in M. Smith and D. George (eds) (1992) Selection Methods. *International Review of Industrial and Organizational Psychology*, 7, 55–97.

Nicholson, N. and Johns, G. (1985) Absence culture and the psychological contract – Who's in control of absence? *Academy of Management Review*, 3, 397–407.

Noe, R.A. (1986) Trainees' attributes and attitudes: neglected influences on training effectiveness. *Academy of Management Review*, 11(4), 736–49.

O'Brien, G. (1986) *Psychology of Work and Unemployment*. (Chichester, Wiley).

Oborne, D.J. (1995) *Ergonomics at Work*. 3rd edn. (Chichester, Wiley).

Olea, M.M. and Ree, M.J. (1994) Predicting pilot navigator criteria: not much more than 'g'. *Journal of Applied Psychology*, 79, 845–51.

Orpen, C. (1985) Patterned behaviour description interviews versus unstructured interviews: a comparative validity study. *Journal of Applied Psychology*, 70, 774–6.

Osborn, A.F. (1953) *Applied Imagination: Principles and Procedures of Creative Problem-solving*. (New York, Scribner).

Owens, W.A. (1976) Background data. In M.D. Dunnette (ed.) *Handbook of Industrial and Organizational Psychology*. (Chicago, Rand-McNally).

Owens, W.A. and Schoenfeldt, L.F. (1979) Towards a classification of persons. *Journal of Applied Psychology*, 64, 569–607.

Palmore, E.B., Fillenbaum, G.G. and George, L.K. (1984) Consequences of retirement. *Journal of Gerontology*, 39, 109–16.

Parsons, C.K. and Liden, R.C. (1984) Interviewer perceptions of applicant qualifications: a multivariate field study of demographic characteristics and non-verbal cues. *Journal of Applied Psychology*, 69, 557–68.

Pearlin, L.I. and Schooler, C. (1978). The structure of coping. *Journal of Health and Social Behaviour*, 19, 2–21.

Pearlman, I., Schmidt, F.L. and Hunter, J.E. (1980) Validity generalisation results for tests used to predict job performance and training success in clerical occupations. *Journal of Applied Psychology*, 65, 353–406.

Pearlman, K. (1980) Job families: a review and discussion of their implications for personnel selection. *Psychological Bulletin*, 87, 1–28.

Peeters, M. (1994) Production organisation in the clothing sector: analysis of teamwork pioneers in the Netherlands. *European Work and Organizational Psychologist*, 4, 239–50.

Pervin, L. (1980) *Personality Theory and Assessment*. (New York: Wiley).

Peters, L.H., O'Connor, E.J. and Eulber, J.R. (1985) Situational constraints: sources, consequences and future considerations. In K.M. Rowland and G.R. Ferris (eds) *Research in Personnel and Human Resource Management*. 3, 79–114.

Peters, L.H. and Terborg, J. (1975) The effects of temporal placement of unfavourable information and of attitude similarity on personnel selection decisions. *Organizational Behavior and Human Performance*, 13(2), 279–93.

Peters, T.J. and Waterman, R.H. (1982) *In Search of Excellence: Lessons From America's Best Run Companies*. (New York, Harper Row).

Peterson, N.G. (1990) Specifying domains of biographical data and outlining new areas for selection tests. *Personnel Psychology*, 43, 247–76.

Phillips, A.P. and Dipboye, R.L. (1989) Correlational tests of predictions from a process model of the interview. *Journal of Applied Psychology*, 74, 41–52.

Pibal, D.C. (1985) Criteria for effective resumes as perceived by Personnel Directors. *Personnel Administrator*, 30(5), 119–23.

Pignitore, R., Dugoni, B.L., Tindale, R.S. and Spring, B. (1994) Bias against overweight job applicants in a simulated employment interview. *Journal of Applied Psychology*, 79(6), 909–17.

Platt, S. (1984) Unemployment and suicidal behaviour: a review of the literature. *Social Science and Medicine*, 19(2), 93–115.

Platt, S. (1986) Parasuicide and unemployment. *British Journal of Psychiatry*, 149, 401–5.

Platt, S. and Krietman, N. (1984) Trends in parasuicide and unemployment among men in Edinburgh, 1968–1982. *British Medical Journal*, 289, 1029–32.

Porteous, M.A. and Hodgins, J. (1995) A survey of selection practices in Irish organisations. *Irish Journal of Psychology*, 16(4), 397–408.

Porter, L.W. and Lawler, E.E. (1968) *Managerial Attitudes and Performance*. (Homewood, IL, Dorsey).

Porter L.W. and Steers, R.M. (1973) Organizational, work and personal factors in employee turnover and absenteeism. *Psychological Bulletin*, 80, 151–76.

Powers, C.W. and Vogel, D. (1980) *Ethics in the Education of Business Managers*. (Hastings, CIS).

Preece, J. (1994) *Human–computer Interaction*. (Wokingham, Addison-Wesley).

Price Waterhouse Cranfield Project (1992) *Human Resource Management in Ireland*, University of Limerick.

Pritchard, R.D. (1969) Equity theory: a review and critique. *Organisational Behavior and Human Performance* 4, 176–211.

Pulakos, E.D., Schmitt, N., Whitney, D. and Smith, M. (1996) Individual differences in interviewer ratings: the impact of standardization, consensus discussion, and sampling error on the validity of a structured interview. *Personnel Psychology*, 49, 85–102.

Pursell, E.D., Campion, M.A. and Gaylord, R.S. (1980) Structured interviews: avoiding selection problems. *Personnel Journal*, 59, 907–12.

Quinn, R.P. and Staines, G.L. (1979) The 1977 Quality of Employment Survey. Cited in D.C. Ganster and J. Schaubroeck (1991). Work stress and employee health. *Journal of Management*, 17, 235–71.

Rafaeli, A. (1989) When clerks meet customers: a test of variables related to emotional expression on the job. *Journal of Applied Psychology*, 74(3), 385–93.

Rafaeli, A. and Klimoski, R.J. (1983) Predicting sales success through handwriting analysis: an evaluation of the effects of training and handwriting sample content. *Journal of Applied Psychology*, 68, 212–17.

Rasmussen, K.G. (1984) Non-verbal behavior, verbal behavior, resume credentials and selection interview outcomes. *Journal of Applied Psychology*, 61, 551–6.

Redmond, M.R., Mumford, M.D and Teach, R. (1993) Effects of leader behaviour on subordinate creativity. *Organisational Behavior and Human Decision Processes*, 55, 120–51.

Ree, M.J., Earles, J.A. and Teachout, M. (1994) Predicting job performance: not much more than g. *Journal of Applied Psychology*, 79, 518–24.

Reich, R.B. (1987) Entrepreneurship reconsidered: the team as hero. *Harvard Business Review*, 65(3), 77–83.

Reich, R.B. (1991) *The Work of Nations: Preparing Ourselves for 21st Century Capitalism*. (London, Simon and Schuster).

Reilly, R.R., Brown, B., Blood, M.R. and Malatesta, C.Z. (1981) The effects of realistic reviews: a study and discussion of the literature. *Personnel Psychology*, 34, 823–34.

Reilly, R.R. and Chao, G.T. (1982) Validity and fairness of some alternative employee selection procedures. *Personnel Psychology*, 55, 12–37.

Reilly, R.R., Henry, S. and Smither, J.W. (1990) An examination of the effects of using behaviour checklists on the construct validity of assessment dimensions. *Personnel Psychology*, 43, 71–84.

Rhodes, S.R. (1983) Age related differences in work attitudes and behaviour: a review and conceptual analysis. *Psychological Bulletin*, 93(2), 328–67.

Richards, J.R. (1980) *The Sceptical Feminist: A Philosophical Enquiry*. (London, Routledge Kegan Paul).

Richardson, Bellows, Henry & Co. (1981) Supervisory profile record quoted in W.M.M. Altink (1991) *European Work and Organizational Psychologist*, 1(4).

Ritchie, R.J. and Moses, J.L. (1983) Assessment correlates of women's advancement into middle management: a seven year longitudinal study. *Journal of Applied Psychology*, 68, 227–31.

Roberts, G.E. (1994) Maximising performance appraisal systems effectiveness: perspectives from municipal government personnel administrators. *Public Personnel Management*, 23(4), 525–49.

Robertson, I.T. (1994) Personnel selection research: Where are we now? *The Psychologist*, 7(1), 17–21. (BPS Publications).

Robertson, I.T. and Downs, S. (1979) Learning and the prediction of performance: the development of trainability tests in the United Kingdom. *Journal of Applied Psychology*, 64, 42–50.

Robertson, I.T. and Downs, S. (1989) Work sample tests of trainability: a meta-analysis. *Journal of Applied Psychology*, 74, 402–10.

Robertson, I.T., Gratton, L. and Rout, U. (1990) The validation of situational interviews for administrative jobs. *Journal of Organizational Behaviour*, 11, 69–76.

Robertson, I.T. and Kandola, R.S. (1982) Work sample tests: validity, adverse impact and applicant reaction. *Journal of Occupational Psychology*, 55, 171–82.

Robertson, I.T and Kinder, A. (1993) Personality and job competencies: the criterion related validity of some personality variables. *Journal of Occupational Psychology*, 66, 225–44.

Robertson, I.T and Makin, P.J. (1986) Management selection in Great Britain: a survey and critique. *Journal of Occupational Psychology*, 59, 45–57.

Robertson, J. (1985) *Future Work*. (Aldershot, Gower).

Robinson, W.S. (1950) Ecological considerations and the behaviour of individuals. *American Sociological Review*, 15, 352–7.

Roche, F. and Tansey, P. (1992) *Industrial Training in Ireland: A Study Prepared for the Industrial Policy Review Group*. (Dublin, Stationery Office).

Rodgers, R. and Hunter, J.E. (1991) Impact of management by objectives on organisational productivity. *Journal of Applied Psychology*, 76, 322–36.

Roessner, J.D. (1985) *The Impact of Office Automation on Clerical Employment, 1985–2000*, (Westport, VA, Greenwood).

Roethlisberger, F.J. and Dickson, W.J. (1939) *Management and the Worker*. (Cambridge, Harvard University Press).

Rones, P.L. (1985) Using the CPS to track retirement trend among older men. *Monthly Labor Review*, 108, 46–9.

Rosch, E. and Lloyd, B.B. (1978) *Cognition and Categories*. (New York, Erlbaum).

Rosen, B. and Jerdee, T.H. (1988) Managing older workers careers. In G.R. Ferris and K.M. Rowland (eds) *Research in Personnel and Human Resource Management*. Vol. 6. (Greenwich, CT, JAI Press).

Rosse, J.G. and Hulin, C.L. (1985) Adaptation to work: an analysis of employee health withdrawal and change. *Organisational Behaviour and Human Decision Processes*, 36, 324–47.

Rothstein, H.R., Schmidt, F.L., Erwin, F.W., Owens, W.A. and Sparks, C.P. (1990) Biographical data in employment selection: can validities be made generalizable? *Journal of Applied Psychology*, 75, 175–84.

Rotter, J.B. (1966) Generalised expectancies for internal versus external control of reinforcement. *Psychology Monographs*, 80(1, 609).

Rowley, K. and Feather, N.T. (1987) The impact of unemployment in relation to age and length of unemployment. *Journal of Occupational Psychology*, 60, 323–32.

Ruff, M.R., Pert, C.B. and others. (1985) Benzodiazepine receptor-mediated chemotaxis of human monocytes. *Science*, 229, 1281–3.

Ruiz Quintanilla, S.A. and Wilpert, B. (1991) Are work meanings changing? *European Work and Organizational Psychologist*, 1(2/3), 91–109.

Russell, C.J. (1985) Individual decisions in an assessment centres. *Journal of Applied Psychology*, 70, 737–46.

Russell, C.J., Mattson, J., Devlin, S.E. and Atwater, D. (1990) Predictive validity of bio-data items generated from retrospective life experience essays. *Journal of Applied Psychology*, 75, 569–80.

Russell, J.S. and Wexley, K.N. (1988) Improving managerial performance in assessing needs and transferring training. In K.M. Rowland and G.R. Ferris (eds) *Research in Personnel and Human Resource Management*, Vol. 6. (Greenwich, CT, JAI Press).

Rutter, M. and Smith, D.J. (eds) (1995) *Psychosocial disorders in Young People*. (Chichester, Wiley).

Ryan, A.M. and Sackett, P.R. (1989) Exploratory study of individual assessment practices by I/O Psychologists. *Journal of Applied Psychology*, 74, 568–79.

Saal, F.E. and Knight, P.A. (1988) *Industrial/Organizational Psychology, Science and Practice*. (Pacific Grove, CA, Brooks/Cole).

Sackett, P.R., Burns, L.R. and Callahan, C. (1989) Integrity testing for personnel selection: an update. *Personnel Psychology*, 43, 491–529.

Sackett, P.R. and Harris, M.M. (1984) Honesty selection for personnel selection: a review and critique. *Personnel Psychology*, 37, 221–46.

Santy, P.A. (1994) Choosing the 'right stuff': the psychological selection of astronauts and cosmonauts. (Westport, CT, Praeger).

Schaff, A. (1985) *Wohin furht der Weg?* (Vienna, Europa Verlag).

Schmidt, F.L. and Hunter, J.E. (1977) Development of a general solution to the problem of validity generalization. *Journal of Applied Psychology*, 62, 529–40.

Schmidt, F.L. and Hunter, J.E. (1983) Individual differences in productivity: an empirical test of estimates derived from studies of selection procedure utility. *Journal of Applied Psychology*, 68, 407–14.

Schmidt, F.L., Hunter, J.E., McKenzie, R.C. and Muldrow, T.W. (1979) Impact of valid selection procedures on work-force productivity. *Journal Of Applied Psychology*, 64, 609–26.

Schmidt, F.L., Outerbridge, A.N., Hunter, J.E. and Goff, S. (1988) Joint relationship of experience and ability with job performance – a test of 3 hypotheses. *Journal of Applied Psychology*, 73, 46–57.

Schmitt, N. (1976) Social and situational determinants of interview decisions: implications for the employment interview. *Personnel Psychology*, 29, 79–101.

Schmitt, N., Gooding, R., Noe, R. and Kirsch, M. (1984) Meta-analyses of validity studies published between 1964 and 1982 and the investigation of study characteristics. *Personnel Psychology*, 37, 407–22.

Schneider, R.J. and Hough, L.M. (1995) Personality and industrial/organisational psychology. *International Review of Industrial and Organizational Psychology*, 10, 75–129.

Schneier, C.E. (1977) Operational utility and psychometric characteristics of BES: a cognitive reinterpretation. *Journal of Applied Psychology*, 62, 541–8.

Schuler, H., Farr, J.L. and Smith, M. (1993) *Personnel Selection and Assessment*. (Hillsdale, NJ, LEA).

Schwartz, F.N. (1989) Management women and the new facts of life. *Harvard Business Review*, 110, 65–76.

Selye, H. (1956) *The Stress of Life*. (New York, McGraw-Hill).

Shackleton, V. and Newell, S. (1991) Management Selection: a comparative survey of Methods used in top British and French Companies. *Journal of Occupational Psychology*, 64, 45–57.

Shepard, J.M., Shepard, J. and Wokutch, R.E. (1991) The Problem of Business Ethics: Oxymoron or Inadequate Vocabulary. *Journal of Business and Psychology*, 6(1), 9–23.

Shepherd, D.M. and Barraclough, B.M. (1980) Work and suicide: an empirical investigation. *British Journal of Psychiatry*, 136, 469–78.

Shimmin, S. (1989) Selection in the European context. In P. Herriot (ed.) *Assessment and Selection in Organizations*. Ch. 17. (Chichester, Wiley).

Shimmin, S. and Wallis, D. (1994) *Fifty Years of Occupational Psychology*. (Leicester, British Psychological Society).

Shostak, A.B. (1993) The nature of work in the 21st century: certain uncertainties. *Business Horizons*, 36(6), 30–4.

Shostak, A.B. (1980) *Blue Collar Stress*. (Reading, MA, Addison-Wesley).

Siegel, L. (1982) Paired comparisons of managerial effectiveness by peers and supervisors. *Personnel Psychology*, 35, 843–52.

Silverman, M.M., Eichler, A. and Williams, G.D. (1987) Self-reported stress, findings from the 1985 National Health Interview Study. *Public Health Research*, 102(1), 47–53.

Silvestri, G.T. (1993) Occupational employment: wide variations in growth. *Monthly Labor Review*, November, 116(11), 58–86.

Slocum, J.W., Cron, W.L., Hansaen, R.W. and Rawlings, S. (1985) Business strategy and the management of plateaued employees. *Academy of Management Journal*, 28, 133–54.

Slora, K. and Boye, M. (1989a) An empirical approach to determining employee deviance base rates. *Journal of Business and Psychology*, 42 (2), 199–219.

Slora, K.B. and Boye, M.W. (1989b) *The Food Marketing Institute Speaks. Loss Prevention Issues Study Highlights*. (Washington D.C., Institute Reports).

Smith, D.E. (1986). Training programs for Performance appraisal: a review. *Academy of Management Review*, 11(1), 22–40.

Smith, J.M. and Abrahamsen, M. (1992) Patterns of selection in six countries. *The Psychologist*, 5, 205–7.

Smith, M. and George, D. (1992) Selection methods. *International Review of Industrial and Organizational Psychology*, 7, 55–97.

Smith, M. and Robertson, I.T. (1989) *Advances in Selection and Assessment*. (Chichester, Wiley).

Smith, P.C and Kendal, L.M. (1963) Retranslation of expectations: an approach to the construction of unambiguous anchors for rating scales. *Journal of Applied Psychology*, 47, 149–55.

Smither, R.D. (1988) *The Psychology of Work and Human Performance*. (New York, Harper Row).

Smulders, P.G.W. (1980) Comments on employee absence/attendance as a dependent variable in organisational research. *Journal of Applied Psychology*, 65(3), 368–71.

Snyder, C.J. and Barrett, G.V. (1988) The Age Discrimination in Employment Act: a review of court decisions. *Experimental Ageing Research*, 14, 3–47.

Sparrow, P.R. (1995) Organizational competencies: a valid approach for the future? *International Journal of Selection and Assessment*, 3(3), 168–77.

Spector, P.E. (1988). Development of a work locus of control scale. *Journal of Occupational Psychology*, 61(4), 335–40.

Spencer, L.M. and Spencer, S.M. (1993) *Competence at Work: Models for Superior Performance*. (London: Wiley).

Squires, P., Torkel, S.J., Smither, J.W. and Ingate, M.R. (1991) Validity and generalizability of a role play test to select telemarketing representatives. *Journal of Occupational Psychology*, 64(1), 37–47.

Stagner, R. (1985) Ageing in industry. In J.E. Birren and K.W. Schaie (eds). *Handbook of the Psychology of Ageing*, (pp. 789–817). (New York, Van Nostrand Reinhold).

Staw, B.M. and Ross, J. (1985) Stability in the midst of change: a dispositional approach to job attitudes. *Journal of Applied Psychology*, 70(3), 469–80.

Steddon, P. (1990) Protecting the bottom line. *Industrial Management and Data Systems UK*, 90(7).

Steel, R.P. and Ovalle, N.K. (1984) Self appraisal based upon supervisor feedback. *Personnel Psychology*, 37(4), 667–85.

Steers, R.M. and Rhodes, S.R. (1978) Major influences of employee attendance: a process model. *Journal of Applied Psychology*, 63, 391–407.

Steers, R.M. and Porter, L.W. (1991) *Motivation and Work Behavior*. (New York, McGraw-Hill).

Sterns, H.L. and Doverspike, D. (1989) Ageing and the training and learning process. In I.L. Goldstein and associates. *Training and Development in Organisations*. (San Francisco, Jossey-Bass).

Stodgill, R. and Coons, A.E. (1957) Leader behaviour: its description and measurement. *Bureau of Business research, Monograph 88*, Ohio State University.

Stokes, G.S. and Reddy, S. (1992) Use of background data in organisational decisions. *International Review of Industrial and Organisational Psychology*, 7, 285–322.

Stone, E.F. (1986) Job scope-job satisfaction and job–scope–job performance relationships. In E.A. Locke (ed.) *Generalising From Laboratory to Field Settings*. (Lexington, MA, Lexington Books).

Talaga, J. and Beehr, T.A. (1989) Retirement: a Psychological perspective. *International Review of Industrial and Organizational Psychology*, 4, 185–211.

Tang, T.L-P. and Tzeng, J.Y. (1992) Demographic correlates of the Protestant work ethic. *Journal of Psychology* 126(2), 163–70.

Taylor, F.W. (1911) *The Principles of Scientific Management*. (New York, Harper).

Taylor, H.C. and Russell, J.T. (1939) The relationship of validity coefficients to the practical effectiveness of tests in selection. *Journal of Applied Psychology*, 23, 565–78.

Taylor, M.S. and Schmidt, D.W. (1983) A process oriented investigation of recruitment source effectiveness. *Personnel Psychology*, 36, 343–54.

Taylor, S.M. and Sniezek, J.A. (1984) The college recruitment interview: topical content and applicant reactions. *Journal of Occupational Psychology*, 57, 157–68.

Terkel, S. (1975) *Introduction to Work*. (Harmondsworth, Penguin).

Tett, R.P. and Jackson, D.N. (1990) Organisation and personality correlates of participative behaviours using an in-basket exercise. *Journal of Occupational Psychology*, 63, 175–88.

Tett, R.P. and Jackson, D.N. (1991) Personality measures as predictors of job performance. *Personnel Psychology*, 44, 703–42.

Thomas, L.T. and Ganster, D.C. (1995) Impact of family supportive work variables on work–family conflict and strain: a control perspective. *Journal of Applied Psychology*, 80(1), 6–15.

Tiggemann, M. and Winefield, A.H. (1989) Predictors of employment, unemployment and further study among school leavers. *Journal of Occupational Psychology*, 62(3), 213–22.

Toscano, G. and Windau, J. (1993) Fatal work injuries: results from the 1992 national census. *Monthly Labor Review*, 116 (10), 39–48.

Trew, K. and Kilpatrick, R. (1985) Life styles and psychological well being among unemployed in Northern Ireland. *Journal of Occupational Psychology*, 58, 207–16.

Tullar, W.L. (1989) Relation control in the employment interview. *Journal of Applied Psychology*, 74, 971–7.

Turnage, J.J. and Muchinsky, P.M. (1984) A comparison of the validity of assessment center evaluations versus traditional measures in forecasting supervisory job performance: interpretive implications of criterion distortion for the assessment paradigm. *Journal of Applied Psychology*, 69, 595–602.

Turner, F.J. (1921) *The Frontier in American History*. (New York, Krieger). (Reprint 1976).

Ullah, P. (1990) The association between income, financial strain and psychological well being among unemployed youths. *Journal of Occupational Psychology*, 63, 317–30.

Valacich, J.S., Dennis, A.R. and Connolly, T. (1994) Idea generation in computer based groups a new ending to an old story. *Organisational Behavior and Human Decisions Processes*, 57, 448–67.

Van Zwanenberg, N. and Wilkinson, L.J. (1993) The person specification: a problem masquerading as a solution. *Personnel Review*, 22(7), 54–65.

Vecchio, R.P. (1990) Theoretical and empirical explorations of cognitive resource theory. *Journal of Applied Psychology*, 75, 141–7.

Verillo, R.T. and Verillo, V. (1985) Sensory and perceptual performance. In N. Charnes (ed.) *Ageing and Human Performance*. (Chichester, Wiley).

Vineberg, R. and Joyner, J.N. (1982) *Prediction of Job Performance: Review of Military Studies*. (Alexandria, HRRO), (cited in Hunter and Hunter, 1984).

Volwiler, A.T. (1922) Robert Owen and the congress of Aix-la-Chapelle 1818. *The Scottish Historical Review*, 19, 96–105.

Wagel, W.H. (1986) Building excellence through training. *Personnel*, 63(9), 5–10.

Wagner, S.R. and Sternberg, R.J. (1985) Practical intelligence in real world pursuits: the role of tacit knowledge. *Journal of Personality and Social Psychology*, 49, 436–58.

Wahba, M. and Bridwell, L. (1976) Maslow reconsidered: a review of research in the need hierarchy theory. *Organisational Behaviour and Human Performance*, 15, 212–40.

Wainer, H.A. and Rubin, I.M. (1969) Motivation of research and development entrepreneurs: determinants of company success. *Journal of Applied Psychology*, 53, 178–84.

Waldman, D.A. and Avolio, B.J. (1993) Ageing and work performance. In K.M. Rowland and G.R. Ferris (eds) *Research in Personnel and Human Resource Management*, Vol. 11. (Greenwich, CT, JAI Press).

Walker, K.F. (1979) Psychology and industrial relations a general perspective. In G.M. Stephenson and C.J. Brotherton (eds) *Industrial Relations: A Social Psychological Approach*. (Chichester, Wiley).

Wall, T.D., Corbett, J.M., Martin, R., Clegg, C.W. and Jackson, P.R. (1990) Advanced manufacturing technology, work design and performance: a change study. *Journal of Applied Psychology*, 75, 691–7.

Warr, P. (1984) *Economic recession and Mental Health: a review of research*. (Tijdschrift voor Sociale Gezendheidserg).

Warr, P. (1987) *Work, Unemployment and Mental Health*. (Oxford, Oxford University Press).

Warr, P.B. and Payne, R.L. (1983) Social class and reported changes in behaviour after job loss. *Journal of Applied Social Psychology*, 13, 206–22.

Watson vs *Fort Worth Bank and Trust*, 47 FEP cases 102, 1988.

Watts, F.N. and Everitt, B.S. (1980) The factorial structure of the general aptitude test battery. *Journal of Clinical Psychology*, 36, 763–7.

Weber, M. (1958) *The Protestant Ethic and the Spirit of Capitalism*. (Translator T. Parsons). (New York, Scribner), (Original pub. 1904–5).

Webster, E.C. (1964) *Decision Making in the Employment Interview*. (Montreal, Eagle).

Webster, E.C. (1982) *The Employment Interview: A Social Judgement Process*. (Ontario, SIP Pub.).

Wedderburn, Z. and Dalrymple, D. (1992) Structured Interviews: reliable? Yes; humanly acceptable? Dubious; valid? Not this time, but . . . Paper presented at *British Psychological Society, Division of Occupational Psychology Conference*, January 1992, Liverpool.

Weisner, W.H. and Cronshaw, S.F. (1988) A meta-analytic investigation of the impact of interview format and degree of structure on the validity of the employment interview. *Journal of Occupational Psychology*, 61, 275–90.

Wernimont, P.F. and Campbell, J.P. (1968) Signs, samples and criteria. *Journal of Applied Psychology*, 52(5), 372–6.

West, P. and Sweeting, H. (1996) Nae job, nae future: young people and health in the context of unemployment. *Health and Social Care in the Community*, 4(1), 50–62.

Wexley, K.N. (1984) Personnel Training. *Annual Review of Psychology*, 35, 519–51.

Wexley, K.N. (1989) Contributions to the practice of training. In Goldstein and others, Training and Development in Organizations, *Personnel Psychology* 487–500.

Whelan, C.T. (1992) The role of income, life-style deprivation and financial strain in mediating the impact of unemployment on psychological distress: evidence from the Republic of Ireland. *Journal of Occupational Psychology*, 65, 331–44.

Whelan, C.T., Hannan, D.F. and Creighton, S. (1991) Unemployment, poverty and psychological distress. *Economic And Social Research Institute*, Paper Number 150, Dublin.

Wigdor, K.N. and Sackett, P.R. (1993) Employment testing and Public Policy: the case of the General Aptitude Test Battery. In Schuler, H., Farr, J.L. and Smith, M. (eds), *Personnel Selection and Assessment*. (Hillsdale: LEA).

Wilcoxson, L. and Prosser, M. (1996) Kolb's *Learning Style Inventory* (1985): review and further study of reliability and validity. *British Journal of Educational Psychology*, 66, 247–57.

Williamson, O. (1984) Corporate governance. *Yale Law Journal*, 93, 1197–230.

Winefield, A.H. (1995) Unemployment: its psychological cost. *International Review of Industrial and Organizational Psychology*, 10, 170–212.

Winefield, A.H., Tiggemann, M., Winefield, H.R. and Goldney, R.D. (1993) *Growing Up With Unemployment: A Longitudinal Study of its Impact*. (London, Routledge).

Wingrove, J., Glendinning, R. and Herriot, P. (1984) Graduate pre-selection: a research note. *Journal of Occupational Psychology*, 57, 169–71.

Winkler, D.R. (1980) The effects of sick leave policy on teacher absenteeism. *Industrial and Labour Relations Review*, 33, 232–40.

Wolfson, A. (1985) Assessment centres ten years later. Cited in R. Klimoski and M. Brickner (1987). Why do assessment centers work: The puzzle of assessment center validity. *Personnel Psychology*, 40, 243–60.

York, K.L. and John, O.P. (1992) The four faces of Eve: a typological analysis of women's personalities at mid-life. *Journal of Personality and Social Psychology*, 63, 494–508.

Yukl, G. (1981). *Leadership in Organizations*. (Englewood Cliffs, NJ, Prentice Hall).

Zaccaro, S.J., Foti, R.J. and Kenny, D.A. (1991) Self-monitoring and trait based variance in leadership: an investigation of leader flexibility across multiple group situations. *Journal of Applied Psychology*, 76(2), 308–15.

Zeytinoglu, I.U. (1992) Reasons for hiring part-time workers. *Industrial Relations*, 31(3), 489–99.

Index